UNIVERSITY
ENGLISH
READER

余光中的
英文课

英汉
双语版

余光中 编著

商务印书馆
The Commercial Press

图书在版编目(CIP)数据

余光中的英文课/余光中编著.—北京:商务印书馆,2023(2024.9重印)
ISBN 978-7-100-22307-2

Ⅰ.①余… Ⅱ.①余… Ⅲ.①英语—高等学校—教材 Ⅳ.①H319.39

中国国家版本馆 CIP 数据核字(2023)第 075638 号

权利保留,侵权必究。

余光中的英文课

余光中　编著

商　务　印　书　馆　出　版
(北京王府井大街36号　邮政编码100710)
商　务　印　书　馆　发　行
北京盛通印刷股份有限公司印刷
ISBN 978-7-100-22307-2

2023年6月第1版　　开本 880×1230 1/32
2024年9月北京第4次印刷　印张 18¾
定价:88.00元

Write down your own immortal sayings here.
Never mind the saints and bores in the rear.

本书前身《大学英文读本》旧书影

一代中文大师的英文博雅读本

单德兴

楔　子

大二时在余光中老师的英国文学史课堂上,听他说起一则小故事:暑假期间他主编《大学英文读本》(*University English Reader*),为了把长短不一的作者名在封底排成一个长方形,兜来兜去,不知不觉花了一个晚上。少不更事的我,对赫赫有名的诗人竟然花上整晚处理这种戋戋小事,感到有些诧异、好笑,甚至不值。待自己年事稍长,在写作、校对、编辑多所磨炼,才体会到正是先天的才华,加上后天这种狮子搏兔、全力以赴的精神,造就了余老师身为作者/学者/译者此"三者合一"、一代大师的地位。

遗珠之憾:余光中最被忽略的一本编著

余光中于诗歌、散文、评论、翻译"四大写作空间"都有非常亮丽的表现,为中国近当代文学史上罕见的通才。由于文名显赫,以致许多人忽略了一项事实:余光中除了在香港时期(1974—1985)任教于香港中文大学中文系之外,在台湾的漫长岁月都任教于外文系——从赴港前的台湾师范大学英语系、台湾大学外文系、政治大学西洋语文学系(简称"政大西语系"),到离港后的中山大学外文系。他多年讲授英美文学,以英诗与翻译两课程最为人称道。此外，余光中曾于政治大学、台湾师范大学、中山大学等校担任系主任、所长、院长，学术行政经验丰富。因此，若想深入了解余光中，必须谨记他资深外文学者与教育者的身份。

他在学院里的角色与职掌，不论是英美文学教授、英文教育者或外文系所与文学院的行政主管，都涉及学生英文能力的提升以及文学欣赏能力的培养。余光中为政大西语系第五任系主任，任期自1972年8月至1974年7月，实际负责全校英文课程安排与师资调度，带动全校英文与文学风气。《大学英文读本》的编纂不仅涉及主事者心目中大学生学习英文的需求，而且与其他必修课程提供了大学生的基础人文教育。可惜的是，该书以英文印行，读者限于大学校园，加以年代久远，以致成为他所有中英文著作与编著中最被忽略的一本。

《大学英文读本》的时空因素

当时台湾的英美文学界追随美国盛行的新批评，于课程、教材与教法多方锐意革新。于美国取得英美文学博士学位的颜元叔、朱立民，在台大外文系高举改革大纛，风行草偃，英文系／外文系耳目一新，遂有"朱颜改"之说。这股外文教育改革之风进而借由新编英文读本扩及整个校园。流风所及，政大西语系余光中、中兴大学外文系齐邦媛、成功大学外文系马忠良等系主任，也都针对该校需求新编英文读本。

余光中接受笔者访谈时坦言："我是受他（颜元叔）的影响。早年的大一英文课本编得不好，把它当作一种纯语言的课本，不太强调人文深度，其实大一英文、大一国文应该是变相的 liberal education（博雅教育）的教材才对。"因此当他担任西语系主任时便改编英文教科书，着重当代"大学"应有的辽阔视野与英文素养，兼顾宏观的文化胸怀与微观的文本阅读。

此书由余光中担任主编，其他三位编者为该系的杜莉、斯安生，以及美籍教师邓临尔。邓临尔为华盛顿大学博士，专长为语言学。杜莉为夏威夷大学硕士，专长为英语教学。斯安生为纽约州立大学宾汉姆敦校区英美文学硕士。四位编者对中美社会皆有切身体会，对读本的要求对象更有第一手的认知，各依专长选材，并为其选文撰写简介与注释。

余光中除了英文读本的《前言》(Foreword)，另撰《从毕卡索到爱因斯坦——〈大学英文读本〉编后》，说明缘起、理念、特色与意义。邓临尔的四篇选文着重思想性与教育性，斯安生的四篇选文着重文学性，杜莉的六篇选文着重社会性与时代性。[1] 其余十九篇（将近六成）由余光中亲力亲为，以文学与艺术为主，对作家与选文的简介尤其翔实，投入之深、贡献之大超过另三人总和。

由《前言》可知，大学英文读本不仅要厚植当代知识青年的英文能力，并要开拓视野与胸襟，达到宽宏远大的教育与文化目标。因此，本书可谓余光中有关大学英文读本理念的"尝试集"，在其他编者协力下，广搜博纳，悉心编排，仔细批注，以响应教学的需求、时代的演变、学风的转化、教育的目标，遂成为余光中所有中英文出版品中独树一帜之作。

作者与选文分析

此书收录三十三篇选文，来自三十二位作者，入选两篇的是惠特曼，唯一的女性是狄金森，两人为十九世纪美国"诗坛双璧"。

就国籍分析，三十二位作者中，外国作者计二十九位，以美国十六位最多，占全书一半，自十九世纪初出生的林肯，到二十世纪中叶出生的科珀。其次为英国作家十位，自十六世纪的莎士比亚到二十世纪的克拉克。五篇来自其他语文的英译，包括俄国作家契诃夫的短篇小说、西班牙画家毕加索的艺术论，以及三篇中国文史哲经典：《论语》《庄子》与《史记》。

---

1 见本书英文前言末尾说明。——编者注

就选文类别分析,除了三篇中文文史哲经典英译,其余三十篇包括诗歌六篇、短篇小说一篇、非虚构类散文二十三篇,细分为人文社会科学十篇、文学艺术六篇、抒情散文与传记回忆录四篇、自然科学三篇。

《大学英文读本》收录的作者多为名人,莎士比亚、济慈、惠特曼、狄金森、梭罗、马克·吐温等文学大家姑且不论,近代作家中,萧伯纳、艾略特、罗素分别是一九二五、一九四八、一九五〇年诺贝尔文学奖得主,爱因斯坦为一九二一年诺贝尔物理学奖得主。毛姆于一九一九年游历中国,罗素于一九二〇年担任北京大学客座哲学教授,萧伯纳于一九三三年访问中国,汤因比于一九二九年、一九六七年两次访问中国。

《大学英文读本》内容大要与有机结构

余光中在《前言》未提,也是阅读选文时容易忽略的,就是全书自成一体。零散阅读难免"见树不见林"之憾。若能认知全书有机结构,可收"见树又见林"之效。

全书以本涅特的《经典何以为经典》领衔,主张经典之所以为经典,是因为热情的少数人对文学的乐趣与经验,以品位维系其地位,代代相传。作品之所以成为经典,文字造诣高超是基本条件。毛姆在《怎样写作才完美》拈出清晰、简洁、悦耳三要诀。萧伯纳的《戏剧评论家》力主剧评家须独立不群,具备"追求完美艺术的激情"。

剧评后的两篇选文扩及电影与绘画。希区柯克以《新铸的语言》形容自己从事的艺术,现身说法,示范如何运用电影语言。毕加索的《艺术宣言》主张绘画是为了"发现",其本质是"或多或少令人信服的谎言",只着重当下,并强调兴趣、"发现的喜悦、意外的喜悦"。

艾略特的诗作与评论影响深远。其《论诗歌》第一节"品味的发展"分述孩提、青春期到成熟后对诗的欣赏,从单纯好恶,到区分真伪,到辨识杰出的程度。第二节"诗歌的鉴赏"主张评论是甄别诗的好坏良窳。他把诗歌的鉴赏分为三阶段,由初期选佳弃劣的享受,到加入知性的组织与鉴赏,再到遇见当代新作能参酌经验加以重新组织。第三节"诗歌评论家"强调各代都须以自己的世代重新品评诗歌。此篇不仅供读者管窥艾略特的风格与论点,并可作为阅读诗歌的参考。

紧接的六首英美诗歌,依序从十六世纪的莎士比亚,到二十世纪的弗罗斯特。莎翁的《乡村之歌》来自喜剧《皆大欢喜》,活泼的节奏、轻巧的内容、接连的叠句,引领读者进入诗歌的园地。济慈的十四行诗《久困在都市的人》则格律严谨、节奏稳重,传达出久困城市中人的无奈,以及对大自然的向往。

英诗横越大西洋来到美国,因应民族性与风土人情,产生自己的特色。惠特曼的两首短诗均为自由诗,看似不讲究韵式,其实自有节奏与章法。《我歌唱自己》歌颂自我,拥抱自尊自信,展现美国民主平等的信念。《一堂天文课》对比了科学家满是数据、图表的知识,以及诗人在寂静中仰望星空,对大自然的直观与敬畏。狄金森如隐士般深居简出,对大自然观察入微,《蛇》以歌谣体表达骤然遇到草丛中长虫的惊悚。惠特曼因作品在形式与精神上的自由解放,成为现代诗歌的先驱。狄金森则因形式与内容自成一格,意象突出,成为意象派诗歌的先驱。与余光中有一面之缘的弗罗斯特经常触景生情,因物起兴,将日常素材化为深具哲思的诗篇。《雪夜林畔小住》表面上是雪夜即景的自然诗歌,其实深具象征意味,格律严谨。

英诗无数,不胜枚举,选诗固然不易,注诗尤其困难。余光中使出英诗教授看家本领,用心批注,包括形式与内容、意象与意义、表面与象征、观察与想象、文体的发展及文学史上的意义,强调朗读以欣赏音韵之美。这些都来自多年读诗、译诗、教诗的心得,厚积薄发,深入浅出,言简意丰。若能善加体会,依教奉行,有如跟着余光中上了一堂英诗课。

契诃夫的《哀歌》是全书唯一的短篇小说。读者经由简单的文字与情节,感受到作者笔下小人物的丧子之恸、无处可诉的孤绝,以及人与动物的关系。

其余各篇均为散文作品,风格迥异,内容多样。《琐事》为典型小品文,十四则素描长短不一,篇篇巧思,字字珠玑,俱见作者个性,平凡中见妙趣。马克·吐温的《回忆母亲》透过一则则小故事，生动呈现十九世纪美国女性的真诚、坦率、幽默、悲悯与勇气，令读者如见其人。梭罗以特立独行、离群索居闻名。《论忙碌》提醒世人检视人生。他批评忙碌谋生、蝇营狗苟的态度，主张自动自发，以爱谋生。霍弗在《人、游戏和创造力》中指出游戏与艺术在人类文明发展过程中的重要性，呼吁摆脱功利目的，以游于艺的心态面对人生，发挥创意。

接下来四位作者的时代、背景与身份各异，主题却都涉及大学生、阅读、教育、知识与学习。科珀写《离家》时只是大二学生。文中描绘四位美国大学新鲜人如何面对新生活，运用新自由，由想家而自立。埃尔斯沃思在《大学生和阅读》中警示大学生缺乏阅读，忧虑这种非智主义的现象，并剖析其成因。作者强调求知欲，为学习而学习，广泛阅读，严加比较，培养判断力与品味，认为这些都是好公民的素养。年仅三十岁就担任芝加哥大学校长的传奇人物哈钦斯，以推动阅读经典闻名。《教育的基础》主张教育的目标在于改善人与社会。他强调哲学、历史、文学和艺术能提供有关关键议题的重要知识。而年轻人的博雅教育目标是"教给他们日后自我教育所需要的习惯、思想和技巧"，并强调成人教育的重要，呼吁"持续的学习和温故知新"，以建立理想的"学习的共和国"。最早深入探讨大学教育的是十九世纪的纽曼枢机主教。《从与学习的关系看待知识》指出，为确保对严肃议题能形成个人见解，需大量的阅读与信息，否则思而不学则殆。而大学的作用在于广其心志。博雅教育的目标则是心灵的启蒙与扩展。作者把博览群籍、融会贯通的知识称为普遍知识，而大学就是培养普遍知识的场所。

林肯的《葛底斯堡演说》是全书最短而有名的散文，仅两百六十字，却是标举美国立国精神与自由平等思想的重要文献，强调民有、民治、民享的政府，广泛收入各种文选，也是极少数保留先前读本之文。《战胜孤独》来自布鲁斯一九七三年（此读本出版同一年）问世的《贝尔传》，以传记文学手法记述既盲又聋的凯勒与发明家贝尔、老师莎莉文三人多年的情谊与合作。蒙塔古的《女人天生优越论》以风趣幽默的口吻传达科学新知。作者举出许多科学证据，说明女人在生理与心理上都比男性优越,此篇既是平易近人的科普文章,又充满女性主义意识。同为科普文章,皮蒂的《镜头》大异其趣,细描漫步乡野自然观察的优美笔法让人联想起梭罗。出外采样后,回到家里,取出显微镜悉心观察,另一个截然不同的世界随即映入眼帘。

爱因斯坦深具人文精神,《宗教与科学》区分原始先民因恐惧自然环境而产生的"恐惧宗教",以及文明人出于道德意识与社会感情而产生的"道德宗教",两者共同之处是"它们的上帝观念都有拟人化特征"。作者从多年科学探索的体悟,拈出"宇宙宗教感情",认为不仅层次最高,而且可得自超过日常功利思维的艺术与科学研究。科幻小说作家克拉克兼具文学与科学之长。《我们永远无法征服太空》以具体数据论证,即使科技发展一日千里,再先进的飞行器速度依然有限,人类面对浩瀚宇宙只能望而兴叹。

《技术与世界政局》作者斯柯尼科夫已臻九五高龄,是全书唯一健在的作者。全文主张科技的发展与影响早已跨越人为国界,必须以全球视角看待。文中提到全球暖化、生态污染、海洋资源与外层空间的争夺等议题,甚至信息战、"自然资源管理、人口增长、信息处理、遗传工程"以及"军事技术"等问题,并呼吁建立国际监管机制,都是今日迫在眉睫的事,却早出现于半世纪之前的英文读本。

余光中一向关切中西文学、思想与文化,授课时经常带入中西比较的观点。《〈论语〉五十节》自狄百瑞、陈荣捷、华兹生合编的《中国传统文献》精选而来,让习于从《论语·学而篇》读起的中文读者,得以透过英译以及比原著更有系统的分类,不仅重新认识这部儒家奠基文本,也能学到儒家重要观念的英文表达方式,有利于向外国人士介绍中华文化。《〈庄子〉五节》选文集中于生死,录自《至乐》《大宗师》《齐物论》《秋水》诸篇,英译者为韦礼、华兹生与梅贻宝,足见取材之广泛,编选之用心。读者借道三位中西学者的英译,再次领会道家圣哲思想之超脱与想象力之丰富。来自《史记》的《李将军列传》以英文再现兼具历史之真与文学之美的名作。余光中建议读者对照中文阅读,以见太史公雄深雅健的风格。

压卷的两篇名家之作别具深意。罗素的《中西文明的比较》以跨文化的视野,对比中西文明,说明各自的特色与优劣。文中论及欧美文明的三个共同源头——希腊文化、基督宗教与现代工业主义——也介绍中国的老庄、孔子以及诗歌与艺术,并提到中华文化接受佛教,以示其兼容并蓄。他对比老子的"生而不有,为而不恃,长而不宰"与西方的"占有、自恃,以及统治",指出中国人天性宽容、友善,以礼相待,而西方白人到中国则出于三个动机:打仗、赚钱、传教。罗素认为中西双方相互学习必然有益彼此。

汤因比写《我为什么不喜欢西方文明》时已七十五岁,为汇集多年研究世界各大文明心得后的反思。他之所以不喜欢西方文明,是因为在他有生之年"西方世界爆发了两次世界大战","出现了墨索里尼、希特勒、麦卡锡等领导人物"。他也细数当前西方文明让他不满之处:个人主义、嫌弃老人、广告业、标准化、性意识、专业化、机械化等。

读本最后五篇选文中,前三篇介绍中国儒家、道家与史家的代表文本,续以罗素与汤因比的两篇思想性文章。余光中特别提到,"压卷的五篇选文(……)这样子的取材和编排,我自命是'革命性的',不免有点沾沾自喜"。

要言之,全书始于经典的定义与功能,接着重视文字与修辞的作用,经由广泛的艺术引入诗论,继而赏析英美诗作与短篇小说,再进入面貌繁复、具有文学性与启发性的散文,衔之以英文重新阅读、诠释的中华文学与文化经典,总结于中西文明的比较与批判。细读各篇固然开卷有益,总体观之更见其结构有机,井然有序,前后呼应,体现余光中如何透过语文学习达到博雅教育的理念。

余氏美学与读本特色

余编《大学英文读本》采用高雅光滑的乳白色系以及较大的开数,颇显亮丽、脱俗、大气。封面插图为他心仪的克利画作《满月时的动物》,寥寥几笔,童趣中带有深意,仿佛召唤读者参加一场知识派对。扉页后的两页，左侧底下的十音节双行体诗："Write down your own immortal sayings here. / Never mind the saints and bores in the rear."（"此处写下自己不朽格言。／别理后面无聊人与圣贤。"）出自精通英诗的余老师，格律工整，语带幽默，期许读者的同时调侃书中作者。右侧硬笔画也出自他的手笔，只见一位头戴高帽、身穿燕尾服的男子，手持捕蝶网正蹑手蹑脚要捕捉前方地上的"问号"，一如书中多篇文章所强调的求知欲。这些编排在在体现"余氏美学"。

综上所述，余编《大学英文读本》特色有四：

第一，博雅理念，具体实践：余光中身为大学西语系系主任，因应时代与教学需求，新编英文教材，以强化学生的语文能力。他的理念高超，视野广阔，秉持博雅教育理念，落实于具体文本，以期培养出兼具英文能力、人文素养、现代感与国际观的知识青年。

第二，推陈出新，设计多元：四位编者对跨文化的语言学习都有深切认知，体认大学英文教育的需求，深悉旧有教材的贫乏与缺失，力求创新与多元，若干选材甚至是几年内的新文，显示触角的敏锐、与时俱进的精神、接轨国际的作为。

第三，古今兼容，中西并蓄：选文上自中国传统经典，下至当代美国大学生的回顾，既有莎士比亚诗歌、艾略特诗论、契诃夫短篇小说、希区柯克电影论、毕加索艺术论，也有二十世纪小品文、科普文，及其他领域论述。内容既涉及大学理念、教育目标、阅读与学习，以及中西文化比较与批判的思想性文章，也涉及女性意识、科技发展、宗教观点、环保议题与国际政治等文章，熔古今中外于一炉，以成就大学之"大"与"学"。

第四，浑然有机，六"文"兼具：此书小到一字一词批注，中到作者简介与选文提要，大到文章的精挑细选、排列组合与有机结构，在在透露出主事者目标明确，大处着眼，小处着手，由文字、文句，而文本、文学、文化、文明，层层向上，统揽古今中外，开拓学生视野，达到博雅教育的目标。

此书在一九七〇年代台湾外文学界改革运动中应运而生，内容与形式独树一帜，带有浓厚余氏色彩，遂能异军突起，引人瞩目。惟年代久远,时过境迁,罕为人知,殊为可惜。北京商务印书馆慧眼独具,在半世纪后以英汉双语形式重新印行,供今日读者阅读,更能体认此读本历久弥新之处。

余老师于二〇一七年辞世,为中文世界留下丰厚遗产,成为现当代文学史上一枚巨星。却也因文名闪耀,难免遮掩他身为英美文学教授,尤其英语教育者的角色。《大学英文读本》以崭新面貌问世,再现余光中罕为人知的一面,就"余学"而言,固然有寻幽探微、钩沉出新的意义,一般读者也可运用昔今的双重视角,精读细品,依文索意,体会其中的微言大义与博雅教育。

2023 年 3 月 31 日
台北南港

(单德兴,台湾大学外文研究所博士,现任"中研院"欧美所特聘研究员,专长为比较文学、文化研究、翻译研究。)

从毕卡索[1]到爱因斯坦
——《大学英文读本》编后

余光中

"我们所以博览群书,是因为无法广交益友。"一位现代诗人这样说过。生也有涯,恓恓惶惶的现代人,谁也不能识尽天下的智士。退而求其次,只好博览群书了。可是现代的知识,不但日积月累,抑且日新月异,书刊之多,何止汗牛充栋?无论一个人多么博览,而且精选,迟早他得承认,永远有更多更多的书等他去读,永远有卷帙浩繁的名著、杰作,在内行人看来,都是那一行那一科的基本常识,可是对于一般的读者,恐怕只能始于传闻,终于纳罕,永远是一个谜了。折中之道,便是将各行各门的大师和专家汇于一卷之中,人各一篇,逐篇读来,该有遍访名师之趣,而无单调偏狭之感。政治大学西洋语文系新编的《大学英文读本》,便是这种构想的尝试。

我一直认为,大学的英文读本,应该一箭双雕,不仅旨在提高学生的英文程度,更应在课文的编选和阐扬上,扩大他们的见识,恢宏他们的胸襟,锻炼他们的美感,并且鼓舞青年特有的旺盛的好奇心。新编《大学英文读本》,对于课文的要求,除了内容的深度和时代性之外,强调的正是这种兴趣的多般性。三十三篇课文,以内容而言,有诗,有散文,有文学和艺术的论述,也有教育、哲学、历史、生理、太空、宗教与科

---

[1] 这里的毕卡索,下文的希区考克、汤恩比、史科尼考夫、孟太古均为台湾译法,本书正文中均采用大陆通行译法。——编者

学等等的文章。至于作者的阵容，从萧伯纳到弗罗斯特，从济慈到希区考克，从爱因斯坦到毕卡索，更是多彩多姿，并不限于英美的大师。

本书的编选，纯然针对中国的大学生，因此在取材上，也兼顾到中国古典的英译。压卷的五篇选文，依次是《论语》五十节（超过《论语》全书的十分之一），《庄子》五节（摘自《至乐》《大宗师》《齐物论》《秋水》诸篇），《史记》的《李将军列传》，罗素的《中西文明的比较》，汤恩比的《我为什么不喜欢西方文明》。这样子的取材和编排，我自命是"革命性的"，不免有点沾沾自喜。我这样做，一则希望中国的大学生，在西方文化的对照甚至挑战之下，对于本国文化能有更客观也是更深切的体认；二是希望他们，在国际文化交流日益频繁也日益重要的七十年代，面对外国人士的问题，不致茫然，如果他们有志在国际的学术界研阐中国的文化，这几篇选文的浅尝，未始不是一个好的开端。

英文教师可针对他班上学生的程度和背景，调整自己的进度和比重。如果学生程度不高，不妨先教《离家》和《回忆母亲》等几篇。如果是法学院和理工学院的学生，该会喜欢史科尼考夫的那篇《技术与世界政局》。中文、历史、哲学、教育等系的学生，对于中国文化的几篇，该有共同的兴趣。而无论是男生或女生（也许我该说"无论女生或男生"吧），尤其是可怜的男生，读罢孟太古《女人天生优越论》，是不可能没有一肚子的话要说的，也许教师正可借此引发一次轰轰烈烈的辩论比赛吧。有不爱看电影的大学生吗？如果没有，老师啊，教到希区考克导演的《新铸的语言》时，包你班上没有人对着窗外发愣——如果你对电影不太外行的话。

本书的注解全用英文，附于课文之末，共分三部分：第一部分抉发题旨与文义，第二部分简述作者生平，第三部分则为生字与成语等等的逐条诠释，可谓详尽，甚至便于自修。注解应用中文或英文，诚然见仁见智，难有定论。本书用英文注释英文，无非意在迫使学生放弃中文这根"拐杖"，破釜沉舟，义无反顾而已。有些地方，也许注解本身也需要注解，不是有了注解，便没了问题。不过，既然是来游泳的，何惧乎水？不呛几口水，怎么学得会游泳呢？

一九七三年九月二十日
于指南山下

FOREWORD

Yu Kwang-chung

"We read books because we don't know enough friends," sighed a modern poet fifty years ago. But books are also legion, and sooner or later even the most omnivorous of readers will realize in despair that they cannot know enough books. The monstrous multiplicity of knowledge in the twentieth century easily discourages the most ambitious scholars. Selective as we may be, there will always remain books which the initiated insist are the cornerstones of culture but of which general readers must settle for a faint, even false acquaintance. A happy compromise, however, is to frequent where the best minds meet in their best moods: a book of selections from widely different authors on topics as widely different.

It is our conviction that such a book, compiled in English for freshman reading, is meant not merely to enhance language proficiency in a foreign tongue, but, more emphatically, to widen intellectual scope, refine aesthetic taste, and arouse youthful curiosity in the healthiest terms. Diversity of interests, no less than the excellence of the selections and their relevance to the modern reader, was the editors' aim when they made the selection. From religion to science, from philosophy and the arts to current international politics, the subjects are as varied as the authors who range from Picasso to Einstein. It is hoped that an exposure to such disciplinary variety will acquaint the students with diverse terminologies and expressions and result in the enrichment of their vocabulary.

Since this reader was made exclusively for Chinese students, we have included several selections from Chinese classics not so much to refresh fond memories of the tradition as to give it a new dimension in a Western context and to encourage young Chinese minds to take the first steps towards self-knowledge as a people and comparative culture as a means of international understanding. We hope the students will find this inclusion helpful when they interpret their native culture, as they often will in this age of growing cultural exchange and interdisciplinary encounter, to a foreign audience.

The selections are all by masters or experts of their respective fields, with one exception. Peter Koper's *Away from Home* is used because we believe the challenge and excitement of becoming a freshman are better expressed by a newcomer on campus than an experienced old scholar and because Peter's diction, being practical and up-to-date, may prove more useful to our students than that of such time-honored advice as *If I Were a Freshman Again*.

The instructor is certainly justified to adapt his emphasis and progress to the specific needs of his class. If, for instance, he finds his students of poorer backgrounds, he should by all means begin with shorter and simpler pieces like *Away from Home* and *This Was My Mother*, and probably should exclude the longer and more sophisticated ones. On the other hand, while it is our wish to stimulate the students with the greatest possible diversity, relevance to their own fields of study should also be stressed. Naturally, Western Languages and Literature majors are expected to read all the poems and all the essays on arts and literature, while students of Chinese, History, Education, and Philosophy may find Confucius, Russell, and Toynbee of common interest.

The notes consist of three parts: about the selection, about the author, and itemized annotations, none of which is meant to be exhaustive. Some of the observations in the first and second parts are the editors' and should not be taken as definitive. The student would be grossly mistaken if he should depend entirely on the notes and leave his dictionary unconsulted. The instructor, on his part, is expected to help in pronunciation and other aspects that are not covered in the notes.

The making of this book has kept me almost fully occupied throughout the summer, one of the busiest vacations I have ever had. Yet my labor was shared in sweet fellowship. Thanks are due to Dr. Paul Denlinger for his annotations on Newman, Hutchins, Toynbee, and Clarke; to Loretta Lee Tu for her part on Hoffer, Koper, Ellsworth, Bruce, Montagu, and Skolnikoff; and to An-sun Sze for hers on Thoreau, Chekhov, Smith, and Peattie.

September, 1973

目录
CONTENTS

1. WHY A CLASSIC IS A CLASSIC Arnold Bennett / 1
   经典何以为经典 阿诺德·本涅特

2. HOW TO WRITE PERFECTLY William Somerset Maugham / 15
   怎样写作才完美 威廉·萨默塞特·毛姆

3. THEATER CRITIC George Bernard Shaw / 33
   戏剧批评家 萧伯纳

4. FRESHLY COINED LANGUAGE Alfred Hitchcock / 41
   新铸的语言 阿尔弗雷德·希区柯克

5. STATEMENT ON ART Pablo Picasso / 57
   艺术宣言 巴勃罗·毕加索

6. ON POETRY T. S. Eliot / 73
   论诗歌 T. S. 艾略特

7. COUNTRY SONG William Shakespeare / 91
   乡村之歌 威廉·莎士比亚

8. TO ONE WHO HAS BEEN LONG IN CITY PENT John Keats / 99
   久困在都市的人 约翰·济慈

9. ONE'S-SELF I SING Walt Whitman / 107
   我歌唱自己 沃尔特·惠特曼

10. WHEN I HEARD THE LEARN'D ASTRONOMER Walt Whitman / 115
    一堂天文课 沃尔特·惠特曼

11. A NARROW FELLOW IN THE GRASS Emily Dickinson / 121
    蛇 艾米莉·狄金森

12. STOPPING BY WOODS ON A SNOWY EVENING Robert Frost / 127
    雪夜林畔小驻 罗伯特·弗罗斯特

13. THE LAMENT Anton Pavlovich Chekhov / 135
    哀歌 安东·巴甫洛维奇·契诃夫

14. TRIVIA Logan Pearsall Smith / 153
    琐事 洛根·皮尔索尔·史密斯

15. THIS WAS MY MOTHER Mark Twain / 173
    回忆母亲 马克·吐温

16. ON BEING BUSY Henry David Thoreau / 187
    论忙碌 亨利·戴维·梭罗

17. MAN, PLAY, AND CREATIVITY Eric Hoffer / 201
    人、游戏和创造力 埃里克·霍弗

18. AWAY FROM HOME Peter Koper / 221
    离家 彼得·科珀

19. COLLEGE STUDENTS AND READING Ralph E. Ellsworth / 241
    大学生和阅读 拉尔夫·E.埃尔斯沃思

20. THE BASIS OF EDUCATION Robert M. Hutchins / 265
    教育的基础 罗伯特·M.哈钦斯

21. KNOWLEDGE VIEWED IN RELATION TO LEARNING
    John Henry Newman / 287
    从与学习的关系看待知识 约翰·亨利·纽曼

22. GETTYSBURG ADDRESS Abraham Lincoln / 313
    葛底斯堡演说 亚伯拉罕·林肯

23. A CONQUEST OF SOLITUDE Robert V. Bruce / 321
    战胜孤独 罗伯特·V.布鲁斯

24. THE NATURAL SUPERIORITY OF WOMEN Ashley Montagu / 347
    女人天生优越论 阿什利·蒙塔古

25. LENSES Donald Culross Peattie / 375
    镜头 唐纳德·卡尔罗斯·皮蒂

26. RELIGION AND SCIENCE Albert Einstein / 391
    宗教与科学 阿尔伯特·爱因斯坦

27. WE'LL NEVER CONQUER SPACE Arthur C. Clarke / 403
    我们永远无法征服太空 亚瑟·查尔斯·克拉克

28. TECHNOLOGY AND WORLD POLITICS Eugene B. Skolnikoff / 425
    技术与世界政局 尤金·B.斯柯尼科夫

29. SELECTIONS FROM THE ANALECTS Confucius / 457
    《论语》五十节 孔子

30. SELECTIONS FROM CHUANG TZU Chuang Tzu   / 477
    《庄子》五节 庄子

31. THE BIOGRAPHY OF GENERAL LI KUANG Ssu-ma Ch'ien   / 495
    《史记·李将军列传》 司马迁

32. CHINESE AND WESTERN CIVILIZATION CONTRASTED
    Bertrand Russell   / 521
    中西文明的比较 伯特兰·罗素

33. WHY I DISLIKE WESTERN CIVILIZATION Arnold Toynbee   / 551
    我为什么不喜欢西方文明 阿诺德·汤因比

1

Why a Classic Is a Classic

经典何以为经典

ARNOLD BENNETT
阿诺德·本涅特

(1867–1931)

ABOUT THE AUTHOR

Arnold Bennett (1867–1931), English novelist, dramatist, and journalist, was born in Hanley, son of a solicitor, and educated at Burslem and Middle School, Newcastle. He began studying law, but turned to journalism instead. As a novelist he is best known for the nostalgic *The Old Wives' Tale* (1908) and the novels in the Clayhanger series. *Milestones* was a successful play which he wrote in collaboration with Edward Knoblock.

作者简介

阿诺德·本涅特（1867—1931），英国小说家、剧作家和记者，生于汉利，父亲是律师，他在伯斯勒姆和纽卡斯尔的中学接受教育。起初攻读法律，后来转学新闻。作为小说家，他最知名的作品是怀旧性质的《老妇人的故事》(1908)，以及《克莱汉格》小说三部曲。他还与爱德华·诺布洛克合作创作了一部成功剧本《里程碑》。

* **ABOUT THE SELECTION** A "classic" is a literary work which, having stood the test of time, is universally accepted as of indisputable superiority. Its universality, however, is not won by general voting but, as Arnold Bennett views it, by the élite, "the passionate few," who have enjoyed it so much that they insist upon its excellence and its acceptance by the majority of indifferent and inferior tastes. Likewise, the immortality of a classic is maintained only by generation after generation of enthusiasts who refuse to forget and make history remember. The essay is taken from Arnold Bennett's *Literary Taste* (1909).

内容简介 所谓"经典"指的是那些久经时间考验的文学作品，它们的优越地位毫无争议，举世公认。但是，在阿诺德·本涅特看来，这些作品受到的普遍认可，并非通过大众投票赢得的，而是由精英，即"热情的少数读者"来推动的，这些少数人从中获得了巨大的乐趣，对它的卓越品质充满信心，认为大众读者都应该阅读它，而后者对文学要么冷漠疏远，要么品位低劣。而一部经典作品的不朽性也是由一代又一代的热情读者来维护的，他们拒绝遗忘，立志让历史铭记。本文选自阿诺德·本涅特的《文学的品位》(1909)。

The large majority of our fellow citizens care as much about literature as they care about archaeology or the program of the Legislature.[1] They do not ignore it; they are not quite indifferent to it. But their interest in it is faint and perfunctory;[2] or, if their interest happens to be violent, it is spasmodic.[3] Ask the two hundred thousand persons whose enthusiasm made the vogue of[4] a popular novel ten years ago what they think of that novel now, and you will gather[5] that they have utterly forgotten it, and that they would no more dream of reading it again than of reading Bishop Stubbs's *Select Charters*.[6] Probably if they did read it again they would not enjoy it—not because the said novel is a whit worse now than it was ten years ago; not because their taste has improved—but because they have not had sufficient practice to be able to rely on their taste as a means of permanent pleasure. They simply don't know from one day to the next what will please them.

In the face of[7] this one may ask: Why does the great and universal fame of classical authors continue? The answer is that the fame of classical authors is entirely independent of the majority. Do you suppose that if the fame of Shakespeare[8] depended on the man in the street[9] it would survive a fortnight? The fame of classical authors is originally made, and it is maintained, by a passionate few.[10] Even when a first-class author has enjoyed immense success during his lifetime, the majority have never appreciated him so sincerely as they have appreciated second-rate men. He has always been reinforced by the ardor of the passionate few. And in the case of an author who has emerged into glory after his death the happy sequel[11] has been due solely to the obstinate perseverance of the few. They could not leave him alone; they would not. They kept on savoring him, and talking about him, and buying him, and they generally behaved with such eager zeal, and they were so authoritative and sure of themselves, that at last the majority grew accustomed to the sound of his name and placidly agreed to the proposition that he was a genius; the majority really did not care very much either way.

And it is by the passionate few that the renown of genius is kept alive from one generation to another. These few are always at work. They are always rediscovering genius. Their curiosity and enthusiasm are exhaustless, so that there is little chance of genius being ignored. And, moreover, they are always working either for or against the verdicts of the majority.[12] The majority can make a reputation, but it is too careless to maintain it. If, by accident, the passionate few agree with the majority in a particular instance, they will frequently remind the majority that such and such a reputation has been made, and the majority will idly concur: "Ah, yes. By the way, we must not forget that such and such a reputation exists." Without that persistent memory-jogging[13] the reputation would quickly fall into the oblivion which is death. The passionate few only have their way[14] by reason of the fact that they are genuinely interested in literature, that literature matters to them. They conquer by their obstinacy alone, by their eternal repetition of the same statements. Do you suppose they could prove to the man in the street that Shakespeare was a great artist? The said man would not even understand the terms they employed. But when he is told ten thousand times, and generation after generation, that Shakespeare was a great artist, the said man believes—not by reason, but by faith. And he too repeats that Shakespeare was a great artist, and he buys the complete works of Shakespeare and puts them on his shelves, and he goes to see the marvellous stage effects which accompany *King Lear*[15] or *Hamlet*,[16] and comes back religiously convinced[17] that Shakespeare was a great artist. All because the passionate few could not keep their admiration of Shakespeare to themselves.[18] This is not cynicism; but truth. And it is important that those who wish to form their literary taste should grasp it.

What causes the passionate few to make such a fuss about[19] literature? There can be only one reply. They find a keen and lasting pleasure in literature. They enjoy literature as some men enjoy beer. The recurrence of this pleasure naturally keeps their interest in literature very much alive. They are forever making new researches, forever practising on themselves. They learn to understand themselves. They learn to know what they want. Their taste becomes surer and surer as their experience lengthens. They do not enjoy today what will seem tedious to them tomorrow. When they find a book tedious, no amount of popular clatter will persuade them that it is pleasurable; and when they find it pleasurable no chill silence of the street crowds will affect their conviction that the book is good and permanent. They have faith in themselves. What are the qualities in a book which give keen and lasting pleasure to the passionate few? This is a question so difficult that it has never yet been completely answered. You may talk lightly about truth, insight, knowledge, wisdom, humor, and beauty, but these comfortable words do not really carry you very far, for each of them has to be defined, especially the first and last.[20] It is all very well for Keats in his airy manner to assert that beauty is truth, truth beauty, and that that is all he knows or needs to know.[21] I, for one, need to know a lot more. And I shall never know. Nobody, not even Hazlitt[22] nor Sainte-Beuve,[23] has ever finally explained why he thought a book beautiful. I take the first fine lines that come to hand—

> *The woods of Arcady[24] are dead,*
> *And over is their antique joy—*

and I say that those lines are beautiful, because they give me pleasure. But why? No answer! I only know that the passionate few will, broadly, agree with me in deriving this mysterious pleasure from those lines. I am only convinced that the liveliness of our pleasure in those and many other lines by the same author will ultimately cause the majority to believe, by faith, that W. B. Yeats is a genius. The one reassuring aspect of the literary affair is that the passionate few are passionate about the same things. A continuance of interest does, in actual practice, lead ultimately to the same judgments. There is only the difference in width of interest. Some of the passionate few lack catholicity,[25] or, rather, the whole of their interest is confined to one narrow channel; they have none left over. These men help specially to vitalize the reputations of the narrower geniuses: such as Crashaw.[26] But their active predilections[27] never contradict the general verdict of the passionate few; rather they reinforce it.

A classic is a work which gives pleasure to the minority which is intensely and permanently interested in literature. It lives on because the minority, eager to renew the sensation of pleasure, is eternally curious and is therefore engaged in an eternal process of rediscovery. A classic does not survive for any ethical reason. It does not survive because it conforms to certain canons, or because neglect would not kill it. It survives because it is a source of pleasure, and because the passionate few can no more neglect it than a bee can neglect a flower. The passionate few do not read "the right things" because they are right. That is to put the cart before the horse.[28] "The right things" are the right things solely because the passionate few *like* reading them. Hence—and I now arrive at my point—the one primary essential to literary taste is a hot interest in literature. If you have that, all the rest will come. It matters nothing that at present you fail to find pleasure in certain classics. The driving impulse of your interest will force you to acquire experience, and experience will teach you the use of the means of pleasure. You do not know the secret ways of yourself: that is all. A continuance of interest must inevitably bring you to the keenest joys. But, of course, experience may be acquired judiciously or injudiciously, just as Putney may be reached via Walham Green or via Moscow.[29]

NOTES

1. the Legislature: (in this case) the British Parliament.
2. perfunctory: done routinely and indifferently; superficial.
3. spasmodic: fitful; intermittent.
4. made the vogue of: made...popular.
5. gather: conclude; infer.
6. Bishop Stubbs's *Select Charters*: Willian Stubbs (1825-1901), Rector of Navestock in Essex for seventeen years and Regius professor of history at Oxford, is best known for his contributions to English constitutional history such as *Select Charters* and *Other Illustrations of English Constitutional History* (1870).
7. in the face of: in spite of.
8. Shakespeare: See "about the author" of *It Was a Lover and His Lass*.
9. the man in the street: the ordinary person.
10. a passionate few: a few enthusiastic people; the devoted minority.
11. the happy sequel: the happy result.
12. the verdicts of the majority: the judgment of the common readers.
13. memory-jogging: stirring up the memory; reminding.
14. have their way: have things under their control.
15. *King Lear*: a tragedy by Shakespeare, first published in 1608.
16. *Hamlet*: a tragedy by Shakespeare, first published in 1604.
17. religiously convinced: convinced by faith and worship, not by

reason.
18. All because the passionate few could not keep their admiration of Shakespeare to themselves: All because the passionate few had such strong admiration of Shakespeare that they wanted to share it with the majority.
19. make a fuss about: make an important thing of. Originally, the expression means "be needlessly active about or feel too much concerned with (something insignificant)." It is used here ironically.
20. especially the first and last: especially truth and beauty.
21. that beauty is truth, truth beauty, and that that is all he knows or needs to know: a reference to the closing lines of Keats's *Ode on a Grecian Urn*:

> When old age shall this generation waste,
>   Thou shalt remain, in midst of other woe
> Than ours, a friend to man, to whom thou say'st,
>   "Beauty is truth, truth beauty,"—that is all
>   Ye know on earth, and all ye need to know.

22. William Hazlitt (1778-1830): English essayist and critic.
23. Charles Augustin Sainte-Beuve (1804-1869): French literary historian and critic.
24. Arcady: poetic name for Arcadia, a mountainous region in Greece, celebrated by pastoral poets as a place of rustic happiness.
25. catholicity: broad-mindedness.
26. Richard Crashaw (1613-1649): English poet of the metaphysical school.
27. predilection: personal preference; partiality.
28. That is to put the cart before the horse: That is to take the effect for the cause (or to reverse the order of reasoning).
29. Putney may be reached via Walham Green or via Moscow: Putney is a district of SW London, to which Walham Green is very close but Moscow is very far. To reach Putney via Moscow is sheer waste of time and, therefore, injudicious.

参考译文

我们大部分民众对文学的关心程度犹如他们对待考古或议会纲领的态度，不忽视也不十分漠视。但他们对文学的兴趣却是微不足道且敷衍了事的，即使这种兴趣碰巧十分强烈，可能也是一时心血来潮。在二十万人中做个调查，十年前他们的热情曾使一部小说盛行一时，现今，当问及他们对那部小说的印象时，你会发现他们已经将其彻底遗忘，而且他们宁可阅读斯塔布斯主教的《宪章精选》，也不会想起再次阅读那本小说。即使他们开卷重阅，也可能不会乐在其中了——并不是因为这本小说的可读性不如十年前，也不是因为人们的鉴赏力有所精进——而是因为人们没有足够的实践来依赖自己的品位获取持久的快乐。连他们自己也不知道，明天带给他们快乐的会是什么。

　　面对这个问题，有人可能会问：经典作家享有的那伟大而普世的声誉为何能够延续？答案在于：经典作家的声誉独立于大众读者而存在。试想一下，如果莎士比亚的声誉仅仅依靠普通民众来维持，你能指望这种声誉持续多久呢？经典作家的声望，源起于少数对他们情有独钟的读者并由他们所维系。有时某位一流作家在其一生中获得了巨大成功，然而，人们对他表现出的真诚欣赏可能还不及对某个二流作家。他的声誉得以巩固是因那些热情的少数读者。而有些作家在其死后才荣誉加身，这样的圆满结果也仅仅是因为少数人的坚持不懈。这类少数人无法也永不会将他们的"偶像"遗忘，而是继续讨论他，品味他，购买他的经典作品，表现得充满热忱。他们对自己的权威判断充满自信，最终，其他大多数人也耳濡目染，都对这位作家的名字耳熟能详，进而自然地认可其文学天赋。其实，大部分人对此并不十分关心。

　　正因为少数人对文学的执着和热情，文学巨匠的声誉才得以代代相传。这些少数人孜孜不倦，凭借着浓重的好奇心和无限的热情，不断地挖掘天才，极少使得文学巨匠遭到埋没。而且，这些少数人总是在支持或反对大众的观点。大众可以制造声望，但却无心将其维系下去。倘若在某特定情形下，少数人与大众的观点达成一致，他们也会不断地提醒大众，某种声誉已经建立。而大众也会敷衍地同意道："哦，是的。顺便说一下啊，我们绝不能忘了某某声誉存在着。"若没有少数人的不断提醒，经典作家的声望就会迅速湮没无闻。这些少数人的坚持，是建立在自己对文学的热情，以及文学对于他们的重要性之上。他们征服大多数人靠的仅仅是自身的坚持和反复强调同一个观点。你相信这些少数人能向普通民众证明莎士比亚是一位伟大的文学艺术家吗？民众甚至连他们使用的言辞术语都理解不了。但是，如果继续口口相传、代代因袭，那么民众就会认可莎士比亚是个伟大的文学艺术家，这种认可并非源于理性，而是出自信仰。而且，他还会重复前人的观点，认为莎士比亚是一位伟大的文学艺术家，会购买莎士比亚全集，放到家里的书架上，也会去剧院欣赏《李尔王》或《哈姆莱特》的精彩舞台剧，然后笃定莎士比亚就是一位文学大师。所有这些的发生只是因为那些少数人不愿将对莎士比亚的膜拜局限于自身。这并非愤世嫉俗，而是实事求是。对于那些想塑造自己文学品位的人而言，明白这一点极为重要。

是什么让这些狂热的少数人对文学如此热衷？答案只有一个：他们能从文学中获得强烈而持久的乐趣。他们痴迷于文学，就像有些人沉醉于啤酒。这种乐趣的反复重现自然而然地维系着他们对于文学的热情。他们总是孜孜不倦地进行新探索，并身体力行去展开实践。他们学着理解自我，明确自己真正想要什么。随着经验的增长，他们对自己的文学品位越发笃定。他们不会去欣赏一部未来可能使他们感到无趣的作品。当他们发现一本书索然无味时，任何舆论的喧嚣都不能使他们认为此书有一丝乐趣。相反，当他们发觉那本书趣味盎然时，任何来自众人的冷漠都无法改变他们对此书的永久认可。他们对自己的鉴赏力充满了信心。什么样的文学作品会为少数人带来那强烈而持久的乐趣呢？这个问题难以回答，到现在都没人能给出确切的答案。你可能会轻率地认为应该是作品中的真理、洞见、知识、智慧、幽默和美感。但是这些美辞并不能使你真切体会到那种乐趣，因为每个词都需要有确切的含义，尤其是何为"真理"，何为"美感"。不错，济慈用他轻快的文风证明了美即是真，真即是美，而这也正是他所了解或需要了解的全部。但对我而言，我需要了解更多。即便如此，我也很难真正理解它们的含义。任何人，包括哈兹里特和圣伯夫，到最后都没能解释为什么一本文学作品可以被称许优美。我手头有两行文学作品中的诗句——

> 阿卡狄的森林已然死亡，
> 它们那古朴的欢乐也已结束。[1]

我认为这两句诗十分优美，它们让我心情愉悦。但为什么会这样？没有答案。我只知道，那些痴迷于文学作品的少数人大体上能与我达成共识，他们能从这些诗行中获得神秘的乐趣。我们从同一个作家的这些诗行和其他诗行中体会到的快乐，会使得大众坚信威廉·巴特勒·叶芝是一个文学巨匠，对此我深信不疑。令人欣慰的是，这些少数文学爱好者的品位高度趋同。在实践中，持之以恒的兴趣可以最终形成具有共性的观点，不同的只是兴趣的广度。在这些少数人中，有些人的兴趣由于缺乏广泛性，常常局限于某一狭窄领域内，对其他方面则兴趣寥寥。因此他们对作家声誉的促进尤其能作用于更为小众的作家，如克拉肖。但是，这些人的文学偏好并不会和其他少数文学爱好者的文学主张相龃龉，相反，是对他们文学主张的巩固。

所谓经典著作，就是那些作品，它们能够给那些对文学表现出持久且浓厚兴趣的少数人带来快乐。这种快乐之所以存在，是因为这类少数人愿意体验新的快感，于是怀揣一颗永无止境的好奇心，投入于永不止步的再发现当中。成就一部经典之作并不倚仗于伦理道德。经典作品能够流芳百世，并不是因为其符合某种

---

[1] 这两句为叶芝的《快乐的牧人之歌》一诗的开篇。此处引用傅浩译文。

正典标准，也不是因为其注定不会湮灭无闻，而是因为经典作品是快乐的源泉。狂热的少数人绝不会对经典视而不见，就像蜜蜂绝不会对花朵视而不见一样。这类少数人不会因为作品内容"正确"而去阅读它们。逻辑恰恰相反，正是因为这类少数人对作品的喜爱，才使得它们的内容"正确"。因此，我的观点是：文学品位的一个基本要素就是对文学的极度热爱。你做到了这一点，那剩下的则是水到渠成。目前，你没有在某些经典文学作品中获得快乐，这并无大碍。你对文学的兴趣，会驱使你获得更多经验。这些经验会教你运用快乐的方法，那就是你本人也不知道的快乐秘诀，仅此而已。持久的兴趣一定会带给你强烈的快乐感。但是，经验的获得既可能是明晰顺理，也可能无章可循，就如同去帕特尼，既可以经由沃尔哈姆格林，也可以经由莫斯科一样。

（罗选民 译）

How to Write Perfectly

怎样写作才完美

WILLIAM SOMERSET MAUGHAM

威廉·萨默塞特·毛姆

(1874–1965)

ABOUT THE AUTHOR

William Somerset Maugham (1874–1965), English novelist, dramatist, and short story writer, was born in Paris and brought up in Kent. During World War I he served in the Red Cross and later in British Intelligence. He traveled extensively, particularly in the Orient. His experience as a student of medicine at St. Thomas's was turned to account in his major novel *Of Human Bondage*. Other popular novels include *The Moon and Sixpence*, *Cakes and Ale*, and *The Razor's Edge*.

作者简介

威廉·萨默塞特·毛姆（1874—1965），英国小说家、戏剧家、短篇小说家。毛姆出生于法国巴黎，在英国肯特郡长大。一战期间，他先后在英国红十字会和军情处工作过。毛姆游历广泛，尤其是到过许多东方国家。他的代表作《人生的枷锁》很大程度上源于他在圣托马斯医学院学医的经历。毛姆的其他作品也广受欢迎，例如《月亮与六便士》《寻欢作乐》《刀锋》。

ABOUT THE SELECTION

These passages are taken from *The Summing Up*, a literary autobiography by W. Somerset Maugham, published in 1938. Maugham recommends lucidity, simplicity and euphony as the three basic virtues of prose and advises writers to write within their limitations, that is, to write as best they *can* and not as they imagine they *should*. He warns them not to walk into the pitfalls of the three opposite vices of obscurity, grandiloquence and cacophony. While to many Maugham is not a great writer, he is certainly a distinguished writer of prose and it would be more healthful for a literary novice to take lessons from his lucid, simple style than, spurred by youthful vanity, tutor himself on the model of George Meredith or James Joyce.

内容简介

本文选自威廉·萨默塞特·毛姆1938年出版的文学自传《写作回忆录》。在该书中,毛姆主张文字的清晰、简洁和悦耳是散文写作的三项基本要求,并建议写作者在自己的能力范围之内进行创作,即力求写到最好,而不是凭空想象着"应当"如何写作。他提醒写作者们注意不要陷入三个相反的表达误区,即表达不清、卖弄辞藻和选用冗长刺耳的词汇。在很多人看来,毛姆并不是一个伟大的作家,但他无疑是一位杰出的散文家。对于文学领域的初学者而言,与其年少自负,以乔治·梅瑞狄斯或者詹姆斯·乔伊斯为学习典范,还不如借鉴毛姆清晰简洁的文风,后者对初学者更有助益。

I have continued with increasing assiduity[1] to try to write better. I discovered my limitations and it seemed to me that the only sensible thing was to aim at what excellence I could within them.[2] I knew I should never write as well as I could wish, but I thought with pains I could arrive at writing as well as my natural defects allowed. On taking thought it seemed to me that I must aim at lucidity,[3] simplicity and euphony.[4] I have put these three qualities in the order of the importance I assigned to them.

I have never had much patience with the writers who claim from the reader an effort to understand their meaning. You have only to go to the great philosophers to see that it is possible to express with lucidity the most subtle reflections.[5] You may find it difficult to understand the thought of Hume,[6] and if you have no philosophical training its implications[7] will doubtless escape you; but no one with any education at all can fail to understand exactly what the meaning of each sentence is. There are two sorts of obscurity[8] that you find in writers. One is due to negligence and the other to wilfulness.[9] People often write obscurely because they have never taken the trouble to learn to write clearly. This sort of obscurity you find too often in modern philosophers, in men of science, and even in literary circles. Here it is indeed strange. You would have thought that men who passed their lives in the study of the great masters of literature would be sufficiently sensitive to the beauty of language to write if not beautifully at least with perspicuity.[10] Yet you will find in their works sentence after sentence that you must read twice to discover the sense. Often you can only guess at it,[11] for the writers have evidently not said what they intended.

Another cause of obscurity is that the writer is himself not quite sure of his meaning. He has a vague impression of what he wants to say, but has not, either from lack of mental power or from laziness, exactly formulated[12] it in his mind and it is natural enough that he should not find a precise expression for a confused idea. This is due largely to the fact that many writers think, not before, but as they write. The pen originates the thought.[13] But this sort of obscurity merges very easily into the wilful. Some writers who do not think clearly are inclined to suppose that their thoughts have a significance greater than at first sight appears. It is flattering to believe that they are too profound to be expressed so clearly that all who run may read,[14] and very naturally it does not occur to such writers that the fault is with their own minds which have not the faculty of precise reflection. It is very easy to persuade oneself that a phrase that one does not quite understand may mean a great deal more than one realizes. From this there is only a little way to go to fall into the habit of setting down one's impressions in all their original vagueness. Fools can always be found to discover a hidden sense in them.[15] There is another form of wilful obscurity that masquerades[16] as aristocratic exclusiveness.[17] The author wraps his meaning in mystery so that the vulgar shall not participate in it. His soul is a secret garden into which the elect[18] may penetrate only after overcoming a number of perilous obstacles. But this kind of obscurity is not only pretentious; it is shortsighted. For time plays it an odd trick.[19] If the sense is meagre time reduces it to a meaningless verbiage[20] that no one thinks of reading.

Simplicity is not such an obvious merit as lucidity. I have aimed at it because I have no gift for richness. Within limits I admire richness in others, though I find it difficult to digest in quantity.[21] I can read one page of Ruskin[22] with delight, but twenty[23] only with weariness. The appeal is sensuous rather than intellectual, and the beauty of the sound leads you easily to conclude that you need not bother about the meaning. But words are tyrannical things, they exist for their meanings, and if you will not pay attention to these, you cannot pay attention at all. Your mind wanders. This kind of writing demands a subject that will suit it. It is surely out of place to write in the grand style of inconsiderable things. No one wrote in this manner with greater success than Sir Thomas Browne,[24] but even he did not always escape this pitfall.[25] In the last chapter of *Hydriotaphia*[26] the matter, which is the destiny of man, wonderfully fits the baroque[27] splendor of the language, and here the Norwich doctor[28] produced a piece of prose that has never been surpassed in our literature, but when he describes the finding of his urns in the same splendid manner the effect (at least to my taste) is less happy. When a modern writer is grandiloquent to tell you whether or no a little trollop[29] shall hop into bed with a commonplace young man you are right to be disgusted.

To my mind King James's Bible[30] has been a very harmful influence on English prose. I am not so stupid as to deny its great beauty. It is majestical. But the Bible is an oriental book. Its alien imagery has nothing to do with us. Those hyperboles,[31] those luscious metaphors,[32] are foreign to our genius.[33] I cannot but think that not the least of the misfortunes that the secession from Rome[34] brought upon the spiritual life of our country is that this work for so long a period became the daily, and with many the only, reading of our people. Those rhythms, that powerful vocabulary, that grandiloquence, became part and parcel[35] of the national sensibility. The plain, honest English speech was overwhelmed with ornament. Blunt Englishmen twisted their tongues to speak like Hebrew prophets...ever since, English prose has had to struggle against the tendency to luxuriance.

The dictum that the style is the man[36] is well known. It is one of those aphorisms[37] that say too much to mean a great deal. I suppose that if a man has a confused mind he will write in a confused way, if his temper is capricious his prose will be fantastical, and if he has a quick, darting intelligence that is reminded by the matter in hand of a hundred things he will, unless he has great self-control, load his pages with metaphor and simile.[38] I can read every word that Dr. Johnson[39] wrote with delight, for he had good sense, charm and wit. No one could have written better if he[40] had not wilfully set himself to write in the grand style. He knew English when he saw it. No critic has praised Dryden's[41] prose more aptly. He[42] said of him[43] that he[44] appeared to have no art other than that of expressing with clearness what he thought with vigor. And one of his *Lives*[45] he finished with the words: "Whoever wishes to attain an English style, familiar but not coarse, and elegant but not ostentatious, must give his days and nights to the volumes of Addison."[46] But when he himself sat down to write it was with a very different aim. He mistook the orotund[47] for the dignified. He had not the good breeding to see that simplicity and naturalness are the truest marks of distinction. For to write good prose is an affair of good manners. It is, unlike verse, a civil art.[48] It has been said that good prose should resemble the conversation of a well-bred man (and have we not also been told that good prose should be like the clothes of a well-dressed man, appropriate but unobtrusive?).

Whether you ascribe importance to euphony, the last of the three characteristics that I mentioned, must depend on the sensitiveness of your ear. A great many readers, and many admirable writers, are devoid of[49] this quality. Poets as we know have always made a great use of alliteration.[50] They are persuaded that the repetition of a sound gives an effect of beauty. I do not think it does so in prose. It seems to me that in prose alliteration should be used only for a special reason, when used by accident[51] it[52] falls on the ear very disagreeably. But its accidental use is so common that one can only suppose that the sound of it is not universally offensive.[53] Many writers without distress will put two rhyming words together, join a monstrous long adjective to a monstrous long noun, or between the end of one word and the beginning of another have a conjunction of consonants that almost breaks your jaw.[54] These are trivial and obvious instances. I mention them only to prove that if careful writers can do such things it is only because they have no ear. Words have weight, sound and appearance; it is only by considering these that you can write a sentence that is good to look at and good to listen to.

I have read many books on English prose, but have found it hard to profit by them; for the most part they are vague, unduly theoretical, and often scolding. But you cannot say this of Fowler's *Dictionary of Modern English Usage*.[55] It is a valuable work. Fowler liked simplicity, straightforwardness and common sense. He had a sound feeling that idiom was the backbone of a language and he was all for the racy phrase. He was no slavish admirer of logic and was willing enough to give usage right of way through the exact demesnes of grammar.[56] English grammar is very difficult and few writers have avoided making mistakes in it. It is necessary to know grammar, and it is better to write grammatically than not, but it is well to remember that grammar is common speech formulated. Usage is the only test. I would prefer a phrase that was easy and unaffected to a phrase that was grammatical. I have given the matter of style a great deal of thought and have taken great pains.[57] I have written few pages that I feel I could not improve and far too many that I have left with dissatisfaction. I cannot say of myself what Johnson said of Pope,[58]

"He never passed a fault unamended by indifference, nor quitted it by despair."⁵⁹ I do not write as I want to; I write as I can.

Anything is better than not to write clearly. There is nothing to be said against lucidity, and against simplicity only the possibility of dryness.⁶⁰ This is a risk that is well worth taking when you reflect how much better it is to be bald than to wear a curly wig. But there is in euphony a danger that must be considered. It is very likely to be monotonous. I do not know how one can guard against this. I suppose the best chance is to have a more lively faculty of boredom than one's readers so that one is wearied before they are. One must always be on the watch for mannerisms⁶¹ and when certain cadences come too easily to the pen ask oneself whether they have not become mechanical.

If you could write lucidly, simply, euphoniously and yet with liveliness you would write perfectly; you would write like Voltaire.⁶² And yet we know how fatal the pursuit of liveliness may be; it may result in the tiresome acrobatics of Meredith.⁶³ Macaulay⁶⁴ and Carlyle⁶⁵ were in their different ways arresting,⁶⁶ but at the heavy cost of naturalness.⁶⁷ Their flashy effects distract the mind. They destroy their persuasiveness; you would not believe a man was very intent on ploughing a furrow if he carried a hoop with him and jumped through it at every other step. A good style should show no sign of effort. What is written should seem a happy accident.⁶⁸

NOTES

1. assiduity: diligence.
2. to aim at what excellence I could within them: to aim at what excellence I could aim at within my limitations.
3. lucidity: clearness; clarity.
4. euphony: harmony of sound; pleasing effects to the ear.
5. reflections: thoughts.
6. David Hume (1711-1776): Scottish philosopher and historian.

7. its implications: the implications of Hume's thought.
8. obscurity: lack of clearness; difficulty in being understood.
9. wilfulness: stubbornness; deliberate choice.
10. perspicuity: lucidity.
11. guess at it: guess at the sense.
12. formulate: state definitely; express clearly.
13. The pen originates the thought: With a good writer, the thought dictates the pen. With a poor writer, the pen wanders on thoughtlessly. He does not bother to think carefully in advance, but lets his thoughts come at random the moment he applies pen to paper.
14. so clearly that all who run may read: so clearly that everybody can understand even in a great hurry.
15. in them: in those impressions.
16. masquerades: disguises oneself.
17. aristocratic exclusiveness: the élite's fastidiousness in choosing friends; the superior class keeping its own company and shutting others out.
18. the elect: the chosen minority; the privileged people.
19. For time plays it an odd trick: For time plays mischief with such kind of obscurity; for time eventually holds such obscurity to ridicule.
20. verbiage: use of too many words.
21. in quantity: in large amount; in abundance.
22. John Ruskin (1819-1900): English art critic and essayist, remarkable for his poetic and richly ornate style in prose.
23. twenty: twenty pages.
24. Sir Thomas Browne (1605-1682): English prose writer, famous for his wide learning and quaint style.
25. this pitfall: the trap of writing of triviality in the grand style.
26. *Hydriotaphia*: also entitled *Urn Burial*, a treatise, by Sir Thomas Browne on the various modes of burial of the dead recorded in history and practiced in Britain, urns and their contents, funeral ceremonies, immortality or annihilation. The tone is meditative and mystical and the style reaches the height of rhetorical prose.
27. baroque: fantastic; grotesque; artistically irregular.
28. the Norwich doctor: Sir Thomas Browne was a practicing physician at Norwich.
29. trollop: prostitute.

30. King James's Bible: also called King James Version or the Authorized Version, English translation of the Bible published in 1611 in the reign of James I.
31. hyperbole: the use of exaggeration for effective emphasis. Example: The waves were mountains high.
32. metaphor: figure of speech in which a word or phrase that ordinarily means one thing is used of another thing to suggest a likeness between the two. To put it in a more simple way, metaphor is an implied comparison between two things essentially unlike. Example: Merry larks are ploughmen's clocks (Shakespeare).
33. our genius: our (English) national character.
34. secession from Rome: formal separation from Roman Catholicism. In 1534 King Henry VIII of England signed the Act of Supremacy and rejected papal control (control by the Roman Catholic Church) to establish Church of England.
35. part and parcel: a necessary part.
36. the style is the man: Le style est l'homme meme, a statement taken from the *Discourse* by Georges Louis Leclerc de Buffon.
37. aphorism: maxim; proverb.
38. simile: an explicit comparison of two things essentially unlike. Example: And like a thunderbolt he falls (Tennyson).
39. Dr.Johnson: Samuel Johnson (1709-1784), a master of English prose.
40. he: Dr. Johnson.
41. John Dryden (1631-1700): English poet, critic, and dramatist.
42. He: Johnson.
43. him: Dryden.
44. he: Dryden.
45. *Lives*: *Lives of the Poets* (1781), a book of critical and biographical studies of English poets by Johnson.
46. Joseph Addison (1672-1719): English essayist.
47. the orotund: the pompous or bombastic (style).
48. It is, unlike verse, a civil art: Prose is a polite and graceful art, it is different from verse, which is wild with "passion, pulse, and power".
49. devoid of: lacking.
50. alliteration: explained in note 8 to *One's-Self I Sing*. "The hero's harp, the lover's lute" is another example.
51. by accident: accidentally; unawares.
52. it: alliteration.

53. universally offensive: unpleasant to all people.
54. Many writers...will put two rhyming words together, join a monstrous long adjective to a monstrous long noun, or between the end of one word and the beginning of another have a conjunction of consonants: Examples of such violations of euphony: (1) late date; (2) objectionable misdemeanor; (3) the obstructed traffic.
55. Fowler's *Dictionary of Modern English Usage*: Henry Watson Fowler (1858-1933), English lexicographer, published the dictionary in 1926.
56. to give usage right of way through the exact demesnes of grammar: to give usage (idiomatic use of words) the right to pass the heavily guarded estate of grammar; to give usage priority over grammar; to let usage pass in spite of the red light of grammar.
57. have taken great pains: have made a great effort; have taken great care. Hence "painstaking".
58. Alexander Pope (1688-1744): English poet and critic whose shapely couplets are flawless in the Neo-Classic tradition.
59. "He never passed a fault unamended by indifference, nor quitted it by despair": He never found a fault without correcting it carefully, nor ever gave it up because he could not improve it.
60. dryness: dullness.
61. be on the watch for mannerisms: be careful not to repeat the same manner of writing.
62. Voltaire: pseudonym of Francois Marie Arouet (1694-1778), French philosopher and author, one of the leaders of the Enlightenment movement in eighteenth-century Europe. His prose style is lucid and forceful.
63. acrobatics of Meredith: George Meredith (1828-1909) was an English novelist and poet whose rich but difficult style is comparable to the gymnastic feat of an acrobat.
64. Thomas Babington Macaulay (1800-1859): English historian and author.
65. Thomas Carlyle (1795-1881): English historian and author.
66. arresting: striking; attractive.
67. at the heavy cost of naturalness: at the heavy expense of naturalness; at the high price of losing spontaneity.
68. happy accident: happy surprise; inspired improvisation; or (in the words of Keats) the magic hand of chance.

参考译文

一直以来,我刻苦勤勉,不断地努力提高自己的写作水平。在这个过程中,我也发现了自己的水平有限,但在我看来,唯一要做的合理的事情就是力求在能力范围之内做到最好。我知道我的写作水平可能永远也达不到自己的期望,但我还是苦思冥想地创作。尽管天赋不足,但我依然可以竭尽所能去提高写作水平。思考再三,我认为写作应当追求清晰性、简洁性、悦耳性(我是按照这三项要求的重要性而排序的)。

一些作家的文字晦涩难懂,要求读者绞尽脑汁去揣摩其中深意,我从来都没有耐心去阅读该类作品。其实你只需要去阅读那些伟大哲人的作品,就会发现再高深的思想也能通过清晰的文字表达出来。比如说休谟,你也许会觉得休谟的思想深奥难懂,如果没有接受过哲学思维训练的话,肯定很难理解其中的内涵,但是任何受过教育的人都能读懂其作品中每句话的确切意思。作家的作品晦涩难懂,可能有两种情况:一种是作家的无心之过,另一种则是有意为之。人们常常因为不愿意费工夫学习如何用清晰的语言写作,从而导致写出的文字晦涩难懂。这种情况在现代的哲学家、科学乃至文学界人士中屡见不鲜。这的确令人费解。我们通常会认为,那些毕生都在研究大师作品的人,往往能够充分领悟语言的美感,因此能够写出优美,或者至少清晰的文字。但事实是,你在阅读他们的作品时,很多句子都需要通读两遍才能知晓其中含义。甚至很多时候因为作者没有表达清楚自己的意思,你只能揣测一番。

造成文章晦涩难懂的另一个原因是作者本人也不清楚自己想要表达什么。如果作者对于自己想要表达的东西只有一个模糊的印象,因为缺乏思考力或者怠于思考而没有在脑海中形成一个明确的想法,那么自然也就无法用精确的语言表达出来。这在很大程度上是因为作者在写作前没有构思清楚,而是边写边想。(毕竟)只有做到胸有成竹,才能下笔有神。这种情况下,读者很可能会误以为文字的模糊性是作者有意为之。一些没有思考清楚就下笔的作者,倾向于认为他们的想法意义重大,至少要比乍看之下的意义来得重要。如果认为那些作家们的想法高深莫测,无法用通俗易懂的语言表达出来,那就明显是在吹捧奉承了。作家们如果抱有这种想法,自然也就无法意识到问题的根源在于,写作前自己未能在脑海中形成一个清晰的思路。当人们对某个短语的含义有所疑惑时,往往很容易说服自己,认为该短语的实际含义远远超出自己的理解范围。在这种观念的影响下,人们很容易养成习惯,不加思考就直接将自己脑海中关于某个想法的模糊印象记录下来(由此形成的文字晦涩难懂)。其实,就连傻子也时常能发现这些文字背后的隐藏含义(但作者就是无法清楚地表达出来)。此外还有另一种有意为之的晦涩文风,那就是作者遣词用句故作高深,以示自身尊贵。这些作者希望通过晦涩的语言将其想要表达的意思隐藏起来,让他们所谓的"凡夫俗子"无法理解其中之义。他们的内心世界就像一个秘密花园,只有少部分人在艰难地克服重重障碍之后方能一探究竟。这种晦涩的文风不仅反映出写作者自命不凡、目光短浅,而且也经不起时间的检验。因为如果作品文字含糊不清,那么随着时间推移,终将会变成无人问津、毫无意义的晦涩冗文。

  与清晰性相比,文章的简洁性并不是一个明显的优点。我之所以追求简洁的文风,是因为自己没有使用丰富词汇进行表达的天赋。在有限的范围内,我很欣赏别人作品中用词的丰富多彩,但如果华丽辞藻堆砌过多,我会难以理解其中的含义。阅读一页约翰·拉斯金的作品会让我感到身心愉悦,但如果读上个 20 页,我就会疲惫不堪。华丽文辞的魅力并不在于能够启发读者思考而在于使读者在阅读时感到赏心悦目,美妙的发音很容易使读者觉得文字本身的意思已经无关紧要。但是，文字并不能离开其自身的含义而存在，同时文字也是"蛮横任性"的，如果阅读时你不关注它的含义，那么最终的结果就是神游天外，一无所知。如果作者打算采用这样的文风进行写作，就需要事先设定一个合适的主题。显然，用宏大的叙事风格描述鸡毛蒜皮的小事是不合适的。在喜用这种文风的作家中，最为成功者当数托马斯·布朗先生，但即使是这位大师，有时也会陷入这种"小题大做"的误区。托马斯·布朗在其作品《瓮葬》的最后一章中探讨的是人的命运。他在这章中采用的"巴洛克式"的宏大的语言风格就完美地契合这一主题。这位诺维奇的医生（即托马斯·布朗）写下了一篇文学史上无人能超越的散文。但是，这位大师用同样宏大华美的文风描绘其发现瓮的过程，其表达效果，至少在我看来，并不尽如人意。试想一下，如果一个现代作家用极其华丽浮夸的文字论述"一个雏妓和一个普通青年上床的行为是否恰当"，你肯定会觉得恶心。

在我看来，英王詹姆斯译本《圣经》（"钦定版"《圣经》）对于英国散文创作产生了恶劣的影响。该译本的文风庄严高贵，我并不会愚蠢到质疑它所表现出来的超然美感。但是《圣经》毕竟源于东方，其文本中所描绘的他国意象与我们（西方国家）关联不大。书中那些夸张的表达和悦耳的比喻于我们的国民性而言都是异质的。我不禁会想，英国教会脱离罗马教会给国民精神生活带来了诸多不幸，这种不幸不仅仅表现为"钦定版"《圣经》在相当长一段时间内成为国民日常生活的唯一读物，而且书中那些音节、那些掷地有声的表达以及华丽优美的辞藻，已经成为国民品性中不可或缺的一部分。自此，人们开始用华丽的辞藻修饰覆盖平实真诚的英语表达，直率的英国人开始卷起舌头像希伯来先知那样说话，传统风格的英文散文也不得不抵抗盛行的华丽文风。

人们都说，文如其人。但这句俗语只是泛泛而谈，并未落到实处。在我看来，如果写作者思路混乱，那么写出的文字就会含糊不清；如果写作者个性乖张，那么他所创作的散文就会荒诞不经；如果写作者神思敏捷，善于从万千世界中找到事物之间的关联，那么除非他时刻有意克制自己，否则他的文章字里行间将会遍布各种或明或隐的比喻。我可以满怀喜悦，逐字逐句地阅读塞缪尔·约翰逊博士的作品，因为他理智、风趣、富有魅力。若不是他执意采用宏大的叙事风格进行写作，那么我想他的写作水平是无人能及的。他的遣词用句浑然天成。约翰逊博士对约翰·德莱顿散文的评价最为恰当不过。他指出，德莱顿的艺术造诣主要在于能够用清晰的语言表达内心激情澎湃的想法。塞缪尔·约翰逊在其著作《诗人轶事》某一篇的结束语中这样写道："要想追求一种平实而不粗俗、优美而不浮夸的写作风格，那就必须夜以继日地研习约瑟夫·艾迪生的著作。"但当他自己开始下笔写作时，他所追求的就是另一个不同的目标了。他误以为华丽的言辞代表着庄严与高贵。如果说写作好的散文能体现一个人的良好修养，那他的修养还不足以让他明白简洁性和自然性是区分写作水平最为可靠的标准。与诗歌不同，散文是优雅得体的艺术。有人说，好的散文就像一个有着良好教养的人的谈吐一样令人感到舒适（不是还有人说过，好的散文应该像衣着讲究的人身上穿的衣服一样，得体而不张扬吗？）。

悦耳性是前述三项要求中的最后一项，在写作过程中是否重视文字的悦耳性，取决于你耳朵的敏锐程度。许多读者，甚至许多知名作家都不具备这种敏锐性。很多我们熟知的诗人都认为音素的重复能够带来美感，所以在诗歌创作中总是会大量地使用"头韵法"，即相连单词的开头使用同样的字母或语音。但我认为在散文创作中，重复的音素并不能带来美感，因此写作者仅应基于特定目的使用"头韵法"。若是无意识地使用这种方法，将会使散文读起来十分刺耳。但这种无意识的使用十分普遍，以至于我们只能认为，并不是所有人都无法接受这些重复的音律。许多可以接受（重复音律）的作家，在写作中总是热衷于将两个押韵的单词连接起来，在一个很长的名词前添加一个很长的形容词，或者在一个单词结尾和另一个单词开头之间，加入十分拗口的辅音字母进行连接。我列举这些细微琐碎但是通俗易懂的例子，仅仅是为了证明细心的（散文）写作者绝对不会犯下这种错误。凡文字皆有其质、有其音、有其形，在写作过程中只有考虑这些方面的因素，才能写出形美悦耳的句子。

我读过许多关于英国散文的著作，但大都言之无物、脱离实际，或者经常满是牢骚，因此获益不多。但福勒的《现代英语用法词典》并非如此，相反，它是一部有价值的著作。福勒追求语言文字的简洁、直接和通俗易懂。他正确地认识到，习语是语言的支柱，并极力主张使用活泼的短语表达来进行写作。福勒没有盲目地遵从逻辑，即使一些习语的用法不符合传统的语法规则，他也极力主张其适用的合理性。英语语法复杂难懂，几乎没有作家在写作时能够完全避免语法错误。尽管写作者有必要通晓语法，符合语法规则总比违背语法规则要好，但同时需要注意的是，语法规则也是在日常生活的对话中形成的。语言的适用性是唯一的评价标准。相较于符合语法的表达，我更喜欢那些简单的自然表达。我曾煞费功夫，苦苦思索写作的语言风格问题。在我迄今为止写作的文章中，几乎没有让我觉得无需进一步修改完善的，实际上，绝大部分文章都无法令我满意。约翰逊曾这样评价蒲柏："他从来不会忽视任何需要修改的（语言）错误，也不会绝望地放弃修改（这些）错误。"我无法做到这点。对于写作，我会尽我所能，但做不到随心所欲。

在写作中，表达不清是最差的结果。清晰的表达无可诟病，但简洁的表达可能会显得枯燥乏味。但是，如果你认为，"自然的秃头好过戴着假发"（自然纯粹胜于花里胡哨），那么你在写作中仍然值得（冒着表达枯燥的风险）去追求文字的清晰和简洁。追求文字悦耳性的同时需要考虑与之伴随的陷阱，即表达过于冗长。我不知道如何才能避免掉进这一陷阱。可能最好的办法是写作者比自己的读者更加敏捷，更容易对那些烦冗的表达感到厌倦。写作者应时刻注意避免"矫饰主义"的文风，同时，（在写作中）当一些抑扬顿挫的表达信手拈来时，需要警惕这些表达是否过于僵化。

如果你能用清晰、简洁、悦耳而且生动的文字进行写作，那你的水平已经臻于完美，可以像伏尔泰那样写出优美的作品。但我们都知道，过分追求文字的生动性可能会带来严重的后果，可能会形成像乔治·梅瑞狄斯那样"炫技式"的文风，令读者厌烦。托马斯·麦考莱和托马斯·卡莱尔都凭借各自独特的文风吸引读者眼球，但其文字都失去了本真的特性。他们浮夸的文风让人难以静下心来阅读，同时也减损了文字的说服力。显然，如果一个犁地的人同时还带着一个铁圈，每走一步就跳过去，你肯定不会相信他是真心实意想要犁地的。好的写作风格应当看不出雕琢的痕迹，好的作品应当是即兴创作的，能给人一种意外之喜。正所谓"文章本天成，妙手偶得之"。

（罗选民 译）

Theater Critic

戏剧批评家

George Bernard Shaw
萧伯纳

(1856–1950)

ABOUT THE AUTHOR

George Bernard Shaw (1856–1950), Irish dramatist and critic, was born and educated in Dublin, but moved to London in 1876. He began his long and brilliant literary career as a critic of music and drama. After 1900 he turned to writing plays himself and became one of the most influential authors of early twentieth century. His writing for the stage brought to people's attention his unorthodox turn of mind and his distrust of conventions and accepted institutions. General readers, however, remember him mostly for his witticisms in innumerable quotations. In 1925 Shaw was awarded the Nobel Prize for Literature. In 1933 he came to China for a brief but much publicized visit, and met some of the leading authors of the country.

作者简介

萧伯纳（1856—1950），爱尔兰剧作家和批评家，在都柏林出生长大、接受教育，1876年迁居伦敦。他的文学生涯漫长而光辉灿烂，起步伊始，他的身份是音乐和戏剧批评家。1900年后，他转向剧本创作，成为20世纪初最有影响力的作家之一。他的舞台创作，让人们注意到他的离经叛道，以及他对传统和陈规旧俗的不信任。然而，大众读者记住他，主要是因为他贡献了无数精妙语录。1925年，萧伯纳被授予诺贝尔文学奖。1933年，他曾短暂来访中国，轰动一时，访问期间曾和中国最优秀的一些作家会面。

ABOUT THE SELECTION

This selection is taken from *Shaw on Music*, edited by Eric Bentley and published by Doubleday in 1955. Originally, it was written for a newspaper column whose space was limited; hence the teasing reference in the last sentence. A theater critic is a person who writes criticism, usually for a newspaper column, on current dramatic performances. As a columnist whose critical comments appear regularly and often immediately after the dramatic performance, he is expected to be quick, terse, and incisive. Shaw was all that, and much more. Shaw was a delightful and formidable satirist who never spoke but in paradox and overstatement. He slashed away with great gusto, leaving no head unturned. An implacable enemy to clichés, Shaw laughed in the face of demureness and dispassionateness in defence of personal commitment to criticism. He insisted that genuine and earnest response to the performing arts was at once intellectual and emotional and that no criticism which was "impersonal" was worth our attention.

内容简介

本文选自埃里克·本特利所编的《萧伯纳论音乐》，1955年由道布尔戴出版社出版。起初，这是一篇为报纸撰写的专栏文章，有空间限制，所以才有了文章最后那句玩笑话。戏剧批评家是为时下戏剧演出撰写批评文章的人，通常发表在报纸专栏上。专栏作家要定期发表文章，常常是一场戏剧演出结束后就要立即刊出，人们希望批评家能快速、简洁、精辟地对演出做出及时的评论。这些萧伯纳都能做到，他的能力又不限于此。萧伯纳是一位令人愉悦也让人畏惧的讽刺作家，一开口就能抓住矛盾关键，措辞夸张猛烈。他精力充沛地四处出击，引人注目。萧伯纳厌恶套路，在为自己的戏剧批评辩论时，他对剧评人的故作公正和冷静嗤之以鼻。他坚持认为，对表演艺术的真挚反应发生在思想和情感两个层面，任何所谓"客观"的批评都不值得关注。

戏剧批评家
Theater Critic

S omebody has sent me a cutting[1] from which I gather that a proposal to form a critics' club has reached the very elementary stage of being discussed in the papers[2] in August. Now clearly a critic should not belong to a club at all. He should not know anybody: his hand should be against every man, and every man's hand against his. Artists insatiable by the richest and most frequent doses of praise;[3] entrepreneurs[4] greedy for advertisement; people without reputations who want to beg or buy them ready made; the rivals of the praised;[5] the friends, relatives, partisans, and patrons of the damned:[6] all these have their grudge against the unlucky Minos in the stalls,[7] who is himself criticized in the most absurd fashion.

People have pointed out evidences of personal feeling in my notices[8] as if they were accusing me of a misdemeanor,[9] not knowing that a criticism written without personal feeling is not worth reading. It is the capacity for making good or bad art a personal matter[10] that makes a man a critic. The artist who accounts for my disparagement by alleging personal animosity on my part[11] is quite right: when people do less than their best,[12] and do that less at once badly and self-complacently, I hate them, loathe them, detest them, long to tear them limb from limb and strew them in gobbets[13] about the stage or platform. (At the Opera,[14] the temptation to go out and ask one of the sentinels for the loan of his Martini,[15] with a round or two of ammunition,[16] that I might rid the earth of[17] an incompetent conductor or a conceited and careless artist, has come upon me so strongly that I have been withheld only by my fear that, being no marksman,[18] I might hit the wrong person and incur the guilt of slaying a meritorious singer.)

In the same way, really fine artists inspire me with the warmest personal regard,[19] which I gratify in writing my notices without the smallest reference to such monstrous conceits as justice, impartiality, and the rest of the ideals. When my critical mood is at its height, personal feeling is not the word: it is passion: the passion for artistic perfection—for the noblest beauty of sound, sight, and action—that rages[20] in me. Let all young artists look to[21] it, and pay no heed to the idiots who declare that criticism should be free from personal feeling. The true critic, I repeat, is the man who becomes your personal enemy on the sole provocation of a bad performance, and will only be appeased by good performances. Now this, though well for art and for the people, means that the critics are, from the social or clubable[22] point of view, veritable fiends.[23] They can only fit themselves for other people's clubs by allowing themselves to be corrupted by kindly feelings foreign to[24] the purpose of art, unless, indeed, they join Philistine clubs,[25] wherein neither the library nor the social economy of the place will suit their nocturnal, predatory habits.[26] If they must have a club, let them have a pandemonium[27] of their own, furnished with all the engines of literary vivisection.[28] But its first and most sacred rule must be the exclusion of the criticized, except those few stalwarts[29] who regularly and publicly turn upon[30] and criticize their critics. (No critics' club would have any right to the name unless it included—but the printer warns me that I have reached the limit of my allotted space.)

NOTES

1. cutting: newspaper clipping.
2. papers: newspapers.
3. Artists insatiable by the richest and most frequent doses of praise: artists who are not satisfied with the richest and most frequent of favorable criticisms. Dose is the amount of medicine to be taken at a time, by this it is suggested that vanity is a disease that needs the medication of praise.
4. entrepreneur: person who organizes and manages a business or industrial enterprise, taking the risk of loss and getting the profit when there is one; especially an opera or concert impresario.
5. the praised: the artists, directors, conductors, etc. who are praised by the critics.
6. the damned: the artists who receive unfavorable criticisms.
7. the unlucky Minos in the stalls: the theater critic. Minos was a legendary king of Crete, made at death supreme judge of the lower world, where all the dead appeared before him for judgment of their deeds. The situation is comparable to a theater critic sitting in judgment of the performing artists. The "stalls" are the front seats in a theater, usually reserved for the critics.
8. notice: a printed critical review of a play, book, or other cultural work.
9. misdemeanor: wrong deed; bad behavior.
10. making good or bad art a personal matter: making good or bad art a personal as well as professional concern.
11. accounts for my disparagement by alleging personal animosity on my part: explains my depreciation by attributing it to personal hatred on my part; attributes my unfavorable criticism of him to my personal ill will towards him.
12. do less than their best: do well enough but not the best they can do.
13. strew them in gobbets: scatter their bodies piece by piece.
14. the Opera: an opera house in London.
15. Martini: Martini-Henry rifle, a single-loading, 45 caliber rifle used in the British service in 1876-1886.
16. with a round or two of ammunition: with ammunition (bullets or gunpowder) for a single shot or two.
17. rid the earth of: get rid of; kill.
18. being no marksman: being poor at shooting.
19. personal regard: personal esteem or favor.

20. rage: act violently; move strongly.
21. look to: attend to; take care of.
22. clubable: suited for membership in a social club; social. Also spelt clubbable.
23. veritable fiends: real devils; truly wicked people.
24. foreign to; not suited for.
25. Philistine clubs: clubs for the lowbrows. The Philistines were a warlike, uncivilized people in Palestine. The name now stands for a person who is low in mind and poor in taste. In the writings of Wilde and Shaw, the name refers to the middle class.
26. nocturnal, predatory habits: nightly plundering habits.
27. pandemonium: abode of all the demons; hell.
28. literary vivisection: Vivisection is cutting into living animals for scientific study. The expression means close and ruthless analysis of a literary work by a critic.
29. stalwarts: strong and brave persons.
30. turn upon: attack.

参考译文

从收到的一则剪报看，组建批评家俱乐部的倡议得到初步响应，已在8月份的报纸上议论起来了。确实，批评家绝不应属于任何俱乐部。他不应和任何人过从甚密：他那支笔对每个人都不应客气，任何人对他也同样不用手软。那些渴望美言不绝于耳的艺术家，那些贪求知名度的经理人，那些为获声望不惜沽名钓誉的人，那些好评如潮者的对手，那些负评缠身者的友人、亲属、支持者、赞助人，所有这些人都恨透了坐在舞台前排定夺演出生死的批评家，而倒霉的批评家自己也饱受妄语谗言。

有人拿出证据，说我的评论有掺杂个人情感之嫌，好像是在指控我犯了行规，殊不知文艺批评若不带个人情感是不值一读的。恰恰是能牵艺术之优劣于己心者才称得上是批评家。说我挟带私愤诋毁他人的艺术家并没说错：能做得更好却满足于次好，就这样仍做得很糟糕，还能心安理得，这种人我怨恨他们，讨厌他们，憎恶他们，真想把他们大卸八块，再把肢解物散抛在舞台上。（在剧场里，我真有一种强烈的欲望，冲出剧院向守卫借一支枪、要几颗子弹，也许能从地球上把那个无能的指挥或自负粗心的艺术家给消灭掉，我忍着未开杀戒，只因我不能百发百中，生怕误伤他人，断送了某位出色歌手的性命而追悔莫及。）

  同样，真正好的艺术家激起我由衷的尊敬，我会在评论中尽情地赞美他们，丝毫不会去唱公正、公平等冠冕堂皇的高调。当我艺术批评的心潮高涨时，用个人情感来形容是不确切的，那是激情在我胸中奔腾，即追求完美艺术的激情，追求听觉、视觉、动作完美的激情。愿所有年轻的艺术家都牢记我上面的话，不要去听信那些宣称文艺批评应与个人情感绝缘的白痴。我再说一次，真正的批评家之所以成了你的敌人只是因为你拙劣的表演，而你得呈上一个上乘的演出才能平息他的敌意。不过，批评家的这种态度，虽然对艺术、对人来说是有益的，但从社会或社群关系的角度看，却使他们成了千夫所指的恶魔。他们只有违背艺术宗旨，态度和风细雨，才能和他人结团合伙。当然，他们可以加入平庸者的俱乐部，可那里的藏书和社交氛围都与批评家喜欢夜晚操刀解剖作品的习性格格不入。如果他们一定要有个俱乐部，那就让他们组建一个自己的魔窟，在那里解剖作品所需的工具应有尽有。但这个魔窟至高无上的入会规则是排除那些饱受批判的艺术家，不过其中的少数勇者不在此列，因为这些人会攻击批评家，常常公开对他们进行批评（一个批评家的俱乐部想要不辱其名，就得包括……因版面所限，就不写下去了）。

（叶子南 译）

Freshly Coined Language

新铸的语言

Alfred Hitchcock
阿尔弗雷德·希区柯克

(1899–1980)

ABOUT THE AUTHOR

Alfred Hitchcock (1899–1980) is the supreme technician of the American cinema famous for his carefully devised suspense stories and movie scripts. Like John Ford, he cuts in his mind, and not in the cutting room with five different set-ups for every scene. His is the only contemporary style that unites the divergent classical traditions of Murnau (camera movement) and Eisenstein (montage). Hitchcock's art is built on paradox. He requires a situation of normality, however dull it may seem on the surface, to accentuate the evil abnormality that lurks beneath it. It would be difficult to commit a murder in a haunted house or dark alley and make a meaningful statement to the audience; for then the spectators simply withdraw from these bizarre settings, let the decor dictate the action. It is not *us* up there but some actors trying to be sinister. However, when murder is committed in a gleamingly sanitary motel bathroom (as in *Psycho*), the incursion of evil into our well-laundered existence becomes intolerable. Of the fifty odd films that Hitchcock has made in a long career dating from 1925, the most important are *Rebecca* (1940), *The Paradine Case* (1947), *Rear Window* (1954), *The Man Who Knew Too Much* (1956), *Psycho* (1960), *The Birds* (1963), and *Topaz* (1969).

作者简介　阿尔弗雷德·希区柯克（1899—1980）是美国电影界最负盛名的技术大师，他以其精心设计的悬念故事和电影剧本而著称于世。和约翰·福特一样，他对镜头的剪辑是在脑海中进行的，而不是在剪辑室中面对着每场戏的不同布景来工作。他的风格在当代是独一无二的，将茂瑙的镜头移动和爱森斯坦的蒙太奇这两种有分歧的古典传统完美融合。希区柯克的艺术建立在悖论之上。根据他的要求，一种正常的情况无论表面上看起来多么平淡无奇，都需要凸显出隐藏其下的邪恶反常面。在闹鬼的屋子或是昏暗的街巷实施谋杀，同时让观众有代入感是困难的，因为观众会主动从怪异的场景中抽身出来，让布景来支配人物行动。他们不会沉浸其中，因为知道那都是些假扮邪恶的演员。但是如果谋杀地点换成汽车旅馆干净整洁得闪闪发亮的洗手间（比如在电影《惊魂记》中），那么邪恶入侵我们美好生存环境的场景就会令人无法忍受。从1925年起，希区柯克在漫长的职业生涯中拍摄了五十多部电影，其中最重要的作品有《蝴蝶梦》(1940)、《凄艳断肠花》(1947)、《后窗》(1954)、《擒凶记》(1956)、《惊魂记》(1960)、《群鸟》(1963)和《谍魂》(1969)。

* **ABOUT THE SELECTION**

Cinema is to the twentieth century what novel was to the nineteenth and drama was to the sixteenth. The most recent of art forms, the cinema is also the most complex, synthetic, and overwhelming. In the short space of two hours a whole world comes alive on the screen, rich and vivid with images and sounds, ideas and feelings. Ever since the 1920's the cinema has been the most influential of the arts in its capacity to transcend national and language barriers and to immerse the audience instantly and intently in a situation or mood. Creative film directors write their works, not with a pen, but a camera. Masters in this medium, such as Ingmar Bergman, Charles Chaplin, Federico Fellini, Akira Kurosawa, Alain Resnais, and Orson Welles, have been widely respected not only as directors but also as intellectual leaders of international stature. Not the least of them, certainly, is Alfred Hitchcock. In this short article the Master of Suspense shares the tricks of his trade with us by telling the essential differences between presentations on the stage and the screen. On the stage, the distance of the scene and the angle at which it is viewed can hardly be changed. Not so on the screen, where the director is free to shift the angle, adjust the distance, and change the scenes in rapid succession as in a montage. To Hitchcock the essential of making a film is not to stand by and passively record what is being enacted before the camera, but to select and arrange the details of action and objects through concentration and exaggeration so that an event is made to happen in a most effective way. The selection is taken from Alfred Hitchcock's "Direction" in *Footnotes to the Film*, edited by Charles Davy (London: Peter Davies, Ltd., 1939.)

内容简介　就重要意义而言，20世纪的电影与19世纪的小说和16世纪的戏剧是一样的。电影作为最前沿的艺术形式，也是最为复杂、最为综合和最令人震撼的。在短短的两个小时之内，银幕上出现了一个活灵活现的完整世界，其中的影像、声音、思想和情感既丰富又生动。自20世纪20年代以来，电影一直都是最具影响力的艺术，它能超越国界和语言的障碍，能让观众即刻专注地沉浸于某种情景或情绪中。有创造力的电影导演在书写作品时不是用笔而是用摄像机来完成的。在这一领域有很多大师，如英格玛·伯格曼、查理·卓别林、费德里科·费里尼、黑泽明、阿伦·雷乃和奥逊·威尔斯，他们作为导演和具有国际声望的知识领袖而受到广泛的尊重。当然，最重要的一位便是阿尔弗雷德·希区柯克。在这篇短文中，这位悬疑大师与我们分享了他拍摄电影的技巧，讲述了舞台表演和银幕表演之间的本质区别。在舞台表演过程中，观众与舞台之间的距离以及观看的角度很难改变。而在银幕上则不然，导演可以自由改变角度，调整距离，像蒙太奇一样迅速转换场景。对希区柯克而言，拍摄电影的关键点不是站在一旁被动地记录摄像机前正在发生的事情，而是通过特写和夸张的手段来选择和安排人物动作以及聚焦对象的细节，这样才能使一个事件以最有效的方式发生。本文选自阿尔弗雷德·希区柯克的文章《拍摄方法》(查尔斯·戴维编，《电影脚注》，伦敦: 彼得·戴维斯有限公司，1939年)。

In time the script and the sets[1] are finished, and we are ready to start shooting.[2] One great problem is to get the players to adapt themselves to film technique. Many of them, of course, come from the stage;[3] they are not cinema-minded[4] at all. So, quite naturally they like to play long scenes straight ahead.[5] I am willing to work with the long uninterrupted shot:[6] you can't avoid it altogether and you can get some variety by having two cameras running, one close up and one farther off, and cutting[7] from one to the other when the film is edited. But if I have to shoot a long scene continuously, I always feel I am losing grip on it, from a cinematic point of view. The camera, I feel, is simply standing there, hoping to catch something with a visual point to it. What I like to do always is to photograph just the little bits of a scene that I really need for building up a visual sequence,[8] I want to put my film together on the screen, not simply to photograph something that has been put together already in the form of a long piece of stage acting. This is what gives an effect of life to a picture: the feeling that when you see it on the screen you are watching something that has been conceived and brought to birth directly in visual terms.[9] The screen ought to speak its own language, freshly coined, and it can't do that unless it treats an acted scene as a piece of raw material which must be broken up, taken to bits, before it can be woven into an expressive visual pattern.

You can see an example of what I mean in *Sabotage*.[10] Just before Verloc[11] is killed, there is a scene made up entirely of short pieces of film, separately photographed. This scene has to show how Verloc comes to be killed, how the thought of killing him arises in Sylvia Sidney's mind and connects itself with the carving knife she uses when they sit down to dinner. But the sympathy of the audience has to be kept with Sylvia Sidney; it must be clear that Verloc's death, finally, is an accident. So, as she serves at the table, you see her unconsciously serving vegetables with the carving knife, as though her hand were keeping hold of the knife of its own accord.[12] The camera cuts from her hand to her eyes and back to her hand, then back to her eyes as she suddenly becomes aware of the knife making its error. Then to a normal shot, the man unconcernedly eating; then back to the hand holding the knife. In an old style of acting, Sylvia would have had to show the audience what was passing in her mind by exaggerated facial expression. But people today in real life often don't show their feelings in their faces; so the film treatment showed the audience her mind through her hand, through its unconscious grasp on the knife. Now the camera moves again to Verloc, back to the knife, back again to his face. You see him seeing the knife, realizing its implication. The tension between the two is built up with the knife as its focus.[13]

Now when the camera has immersed[14] the audience so closely in a scene such as this, it can't instantly become objective again. It must broaden the movement of the scene without loosening the tension. Verloc gets up and walks round the table, coming so close to the camera that you feel, if you are sitting in the audience, almost as though you must move back to make room for him.[15] Then the camera moves to Sylvia Sidney again, then returns to the subject: the knife.

So you gradually build up the psychological situation, using the camera to emphasize first one detail, then another. The point is to draw the audience right inside the situation instead of leaving them to watch it from outside, from a distance. And you can do this only by breaking the action up into details and cutting from one to the other, so that each detail is forced in turn on the attention of the audience and reveals its psychological meaning. If you played the whole scene straight through and simply made a photographic record of it with the camera always in one position, you would lose your power over the audience. They would watch the scene without becoming really involved in it, and you would have no means of concentrating their attention on what the characters are feeling.

One way of using the camera to give emphasis is the reaction shot. By the reaction shot I mean any close-up[16] which illustrates an event by showing instantly the reaction to it of a person or a group. The door opens for someone to come in, and before showing who it is, you cut to the expressions of the persons already in the room. Or, while one person is talking, you keep your camera on someone else who is listening. This over-running[17] of one person's image with another person's voice is a method peculiar to the talkies;[18] it is one of the devices which help the talkies to tell a story faster than a silent film could tell it and faster than it could be told on the stage.

Or you can use the camera to give emphasis whenever the attention of the audience has to be focused for a moment on a certain player. There is no need for him to raise his voice or move to the centre of the stage or do anything dramatic. A close-up will do it all for him, will give him, so to speak, the stage all to himself.

In recent years I have become more commercially minded,[19] afraid that anything at all subtle may be missed. I have learnt from experience how easily small touches are overlooked. The other day a journalist came to interview me, and we spoke about film technique. "I always remember," he said, "a little bit in one of your silent films, *The Ring*. The young boxer comes home after winning his fight. He is flushed with success,[20] wants to celebrate. He pours out champagne all round. Then he finds that his wife is out, and he knows at once that she is out with another man. At this moment the camera cuts to a glass of champagne; you see a fizz of bubbles rise off it, and there it stands untasted, going flat.[21] That one shot gives you the whole feeling of the scene." Yes, I said, that sort of imagery may be quite good: I don't despise it and still use it now and then. But is it always noticed?

There was another bit in *The Ring*, which I believe hardly anyone noticed. The scene was outside a boxing booth[22] at a fair, with a barker[23] talking to the crowd. Inside the booth a professional[24] is taking on[25] all comers. He has always won in the first round.[26] A man comes running out of the booth and speaks to the barker: something unexpected has happened. Then a cut straight to the ringside:[27] you see an old figure 1 being taken down and replaced by a brand new figure 2. I meant this single detail to show that the boxer now is up against someone he can't put out in the first round. But it went by too quickly. Perhaps I might have shown the new figure 2, being taken out of a paper wrapping; something else was needed to make the audience see in a moment that the figure for the second round had never been used before.

The film always has to deal in exaggerations. Its methods reflect the simple contrasts of black and white photography. One advantage of color is that it would give you more intermediate shades.[28] I should never want to fill the screen with color: it ought to be used economically, to put new words into the screen's visual language when there's a need for them. You could start a color film with a board room scene: sombre paneling and furniture, the directors all in dark clothes and white collars. Then the chairman's wife comes in, wearing a red hat. She takes the attention of the audience at once, just because of that one note of color. Or suppose a gangster story: the leader of the gang is sitting in a café with a man he suspects. He has told his gunman to watch the table. "If I order a glass of port, bump him off.[29] If I order green chartreuse,[30] let him go."

This journalist asked me also about distorted sound, a device I tried in *Blackmail*[31] when the word "knife" hammers on the consciousness of the girl at breakfast on the morning after the murder. Again, I think this kind of effect may be justified. There have always been occasions when we have needed to show a phantasmagoria[32] of the mind in terms of visual imagery. So we may want to show someone's mental state by letting him listen to some sound—let us say church bells—and making them clang with distorted insistence in his head. But on the whole nowadays I try to tell a story in the simplest possible way, so that I can feel sure it will hold the attention of any audience and won't puzzle them.

NOTES

1. the script and the sets: Script is the manuscript of a play or actor's part. Sets are the sceneries of a play.
2. shooting: taking (a picture) with a camera.
3. the stage: the theater; the drama.
4. cinema-minded: thinking in terms of the art of motion picture.
5. straight ahead: continuously.
6. shot: picture taken with a camera, photograph.
7. cutting: editing (film or audio tape); changing suddenly from one scene to the other.
8. visual sequence: order in which images and visions are presented (to the spectator).
9. something that has been conceived and brought to birth directly in visual terms: something that has been designed and presented directly to the eye.
10. *Sabotage*: a film made by Hitchcock in 1937.
11. Verloc: Both Verloc and Sylvia Sidney are characters in *Sabotage*.
12. of its own accord: without being asked or (in this case) dictated (by Sylvia's mind).
13. focus: the central point of attention.
14. immersed: plunged; absorbed.
15. to make room for him: so that he has space enough to move about.
16. close-up: picture taken at close range.

17. over-running: overlapping; superimposition.
18. talkies: motion pictures with sound.
19. commercially minded: catering to popular taste for the box office.
20. flushed with success: excited with success.
21. going flat: becoming flavorless.
22. boxing booth: a covered structure in a fair for boxing.
23. barker: person who stands in front of a show to urge people to go in.
24. professional: person who makes a business of something (in this case boxing) not properly regarded as a business; person who is properly trained for some performance and not an amateur.
25. taking on: undertaking to deal with.
26. the first round: the first part of a game or sport. 第一回合.
27. a cut straight to the ringside: a sudden shift of scene from in front of the booth to the place just outside the ring (of boxing). Cut is a sharp transition between shots or scenes in a film.
28. intermediate shades: degrees from lightness to darkness.
29. bump him off: kill him.
30. chartreuse: a liqueur first made by Carthusian monks. It may be green, yellow, or white. Port wine is usually red. Thus color becomes the focus of uneasy anticipation because red means death and green means luck.
31. *Blackmail*: a film Hitchcock made in 1929.
32. phantasmagoria: a fantastic sequence of haphazardly associative imagery, as seen in dreams or fever.

参考译文

在剧本和布景完成之后，我们就可以准备开始拍摄了。一个很大的问题就是如何让演员适应电影的拍摄手法。他们当中很多人都来自戏剧舞台，根本没有拍电影时的镜头意识。所以，他们自然喜欢远景镜头下不间断的表演。我也愿意使用不间断的长镜头，因为这是无法完全避免的。如果想要增添些变化，可以同时使用两台摄像机，一台近景，一台远景，在剪辑影片时再进行场景切换。然而如果我必须得连续拍摄一个场景，从电影的角度来看，我总感觉自己丧失了对镜头的把控力。我认为，摄像机立在那里为的是要捕捉到一些具有视觉意义的镜头。我常常喜欢只拍摄一个场景中自己真正需要的一小部分镜头，然后构成一个视觉的序列呈现在银幕上，而不是简单地将一些舞台表演的长镜头组合在一起。这样就能赋予电影一种活灵活现的效果：观众在银幕上看到影片的时候，就会感觉到导演的构思直接被视觉影像赋予了生命。银幕应该使用它自己的语言，一种新铸的语言，要做到这一点就必须将一个表演场景视为一块原材料，要打破整体性，拆成碎片，这样才可以编织出一种富有表现力的视觉模式。

在电影《阴谋破坏》中就能看到典型的例子。就在维洛克被杀之前，有一场戏完全由短小的片段组成，它们是分别拍摄完成的。这场戏必须展示出维洛克是如何被杀的，也要交代杀死他的想法是如何在西尔维娅·西德尼的脑中浮现的，得和她在餐桌旁使用的餐刀联系起来。然而观众的同情必须放在西尔维娅·西德尼的身上，必须证明维洛克的死最终只是一场意外。因此，她在餐桌旁备菜时，观众能看到她无意识地用餐刀切分蔬菜，好像她的手不自觉地主动握住了餐刀。镜头从她的手切换到她的眼睛，再切换回她的手，然后又切换到她的眼睛，因为她突然意识到刀用错了地方。接着是一个正常的镜头，男人在漫不经心地吃着东西，然后镜头又切回拿刀的手上。在旧式的表演风格中，西尔维娅不得不通过夸张的面部表情向观众展示她的内心活动。但是今天的人们在现实生活中往往不会将自己的感情表露在脸上，因此电影的处理手法是通过她的手和无意识的握刀镜头向观众展现她的内心。镜头再次移向维洛克，又转向餐刀，再又切回他的脸。观众看到他在看刀，也就明白了其中的深意。餐刀作为焦点建立起了两者之间的紧张关系。

镜头让观众沉浸在这样的场景中，代入感十分强烈，很难立即返回客观的立场。此时人物的活动空间必须拓展，还要继续保持情节的紧张。维洛克起身绕过桌子，逼近镜头，要是你坐在观众席上，就会感觉必须得后退才能给他腾出空间。随后镜头再次转向西尔维娅·西德尼，然后回到场景的主题：餐刀。

因此，用镜头先强调一处细节，然后强调另一处细节，这样就逐渐构建出一种心理状况。关键是要把观众吸引到这种状况中来，而不是让他们在外部和远处观看。要做到这一点，就只能把动作分解成细节，从一处细节切换到另一处细节，每一处细节轮番吸引观众的注意力，也揭示出其心理意义。一场戏从头到尾表演一遍，如果只是简单地用一个固定机位的摄像机进行记录，那你就会失去对观众的掌控力。他们在观看时不能真正融入其中，你也无法将观众的注意力集中在剧中人物的感受上。

有一种用摄像机来进行强调的方式称为"反应镜头"。所谓的"反应镜头"，就是指通过展示个体或群体的即时反应来描绘事件的任何特写镜头。门敞开着，有人要进来，在展示谁要进来之前，要先切换到屋里人的表情。或者，一个人说话时，镜头要聚焦在听话人的身上。用一个人的声音重叠覆盖另一个人的形象，这是有声电影独特的手法。在讲述同样的故事时，它让有声电影比无声电影的速度更快，也比舞台上讲述的速度更快。

当观众的注意力需要集中在某位剧中人身上时，你也可以使用镜头来进行强调。人物不需要提高嗓门，不需要走到舞台中央，也不需要做任何夸张的表演。一个特写镜头就已足够，特写镜头可以让人物成为剧中唯一的主角。

近年来，我变得更具商业眼光了，生怕错过任何细微的东西。经验告诉我，细微的感触是很容易被忽视的。有一天，一位记者来采访我，我们谈到了电影的技术。他说："我一直记得你那部无声电影《拳击场》中的一个小片段。年轻的拳击手在赢得比赛后回到家中，他带着胜利的喜悦想要庆祝一下。他将香槟酒杯斟满，却发现自己的妻子没在家。他立刻明白妻子和另一个男人在外逍遥。此时，镜头切换到一杯香槟上，可以看到气泡在杯中上升，然而这杯酒却无人品尝，随即变得香味全无。这一个镜头给足了整段戏的全部感觉。"我回答道，是的，这种画面或许很不错，我并不鄙视它，而且还时常在使用该手法。可是人们会常常注意到这种细节吗？

《拳击场》中还有另一个片段，我相信几乎没人注意过。该场景设在集市，一名招徕顾客的人站在拳击棚外与众人交谈。一位职业拳击手在棚中正与挑战者交手，他总能在第一回合就赢过对方。一个人从棚中跑出来，对招徕顾客的人说：发生了点意外。然后镜头直接切换到擂台边上：你能看到一个旧的数字"1"被拿下，取而代之的是一个崭新的数字"2"。我突出这一细节是想表明，拳击手现在面对的是一个他无法在第一回合就解决掉的人。但该细节在电影中一闪而过，或许我应该向观众展示新数字"2"从包装纸中拿出的过程，也需要增添其他内容让观众明白，第二回合的这个数字以前从未使用过。

电影中总是要有夸张的处理手法，可以反映出黑白摄影中明显的色调差。使用色彩的好处之一就是可以呈现更多的色度。我不会总是想着用色彩来填满银幕：色彩的使用要有节制，只有在需要的时候才应该把新词汇放入银幕的视觉语言中去。一部彩色电影的开头场景可以是一个会议室：木板墙与桌椅都是暗淡的色调，所有董事的衣服是深黑色的，领子是亮白色的。这时，董事长的妻子走了进来，戴着一顶红帽子。单凭这颜色，她立刻就能吸引观众的注意力。或者再设想一个有关黑帮的故事：黑帮头目和他怀疑的人坐在一家咖啡馆里。头目告诉杀手要注意观察桌子："如果我点了一杯波特酒，就干掉他。如果我点了一杯荨麻酒，就放他走。"

这位记者还问到有关声音失真的问题，这是我在电影《讹诈》

中使用过的手法。女孩在谋杀案发生后的早晨用餐时，"刀"这个词就以扭曲失真的音效敲打着她的意识。同样，我认为使用这种效果是合理的。有些时候，我们需要用视觉图像来展现心灵上的幻影。因此，我们或许可以让一个人来聆听某种声音，比如说教堂的钟声，这样就可以展现出他的精神状态，让这些声音与他头脑中那扭曲的固执产生共鸣。但总体而言，现在的我会尽量用最简单的方式来讲述故事，这样我就能确保故事可以吸引任何观众的注意力，而不会让他们感到困惑。

（吴思远 译）

Statement on Art

艺术宣言

Pablo Picasso
巴勃罗·毕加索

(1881–1973)

ABOUT THE AUTHOR

Pablo Picasso (1881–1973) enjoyed a long and fruitful life as the greatest Western painter whose universal influence few artists in the twentieth century have escaped. Born in Malaga, Spain, he established his great fame in Paris and, after 1904, made France his home in token of his disapproval of Franco's government. Early in his career he had impressed the world of modern art with his leadership of the Cubist movement, but his genius was so fecund that in his art periods and styles continually rose, sometimes alongside one another, only to reappear in new combinations in painting or sculpture. Among his masterpieces is the monumental *Guernica*, painted in protest of German air raid on a Spanish town of the same name.

作者简介　巴勃罗·毕加索（1881—1973），西方最伟大的画家，他漫长的一生成果累累，20世纪鲜有艺术家能不受其影响。他出生于西班牙马拉加，成名于巴黎，1904年后，他移居法国，以示对佛朗哥政府的不满。在职业生涯早期，他作为立体主义的领头羊给现代艺术界留下了深刻印象，他的创造力非常旺盛，其艺术生涯划分为不同时期，作品呈现出多样的风格，有时不同的风格并驾齐驱，在他的绘画或雕塑中以新的组合出现。其杰作包括不朽的《格尔尼卡》，这幅作品是为抗议德国空袭一个同名西班牙小镇而作的。

ABOUT THE SELECTION

The above statement was dictated by Picasso in Spanish to Marius de Zayas. Picasso approved the manuscript before it was translated and published in 1923. Early in the twentieth century, theorists like Wilhelm Worringer contrasted naturalistic art (which mirrors the organic world and wins our vitalistic empathy for it) with abstract art (which revolts from such naturalism and escapes to a timeless world of inorganic and geometric forms). To such a dualism in art Picasso stood firmly opposed. As the foremost artist in the West, Picasso made a more fundamental distinction—one that is between all art and reality. "There are no concrete or abstract forms, but only forms which are more or less convincing lies." Yet art is more than the artificial, Picasso hastened to say: "Art is a lie that makes us realize truth." In a career of so many periods and styles, it should not surprise us that Picasso rejected superficial notions of "rise and decline" in the arts. He viewed each work in terms of its intrinsic value in confronting reality with its lies and its truth. Picasso believed that a work of art must live always in the present, that arts of transition do not exist, and that there is no evolution or progress in art. This reminds us strongly of T. S. Eliot's conviction in the simultaneous presence of all works of art when he said: "No poet, no artist of any art, has his complete meaning alone. His significance, his appreciation is the appreciation of his relation to the dead poets and artists... What happens when a new work of art is created is something that happens simultaneously to all the works of art which preceded it... The poet must be very conscious of the main current, which does not at all flow invariably through the most distinguished reputations. He must be quite aware of the obvious fact that art never improves, but that the material of art is never quite the same. He must be aware that the mind of Europe... is a mind which changes, and that this change is a development which abandons nothing *en route*, which does not superannuate either Shakespeare or Homer... that this development, refinement perhaps, complication certainly, is not, from the point of view of the artist, any improvement."

内容简介 本文是毕加索用西班牙语口述给马里乌斯·德·萨亚斯的。在 1923 年翻译出版之前，毕加索核准了手稿。在 20 世纪早期，威廉·沃林格等理论家将自然主义艺术（自然主义艺术反映了有机世界，并赢得了我们的强烈共鸣）与抽象艺术（抽象艺术反抗这种自然主义，逃避到无机和几何形式的永恒世界）进行了对比。毕加索坚决反对艺术上的这种二元论。作为西方最重要的艺术家，毕加索提出了一个更根本的区别——所有艺术与现实之间的区别。"没有具体或抽象的形式，只有或多或少令人信服的谎言形式。"然而，艺术并不全然是人造的，毕加索很快补充说："艺术是一种谎言，能让我们认识真理。"毕加索的职业生涯分为多个时期，风格多变，所以他拒绝肤浅的艺术"兴衰"论，并不令人意外。他衡量每一部作品是看它的内在价值，即它如何以谎言和真理来对照现实。毕加索认为，艺术作品必须永远活在当下，不存在什么过渡的艺术，艺术没有演变或进步之说。这不由得让我们想起 T. S. 艾略特关于所有艺术作品同时并存的信念，他说："任何诗人，任何艺术的艺术家，都不能独自拥有自己完整的意义。他的意义，他的欣赏说到底是对自己与死去的诗人和艺术家之间关系的欣赏……一件新艺术作品创作出来时出现的情况，会同时出现在之前的所有艺术作品上……诗人必须对主流有非常清醒的认识，因为主流并不见得总是从最显赫的名声中流出。他必须非常清楚一个显而易见的事实：艺术永远不会改进，而艺术的材料也永远不会完全相同。他必须意识到欧洲的思想……是一种变化的思想，这种变化是一种发展，而这种发展在途中不会抛弃任何东西，不会淘汰莎士比亚，也不会淘汰荷马……这种发展，也许有改进，肯定会遇到困难，但从艺术家的角度来看，不是什么进步。"

I can hardly understand the importance given to the word *research* in connection with modern painting. In my opinion to search means nothing in painting. To find, is the thing. Nobody is interested in following a man who, with his eyes fixed on the ground, spends his life looking for the pocketbook[1] that fortune should put in his path. The one who finds something no matter what it might be, even if his intention were not to search for it, at least arouses our curiosity, if not our admiration.

Among the several sins that I have been accused of committing,[2] none is more false than the one that I have, as the principal objective[3] in my work, the spirit of research. When I paint my object is to show what I have found and not what I am looking for. In art intentions are not sufficient and, as we say in Spanish: love must be proved by facts and not by reasons. What one does is what counts[4] and not what one had the intention of doing.

We all know that art is not truth. Art is a lie that makes us realize truth, at least the truth that is given us to understand.[5] The artist must know the manner whereby[6] to convince others of the truthfulness of his lies. If he only shows in his work that he has searched, and researched, for the way to put over[7] his lies, he would never accomplish anything.

The idea of research has often made painting go astray,[8] and made the artist lose himself in mental lucubrations.[9] Perhaps this has been the principal fault of modern art. The spirit of research has poisoned[10] those who have not fully understood all the positive and conclusive elements in modern art and has made them attempt to paint the invisible and, therefore, the unpaintable.[11]

They speak of naturalism[12] in opposition to modern painting. I would like to know if anyone has ever seen a natural work of art. Nature and art, being two different things, cannot be the same thing. Through art we express our conception of what nature is not.

Velásquez[13] left us his idea of the people of his epoch. Undoubtedly they were different from what he painted them, but we cannot conceive a Philip IV[14] in any other way than the one Velásquez painted. Rubens[15] also made a portrait of the same king and in Rubens' portrait he seems to be quite another person. We believe in the one painted by Velásquez, for he convinces us by his right of might.[16]

From the painters of the origins; the primitives,[17] whose work is obviously different from nature, down to those artists who, like David, Ingres and even Bouguereau,[18] believed in painting nature as it is, art has always been art and not nature. And from the point of view of art there are no concrete or abstract forms, but only forms which are more or less convincing lies. That those lies are necessary to our mental selves is beyond any doubt, as it is through them that we form our esthetic point of view of life.

Cubism[19] is no different from any other school of painting. The same principles and the same elements are common to all. The fact that for a long time cubism has not been understood and that even today there are people who cannot see anything in it, means nothing. I do not read English, an English book is a blank book to me. This does not mean that the English language does not exist, and why should I blame anybody else but myself if I cannot understand what I know nothing about?

I also often hear the word evolution.[20] Repeatedly I am asked to explain how my painting evolved. To me there is no past or future in art. If a work of art cannot always live in the present it must not be considered at all. The art of the Greeks, of the Egyptians, of the great painters who lived in other times, is not an art of the past; perhaps it is more alive today than it ever was. Art does not evolve by itself, the ideas of people change and with them their mode of expression. When I hear people speak of the evolution of an artist, it seems to me that they are considering him standing between two mirrors that face each other and reproduce his image an infinite number of times, and that they contemplate the successive images of one mirror as his past, and the images of the other mirror as his future, while his real image is taken as his present. They do not consider that they all are the same images in different planes.

Variation[21] does not mean evolution. If an artist varies his mode of expression this only means that he has changed his manner of thinking, and in changing, it might be for the better or it might be for the worse.

The several manners I have used in my art must not be considered as an evolution, or as steps toward an unknown ideal of painting. All I have ever made was made for the present and with the hope that it will always remain in the present. I have never taken into consideration the spirit of research. When I have found something to express, I have done it without thinking of the past or of the future. I do not believe I have used radically different[22] elements in the different manners I have used in painting. If the subjects I have wanted to express have suggested different ways of expression I have never hesitated to adopt them. I have never made trials nor experiments. Whenever I have something to say, I have said it in the manner in which I have felt it ought to be said. Different motives inevitably[23] require different methods of expression. This does not imply either evolution or progress, but an adaptation of the idea one wants to express and the means to express that idea.

Arts of transition[24] do not exist. In the chronological[25] history of art there are periods which are more positive, more complete than others.

This means that there are periods in which there are better artists than in others. If the history of art could be graphically[26] represented, as in a chart used by a nurse to mark the changes of temperature of her patient, the same silhouettes of mountains[27] would be shown, proving that in art there is no ascendant progress,[28] but that it follows certain ups and downs[29] that might occur at any time. The same occurs with the work of an individual artist.

Many think that cubism is an art of transition, an experiment which is to bring ulterior[30] results. Those who think that way have not understood it. Cubism is not either a seed or a foetus,[31] but an art dealing primarily with forms, and when a form is realized it is there to live its own life. A mineral substance, having geometric formation, is not made so for transitory[32] purposes, it is to remain what it is and will always have its own form. But if we are to apply the law of evolution and transformism to art, then we have to admit that all art is transitory. On the contrary,[33] art does not enter into these philosophic absolutisms.[34] If cubism is an art of transition I am sure that the only thing that will come out of it is another form of cubism.

Mathematics, trigonometry, chemistry, psychoanalysis, music, and whatnot,[35] have been related to cubism to give it an easier interpretation.[36] All this has been pure literature,[37] not to say nonsense, which brought bad results, blinding people with theories.

Cubism has kept itself within the limits and limitations of painting, never pretending to go beyond it. Drawing, design and color are understood and practiced in cubism in the same spirit and manner that they are understood and practiced in all other schools. Our subjects might be different, as we have introduced into painting objects and forms that were formerly ignored. We have kept our eyes open to our surroundings, and also our brains.[38]

We give to form and color all their individual significance, as far as we can see it; in our subjects we keep the joy of discovery, the pleasure of the unexpected; our subject itself must be a source of interest. But of what use is it to say what we do when everybody can see it if he wants to?

NOTES
1. pocketbook: small case or folder to hold money or paper, etc.; wallet.
2. commit: do (something wrong).
3. objective: aim, goal.
4. what counts: what matters; what is important.
5. the truth that is given us to understand: the truth that is in our power to understand.
6. whereby: by which.
7. put over: present.
8. go astray: go off the right way.
9. lose himself in mental lucubrations: lose his way in hard but dull work of the mind.
10. poisoned: had a harmful effect on.
11. unpaintable: impossible to paint.
12. naturalism: accurate depiction of things as they are, not as they are imagined, idealized or intellectualized. It should not be confused with Realism, which is the depiction of the squalid, the lowly and the depressing.
13. Diego Rodriguez de Silva y Velásquez (1599-1660): Spanish painter.
14. Philip IV (1605-1665): King of Spain who ruled during 1621-1665.
15. Peter Paul Rubens (1577-1640): Flemish painter, a friend of Velásquez.
16. right of might: claim of exquisite artistic achievement; claim of superiority.
17. the primitives: Netherlandish painters of the late fourteenth and all the fifteenth centuries, and all Italian painters between Giotto and Raphael.
18. David, Ingres, Bouguereau: Jacques Louis David (1748-1825), Jean Auguste Dominique Ingres (1780-1867), and Adolphe William Bouguereau (1825-1905) were all followers of Neo-Classicism. Their themes, removed from contemporary life, were either historical, mythological, or religious; their styles were academic in

contrast to the Impressionist school.
19. Cubism: a movement in painting led by Picasso and Braque during 1908-1920 as a reaction against the diffuse, formless character of Impressionism. It derived its name from the critic Louis Vauxcelles who referred to certain elements in a work by Braque as "little cubes". Taking up Cezanne's search for basic, geometric elements, the bones of nature, Cubism aimed first of all at their realization through a process of breaking down and taking apart the forms of nature (analytical cubism) and secondly, at an imaginative reorganization of these geometric elements in various contexts (synthetic cubism). The final aim of Cubism was the realization of new combinations of fundamental forms. While Impressionism was concerned primarily with the liberation of color, Cubism sought the liberation of form. Important painters of this school included, besides Picasso and Braque, Fernand Leger and Juan Gris. No school of modern painting is free from the radical influence of Cubism.
20. evolution: process of growth from a crude to an advanced state.
21. variation: a varying in condition, degree, etc.; change.
22. radically different: fundamentally different; thoroughly different.
23. inevitably: unavoidably.
24. transition: change from one condition or state to another.
25. chronological: arranged in the order of happening.
26. graphically: in a diagram, chart or picture; pictorially.
27. silhouettes of mountains: lines that go up and down sharply.
28. ascendant progress: steadily rising progress.
29. ups and downs: rises and falls.
30. ulterior: hidden; further; more distant.
31. foetus: an animal embryo during the later stages of its development. Also spelt "fetus".
32. transitory: lasting for a short time.
33. on the contrary: from an opposite point of view; conversely.
34. absolutism: despotism; tyranny. Here "philosophic absolutisms" means "philosophic dogmatisms".
35. and whatnot: and so on.
36. interpretation: explanation; explication.
37. pure literature: sheer imagination; pure invention, something made up.
38. brains: mind; intelligence.

参考译文

"探索"一词在现代绘画中的重要性，我很难理解。在我看来，探索在绘画中毫无意义。发现，才是关键。谁都不会有兴趣追随一个两眼盯着地面、一辈子都想撞大运、在路上捡到钱包的人。一个人有所发现，不论发现的是什么，哪怕是无意之中的发现，不说会令我们肃然起敬，起码也会令我们油然感到好奇。

有人给我头上安了好几个罪名，但最莫须有的一个还是说我有探索精神，而且说成了我作品的主要宗旨。作画时，我的宗旨是画出我所发现的东西，而不是我要寻找的东西。在艺术中仅有这样那样的意图是不够的，正如西班牙俗语所言：爱必须拿事实来证明，不能用情理来证明。重要的是看一个人做了什么，而不是他打算做什么。

众所周知，艺术不是真理。艺术是一种谎言，能让我们认识真理、至少是我们能明白的真理的谎言。艺术家须深谙一套以假乱真的本领，令人对自己的谎言信以为真。倘若他在作品中只是表现出自己寻找和探索过掩盖谎言的方法，那他就将一事无成。

探索的念头往往会使绘画误入歧途，让艺术家绞尽脑汁，冥思苦想而不能自拔。也许这就是现代艺术的主要缺陷之所在。探索精神把那些没有吃透现代艺术中所有积极的、决定性元素的人给毒害了，诱使他们画那些看不见，因而也画不出来的东西。

他们张口闭口都是写实主义，也叫自然主义，以此来反对现代绘画。我想知道有没有谁见过自然的艺术作品。自然和艺术，是两种不同的东西，不可能是一回事。我们用艺术所表达的就是我们认为自然就是自然，不是艺术的概念。

委拉斯凯兹给我们留下了他对同时代人民的看法。毫无疑问，他笔下的人与现实中的是不一样的，但除了委拉斯凯兹所画的费利佩四世，我们根本无法以别的任何方式想象出一个费利佩四世来。鲁本斯也画过同一位国王的肖像，在鲁本斯的肖像画中，费利佩四世看上去完全是另一个人。我们相信委拉斯凯兹画的那一幅，因为他高超的艺术感染力，让我们心悦诚服。

　　从作品显然有别于自然的最早的原始派画家，到像大卫、安格尔，乃至布格罗等崇尚写实的艺术家，艺术都一直是艺术，而不是自然。从艺术的角度来看，没有具体或抽象的形式，只有或多或少令人信服的谎言形式。毫无疑问，这些谎言对我们精神上的自我来说是必要的，因为正是凭借这些谎言，我们才形成了对生活的审美观。

　　立体主义与任何其他画派都没有什么不同。绘画的原则和要素都是一模一样的。很长一段时间以来，人们都理解不了立体主义，即使在今天，也有人看不出其中的任何东西，这并不意味着什么。我不懂英文，英文书对我来说就是一本天书，但这并不意味着英语不存在。理解不了自己一无所知的东西，为什么要怪别人而不是怪自己呢？

　　我也经常听到"演变"这个词。人们一再要求解释我的绘画是如何演变的。对我来说，艺术无所谓演变，没有过去，也没有未来。倘若一件艺术作品不能永远活在当下，那就根本不值一顾。希腊人、埃及人以及生活在其他时代的伟大画家的艺术，都不是过去的艺术，说不定它今天比以往任何时候都更有活力。艺术不会自行演变，但人们的观念会改变，他们的表达方式也会随之改变。听到人们大谈特谈某个艺术家的演变，给我的感觉是，他们仿佛是在端详自己站在两面相对的镜子之间的样子，无数次地复制其形象，把一面镜子中的连续形象视为他的过去，另一面镜子中的形象视为他的未来，而他的真实形象则被视为他的现在。他们看不到这些形象其实是不同平面上的同一映像。

艺术宣言
Statement on Art

改变并不意味着演变。如果一个艺术家改变了自己的表现方式，只意味着他改变了自己的思维方式，而且在改变的过程中，可能会变得更好，也可能变得更糟。

我在艺术中使用的几种方式不能视为演变，也不能视为迈向未知绘画理想的步骤。我所做的一切都是为了当下，而且希望这一切永远停留在当下。我从来没有考虑过探索精神。一旦找到要表达的东西，我就表达出来，而不考虑过去或未来。在我不同的画法中，我不认为自己使用过完全不同的元素。如果我想表达的主题要求采用不同的表达方式，我就会毫不犹豫地采用。我从来没做过任何实验，也没进行过任何试验。只要我有话要说，我就会以自认为应该的方式说出来。动机不同，必然要求表达方式也随之改变。但这并不意味着演变或进化，而是对一个人要表达的想法和表达该想法的方式的适应。

不存在什么过渡的艺术。在艺术的编年史中，有些时期的艺术成就比其他时期更为斐然。这意味着，比起别的时期来，某些时期有更出色的艺术家。如果艺术史可以用护士标记病人体温变化的图表来表示的话，那么同样的山脉轮廓也会显示出来，也就证明了艺术不可能只上不下，而是随时都可能会有起有伏。一个艺术家的作品也是如此。

很多人认为立体主义是一种过渡的艺术，是一场影响未来的实验。有这种想法的人还没有理解立体主义。立体主义既不是一粒种子，也不是一个胎儿，而是一门主要与形式打交道的艺术，而某种形式诞生之后，就有了自己的生命。就如一种几何形态的矿物，不是为了暂时的目的而形成的，它会保持原样，并且会永远有其自己的形态。如果我们要把演变和进化论的规律应用到艺术上，那就必须承认，所有的艺术都是短暂的。但恰恰相反，艺术并没有步入这种哲学上的绝对主义。如果说立体主义是一种过渡的艺术，那么我确信，能从中产生的唯一东西就是另一种形式的立体主义。

　　有些人为了解释起来省事一些，把数学、三角学、化学、精神分析学、音乐等等都与立体主义扯到了一起。这一切虽不能说是胡说八道，但都是纯粹臆想出来的东西，影响很坏，用各种各样的理论蒙蔽了人们。

　　立体主义一直把自己限制在绘画的范畴之内，从不妄称超越了这个界限。从精神和方式上说，立体派对绘画、设计和色彩的理解和实践与其他所有流派并无二致。我们的主题可能会有所不同，那是因为我们在绘画中引入了以前被忽略的对象和形式。我们一直睁大眼睛，关注周围的环境，也关注我们的头脑。

　　形式与色彩的与众不同的意义，我们能看出多少，都会毫无保留地表现出来；我们把发现的喜悦、意外的喜悦保存在自己的主题中；我们的主题本身必须能引起人们的兴趣。如果人们只要想看就能看出其中门道的话，我们又何必明说自己做了什么呢？

（覃学岚 译）

On Poetry

论诗歌

T. S. Eliot
T. S. 艾略特

(1888–1964)

ABOUT THE AUTHOR

Thomas Stearns Eliot (1888–1964), American poet, critic and dramatist, was the most influential literary figure in the English-speaking world in the first half of the twentieth century. Educated at Harvard, the Sorbonne and Oxford, Eliot began his literary career in London in 1915 and became a British subject in 1927. Among other honors he was awarded the Nobel Prize in 1948 for his work "as a trail-blazing pioneer of modern poetry." Whether as a poet or a critic, Eliot was chiefly responsible, early in the last century, in turning popular poetic taste from Romanticism to Classicism.

作者简介 托马斯·斯特恩斯·艾略特（1888—1964），美国诗人、批评家、剧作家，20世纪上半叶英语世界最具影响力的文学人物。艾略特先后就读于哈佛大学、索邦大学和牛津大学，1915年在伦敦开始了其文学生涯，1927年加入英国籍。1948年，因其"作为现代诗歌的开拓者"的工作而获得诺贝尔奖。作为诗人和批评家，艾略特领导推动了20世纪初大众的诗歌品味从浪漫主义转向古典主义。

ABOUT THE SELECTION

The three selections here are all taken from *The Use of Poetry and the Use of Criticism* (1933), which incorporated the lectures T. S. Eliot gave at Harvard in 1932-1933 as Charles Eliot Norton Professor of Poetry. The three separate titles were provided by John Hayward, editor of *T. S. Eliot: Selected Prose* in the Penguin series. As a leader of the classical movement in early twentieth century which strongly opposed the sentimental and the didactic in Romantic and Victorian poetry, Eliot emphasizes the cultivation of poetic taste from a purely emotional approach in one's adolescence to a more balanced intellectual approach in one's maturity. The development of taste which Eliot would like to see in a reader of poetry is one from the subjective attitude towards a poem or a poet to an objective one in which poetry is viewed not in its personal relation to the reader, but by its intrinsic value and its independent existence. To Eliot the basic requirement of a critic of poetry is the ability to tell the good from the bad, the genuine from the sham; but, in a more advanced state, he should be able to view a good poem in connection with other good poems and tell if it is superior and, if so, how much. Eliot further warns us that the two extremes of criticism are looking for other meanings than poetry to the neglect of poetry itself and viewing poetry purely as poetry to the exclusion of moral, social, religious and other implications.

内容简介　本文三个选段均出自《诗歌的功能与批评的功能》(1933)，其中收录了 T. S. 艾略特 1932 至 1933 年在哈佛大学任查尔斯·艾略特·诺顿诗歌教授时所做的演讲。三个小标题是由企鹅丛书中《T. S. 艾略特散文选》的编辑约翰·海沃德拟定的。艾略特是 20 世纪早期古典主义运动的领袖，他强烈反对浪漫主义和维多利亚时期诗歌的感伤与说教，强调诗歌品味的培养，认为青少年时期的诗歌应注重情感为主，步入成熟阶段则应更为平衡，更注重思想性。艾略特所希望看到的读者品味的发展是从对诗歌或诗人的主观态度到客观态度的发展，在这种态度中，诗歌不是以其与读者的个人关系，而是以其内在价值和独立存在来被看待的。对艾略特来说，诗评家的基本要求是能够甄别优劣、区分真伪，但层次更高的诗评家应该能够将一首好诗与其他好诗联系起来，并判断其是否优秀，如果优秀，又有多优秀。艾略特进一步警告我们，两种极端的批评都在寻找诗歌以外的意义，而忽视了诗歌本身，且将诗歌纯粹视为诗歌，而排除了道德、社会、宗教等其他含义。

The Development of Taste

The majority of children, up to say twelve or fourteen, are capable of a certain enjoyment of poetry; at or about puberty[1] the majority of these find little further use for it, but a small minority then find themselves possessed of a craving[2] for poetry which is wholly different from any enjoyment experienced before. I do not know whether little girls have a different taste in poetry from little boys, but the responses of the latter I believe to be fairly uniform. *Horatius*,[3] *The Burial of Sir John Moore*,[4] *Bannockburn*;[5] Tennyson's *Revenge*, some of the border ballads: a liking for martial[6] and sanguinary[7] poetry is no more to be discouraged than engagements with lead soldiers and pea-shooters.[8] The only pleasure that I got from Shakespeare was the pleasure of being commended for reading him; had I been[9] a child of more independent mind I should have refused to read him at all. Recognizing the frequent deceptions of memory, I seem to remember that my early liking for the sort of verse that small boys do like vanished at about the age of twelve, leaving me for a couple of years with no sort of interest in poetry at all. I can recall clearly enough the moment when, at the age of fourteen or so, I happened to pick up a copy of Fitzgerald's *Omar*[10] which was lying about, and the almost overwhelming introduction to a new world of feeling which this poem was the occasion of giving me. It was like a sudden conversion, the world appeared anew[11], painted with bright, delicious, and painful colors. Thereupon I took the usual adolescent course[12] with Byron, Shelley, Keats, Rossetti, Swinburne[13].

I take this period to have persisted until about my twenty-second year. Being a period of rapid assimilation[14] the end may not know the beginning, so different may the taste become. Like the first period of childhood, it is one beyond which I dare say many people never advance; so that such taste for poetry as they retain[15] in later life is only a sentimental memory of the pleasures of youth, and is probably entwined[16] with all our other sentimental[17] retrospective[18] feelings. It is, no doubt, a period of keen enjoyment; but we must not confuse the intensity of the poetic experience in adolescence with the intense experience of poetry. At this period, the poem, or the poetry of a single poet, invades[19] the youthful consciousness and assumes complete possession[20] for a time. We do not really see it as something with an existence outside ourselves; much as in our youthful experiences of love, we do not so much see the person as infer the existence of some outside object which sets in motion[21] these new and delightful feelings in which we are absorbed. The frequent result is an outburst of scribbling[22] which we may call imitation, so long as we are aware of the meaning of the word "imitation" which we employ. It is not deliberate choice of a poet to mimic, but writing under a kind of daemonic possession[23] by one poet.

The third, or mature stage of enjoyment of poetry, comes when we cease to identify ourselves with the poet we happen to be reading; when our critical faculties[24] remain awake; when we are aware of what one poet can be expected to give and what he cannot[25]. The poem has its own existence, apart from us; it was there before us and will endure after us.[26] It is only at this stage that the reader is prepared to distinguish between degrees of greatness in poetry; before that stage he can only be expected to distinguish between the genuine and the sham[27]—the capacity to make this latter distinction must always be practiced first. The poets we frequent[28] in adolescence will not be arranged in any objective order of eminence, but by the personal accidents[29] which put them into relation with us; and this is right. I doubt whether it is possible to explain to school children or even undergraduates the differences of degree among poets, and I doubt whether it is wise to try; they have not yet had enough experience of life for these matters to have much meaning.[30] The perception of why Shakespeare, or Dante[31], or Sophocles[32] holds the place he has is something which comes only very slowly in the course of living. And the deliberate attempt to grapple with poetry which is not naturally congenial,[33] and some of which never will be, should be a very mature activity indeed; an activity which well repays the effort, but which cannot be recommended to young people without grave danger[34] of deadening their sensibility to poetry and confounding the genuine *development* of taste with the sham acquisition of it[35].

The Appreciation of Poetry

The rudiment[36] of criticism is the ability to select a good poem and reject a bad poem; and its most severe test is of its ability[37] to select a good *new* poem, to respond properly to a new situation. The experience of poetry, as it develops in the conscious and mature person, is not merely the sum of the experiences of good poems. Education in poetry requires an organization of these experiences. There is not one of us who is born with, or who suddenly acquires at puberty or later, an infallible discrimination[38] and taste. The person whose experience is limited is always liable to be taken in by the sham or the adulterate article[39], and we see generation after generation of untrained readers being taken in by the sham and the adulterate in its own time—indeed preferring them,[40] for they are more easily assimilable than the genuine article. Yet a very large number of people, I believe, have the native capacity[41] for enjoying *some* good poetry: how much, or how many degrees of capacity may profitably be distinguished, is not part of my present purpose to inquire. It is only the exceptional reader, certainly, who in the course of time comes to classify and compare his experiences, to see one in the light of others;[42] and who, as his poetic experiences multiply,[43] will be able to understand each[44] more accurately. The element of enjoyment is enlarged into appreciation, which brings a more intellectual addition to the original intensity of feeling. It is a second stage in our understanding of poetry, when we no longer merely select and reject, but organize.[45] We may even speak of a third stage, one of reorganization; a stage at which a person already educated in poetry meets with something new in his own time, and finds a new pattern of poetry arranging itself in consequence.

The Critic of Poetry

Such writing as Johnson's *Lives of the Poets*[46] and his essay on Shakespeare loses none of its permanence[47] from the consideration that every generation must make its own appraisal[48] of the poetry of the past, in the light of the performance of its contemporaries and immediate predecessors.[49] Criticism of poetry moves between two extremes. On the one hand the critic may busy himself so much with the implications of a poem,[50] or of one poet's work—implications moral, social, religious, or other—that the poetry becomes hardly more than a text[51] for a discourse. Such is the tendency of the moralizing critics of the nineteenth century, to which[52] Landor[53] makes a notable exception. Or if you stick too closely to the "poetry" and adopt no attitude towards what the poet has to say,[54] you will tend to evacuate it of all significance.[55] And furthermore there is a philosophic borderline,[56] which you must not transgress too far or too often, if you wish to preserve your standing as a critic, and are not prepared to present yourself as a philosopher, metaphysician, sociologist, or psychologist instead. Johnson, in these respects, is a type of critical integrity.[57] Within his limitations, he is one of the great critics, and he is a great critic partly because he keeps within his limitations. When you know what they are, you know where you are.[58] Considering all the temptations to which one is exposed in judging contemporary writing, all the prejudices which one is tempted to indulge in judging writers of the immediately preceding generation, I view Johnson's *Lives of the Poets* as a masterpiece of the judicial bench.[59] His style is not so formally perfect[60] as that of some other prose writers of his time.[61] It reads often like the writing of a man who is more habituated to talking than to writing; he seems to think aloud, and in short breaths, rather than in the long periods of the historian or the orator.[62] His criticism is as salutary against the dogmatic excesses of the eighteenth century—more indulged in France than in England—as it is against excessive adulation of individual poets with their faults as well as virtues. For Johnson poetry was still poetry, and not another thing. Had he lived a generation later, he would have been obliged to look more deeply into the foundations, and so would have been unable to leave us an example of what criticism ought to be for a civilization which, being settled, has no need, while it lasts, to inquire into the functions of its parts.[63]

NOTES

1. puberty: the physical beginning of manhood and womanhood. It comes at about 14 in boys and about 12 in girls.
2. craving: strong desire; longing.
3. *Horatius*: a ballad of patriotic spirit by T. B. Macaulay.
4. *The Burial of Sir John Moore*: a short poem by Charles Wolfe (1791-1823), based on Southey's narrative in the *Annual Register*.
5. *Bannockburn*: a patriotic song by Robert Burns. The full title is *Bruce's March to Bannockburn*.
6. martial: of war; warlike.
7. sanguinary: delighting in bloodshed; militant.
8. lead soldiers and pea-shooters: toy soldiers and toy shooters of dried peas or other pellets.

9. had I been: if I had been.
10. Fitzgerald's *Omar*: *The Rubaiyat of Omar Khayyam*, translated from Persian into English by Edward FitzGerald (1809-1883). The quatrains sing the transitory pleasures of earthly life in a romantic tone.
11. anew: once more, in a new way.
12. adolescent course: youthful study. An adolescent is a person from 12 to 22.
13. Byron, Shelley, Keats, Rossetti, Swinburne: English poets of the Romantic school in early and middle nineteenth century. Rossetti refers to Dante Gabriel Rossetti.
14. assimilation: taking in; absorption.
15. retain: keep.
16. entwined: confused; mixed.
17. sentimental: excessively emotional, often because of self-pity. "Sentimental" is a very unfavorable critical term when it is applied to a literary or artistic work to mean "expressing more emotion or passion than is needed for the occasion." To modern critics, sentimentalism is one of the weaker aspects of Romanticism.
18. retrospective: adjective of "retrospect" which means "looking back; thinking about the past."
19. invades: occupies.
20. assumes complete possession: takes complete possession.
21. sets in motion: causes to make movement. "Which sets in motion these new and delightful feelings..." = "Which sets these new and delightful feelings in motion..."
22. scribbling: very poor writing.
23. daemonic possession: devilish control; domination by a daemon.
24. critical faculties: powers of judgment.
25. what he cannot: what that poet cannot be expected to give.
26. endure after us: live after us, survive us.
27. the genuine and the sham: the true and the false; the really good and the seemingly good.
28. frequent: go often to, (in this case) often read.
29. accidents: an unexpected or unintended happening. An accident is not necessarily a "bad" or "fatal" happening as in a traffic collision.
30. they have not yet had enough experience of life for these matters to have much meaning: they have not yet had enough experi-

ence of life to see much meaning in these matters. "They" refers to school children or undergraduates.
31. Dante Alighieri (1265-1321): a great Italian poet.
32. Sophocles: a great tragic dramatist of ancient Greece who lived during 495?-406? B. C.
33. congenial: agreeable; pleasant; (in this case) easy to appreciate.
34. grave danger: serious danger.
35. sham acquisition of it: getting a true taste without real conviction, pretending to have acquired good taste.
36. rudiment: beginning; first step.
37. its ability: criticism's ability; (actually) critic's ability.
38. infallible discrimination: ability to find differences and distinctions in an absolutely reliable way. "Infallible" means "free from error; never going wrong."
39. to be taken in by the sham or the adulterate article: to be deceived by the false or the impure thing.
40. preferring them: preferring the sham and the adulterate articles to genuine ones.
41. native capacity: born ability; natural power.
42. to see one in the light of others: to see one experience in its relation to other experiences.
43. multiply: become richer.
44. each: each of his experiences.
45. when we no longer merely select and reject, but organize: when we no longer select a good poem and reject a poor one, but recognize the comparative merits and weaknesses of the poems in their relations to one another.
46. Johnson's *Lives of the Poets*: Samuel Johnson (1709-1784), leading English critic and man of letters of mid-eighteenth century. *Lives of the Poets* is his biographical and critical studies of 52 English poets including Milton and Gray.
47. permanence: everlasting quality.
48. appraisal: evaluation.
49. the performance of its contemporaries and immediate predecessors: the poetic achievements of its (that generation's) contemporary poet and the poets of the preceding generation.
50. implications of a poem: what a poem implies; what a poem indirectly suggests or hints.
51. becomes hardly more than a text: becomes almost a text.

52. to which: to this digressive tendency.
53. Walter Savage Landor (1775-1864): English poet, critic and prose writer who stood out as a fastidious Classicist in a Romantic age.
54. adopt no attitude towards what the poet has to say: adopt a neutral attitude towards the poem in terms of morality, society, religion and other considerations. This also means "make no value judgments on what the poet has to say."
55. evacuate it of all significance: make it empty of all significance; make it meaningless.
56. philosophic borderline: line separating philosophy from (in this case) poetry.
57. critical integrity: critical sincerity; honesty in criticism.
58. When you know what they are, you know where you are: When you know what your limitations are, you are sure of yourself (you know what you are doing).
59. the judicial bench: the judge's seat; the judge's position; (in this case) literary criticism (wherein a critic sits in judgment of the merits and weaknesses of a work or a writer).
60. formally perfect: perfect in form.
61. other prose writers of his time: other prose writers of the eighteenth century such as Addison, Swift, Burke, Gibbon and Goldsmith.
62. long periods of the historian or the orator: long complete sentences of the historian (like Edward Gibbon) or the orator (like Edmund Burke).
63. Had he lived a generation later... to inquire into the functions of its parts: If Johnson had lived a generation later, in the Romantic age of late eighteenth and early nineteenth centuries, he would have been obliged to explore more deeply into the foundations of English society or culture, and so would have been unable to leave us an example of what criticism ought to be for a civilization which, being settled (as English or European civilization in the middle of the eighteenth century certainly was), has no need... to inquire into the functions of its (civilization's) parts.

参考译文

品味的发展

到了十二三岁,孩子大多有一定的诗歌欣赏能力;在青春期或青春期前后,多数孩子会发现诗歌派不上更多的用场,但少数孩子则会发现自己对诗歌产生了一种渴望,诗歌给人的享受与以往经历的任何享受都截然不同。我不知道女孩子的诗歌品味与男孩子是否相同,但我相信男孩子的反应是相当一致的。《桥上的贺雷修斯》《约翰·摩尔爵士的葬礼》《布鲁斯进军班诺克本》[1] 和丁尼生的《复仇》及一些边境民谣,阅读这些军事和血腥诗歌,和玩铅制玩具兵与射豆枪一样得到认可。我从莎士比亚那里得到的唯一乐趣就是,读了他的作品会得到表扬;要是我思想更独立一点的话,就是连哄带逼,我也压根儿不会读他的书。虽然我也承认记忆往往不可靠,但我似乎记得,男孩子喜欢的那种诗歌,我早年也喜欢过,但十二岁左右就不再喜欢了,后来几年我对诗歌一点儿兴趣都没有。我清楚地记得,十四岁左右的时候,我随手捡起了一本菲茨杰拉德译的《鲁拜集》,这本诗集为我打开了一扇门,让我几乎无法抗拒地进入了一个新的情感世界。就像一个突然的转变,世界被涂上了鲜艳、美味和痛苦的色彩,变得焕然一新了。于是,我和拜伦、雪莱、济慈、罗塞蒂、斯文伯恩一起,修了这门人人须修的青春期课程。

1　一译《苏格兰人》(王佐良译本)。这是罗伯特·彭斯所作爱国诗中最著名的一首,写的是苏格兰国王罗伯特·布鲁斯在大破英国侵略军的班诺克本一役(1314)之前向部队所作的号召。——编者

这段时期一直持续到我二十二岁左右。作为一个快速吸收的时期，结局与开头可能迥异，因此品味也可能会截然有别。就像童年的第一个阶段一样，我敢说，许多人都无法超越这个阶段；因此，他们余生中所保留的这种对诗歌的品味，只是对快乐青春的一种感伤的记忆，而且可能与我们所有其他感伤的回忆交织在一起。毫无疑问，这是一段极度享受的时期，但我们不能把青少年时期富有诗意的强烈体验和对诗歌的强烈体验混为一谈。在这一时期，诗，或者说某位诗人的诗，侵入了年轻人的意识，并在一段时间内完全占据了其意识。我们并不真的认为诗是一种存在于我们自身之外的东西；就像我们年轻时的恋爱经历一样，我们与其说是看到了那个人，不如说臆想出某个外物的存在，让自己沉浸在这些新的、愉快的感情中。常见的结果就是"鸦"兴大发，大笔一挥，也来上几首，我们可以称之为模仿，只要我们知道自己所使用的"模仿"一词的含义。模仿并不是诗人的刻意选择，而是诗人在魔鬼控制下的一种写作。

到了第三个阶段，也就是诗歌欣赏的成熟阶段，我们就不再会把自己等同于碰巧读到的那个诗人，就能保持清醒的判断力，就能意识到一个诗人能给予什么，不能给予什么。诗有诗自己的生命，可以不依赖我们而存在；诗在我们之前就存在，在我们之后仍将继续存在。只有在这个阶段，读者才能对诗歌的优劣进行甄别；在这一阶段之前，能区分真伪就不错了——必须首先练习区分真伪这一能力。我们青少年时期经常读到的诗人，其重要性与任何客观的标准无关，而与使他们与我们产生联系的个人偶然事件有关；这也没什么不好。诗人之间在层次上是存在差异的，但能不能跟中小学生甚至本科生讲清楚这些差异，我表示怀疑；讲这些差异是不是明智之举，我也表示怀疑；他们的阅历还不够，研究这些问题对他们意义并不很大。要理解为何莎士比亚、但丁或索福克勒斯拥有那样的地位，只能是人生中非常缓慢的一个水到渠成的过程。诗歌天生就不容易欣赏，有些诗歌永远不会被人欣赏，因而刻意去啃诗歌这块硬骨头，确实应该是一项成熟之后才尝试的活动，也是一项回报颇丰的活动，但如果推荐给年轻人，就会有极大的危险，不仅可能损害他们的诗歌鉴赏力，还会将品味的真正发展与貌似形成混为一谈。

诗歌的鉴赏

品鉴的基本功是要有甄别诗歌优劣的能力；对品鉴最严峻的考验是看品鉴者能否选择一首好的新诗，以及对新情况能否做出恰当的反应。诗歌的体验，由于是在有意识的、成熟的人身上一点点发展起来的，因而不仅仅是好诗体验的简单相加。诗歌教育需要对这些体验进行组织。我们当中没有人生来就有绝对正确的辨别力和鉴赏力，也没有人在青春期或青春期以后突然获得绝对正确的辨别力和鉴赏力。阅历有限的人总是容易被虚假或掺假的东西所吸引，我们看到一代又一代未经训练的读者上当受骗，他们也的确更喜欢这些假货，因为假货比真货容易吸收。不过我相信，有很多人天生就有欣赏某些好诗的能力。我目前要探讨的不是有多少能力，或者说多少等级的能力可以切实区分出来。当然，只有出类拔萃的读者，才会随着时间的推移，对自己的体验加以分类和比较，把一种体验与其他体验联系起来看；也才会随着诗歌体验的增加，对自己的每一种体验有更为准确的理解。喜爱的成分增大，变成了欣赏，给原有的强烈感受增添了更多的智慧成分。这是我们理解诗歌的第二阶段，我们不再只是甄别，而是品评。我们甚至可以说说第三个阶段，即重组阶段；在这个阶段，一个在诗歌方面受过教育的人会遇到自己所处时代的新鲜事物，进而找到一种新的诗歌模式。

诗歌批评家

鉴于每一代人都必须根据同时代人和前辈的表现,对过去的诗歌做出自己的评价,因而类似约翰逊的《诗人列传》及其关于莎士比亚的文章这样的作品是永远的经典。对诗歌的批评一向游走在两个极端之间。一方面,评论家也许会过分专注于某一首诗的意义,或某一位诗人的作品(其道德、社会、宗教等含义),几乎把诗当成了论说文。此乃19世纪道德化批评家的倾向,唯有兰多是一个明显的例外。要不然,就是过度拘泥于"诗"本身,而对诗人要表达的意思不置一词,倾向于把诗的意义抽离一空。此外,还有一个哲学与诗的界限问题,如果想保持自己批评家的地位,而不准备把自己包装成哲学家、玄学家、社会学家或心理学家,就不能过分或频繁逾越这个界限。在这些方面,约翰逊所做的是一种诚挚的批评。他在自己的局限范围内,是一位伟大的批评家,而他之所以是一位伟大的批评家,部分原因在于他没有突破自己的局限范围。明白自身的局限范围,就清楚自己所处的位置。考虑到人们在评判当代作品时所面临的种种诱惑,以及人们在评判上一代作家时往往陷入种种偏见,我认为约翰逊的《诗人列传》是一部文学批评的杰作。他的文体从形式上说并不像他那个时代别的散文作家那样完美,读起来像是一个更习惯于说而不是写的人的作品;他的文字仿佛是在短时间地自言自语,而不是像历史学家或演说家那样长时间地思考。他的批评有利于反对18世纪过分的教条主义(法国对此的沉迷程度比英国有过之而无不及),也有利于反对过度吹捧或夸大个别诗人的优缺点。对于约翰逊来说,诗歌就是诗歌,而不是别的东西。要是他晚生一代的话,他就不得不更深入地研究各种基础问题,也就无法给我们留下一个范例,来展示对一个文明来说,批评应该是什么样的了,因为这个文明已经定型,在其存续期间,不必去探究其各部分的功能了。

(覃学岚 译)

7

Country Song

乡村之歌

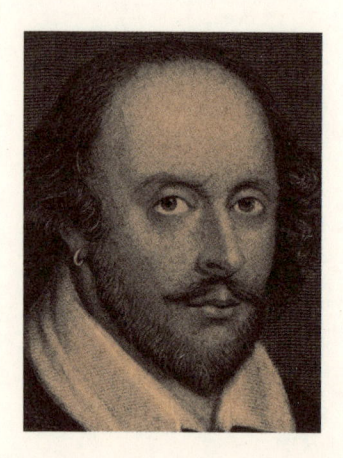

WILLIAM SHAKESPEARE
威廉·莎士比亚

(1564–1616)

> ABOUT THE AUTHOR

William Shakespeare (1564–1616), an English poet and dramatist of the Elizabethan period, is acknowledged as one of the greatest writers in world literature. Born at Stratford-on-Avon, Warwickshire, he received little formal education and in 1582 married Anne Hathaway, who was eight years older than he. As early as 1588 he had moved to London and devoted his life to the stage, probably first as an apprentice and then as an actor and playwright. Before he was fifty, he retired to his native town where he died, in his fifty-second year, on April 23, 1616. Shakespeare's 37 plays, divisible into tragedies, comedies and historical plays, have been widely read and performed not only in their original but in different languages. As a poet, he is remembered more for his 154 sonnets than for his narratives.

作者简介 威廉·莎士比亚（1564—1616），伊丽莎白时代的英国诗人和剧作家，被公认为世界文学史上最伟大的作家之一。他出生于英国沃里克郡埃文河畔斯特拉特福，几乎没有受过正规教育，1582年与大他8岁的安妮·海瑟薇结婚。1588年，他移居伦敦，一生致力于舞台事业，很可能开始是学徒，后来成为演员和编剧。他在50岁之前，退休回到了家乡，1616年4月23日去世，终年52岁。莎士比亚创作的37部戏剧，可以分为悲剧、喜剧和历史剧，英语版本被广泛阅读、上演，还被译成多种语言。作为诗人，他更为后世铭记的是154首十四行诗，而不是他的叙事诗。

ABOUT THE SELECTION

The song is taken from Shakespeare's comedy *As You Like It*, where it is sung, appropriately, by two pages to Touchstone, the court jester, and his country sweetheart, Audrey (V, iii, 17). As a song it is deliberately repetitious in stanzaic structure: in each of the four stanzas, only the first and third lines are new; the rest are refrains. In the words of Louis Untermeyer, such songs were originally written by Shakespeare "as theatrical expedients. They were not composed as poetry per se, but designed to punctuate a scene, to help clear the stage of actors, as excuses for incidental music, as commentaries and epilogues. Primarily Shakespeare wrote his lyrics to be sung. The printed page scarcely does them justice, isolation robs them of their author's masterly stagecraft." Not necessarily knowing the original tune, the modern reader is encouraged to read the "poem" aloud to himself to enjoy the overbrimming lyrical mood through the buoyant rhythm of the lines and the rich echoes of assonance, consonance and rhyme. A poem may appeal to its reader in different ways. Some poems have visual appeal in their vivid imagery. Some have auditory appeal in their metrical pattern. Others may be more complex and may appeal to the reader not only sensuously but also emotionally and intellectually. Country Song is essentially a poem for the ear. To read it in silence is to lose most of its charm. While reading aloud, however, the reader should find out where the accent regularly falls. In the first line, for instance, it falls on every second syllable; in the second line, on every third. The poem is written in rhymed verse. In each stanza, lines 2, and 4 look unrhymed, but, on closer reading, we find "nonino" to be of the same rhyme as "ho", and "ringtime" to be a double echo to "spring-time".

内容简介　这首诗歌选自莎士比亚的喜剧《皆大欢喜》,是两个侍童唱给宫廷小丑"试金石"和他的村姑爱人奥德蕾的(第五幕第三场,17 行)。作为一首歌曲,它在诗节结构上刻意重复:在四个诗节中,只有第一行和第三行是新的,其他都是叠句。用路易斯·昂特迈耶的话说,莎士比亚起初写这些诗歌,是"作为戏剧中的应急手段。它们本身不是作为诗歌来创作的,而是作为解说词或收场白。莎士比亚写下这些词主要是为了演唱。单看印刷本看不出效果,孤立地看文本,看不到作者伟大的编剧艺术"。因为不知道原来的曲调,现代读者被鼓励大声读出这首"诗",通过诗行的轻快节奏,以及准押韵、辅音韵和押韵的丰富回响,来享受其中洋溢的抒情氛围。一首诗可以不同的方式吸引它的读者。诗歌生动的意象会吸引视觉,格律会吸引听觉。其他可能更加复杂,不仅在感官上,也在情感和思想上,吸引读者。《乡村之歌》本质上是一首为耳朵创作的诗歌。默读只会丢掉它大部分的魅力。但是,如果大声读,读者应当找到重音通常落在哪里。比如,在第一行,每隔两个音节一个重音;在第二行,每隔三个音节一个重音。这首诗是押韵的。在每个诗节,第二行和第四行看起来不押韵,但是,细读之下,我们会发现"nonino"和"ho"是同一个韵,"ringtime"是"springtime"的双重回声。

It was a lover and his lass, [1]
    With a hey, and a ho, and a hey nonino, [2]
That o'er[3] the green corn-field did pass
    In the spring-time, the only pretty ring-time, [4]
When birds do sing, hey ding a ding, ding! [5]
    Sweet lovers love the spring.

Between the acres of the rye, [6]
    With a hey, and a ho, and a hey nonino,
These pretty country folks would lie,
    In spring-time, the only pretty ring-time,
When birds do sing, hey ding a ding, ding!
    Sweet lovers love the spring.

This carol[7] they began that hour,
    With a hey, and a ho, and a hey nonino,
How that a life was but[8] a flower
    In spring-time, the only pretty ring-time,
When birds do sing, hey ding a ding, ding!
    Sweet lovers love the spring.

And therefore take the present time, [9]
    With a hey, and a ho, and a hey nonino,
For love is crownéd[10] with the prime[11]
    In spring-time, the only pretty ring-time,
When birds do sing, hey ding a ding, ding!
    Sweet lovers love the spring.

参考译文

一对情人并着肩，
嗳唷嗳唷嗳嗳唷，
走过了青青稻麦田，
春天是最好的结婚天，
听嘤嘤歌唱枝头鸟，
姐郎们最爱春光好。

小麦青青大麦鲜，
嗳唷嗳唷嗳嗳唷，
乡女村男交颈儿眠，
春天是最好的结婚天，
听嘤嘤歌唱枝头鸟，
姐郎们最爱春光好。

新歌一曲意缠绵，
嗳唷嗳唷嗳嗳唷，
人生美满像好花妍，
春天是最好的结婚天，
听嘤嘤歌唱枝头鸟，
姐郎们最爱春光好。

劝君莫负艳阳天，
嗳唷嗳唷嗳嗳唷，
恩爱欢娱要趁少年，
春天是最好的结婚天，
听嘤嘤歌唱枝头鸟，
姐郎们最爱春光好。

（朱生豪 译）

NOTES

1. lass: girl; sweetheart.
2. hey, ho, nonino: Both hey and ho are interjections expressing surprise or joy, though ho is now archaic. Nonino, like "nonny-nonny", is an archaic word in Elizabethan poetry used for a refrain suggesting a lover's croon.
3. o'er: over.
4. ring-time: a nonceword meaning "the season for putting on rings". Ring also suggests a clear, bell-like sound and is, therefore, associated with the singing birds in the next line.
5. hey ding-a ding, ding!: onomatopoeia for chirping birds. Ding is "to sound like a bell" or "a bell-like sound".
6. the acres of the rye: the rye fields.
7. carol: song of joy; hymn.
8. but: only.
9. take the present time: make good use of the present time.
10. crownéd: pronounced "kroun-nid".
11. the prime: Here prime is a word rich in connotations. It is derived from the Latin primus, meaning "first", and has come to suggest "beginning" "the best time" "springtime" and "youth".

8

To One Who
Has Been Long
in City Pent

久困在都市的人

JOHN KEATS
约翰·济慈

(1795–1821)

ABOUT THE AUTHOR

John Keats (1795–1821) is a major poet not only of the Romantic School but of the entire history of English poetry. Narrower in thematic scope than Wordsworth, Byron, and some other Romantics, he surpasses them in depth of feeling, vividness of imagination, closeness of observation, and an almost agonizing immediacy in sensuous experiences. Son of a hostler and stable keeper, John Keats was born in a stable in London. He had little regular schooling and had to earn a living as apprentice to a surgeon. Suffering from tuberculosis and a hopeless love for Fanny Brawne, the young poet sailed to Italy in search of health but died in Rome in his twenty-sixth year.

作者简介 约翰·济慈（1795—1821），英国浪漫主义重要诗人，也是英国诗歌史上的重要诗人。与华兹华斯、拜伦等其他浪漫派诗人相比，他的创作主题较为狭窄，但在感情深度、活跃的想象力、敏锐的观察，以及捕捉令人痛苦的感官经验上，济慈要更胜一筹。他的父亲是一位马厩工人，他本人出生于伦敦一个马厩。他没接受过多少正规教育，后被送去给一位医生做学徒谋生。年轻的诗人后来得了肺结核，又陷入对芬妮·布劳恩的绝望恋情，他前往意大利休养，却不幸在罗马病逝，年仅 26 岁。

ABOUT THE SELECTION

In verse form this is an Italian sonnet: a poem of fourteen lines in iambic pentameter, divided into sections of eight lines (octave) and six lines (sestet), rhyming *abba abba* and *cdecde*. There are many variations of the rhyme scheme in the sestet; the one given above is the most common. In the present case, it is *cdcdcd*. It is conventional for the poet to state the problem in the octave and solve it in the sestet. It is also conventional to use the first line of a sonnet as its title. Founded by the Italian poet Petrarch and introduced into England by Wyatt and Surrey, sonnet in its classic-tradition was mostly used for the expression of love, but since John Milton its thematic scope has been considerably enlarged. The sonnet here selected is both lyrical and descriptive. It expresses the typical Romantic longing for nature and solitude and indicates that, even in Keats's days, poets complained of the stifling labyrinth of city life, a theme which has become very popular in modern literature. Grammatically, this poem consists of three sentences: lines 1–4 make the first sentence; lines 5–8 the second; lines 9–14, the third. In classic Chinese poetry, grammatical division (sentence, clause, etc.) corresponds with metrical division (line), but in English poetry they often overlap. When grammatical and metrical patterns agree, we call the line "end-stopped"; when they do not, we call it "run-on". Lines 2, 3, 6, 7, 9, 10 in this poem are run-on. Thus a classic Chinese poem is read line by line, but a poem in English is often read with due regard to both line and sentence. Take the first four lines of this poem for instance. At the end of the first line there should be a pause. At the end of both the second and third lines the pauses are so fleeting as to be almost imperceptible. At the end of the fourth there should be a complete stop.

内容简介 这首诗从形式而言是一首意大利十四行诗，音步为五步抑扬格，分成前八行和后六行，韵式为 abba, abba, cdecde。后六行有许多不同的韵式，前面提到的这种是最常见的。在这首诗中，后六行的韵式是 cdcdcd。诗人通常会在前八行提出问题，后六行解决问题。十四行诗的第一行常被用来作为题目。十四行诗由意大利诗人彼得拉克始创，后由怀亚特和萨里引入英国，十四行诗在其古典传统中主要用来抒发爱情，但从约翰·弥尔顿以来，它的主题范围大大拓展了。这里选择的十四行诗既抒情又咏物。它抒发了诗人对自然和孤独的渴望，是典型的浪漫派风格，我们从中知道，早在济慈生活的时代，诗人们就在抱怨都市生活像令人窒息的迷宫，这在现代文学中是很受欢迎的主题。从语法而言，这首诗包含三个句子：1—4 行是第一个句子，5—8 行是第二个句子，9—14 行是第三个句子。在中国古典诗歌中，语法分割点（句子、分句等）即是格律分割点（诗行），但在英文诗歌中，它们常常重叠。当语法和格律一致时，我们称之为"结句行"；不一致时，我们称之为"跨行句"。这首诗的第 2、3、6、7、9、10 行是跨行句。所以，一首中国古典诗歌是逐行阅读，但一首英文诗歌在阅读时通常既要考虑诗行，又要考虑句子。以这首诗的前四行为例，第一行行末应该有一个暂停。在二、三行行末，停顿转瞬即逝，几乎感知不到。在第四行行末，则应是一个完全的停顿。

To one who has been long in city pent,¹
    'Tis² very sweet to look into the fair
    And open face of heaven, —to breathe a prayer³
Full in the smile of the blue firmament.⁴
Who is more happy, when, with heart's content,
    Fatigued he sinks into some pleasant lair⁵
    Of wavy grass, and reads a debonair⁶
And gentle tale of love and languishment?⁷
Returning home at evening, with an ear
    Catching the notes of Philomel,⁸ —an eye
Watching the sailing cloudlet's bright career,⁹
    He mourns that day so soon has glided by,
E'en¹⁰ like the passage of an angel's tear
    That falls through the clear ether¹¹ silently.

参考译文

久困在都市的人应感到
最称心是凝望那晴艳
而开朗的天颜——喃喃祈愿
向着笑容广阔的青霄。
谁比他快乐呢,他多逍遥,
倦了,便躺在起伏的草间,
窝得好乐,而且读一篇
优雅的故事,讲为情苦恼。
傍晚的归途,一面追听
夜莺的歌声,一面望断
一帆流云灿烂的生命,
可惜匆匆溜失的一天;
竟似天使的泪珠,全程
寂寂垂落透彻的太清。

(余光中 译)

NOTES

1. pent: past participle of "pen", to confine, to shut in.
2. 'Tis: It is (used mainly in classic poetry).
3. to breathe a prayer: to say a prayer very softly.
4. Full in the smile of the blue firmament: Here full is an adverb meaning "completely" or "entirely". Firmament means "sky".
5. lair: the den or dwelling of a wild animal; or (obsolete) a resting place, a couch.
6. debonair: suave; gracious; genial.
7. languishment: becoming listless as with longing; lovesickness.
8. notes of Philomel: songs of nightingale. Philomel means lover of song and is also spelt Philomela. In Greek legend, Philomela is daughter of King Pandion of Athens and sister of Procne, who is married to Tereus, king of Thrace. Tereus rapes Philomela and cuts her tongue to prevent her from telling it. She weaves a tapestry to depict her disgrace and sends it to Procne. The sisters murder Itylus, Tereus's five-year-old son, and serve him as food to Tereus. The gods change Tereus into a hawk, Philomela into a nightingale, Procne into a swallow, and Itylus into a sandpiper.
9. the sailing cloudlet's bright career: the short life of a small, bright cloud that moves slowly and gracefully. Cloudlet is a happy coinage by Keats, which means "small cloud", "let" being a suffix indicating something small of its kind, as in "booklet" "rivulet" and "starlet". Sailing is an adjective by which the cloudlet is compared to a white, full, smooth-sliding sail. The whole expression is characteristic of Keats's keen observation and imagination.
10. E'en: even.
11. ether: the upper regions of space beyond the earth's atmosphere; clear sky.

9

One's-Self
I Sing

我歌唱自己

WALT WHITMAN
沃尔特·惠特曼

(1819–1892)

ABOUT THE AUTHOR

Walt Whitman (1819–1892), a major American poet of the nineteenth century, is also an inspiring forerunner of modern poetry for his celebration of the common man, his advocacy of democracy, his open treatment of sex, his defiance of institutions, and his free, forceful, rambling style. Like Keats, Whitman had little formal education and little success as a writer during his lifetime. Born in Long Island and brought up in Brooklyn, New York, Whitman earned a precarious living as a journalist and hack writer. After thirty-one he changed his style of writing and living and consorted with ferrymen, bus drivers, and other "powerful, uneducated persons." Whitman came to identify himself with the American people and humanity. His important contribution to American literature was a book of poetry entitled *Leaves of Grass* which he kept expanding until it became a monument in verse.

作者简介　沃尔特·惠特曼（1819—1892），美国 19 世纪重要诗人，也是现代诗歌鼓舞人心的先驱。他歌颂普通人，宣扬民主，在作品中公开探讨性话题，反抗体制。他的写作风格自由奔放，汪洋恣肆，舒卷自如。和济慈一样，惠特曼没有受过多少正规教育，生前也未享受作家身份带来的荣耀。他出生于长岛，在纽约布鲁克林长大，曾经做过记者和写手。三十一岁后，他改变了写作和生活风格，结交船夫、出租车司机和其他"强大的、未受过教育的人"。惠特曼在美国人民和人类全体中找到了身份认同感。他对美国文学的重要贡献是那部名为《草叶集》的诗集，他不断地创作新的诗歌，收入诗集中，使之成为一部不朽之作。

ABOUT THE SELECTION

This is a truly modern poem in both spirit and form. To the poet the complete man is at once an individual by himself and a member of a democratic society. He puts equal emphasis on body and mind, the male and the female; he goes to life with open arms, free and cheerful. He neither dismisses the female sex as inferior nor adores it as angelic. Nor does he escape into the rarified solitude of the soul, away from sweating humanity in the street. In form the poem was written in the so-called "free verse". "Free verse" is so called because there is no rhyme or any established metrical pattern. When applied to *One's-Self I Sing*, however, the term is misleading because, on closer reading, most of the lines are still capable of scansion in loose iambic meter. Line 3, for instance, is in iambic hexameter. Lines 6 and 7 are in iambic pentameter, while the last line is an iambic trimeter. This shows that Walt Whitman was aware of the advantages of traditional versification and made free adaptations of it wherever it helped.

内容简介 这是一首从精神和形式上都真正现代的诗歌。对诗人而言，一个完整的人既是独立的个体，又是民主社会的成员。他对身体和思想，男性和女性给予同样的重视；他张开双臂奔向生活，自由而快乐。他既不轻视女性，也不把她们像天使一样崇拜。他既没有逃进灵魂纯净的孤独中，也没有远离街上汗流浃背的人们。这首诗从形式而言是所谓的"自由诗"。之所以称为"自由诗"，是因为它既没有韵式，也不遵循任何既定的格律。然而，这个术语用在《我歌唱自己》上，是有些误导的，因为进一步分析能看到，绝大多数诗行依然是松散的抑扬格。举例而言，第三行是抑扬格六音步。这显示了沃尔特·惠特曼意识到传统诗律的优势，在需要的时候能够自由地对它加以运用。

One's-self I sing,[1] a simple separate person,
Yet utter the word Democratic, the word En-Masse.[2]

Of physiology[3] from top to toe I sing,
Not physiognomy[4] alone nor brain alone is worthy for the
    Muse,[5] I say the Form complete[6] is worthier far,[7]
The Female equally with the Male I sing.

Of Life immense in passion, pulse, and power,[8]
Cheerful, for freest action form'd under the laws divine,
The Modern Man I sing.[9]

参考译文　我歌唱自己，一个单一的、脱离的人，
然而也说出民主这个词，全体这个词。

我从头到脚歌唱生理学，
值得献给诗神的不只是相貌或头脑，
我是说整个结构的价值要大得多，
女性和男性我同样歌唱。

歌唱饱含热情、脉搏和力量的广阔生活，
心情愉快，支持那些神圣法则指导下形成的、最自由的行动，
我歌唱现代人。

（赵萝蕤 译）

NOTES

1. One's-self I sing: I sing one's-self. Although he is hailed as a forerunner of modern poetry, Whitman still retains some degree of Victorianism, as is evident here in his frequent use of reversed sentence structure. Instead of "I sing the female equally with the male," he says, "The female equally with the male I sing" for greater emphasis on the objects of his singing. The same is true of Lines 3 and 9.
2. En-Masse: in one body; all together.
3. physiology: science dealing with the normal functions of living things or their organs.
4. physiognomy: facial features; the art of judging human character from facial features; physical appearance.
5. the Muse: inspiration for poets, artists and composers. The nine Muses are nine Greek goddesses of the fine arts and sciences.
6. the Form complete: the complete Form; the whole Being; Life in its full balance.
7. worthier far: far worthier; much worthier.
8. passion, pulse, and power: a typical and impressive example of alliteration, which is a verbal musical device by way of repetition of the same first letter or sound, usually consonantal, in a group of words or line of poetry. This device is used abundantly throughout the poem. Repetition of the "s" sound in the first line is another example.
9. The last three lines of the poem can be restored to their "normal" order as: "I sing the modern man of immense life in passion, pulse, and power, cheerful, formed for freest action under the divine laws."

10

When I Heard the Learn'd Astronomer

一堂天文课

Walt Whitman
沃尔特·惠特曼

(1819–1892)

ABOUT THE SELECTION

The poem describes how the poet goes to a lecture on astronomy and soon becomes tired of the presentation of cold facts and figures of the constellations. He steals out of the lecture-room and looks in awe and admiration at the stars themselves. To the poet the stars are the miracle and mystery of God's creation, a spectacle of immortal beauty and glory to be marveled at in speechless contemplation rather than explained away by meaningless statistics and analyses. In the presence of Nature and heavenly splendor, the poet prefers silence to speech, and intuition to intellect. What matters is personal experience, not abstract knowledge. This philosophy comes close to that of William Blake and many other poets and artists. The poem is in "free verse", typical of the racy, rambling style of Whitman, though, on closer analysis, we can still trace traditional meter. The last line, for instance, is a regular iambic pentameter. Notice, too, that the whole poem comprises only one sentence.

内容简介　这首诗描述了诗人去参加一场天文学讲座，很快就对用冰冷的事实和数字介绍星座感到厌倦。他悄悄走出讲演厅，抬头看着天上的星辰，充满敬畏和欣慕。在诗人看来，星辰是上帝创造的神秘奇迹，充满了不朽的美丽和荣耀，人们只应该无言地欣赏和沉思，而不是用没有意义的数据去解释和分析它们。在大自然和天空壮观的景色面前，诗人情愿沉默，不愿开口，更愿感受，而非思考。重要的是个人体验，而非抽象知识。这一哲学和威廉·布莱克等许多诗人和艺术家接近。这首诗是"自由诗"，惠特曼典型的活泼散漫的风格，但是，细加分析，我们依然能看到传统韵律的痕迹。比如最后一行就是标准的五步抑扬格。请注意，整首诗歌是由一个句子构成的。

一堂天文课
When I Heard the Learn'd Astronomer

When I heard the learn'd [1] astronomer,
When the proofs, the figures, were ranged [2] in columns before me,
When I was shown the charts and diagrams, to add, divide, and measure them,
When I sitting heard the astronomer where he lectured with much applause in the lecture-room,
How soon unaccountable [3] I became tired and sick,
Till rising and gliding out I wander'd [4] off by myself,
In the mystical moist night-air, and from time to time,
Look'd [5] up in perfect silence at the stars.

NOTES
1. learn'd: learned; scholarly.
2. ranged: put in groups or classes.
3. unaccountable: unaccountably. In poetry, an adjective can be used instead of its corresponding adverb.
4. wander'd: wandered.
5. look'd: looked.

参考译文   当我听那位博学的天文学家的讲座时,
当那些证明、数据一栏一栏地排列在我眼前时,
当那些表格、图解展现在我眼前要我去加、去减、去
　　测定时,
当我坐在报告厅听着那位天文学家演讲、听着响起一
　　阵阵掌声时,
很快地我竟莫名其妙地厌倦起来,
于是我站了起来悄悄地溜了出去,
在神秘而潮湿的夜风中,一遍又一遍,
静静地仰望星空。

(罗良功 译)

11

A Narrow Fellow in the Grass

蛇

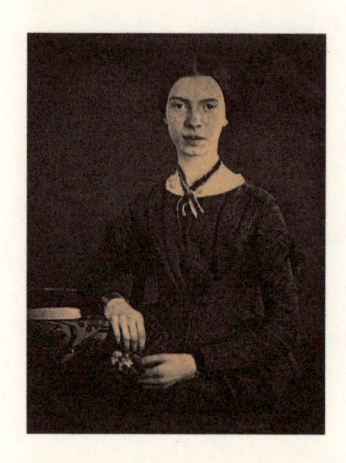

EMILY DICKINSON
艾米莉·狄金森

(1830–1886)

ABOUT THE AUTHOR

Emily Dickinson (1830–1886) was a major American poet of the nineteenth century. Born in Amherst, Massachusetts, she lived there a hermit and died unmarried. Biographers never agree as to whether her singlehood was the result of a frustrated love affair in her youth. Her cryptic lyrics, composed mostly in ballad meter, are metaphysical in style, original in language, and precise in imagery. Nature, love, life, time, and eternity are her favorite themes. Of the 1,200 poems she wrote only four were published during her lifetime. In early twentieth century she was looked upon as a forerunner of the Imagist school of poetry.

作者简介

艾米莉·狄金森（1830—1886），19世纪一位重要的美国诗人。生于马萨诸塞州的阿默斯特镇，她在那里过着隐士的生活，终身未婚。传记作家对她选择独身的原因莫衷一是，也许是因为年少时一段苦涩的恋情所致。她的神秘诗歌，大都是歌谣格律，风格抽象，语言富有原创性，意象精确。自然、爱、人生、时间和永恒是她喜爱的主题。在她创作的1200首诗歌中，只有四首在她生前出版。在20世纪初期，她被视为意象派诗歌的先驱。

ABOUT THE SELECTION

This is a superb example of descriptive poetry. It is lively with the keen observation and vivid imagination of a woman who is at once scared and fascinated by the "narrow fellow in the grass." The poem is delightful in its successful synthesis of a diversity of feelings towards the narrow fellow: it begins in curiosity, but ends in sudden horror and retrospective self-mockery. The author surely deserves admiration for having an eye for both details and drama. A descriptive poem would be unbearably dull if nothing happened. In this poem, however, things do happen and happen fast until they reach a dramatic climax at the end. In verse form this is a free adaptation of ballad meter. The first two stanzas are quite regular: the stress falls on every second syllable; there are eight syllables in the first and third lines, and only six in the second and fourth. In the remaining stanzas, the first and third lines have only three stresses and seven syllables. In a ballad stanza, rhyme usually occurs at the end of the second and fourth lines, but here, with the exception of stanzas 3, 5 and 6, it is irregular.

内容简介

这是一首绝佳的咏物诗。它活泼轻快，带着一个女人敏锐的观察力和生动的想象力，她看到"青草丛中一条细长的东西"，感到恐惧又着迷。这首诗读来令人愉快，它成功地融合了诗人对那个细长的东西多样的情感：以好奇心开始，以突然的恐惧和回顾性的自我嘲弄收尾。作家对细节和戏剧效果的敏锐感知值得赞赏。如果什么事情都没有发生，一篇咏物诗将会单调得令人无法忍受。但是，在这首诗中，事情确实发生了，而且发生的速度如此之快，在诗的末尾达到了一个戏剧化的高潮。从诗歌形式来说，这是对歌谣格律的自由改造。前两个诗节非常规整：重音每隔两个音节一落；第一行和第三行有八个音节，第二行和第四行只有六个音节。在余下的诗节中，第一行和第三行只有三个重音和七个音节。在歌谣体诗节中，通常在第二行和第四行的末尾押韵，但在这首诗中，第三、五和六节除外，押韵是不规则的。

A narrow fellow in the grass
Occasionally rides;[1]
You may have met him—did you not?
His notice sudden is.[2]

The grass divides as with a comb,
A spotted shaft[3] is seen,
And then it closes[4] at your feet
And opens further on.

He likes a boggy acre,[5]
A floor[6] too cool for corn.
Yet when a child, and barefoot,[7]
I more than once, at morn,

Have passed, I thought, a whip-lash
Unbraiding[8] in the sun, —
When, stooping to secure it,[9]
It wrinkled, and was gone.

Several of nature's people[10]
I know, and they know me;
I feel for them a transport
Of cordiality;

But never met this fellow,
Attended or alone,[11]
Without a tighter breathing,
And zero at the bone.[12]

参考译文

青草丛中偶然会驰过
一条细长的东西；
你可能见过他——可不是吗？
他总是来得很急。

丛草像用把梳子给梳开，
露出一把多斑的箭；
然后它在你的脚旁合拢，
又向前分成两边。

他欢喜一块沼泽的地带，
不宜种禾的凉田。
当我还是个赤足的小孩，
曾有几次在晨间，

自以为行经了一根鞭索，
在朝阳之中伸欠——
但是当我俯身去捡拾，
它竟一躬身去远。

有几个自然的孩子我认识，
它们对我也熟悉；
我对于它们总感到一种
发自衷心的欢喜；

可是每一次遇见这家伙，
无论是同行或独步，
总不由呼吸变得紧张，
骨髓里降为零度。

（余光中 译）

NOTES

1. ride: travel on something (like horse, camel, bicycle, train, etc.).
2. His notice sudden is: His notice is sudden. It means "His warning comes suddenly" or "No sooner does he warn us than he comes."
3. shaft: arrow or spear.
4. it closes: the grass closes.
5. boggy acre: wet field; swampy land.
6. floor: ground.
7. Yet when a child, and barefoot: Yet when I was a barefoot child.
8. unbraiding: loosen the strands of.
9. stooping to secure it: when I was bending down to pick it up. Notice the last two lines of stanza 3 and the whole of stanza 4 make up one sentence.
10. nature's people: wild animals.
11. attended or alone: whether I was with friends or by myself.
12. zero at the bone: chill down the spine; sudden freezing shock.

12

Stopping by
Woods on a
Snowy Evening

雪夜林畔小驻

ROBERT FROST
罗伯特·弗罗斯特

(1874–1963)

ABOUT THE AUTHOR

Robert Frost (1874–1963) is one of the greatest of American poets in the twentieth century. He was born in San Francisco, but grew up in New England. Fame came late to him with the publication of *A Boy's Will* (1913) and *North of Boston* (1914). Subsequent books of verse include *Mountain Interval*, *New Hampshire* and *West-Running Brook*. Among his most popular individual poems are: "Mending Wall" "After Apple-Picking" "The Road Not Taken" "Birches" "Fire and Ice" and "Two Tramps in Mud Time". Four times awarded the Pulitzer Prize, Frost enjoyed immense popularity as a facile pastoral poet and was recognized as a "terrifying poet" and profound thinker only towards the end of his life. His self-epitaph is "He had a lover's quarrel with the world."

作者简介　罗伯特·弗罗斯特（1874—1963）是 20 世纪最伟大的美国诗人之一。他出生于美国旧金山，但在新英格兰地区长大。他成名较晚，成名作是《少年的意志》（1913）和《波士顿以北》（1914）。后又出版诗集《山间》《新罕布什尔》《西去的溪流》。他最受欢迎的诗歌有《修墙》《摘苹果之后》《未选择的路》《白桦树》《火与冰》《泥泞时节中的两个流浪工》。他曾四次获得普利策奖。弗罗斯特以田园诗人的身份深受大众欢迎，直到晚年才被视为"一位令人恐惧的诗人"和深刻的思想家。他为自己选定的墓志铭是"我和这个世界有过情人般的争吵"。

* **ABOUT THE SELECTION**

While this is one of the best known and most widely anthologized of modern poems, its "meaning" is so subtly implicit that many readers enjoy it merely as a descriptive "nature poem". This is not to say that the poem should not be appreciated on that level, but to say that, for a fuller understanding of the poem, the reader should also search for the symbolism that lies beneath the description of the beautiful scenery. The lovely, dark and deep woods, the frozen lake, the darkest evening of the year, and, finally, the sweet rest that is sleep—all these may be subtle suggestions of death. To a traveler who finds life too much for him, the idea of death comes as a welcome relief, not to mention the prospect of the village beyond the dark woods, a possible hint at—could it be paradise? But that is only a moment of melancholy contemplation. The speaker in the poem soon collects his mind and turns to this world and the earthly promises he has yet to keep. Thus the poem is an assertion of one's commitment to life in spite of temptations to give in and run away. Yet a successful poem, however richly symbolic, often moves on a dual level: its appeal is at once intellectual and sensuous. It is the happy moment when idea becomes experience. The landscape in the poem is a real experience, not merely a mask for ideas. *Stopping by Woods on a Snowy Evening* is also widely acclaimed for its flawless and resourceful treatment of verse form. The lines are in iambic tetrameter, but the rhyme scheme, instead of the monotony of two couplets, is a successful adaptation of the *aaba* scheme of Omar Khayyám's *Rubáiyát* and the interlocking terza rima of Dante's *The Divine Comedy*. The rhyme scheme of the whole poem is *aaba/bbcb/ccdc/dddd*. What appears at first to be a casual rhyme at the end of the third line proves regular in the following stanza, and an intricate pattern is thus interwoven.

内容简介 这是现代诗歌中最著名和最常被收入诗集的一首，它的"意义"如此隐晦，许多读者只是把它视为一篇描写性的"自然诗歌"。我们并不是说，这篇诗歌不可以在那个层面上欣赏，而是说，要更充分地理解这首诗，读者还应该探寻那潜藏在美景描摹之下的象征意味。那片可爱、幽暗、深邃的树林，冻湖，一年中最黑暗的傍晚，以及那甜美的憩息也即睡眠——所有这些可能是死亡的隐秘暗示。对于一个遭受生活重压的旅人来说，死亡的想法是一种令人愉悦的调剂，还有黑暗树林远处一座村庄的影子，那是对天堂的暗示吗？但那只是忧郁思考的一刻。诗中的讲述者很快冷静下来，转向面前的世界，以及他要信守的尘世的诺言。所以这首诗是在宣示一个人对生活的承诺，尽管有屈服和逃走的诱惑。但是，一首成功的诗歌，不管象征意义如何丰富，通常在双重层面上运行：其吸引力既来自思想又来自感官。当思想变成了经验，便是一个快乐的时刻。诗歌中的风景是真正的经验，不只是思想的面具。《雪夜林边》也因其完美无瑕和设计精巧的诗歌形式而受到广泛赞誉。诗歌采用抑扬格四音步，但是它的韵式不是单调的两行对句，而是对奥马尔·海亚姆《鲁拜集》aaba 韵式以及但丁《神曲》三行诗节隔句押韵法的成功改造。整首诗的韵式是 aaba/bbcb/ccdc/dddd。在每节第三行诗末尾出现一个随意的韵，成为下一节的主韵，一个错综复杂的韵式就这样编织而成。

雪夜林畔小驻
Stopping by Woods on a Snowy Evening

Whose woods these are I think I know.
His house is in the village though;
He will not see me stopping here
To watch his woods fill up with snow.

My little horse must think it queer
To stop without a farmhouse near
Between the woods and frozen lake
The darkest evening of the year.

He gives his harness[1] bells a shake
To ask if there is some mistake.
The only other sound's[2] the sweep
Of easy wind and downy flake.[3]

The woods are lovely, dark and deep.
But I have promises to keep,
And miles to go before I sleep,
And miles to go before I sleep.

NOTES

1. harness: leather straps, bands and other equipment to connect a horse or other animal to a carriage, wagon or plow.
2. sound's: sound is.
3. downy flake: light, feathery pieces of snow.

参考译文

想来我认识这座森林,
林主的庄宅就在邻村,
却不会见我在此驻马,
看他林中积雪的美景。

我的小马一定颇惊讶:
四望不见有什么农家,
偏是一年最暗的黄昏,
寒林和冰湖之间停下。

它摇一摇身上的串铃,
问我这地方该不该停。
此外只有轻风拂雪片,
再也听不见其他声音。

森林又暗又深真可羡,
但我还要守一些诺言,
还要赶多少路才安眠,
还要赶多少路才安眠。

（余光中 译）

The Lament

哀　歌

Anton Pavlovich Chekhov
安东·巴甫洛维奇·契诃夫

(1860–1904)

ABOUT THE AUTHOR

Anton Pavlovich Chekhov (1860–1904) was a Russian dramatist and short story writer. His ancestors having been serfs, Chekhov always felt a sincere sympathy for the poor and oppressed, a feeling which was deepened by his contacts as a physician. His was a stagnant Russia where the poor suffered from severe want, the rich, from idleness and boredom. In his twenties he contracted tuberculosis, which finally led to his death. He began writing short humorous stories for journals while a student of medicine in Moscow. Though he never abandoned this genre, many of his later stories are longer and more serious. An outstanding short story writer, Chekhov is better known as a playwright. His first successful play *Ivanov* (1887) was outshone by *The Sea-Gull* (1896), *Uncle Vanya* (1897), *The Three Sisters* (1901), and *The Cherry Orchard* (1904). Concerned with problems of social reality, Chekhov's dramas are first and foremost artistic portrayals of life. The delineation of characters and insight into life have made their author the forerunner of modern playwrights like Eugene O'Neill, William Saroyan, and Tennessee Williams.

作者简介 安东·巴甫洛维奇·契诃夫（1860—1904），俄国剧作家、短篇小说家。契诃夫的祖先都是农奴，他对穷人和被压迫者始终满怀同情。作为医生，他广泛接触了劳苦大众，使得这种同情愈发深沉。他笔下的俄罗斯是一个停滞不前的国家，穷人因极度贫穷而受苦，富人则因懒惰、百无聊赖而迷茫。他二十多岁的时候，患了肺结核，最终死于这种疾病。契诃夫在莫斯科学医时就开始为杂志写幽默的短篇故事。尽管从未放弃这种体裁，但他后来的许多小说篇幅更长，故事情节更趋严肃。契诃夫是一位杰出的短篇小说作家，但其剧作家的身份更广为人知。他的第一部戏剧作品《伊万诺夫》(1887)虽然大获成功，但被后来的《海鸥》(1896)、《万尼亚叔叔》(1897)、《三姐妹》(1901)和《樱桃园》(1904)所超越。契诃夫的戏剧关注社会现实，他对人物细致的刻画和对生活深邃的洞察使其成为现代剧作家如尤金·奥尼尔、威廉·萨洛扬和田纳西·威廉斯的先驱。

ABOUT THE SELECTION

Simplicity in all its different manifestations has been noted as the most outstanding quality of Chekhov's art. In *The Lament*, a simple story with a simple theme, Chekhov reveals a startling truth about humanity in all its complexity. An old cabdriver has just lost his son. He tries to find an outlet for his grief by seeking someone—among his passengers and fellow cabdrivers—who would willingly listen to his affliction. No one listens, and finally, overwhelmed by his own distress, he finds consolation and peace by confiding in his horse. The theme of this story at times human sympathy can be found only in a beast. The truth of this revelation shocks us and makes this story truly poignant and enduring for all its simplicity. Neither cruel nor hateful, the human beings in *The Lament* are callous in so far as they are engrossed in their own affairs. This is the irony of the theme. Chekhov has been compared to Guy de Maupassant, the French short story writer, for his conciseness as a storyteller. He puts equal emphasis on brevity and depiction of even the least details. This story serves as a good example of his basic style.

内容简介 在诸多表现形式中,人们一直认为"简洁"是契诃夫作品最显著的特点。《哀歌》的故事简单,它所表现的主题也简单。契诃夫揭示了复杂的人性最真实的一面。一位出租马车老车夫刚刚失去儿子,想在乘客和同行伙伴中寻找愿意倾听他痛苦的人,宣泄心中的悲伤,可是没人爱听。心痛欲绝的老车夫只能向马儿倾诉,在倾诉中找到安慰和平静。这个故事的主题是:有时候人只有在动物身上才能找到同情。它所揭示的真谛让人心悸,而其"简洁"更使得这个故事让人读了不但满腹心酸,而且回味无穷。《哀歌》中的人物虽然既不凶残也不可恨,但是只要专注于自己的事务,他们就毫无同情之心。这也使得小说主题颇具讽刺意味。因为笔下的故事简洁,人们常拿契诃夫和法国短篇小说作家莫泊桑相比。他强调简洁的重要性,也注重对哪怕最微小的细节的描绘。这个故事是他创作风格一个很好的例证。

It is twilight. A thick wet snow is twirling around the newly lighted street lamps, and lying in soft thin layers on roofs, on horses' backs, on people's shoulders and hats. The cabdriver Iona Potapov is quite white, and looks like a phantom; he is bent double[1] as far as a human body can bend double; he is seated on his box;[2] he never makes a move. If a whole snowdrift fell on him, it seems as if he would not find it necessary to shake it off. His little horse is also quite white, and remains motionless, its immobility, its angularity, and its straight wooden-looking legs, even close by, give it the appearance of a ginger-bread horse worth a *kopek*.[3] It is, no doubt, plunged in deep thought. If you were snatched from the plow, from your usual gray surroundings, and were thrown into this slough full of monstrous lights, unceasing noise, and hurrying people, you too would find it difficult not to think.

Iona and his little horse have not moved from their place for a long while. They left their yard before dinner, and up to now, not a fare.[4] The evening mist is descending over the town, the white lights of the lamps replacing brighter ray, and the hubbub of the street getting louder. "Cabby[5] for Viborg[6] way!" suddenly hears Iona. "Cabby!"

Iona jumps, and through his snow-covered eyelashes sees an officer in a greatcoat, with his hood over his head.

"Viborg way!" the officer repeats. "Are you asleep, eh? Viborg way!"

With a nod of assent Iona picks up the reins, in consequence of which layers of snow slip off the horse's back and neck. The officer seats himself in the sleigh, the cabdriver smacks his lips to encourage his horse, stretches out his neck like a swan, sits up, and, more from habit than necessity, brandishes his whip. The little horse also stretches its neck, bends its wooden-looking legs, and makes a move undecidedly.

"What are you doing, werewolf!"[7] is the exclamation Iona hears from the dark mass moving to and fro, as soon as they have started.

"Where the devil are you going? To the r-r-right!"

"You do not know how to drive. Keep to the right!" calls the officer angrily.

A coachman from a private carriage swears at him, a passer-by, who has run across the road and rubbed his shoulder against the horse's nose, looks at him furiously as he sweeps the snow from his sleeve. Iona shifts about on his seat as if he were on needles, moves his elbows as if he were trying to keep his equilibrium, and gapes about like someone suffocating, who does not understand why and wherefore he is there.

"What scoundrels they all are!" jokes the officer, "one would think they had all entered into an agreement to jostle you or fall under your horse."

Iona looks round at the officer, and moves his lips. He evidently wants to say something, but the only sound that issues is a snuffle.

"What?" asks the officer.

Iona twists his mouth into a smile, and with an effort says hoarsely:

"My son, barin,[8] died this week."

"Hm! What did he die of?"

Iona turns with his whole body toward his fare, and says:

"And who knows! They say high fever. He was three days in the hospital, and then died....God's will be done."

"Turn round! The devil!" sounds from the darkness. "Have you popped off,[9] old doggie,[10] eh? Use your eyes!"

"Go on, go on," says the officer, "otherwise we shall not get there by tomorrow. Hurry up a bit!"

The cabdriver again stretches his neck, sits up, and, with a bad grace, brandishes his whip. Several times again he turns to look at his fare, but the latter has closed his eyes, and apparently is not disposed to listen. Having deposited the officer in the Viborg, he stops by the tavern, doubles himself up on his seat, and again remains motionless, while the snow once more begins to cover him and his horse. An hour, and another... Then, along the footpath, with a squeak of galoshes, and quarreling, come three young men, two of them tall and lanky, the third one short and humpbacked.

"Cabby, to the Police Bridge!" in a cracked voice calls the humpback. "The three of us for two *griveniks*!"[11]

Iona picks up his reins, and smacks his lips. Two *griveniks* is not a fair price, but he does not mind whether it is a rouble[12] or five kopeks—to him it is all the same now, so long as they are fares. The young men, jostling each other and using bad language, approach the sleigh, and all three at once try to get onto the seat, then begins a discussion as to which two shall sit and who shall be the one to stand. After wrangling, abusing each other, and much petulance, it is at last decided that the humpback shall stand, as he is the smallest.

"Now then, hurry up!" says the humpback in a twanging voice, as he takes his place and breathes in Iona's neck, "Old furry![13] Here, mate,[14] what a cap you have! There is not a worse one to be found in all Petersburg!..."

"He-he! —he-he!" giggles Iona, "Such a..."

"Now you, 'such a,' hurry up, are you going the whole way at this pace? Are you?... Do you want it in the neck?"[15]

"My head feels like bursting," says one of the lanky ones. "Last night at the Donkmasovs,[16] Vaska and I drank the whole of four bottles of cognac."

"I don't understand what you lie for," says the other lanky one angrily; "you lie like a brute."

"God strike me, it's the truth!"

"It's as much the truth as that a louse coughs!"

"He, he," grins Iona, "what gay young gentlemen!"

"Pshaw,[17] go to the devil!" says the humpback indignantly.

"Are you going to get on or not, you old pest? Is that the way to drive? Use the whip a bit! Go on, devil, go on, give it[18] to him well!"

Iona feels at his back the little man wriggling, and the tremble in his voice. He listens to the insults hurled at him, sees the people, and little by little the feeling of loneliness leaves him. The humpback goes on swearing until he gets mixed up in some elaborate six-foot oath,[19] or chokes with coughing. The lankies begin to talk about a certain[20] Nadejda Petrovna. Iona looks round at them several times, he waits for a temporary silence, then, turning round again, he murmurs:

"My son... died this week."

"We must all die," sighs the humpback, wiping his lips after an attack of coughing. "Now, hurry up, hurry up! Gentlemen, I really cannot go any farther like this! When will he get us there?"

"Well, just you stimulate him a little in the neck!"

"You old pest, do you hear, I'll bone[21] your neck for you! If one treated the like of you with ceremony one would have to go on foot! Do you hear, old serpent Gorinytch![22] Or do you not care a spit?"

Iona hears rather than feels the blows they deal him.

"He, he," he laughs. "They are gay young gentlemen, God bless 'em!"

"Cabby, are you married?" asks a lanky one.

"I? He, he, gay young gentlemen! Now I have only a wife and the moist ground... He, ho, ho... that is to say, the grave. My son has died, and I am alive... A wonderful thing, death mistook the door... instead of coming to me, it went to my son..."

Iona turns round to tell them how his son died, but at this moment the humpback, giving a little sigh, announces, "Thank God, we have at last reached our destination," and Iona watches them disappear through the dark entrance. Once more he is alone, and again surrounded by silence, ... His grief, which has abated for a short while, returns and rends his heart with greater force. With an anxious and hurried look, he searches among the crowds passing on either side of the street to find whether there may be just one person who will listen to him. But the crowds hurry by without noticing him or his trouble. Yet it is such an immense, illimitable grief. Should his heart break and the grief pour out, it would flow over the whole earth, so it seems, and yet no one sees it. It has managed to conceal itself in such an insignificant shell that no one can see it even by day and with a light.

Iona sees a hall porter with some sacking, and decides to talk to him.

"Friend, what sort of time is it?" he asks.

"Past nine. What are you standing here for? Move on."

Iona moves on a few steps, doubles himself up, and abandons himself to his grief. He sees it is useless to turn to people for help. In less than five minutes he straightens himself, holds up his head as if he felt some sharp pain, and gives a tug at the reins; he can bear it no longer. "The stables,"[23] he thinks, and the little horse, as if it understood, starts off at a trot.

About an hour and a half later Iona is seated by a large dirty stove. Around the stove, on the floor, on the benches, people are snoring; the air is thick and suffocatingly hot. Iona looks at the sleepers, scratches himself, and regrets having returned so early.

"I have not even earned my fodder."[24] he thinks. "That's what's my trouble. A man who knows his job, who has had enough to eat, and his horse too, can always sleep peacefully."

A young cabdriver in one of the corners half gets up, grunts sleepily, and stretches towards a bucket of water.

"Do you want a drink?" Iona asks him.

"Don't I want a drink!"

"That's so? Your good health! But listen, mate—you know, my son is dead... Did you hear? This week, in the hospital... It's a long story."

Iona looks to see what effect his words have, but sees none—the young man has hidden his face and is fast asleep again. The old man sighs, and scratches his head. Just as much as the young one wants to drink, the old man wants to talk. It will soon be a week since his son died, and he has not been able to speak about it properly to anyone. One must tell it slowly and carefully; how his son fell ill, how he suffered, what he said before he died, how he died. One must describe every detail of the funeral, and the journey to the hospital to fetch the dead son's clothes. His daughter Anissia has remained in the village—one must talk about her too. Is it nothing he has to tell? Surely the listener would gasp and sigh, and sympathize with him? It is better, too, to talk to women; although they are stupid, two words are enough to make them sob.

"I'll go and look after my horse," thinks Iona; "there's always time to sleep. No fear of that!"

He puts on his coat, and goes to the stables to his horse; he thinks of the corn, the hay, the weather. When he is alone, he dares not think of his son; he can speak about him to anyone, but to think of him, and picture him to himself, is unbearably painful.

"Are you tucking in?" Iona asks his horse, looking at its bright eyes; "go on, tuck in, though we've not earned our corn,[25] we can eat hay. Yes! I am too old to drive—my son could have, not I. He was a first-rate cabdriver. If only he had lived!"

Iona is silent for a moment, then continues:

"That's how it is, my old horse. There's no more Kuzma Ionitch.[26] He has left us to live, and he went off pop.[27] Now let's say, you had a foal, you were the foal's mother, and suddenly, let's say, that foal went and left you to live after him. It would be sad, wouldn't it?"

The little horse munches, listens, and breathes over its master's hand...

Iona's feelings are too much for him, and he tells the little horse the whole story.

NOTES

1. bent double: bent or folded in the middle.
2. box: driver's seat on a carriage or coach.
3. kopek: Russian money. 100 kopeks make one rouble.
4. fare: a paying passenger on a public conveyance.
5. cabby: cabdriver.
6. Viborg: also Vyborg, a city to the northwest of St. Petersburg.
7. werewolf: a person transformed into a wolf or capable of assuming a wolf's form. A term of abuse here.
8. barin: person of nobility.
9. popped off: died unexpectedly or suddenly. Abusive language here.
10. doggie: a small dog. A term of abuse here.
11. griveniks: a Russian silver coin worth 10 kopeks or one tenth of a rouble.
12. rouble: also ruble. See note 3.
13. furry: usually an adjective referring to anything that resembles or is covered by fur. The humpback's usage here as noun to address the cabdriver may be a reference to the latter's cap. (Russians wear fur caps in the winter.)
14. mate: friend, pal, chum—often used as a familiar address among seamen. Here also used as an informal address to someone whose name is unknown.
15. Do you want it in the neck: Do you want to receive a beating in the neck? "It" means punishment or chastisement here.
16. at the Donkmasovs: at the house of the Donkmasov family.
17. Pshaw: an interjection used to express irritation, disapproval, contempt, or disbelief.
18. it: See note 15, definition of "it."
19. six-foot oath: a very long oath.
20. certain: particular.
21. bone: remove the bones from.
22. old serpent Gorinytch: a monster with the body of a serpent that haunts the mountains in Russian fairy tales.
23. stables: the buildings where domestic animals (in this case, the horses of the cabdrivers in St. Petersburg) are lodged and fed. The cab-drivers rest in a room nearby.
24. I have not earned enough to feed my horse. Fodder is coarse food fed to domestic animals.
25. earned our corn: earned enough money to buy corn, which is a

better fodder than hay.
26. Kuzma Ionitch: the name of his son.
27. went off pop: died suddenly.

参考译文

薄暮时分。密集的雪花环绕刚刚点亮的街灯旋转,在屋顶、马背、人们的肩膀和帽子上落下薄薄的、轻柔的一层。马车夫伊奥纳·波塔波夫浑身雪白,看起来像个幽灵。他弯腰曲背,一直弯到人体可以"对折"的极限。他坐在赶车人的车座上,一动不动。看起来,即使飘飞的雪都落到身上,他都觉得没有必要抖掉。他那匹小马也是一身白,也一动不动。它纹丝不动、瘦骨嶙峋、直直的、看起来像木棒似的腿,哪怕凑过去细看,也让人觉得只是值一戈比的姜饼马。毫无疑问,它正陷入沉思。如果你被人家从犁杖上卸下来,从平常熟悉的灰色景物中拽出来,突然走进一个充满炫目的灯光、无休止的喧嚣和步履匆匆的人群的世界,你难免不陷入沉思。

伊奥纳和小马已经很长时间没动地方了。他们晚饭前就离开自家的院子,到现在还没有一个人想坐他的雪橇。暮霭笼罩了小镇,街灯的白光替换了明亮的阳光,街上的喧闹声越来越大。"车夫,去维堡!"伊奥纳突然听到有人喊他。"车夫!"

伊奥纳跳了起来,透过挂满雪花的睫毛,看到一个身穿大衣的军官,头上戴着兜帽。

"维堡!"军官又说了一遍。"你睡着了吗?去维堡!"

伊奥纳连忙点点头,拿起缰绳,一层层雪从马背和马脖子上滑落下来。军官坐上雪橇,车夫咂咂嘴吆喝着马,像天鹅一样伸长脖子,直起腰,挥了挥鞭子。其实没什么必要,不过是出于习惯罢了。小马也伸伸脖子,抬起木头

哀歌
The Lament

棒子似的腿，犹豫不决地向前挪动着。

"你在干什么，混蛋！"他们刚出发，伊奥纳就听见从一团黑乎乎的、晃来晃去的东西上传来的大声叫骂。

"你到底要上哪儿去？靠……靠右！"

"你不会赶车吗。靠右边走！"军官生气地喊道。

一辆私人马车的马车夫朝他叫骂。一个行人跑过马路，肩膀蹭在马鼻子上，一边掸袖子上的雪，一边愤怒地看着他。伊奥纳在车座上不自在地挪动身子，如坐针毡，胳膊肘往两旁撑开，仿佛在努力保持平衡。他表情错愕，张着嘴巴，就跟喘不过气来一样，好像不明白自己是在什么地方，也不知道为什么在那儿似的。

"真是些无赖！"军官开玩笑地说，"感觉他们好像商量好了似的，要么挤你，要么倒在你的马下。"

伊奥纳回头看了看军官，嘴唇翕动着显然想说点什么，但唯一发出来的是抽鼻子的声音。

"怎么了？"军官问。

伊奥纳抽动着嘴角，露出一丝苦笑，用嘶哑的声音吃力地说："我的儿子，老爷，这个星期死了。"

"哦！他是怎么死的？"

伊奥纳把整个身子都转向乘客，说道：

"谁知道呢！他们说是高烧。在医院住了三天，就死了……上帝的旨意。"

"拐弯！魔鬼！"黑暗中又传来叫喊声。"你他妈的找死吗，老狗，长眼睛了吗？"

"走吧，走吧，"军官说，"要不然明天也到不了。快点！"

车夫又伸了伸脖子，直起腰，勉强挥了挥手中的鞭子。他又转过身看了几次乘客，但那人已经闭上眼睛，显然不愿意听他唠叨。把军官送到维堡后，他在旅店旁停了下来，在座位上缩成一团，仍旧一动不动。雪又开始覆盖他和他的马。一个小时，又一个小时……然后，人行道上传来胶鞋踩在雪地上的嘎吱声和争吵声。来了三个年轻人，其中两个又高又瘦，第三个身材矮小还驼背。

"车夫，去警察桥！"驼背用沙哑的声音喊道，"我们仨，两格里夫纳。"

伊奥纳挽起缰绳，咂了咂嘴。两格里夫纳太少了，但他不在乎是一卢布还是五戈比。现在对他来说都一样，给钱就行。三个年轻人推推搡搡，满嘴脏话，走近雪橇。三个人都想坐那个座位，争论哪两个人该坐，谁该站着。经过一番争吵，相互谩骂，大发雷霆，最后决定让"驼背"站着，因为他个子最小。

"喂，快点儿吧！""驼背"在他的"立足之地"站定，对着伊奥纳的脖颈儿喘息，带着浓重的鼻音说，"老杂毛！给你钱，伙计。瞧瞧你这顶帽子！走遍彼得堡也找不到比它更糟的了……"

"呵，呵……呵呵！"伊奥纳笑着说，"这样一个……"

"得了，'这样一个'，快点吧，你一路都这么慢吞吞的，是吗？……你的脖子是不是想挨两巴掌了？"

"我头疼，好像要裂开了似的，"瘦高个子中的一个说，"昨天晚上在敦克马瑟夫家，我和瓦斯卡喝了整整四瓶法国白兰地。"

"我不明白你为什么要撒谎，"另一个瘦高个儿生气地说，"你撒起谎来简直像个畜生。"

"我说的都是实话。要是有假，天打雷劈！"

"就像虱子会咳嗽一样，真的不能再真了！"

"呵，呵，"伊奥纳笑着说，"多么快乐的年轻人呀！"

"呸，见鬼去吧！""驼背"愤怒地说。

"能不能快点儿呀，你这个老家伙？你就这么赶车吗？用鞭子抽几下！抽呀，老鬼，抽呀，好好教训教训它！"

伊奥纳觉得那个小个子在他背后扭动，说话的声音颤抖。他听着劈头盖脸的辱骂,看着那些人,孤独感渐渐消散。"驼背"不停地叫骂,直到骂声变成指天画地没完没了的赌咒发誓,或者因为咳嗽喘不过气来。两个瘦高个儿开始谈论一个叫纳德伊达·彼得罗夫娜的人。伊奥纳回过头看了他们几次,终于等到片刻的沉默,连忙转过身,喃喃着说:

"我的儿子……这个星期去世了。"

"谁都得死,"一阵咳嗽过后,"驼背"擦了擦嘴唇,叹了口气说,"快点,快点!先生们,我总这么站着,真的挺不住了!这家伙什么时候才能把我们送到那儿呀?"

"哦,你只要朝他脖子上来两下就行了!"

"你这个老混蛋,听见了吗?我要打断你的脖子!如果有谁对你这种人彬彬有礼,那就只能步行走路了!听到了吗,老蛇精格里尼奇!你是不是一点儿也不在乎?"

伊奥纳虽然听到他们的谩骂,但是不以为意。

"呵,呵,"他笑着说。"快活的年轻人,上帝保佑他们!"

"车夫,你结婚了吗?"一个瘦高个子问道。

"我?呵,呵,快乐的年轻人!现在我只有老婆和那块潮湿的土地……呵呵,唔,唔……也就是说,坟墓。儿子死了,我却活着……一件奇妙的事,死神开错了门……没来找我,而是找我儿子去了……"

伊奥纳转身想告诉他们儿子是怎么死的,但就在这时,"驼背"轻轻地叹了口气,大声说:"谢天谢地,终于到了。"伊奥纳看着他们消失在黑魆魆的大门洞。他又独自一人,又被寂静笼罩,……刚刚减轻了一点点的悲伤又袭上心头,而且更猛烈地撕扯着他的心。他满脸焦急,目光飞快地扫过街道两旁的人群,看是否有人能听他说说话。但是人们都行色匆匆,没有谁注意到他和他的麻烦。然而,那是一种巨大的、无边无沿的悲伤。如果心碎了,悲伤就会喷涌而出,漫过整个大地。事实上,就是这样,可惜没人看到。它设法把自己隐藏在一个微不足道的壳里,即使在白天,阳光明媚的时候也没有人能看到。

伊奥纳看见一个旅馆勤杂工,手里拿着几条麻袋,决定和他谈谈。

"朋友,现在是什么时辰?"他问道。

"九点多了。你站在这儿干什么?快走吧。"

伊奥纳向前走了几步,弯腰曲背,沉浸在悲痛之中。他意识到求人没用。不到五分钟,他又直起腰,抬起头,好像突然感到一阵剧痛,扯了一下缰绳,实在受不了了。"到马厩,"他想,小马好像明白他的意思,小跑起来。

大约一个半小时后,伊奥纳在一个脏兮兮的大火炉旁边坐了下来。火炉周围,地板上,长凳上,都躺着打呼噜的人。屋子里闷热,连气也喘不过来。伊奥纳看了看那些熟睡的人,朝自己身上抓了几把,后悔不该这么早就回来。

"还没挣够草料钱呢,"他心里想,"这就是我的麻烦。一个会干活、能填饱肚子、喂饱马的人,才能睡得安稳。"

墙角,一个年轻车夫坐起来,睡意朦胧地嘟囔着,朝水桶伸了个懒腰。

"想喝水吗?"伊奥纳问道。

"怎么不想喝!"

"是吗?你身体真棒!听着,伙计——你知道,我儿子死了……你听说了吗?这个星期,死在医院……说来话长。"

伊奥纳眼巴巴瞅着,想看看那个年轻人对他的话有什么反应,但是什么也没有看到。他把脸扭过去,又睡着了。老人叹了口气,摇了摇头。就像那个年轻人想喝水一样,老人想说话。儿子离世快一周了,他还没能和任何一个人好好地聊聊这件事。必须慢慢地、仔仔细细地讲:儿子怎么生的病,受了多少罪,临死前说了什么,怎么死的。必须描述葬礼的每一个细节以及去医院取儿子遗物一路上的情况。他的女儿阿尼西亚还留在村里——肯定也要谈谈她。难道他说的一切都无足轻重吗？听他唠叨的人肯定会唉声叹气，表示同情吧？和女人聊更好。虽然她们傻乎乎的，但两个字就能让她们痛哭流涕。

"得去看看马，"伊奥纳想，"睡觉的时间有的是。用不着担心！"

他穿上外套，去马厩找马。他想到了玉米、干草和天气。独自一人的时候，他不敢想儿子。他可以对任何人谈起他，但想到他，在心里描绘他，却是难以忍受的痛苦。

"吃饱了吗？"伊奥纳看着马儿明亮的眼睛问道，"吃吧，尽情地吃吧。虽然我们还没有挣到买玉米的钱，但干草还吃得起。是的！我太老了，赶不了车了——我儿子行，我不行。他是一流的车夫。要是他还活着就好了！"

伊奥纳沉默了一会儿，接着说：

"就是这么回事儿，我的老马。库兹马·伊奥尼奇已经死了。他让我们活着，自己突然就没了。比方说，你有一个小马驹，你是它的妈妈。突然间，比方说，小马驹离你而去，你还活着。那会很悲哀，不是吗？"

小马咀嚼着，倾听着，在主人的手上喘息着……

伊奥纳的情感浓烈得让他无法承受，于是把故事都告诉了小马。

（李尧 译）

14

Trivia

琐　事

LOGAN PEARSALL SMITH
洛根·皮尔索尔·史密斯

(1865–1946)

ABOUT THE AUTHOR

Logan Pearsall Smith (1865–1946), Anglo-American author, was born in Millville, N. J. After 1888 he lived in England, studied at Oxford, and became a man of letters. His brief and exquisite essays were collected as *Trivia* (1902), *More Trivia* (1921), and *All Trivia* (1934). Never married, Smith always wrote as if he were an old man, even when he was young. Bald, thin, and aquiline-featured, he was the typical bachelor of culture and perception who gravitated between his club and his study. His essays are delightful, shrewd, incisive, and witty. His other works include *The English Language* (1912), *On Reading Shakespeare* (1933), *Reperusals and Recollections* (1936), and *Milton and His Modern Critics* (1940). The story of his life can be found in his autobiography, *Unforgotten Years* (1939) and Robert Gathorne-Hardy's *Recollections of Logan Pearsall Smith* (1949).

作者简介 洛根·皮尔索尔·史密斯（1865—1946），现代英国散文作家，生于美国新泽西州米尔维尔。1888年后，在英国生活，在牛津大学学习，成为学者。他的简短而精致的文章收录在《琐事》（1902）、《琐事续篇》（1921）和《尽是琐事》（1934）中。史密斯一生未婚，文字老成，年轻时就是这样。他谢顶、瘦削、鹰钩鼻子，是一位典型的单身汉学者，富有修养和洞察力，穿梭往来于俱乐部和书房之间。他的文章令人愉快、敏锐、深刻、机智。其作品还有《英语语言》（1912）、《读莎士比亚》（1933）、《往事与回忆》（1936）和《弥尔顿及其现代评论者》（1940）。洛根·皮尔索尔·史密斯的生平故事可以在他的自传《忘不了的岁月》（1939）和罗伯特·加索恩－哈代的《洛根·皮尔索尔·史密斯回忆录》（1949）中找到。

ABOUT THE SELECTION

Edmund Wilson, the American writer, said that Smith's *Trivia* revealed "with cool self-mockery his old fogyism, his timidity, his snobbery, his envy, his respect for money, his capacity for being a bore, as well as the touching aspiration, the Quakerish sobriety and purity, of his worship of literature." George Santayana, the poet and philosopher, called the same work "delightfully vivid and humorous" and "a document of importance." In this selection we have a specimen of Smith's work from *Trivia* and *All Trivia*. Both books are sketches of private moods, written with delicate precision. The author depicts different states of mind and employs a variety of stylistic resources to delineate and vivify them as concisely as possible. The state of mind may be analyzed as comprising a notion and a mood. For example, while the notion of "Becalmed" can be stated as "I have a purpose in life," its mood is one of "expectation" or "resolution." The reader will find these sketches not only excellent samples of terse and poetic prose but very delightful reading in which he recognizes his own "wavering, flickering" self.

内容简介 美国作家埃德蒙·威尔逊说,史密斯的《琐事》"带着冷静的自嘲,揭示了他的守旧、胆怯、势利、嫉妒、对金钱的尊重、一个令人厌烦的人的能力以及让人感动的渴望,贵格会信徒的清醒和纯洁,以及他对文学的崇拜。"诗人和哲学家乔治·桑塔亚纳称赞这部作品"生动而幽默",是"一份重要的文献"。我们发表在这里的几则作品,均选自《琐事》和《尽是琐事》,其简洁精练堪称史密斯作品的样本。《琐事》和《尽是琐事》这两本书都是个人情绪的表达,写得非常精确。作者使用各不相同的风格,以尽可能简洁的笔触,描述不同的心理状态,将其生动形象地呈现在读者面前。在他的笔下,精神状态被解析为概念和情绪的组合。例如,"平静"的概念被表述为"我生活中的一个目标",其情绪是"期望"或"决心"。读者会发现,这些小品是简洁而富有诗意的散文的优秀范例,读起来不乏愉悦之感。作者从这些作品中看到了"摇摆不定、忽隐忽现"的自我。

Becalmed

Half-way along the street I stopped; I had forgotten the errand which had brought me out. What was it I wanted? There was nothing on earth[1] I wanted; I stood there, motionless, without desire, like a ship at sea, deserted of all winds. It seemed as if I might stand there for ever.

Then, as with the shadow of a cloud, or ripple of the returning breeze, the wind of impulse[2] darkened over the waters and filled my sails again. Life was again momentous, full of meaning; and radiant to my imagination the stamps, red and green and golden, I had hurried out to buy.

The Busy Bees

Sitting for hours idle in the shade of an apple tree, near the garden-hives, and under the aerial thoroughfares of those honey-merchants—sometimes when the noonday heat is loud with their minute industry, or when they fall in crowds out of the late sun[3] to their nightlong labors,—I have sought instruction from the Bees, and tried to appropriate to myself the old industrious lesson.[4]

And yet, hang it[5] all, who by rights should be the teacher and who the learners? For those peevish, overtoiled, utilitarian insects, was there no lesson to be derived from the spectacle of Me? Gazing out at me with composite eyes[6] from their joyless factories, might they not learn at last—could I not finally teach them—a wiser and more generous-hearted way to improve the shining hours?

Stonehenge[7]

There they sit for ever around the horizon of my mind: that Stonehenge circle of elderly disapproving Faces—Faces of the Uncles, and Schoolmasters and the Tutors[8] who frowned on my youth.

In the bright center and sunlight I leap, I caper, I dance my dance; but when I look up, I see they are not deceived. For nothing ever placates them, nothing ever moves to a look of approval that ring of bleak, old, contemptuous Faces.

Action

I am no mere thinker, no mere creature of dreams and imagination. I pay bills, post letters, I buy new bootlaces and put them in my boots. And when I set out to get my hair cut, it is with the iron face of those men of empire and unconquerable will, those Caesars and Napoleons[9] whose footsteps shake the earth.

High Life

Although that immense Country House was empty and for sale, and I had got an order to view it, I needed all my courage to walk through the lordly gates, and up the avenue, and then to ring the resounding door-bell. And when I was ushered in, and the shutters were removed to illuminate those vast apartments,[10] I sneaked through them, cursing the dishonest curiosity[11] which had brought me into a place where I had no business. But I was treated with such deference, and so plainly regarded as a possible purchaser, that I soon began to give credence to the opulence imputed to me.[12] From all the novels describing the mysterious and glittering life of the Great which I had read (and I have read thousands), there came to me the vision of my own existence in this Palace. I filled those vast halls with the glint of diamonds and stir of voices,[13] I saw a vision of bejewelled Duchesses sweeping[14] in their tiaras down the splendid stairs.

But my Soul, in her swell of pride, soon outgrew these paltry limits. Oh, no! Never could I box up and house under that roof the Pomp, the Ostentation of which I was capable.

Then for one thing there was stabling for only forty horses; and this, of course, as I told them, would never do.[15]

Edification

"I must really improve my mind," I tell myself, and once more begin to patch and repair that crazy structure.[16] So I toil and toil on at the vain task of edification, though the wind tears off the tiles, the floors give way, the ceilings fall, strange birds build untidy nests in the rafters, and owls hoot and laugh in the tumbling chimneys.

The Evil Eye

Drawn by the unfelt wind in my little sail over the shallow estuary, I lay in my boat, lost in the dream of mere existence. The cool water glided through my trailing fingers; and leaning over, I watched the sands that slid beneath me, the weeds that languidly swayed with the boat's motion. I was the cool water, I was the gliding sand and the swaying weed, I was the sea and sky and sun, I was the whole vast Universe.

Then between my eyes and the sandy bottom a mirrored face looked up at me floating on the smooth film of water over which I glided. At one look from that too familiar, and yet how sinister and goblin a face, my immeasurable Soul collapsed like a wrecked balloon; I shrank sadly back into my named personality, and sat there, shabby, hot, and very much bored with myself in my little boat.

Green Ivory

What a bore it is, waking up in the morning always the same person. I wish I were unflinching and emphatic, and had big, bushy eyebrows and a Message for the Age. I wish I were a deep Thinker, or a great Ventriloquist.[17]

I should like to be refined-looking and melancholy, the victim of a hopeless passion; to love in the old, stilted way, with impossible Adoration and Despair under the pale-faced Moon.

I wish I could get up; I wish I were the world's greatest living Violinist. I wish I had lots of silver, and first Editions, and green ivory.[18]

Eclipse

A mild radiance and the scent of flowers filled the drawing-room, whose windows stood open to the summer night. I thought our talk delightful; the topic was one of my favorite topics; I had much that was illuminating to say about it, and I was a little put out[19] when we were called to the window to look at the planet Jupiter, which was shining in the sky just then, we were told, with great brilliance.

In turns through a telescope we gazed at the Planet. I thought the spectacle over-rated. However I said nothing. Not for the world, not for any number of worlds would I have wished them to guess why I was not pleased with that Star.

The Church of England

I have my Anglican[20] moments, and as I sat there that Sunday afternoon, in the eighteenth-century interior of the London Church, and listened to the unexpressive voices chanting the correct service, I felt a comfortable assurance that we were in no danger of being betrayed[21] into any unseemly manifestations of religious fervor.[22] We had not gathered together at that performance to abase ourselves obsequiously, with furious hosannas[23] before any dark Creator of an untamed Universe, no Deity of freaks and miracles and sinister hocus-pocus;[24] but to pay our duty to a highly respected Anglican First Cause[25]—distinguished, undemonstrative, gentlemanly—whom, without loss of self-respect, we could decorously praise.

The Spider

What shall I compare it to, this fantastic thing I call my Mind? To a waste-paper basket, to a sieve choked with sediment, or to a barrel full of floating froth and refuse?

No, what it is really most like is a spider's web, insecurely hung on leaves and twigs, quivering in every wind, and sprinkled with dewdrops and dead flies. And at its geometric centre, pondering for ever the Problem of Existence, sits motionless and spider-like the uncanny Soul.

My Portrait

But after all I am no amoeba, no mere sack and stomach; I am capable of discourse, can ride a bicycle, look up trains in Bradshaw[26]; in fact I am and calmly boast myself a Human Being—that Masterpiece of Nature, and noblest fruit of time;—I am a rational, polite, meat-eating Man.

What stellar collisions and conflagrations, what floods and slaughters and enormous efforts has it not cost the Universe to make me—of what astral periods and cosmic processes am I not the crown, the wonder?

Where, then, is the Esplanade or world-dominating Terrace for my sublime Statue, the landscape of palaces and triumphal arches for the background of my Portrait; stairs of marble, flung against the sunset, not too narrow and ignoble for me to pause with ample gesture on their balustraded flights?

Vertigo[27]

Still, I don't like it; I can't approve of it; I have always thought it most regrettable that earnest and ethical Thinkers like ourselves should go scuttling through space in this undignified manner. Is it seemly that I, at my age, should be hurled with my books of reference, and bedclothes, and hot-water bottle, across the sky at the unthinkable rate of nineteen miles a second? As I say, I don't at all like it. This universe of astronomical whirligigs[28] makes me a little giddy.

That God should spend His eternity—which might be so much better employed—in spinning countless Solar Systems, and skylarking, like a great child, with tops and teetotums[29]—is not this a serious scandal? I wonder what all our circumgyrating Monotheists[30] really do think of it.

Under an Umbrella

From under the roof of my umbrella I saw the washed pavement lapsing beneath my feet, the news-posters lying smeared with dirt at the crossings, the tracks of the busses in the liquid mud. On I went through this world of wetness. And through what long perspectives of the years shall I still hurry down wet streets—middle-aged, and then, perhaps, very old? And on what errands?

Asking myself this question I fade from your vision, Reader, into the distance, sloping my umbrella against the wind.

NOTES

1. on earth: among numberless possibilities—used for emphasis.
2. impulse: inspiration; motivation.
3. The bees return in swarms to their hives at twilight.
4. the old industrious lesson: Idle and indolent men have long been admonished to look to the bee as a model of industriousness.
5. hang it: a mild curse or oath.
6. composite eyes: a double image referring at once to the compound eyes of the bees and the cells of a beehive.
7. Stonehenge: assemblage of monoliths (great stone columns) erected by a prehistoric people on Salisbury Plain in Wiltshire, south England.
8. Tutors: teachers, especially in a British university, ranking below instructors.
9. Caesars and Napoleons: Both Caesar and Napoleon were emperors and iron-willed men. When used in the plural, they represent all men who seek empires and have unconquerable wills.
10. the shutters were removed to illuminate those vast apartments: Always closed, the shutters were opened only when a prospective buyer came to inspect the house.
11. dishonest curiosity: The narrator had come to see the house out of curiosity but with no intention of buying it.
12. to give credence to the opulence imputed to me: to believe that I was as rich as the others thought I was.
13. Diamonds are worn in parties and balls. There is a stir of voices when many people are gathered. The narrator begins to imagine parties, balls, and social gatherings.
14. sweeping: moving swiftly and forcefully with a stately movement.
15. To get out of the awkward situation of explaining why he could

not buy the house, he pretended that the house was too small to accommodate all his possessions. Do: answer the purpose.
16. structure: the author's mind.
17. Ventriloquist: one who is able to produce his voice in such a manner that the sound appears to come from some other source than the vocal organs of the speaker.
18. first Editions and green ivory: both first editions of books and green ivory are rare and, therefore, valuable. To possess them would make one impressive in the eyes of others.
19. put out: annoyed, irritated.
20. Anglican: of or relating to the established episcopal Church of England.
21. betrayed: misled; led astray.
22. unseemly manifestations of religious fervor: the manner of worship in evangelical churches where people are more freely expressive of their devotion—they sing, weep, pray, and shout in praise of God in a way condemned by the Anglicans.
23. hosannas: used as cries of adoration.
24. hocus-pocus: nonsense to disguise deception.
25. First Cause: the self-created source of all causality; God.
26. Bradshaw: short for Bradshaw's Railway Guide, a comprehensive timetable of British railroad trains, named after George Bradshaw, the English printer who first issued it in 1839.
27. vertigo: giddiness; a dizzy confused state of mind.
28. whirligigs: things that continuously whirl or move in a circular course.
29. teetotums: small tops with inscribed letters.
30. circumgyrating Monotheist: Circumgyrating is moving in a circular course. Monotheists are people who believe there is only one God. We are circumgyrating because we are moving around the sun.

参考译文　　　　　　　宁　静

在大街上走了一半，我停下脚步。居然忘记跑出来干嘛，想要什么？世上万物，没有一样东西是我想要的。我站在那儿，一动不动，没有任何欲望，就像海面上的一艘船,风平浪静。我好像要永远站在那里。

然后,天光投下云影,微风掀起涟漪,一股强劲的风将水色变暗,风帆鼓满。生活又充满意义,变得重要起来。我步履匆匆,跑出来要买的红、绿、金黄色的邮票,在想象之中又熠熠生辉。

忙碌的蜜蜂

在一棵苹果树的树荫下懒洋洋地坐了好几个小时,旁边有一个花园里的蜂巢,头顶是"酿蜜者"的空中通道。有时候,热浪滚滚的中午,花丛中采蜜的小蜜蜂大声歌唱;红日西沉的黄昏,归巢的蜂群,嗡嗡营营彻夜辛劳。我从蜜蜂身上寻求启迪,试图把关于蜜蜂勤劳的古训运用到自己身上。

然而,真该死,按理说谁应该是老师,谁应该是学生呢?那些爱发牢骚、日夜操劳、信奉实用主义的昆虫,难道就不能从我身上汲取点经验教训?它们在毫无乐趣的"工厂"里,用复眼傻乎乎地凝望着我。难道它们怎么也学不会、我怎么也教不会它们以一种更聪明、更慷慨大度的方法使闪光的生活更美好吗?

巨 石 阵

他们永远坐在我心灵的地平线上——一圈宛如巨石阵的老年人不以为然的面孔。那是叔叔、校长和指导教师的面孔。总是对年轻人皱着眉头。

阳光下,我在明亮的中心跳跃、欢呼、舞蹈。但是抬头望去,他们并没有为之动容。因为没有什么能抚慰他们,没有什么能让他们露出赞许的表情——那一圈阴郁、苍老、轻蔑的面孔。

行　动

我不只是思想者，不只是耽于梦想、想象力丰富的人。我付账单，寄信，买新鞋带穿到靴子上。在出发前去理发的路上，我面容坚定，像意志不可征服的帝国统治者，像脚步震撼大地的恺撒和拿破仑们。

奢华生活

虽然那座宏伟的乡间别墅已经空空荡荡，正在出售，我又得到允许进去开开眼界，但我还是需要鼓足勇气，才能走进那扇颇具贵族气派的大门，走过浓荫覆盖的大道，按响嘹亮悦耳的门铃。仆人领我进去之后，打开百叶窗，阳光顿时照亮一间间宽敞的厅堂。我蹑手蹑脚地走着，暗自责备不诚实的好奇心把我带到一个与己无关的地方。可是人家对我恭而敬之，显然当作一个潜在的买主。这很快让我产生一种错觉，相信自己真的非常富有。我读过（几千本）描绘大人物神秘奢华生活的小说。这些小说赋予我丰富的想象力，让我看到自己生活在这座宫殿里的情景。大厅里人声鼎沸，流光溢彩。一道风景从我眼前闪过：浑身珠光宝气、头戴冕状头饰的公爵夫人仪态万千沿着华丽的楼梯缓步而下。

但是我的灵魂，随着虚荣心的膨胀，很快就突破了那些不足挂齿的限制。哦，不！我绝对不能住到那座奢华的别墅里，我会大肆炫耀的。

于是我借机推托说，这里的马厩太小，只能容纳四十匹马。这一点，当然，就像我告诉他们的，绝对不行。

提升自我

"必须真正提高心智,"我对自己说,然后又一次开始修补那些不理智的思想和行为。于是,我辛辛苦苦地去干那些徒劳无益的教化工作,尽管风刮掉瓦片,地板塌陷,天花板跌落,陌生的鸟儿在屋檐下筑起乱糟糟的巢,猫头鹰在歪歪斜斜的烟囱上又叫又笑。

邪恶的目光

浅水河口,轻柔得无知无觉的风吹拂小帆。我躺在船里,迷失在"仅仅是存在"的梦境中。清凉的水从滑动的手指间流过,我弯下腰,望着身下游动的细沙,望着水草随小船荡漾,懒洋洋地摇摆。我是清凉的水,我是游动的沙,我是摇曳的草,我是大海,我是天空,我是太阳,我是浩瀚的宇宙。

然后,在我的眼睛和细沙河床之间,一张仿佛映照在镜子里的脸在光滑的水面上漂浮,仰望着我。那张脸那么熟悉,却又那么邪恶、小妖精一般,只瞥我一眼,我那深不可测的灵魂就变成泄了气的皮球。我十分难过,又缩回到我那被确定的人格中,坐在我的小船上,寒酸、燥热,对自己非常不耐烦。

绿象牙

真烦人,每天早上醒来总是同一个自我。我希望成为一个不屈不挠、坚定不移的人,一个眉毛浓重的智者,告诉世界重要的信息。我希望我是一个深刻的思想者,或者一个伟大的腹语者。

我愿意看上去文雅而忧郁,成为无望的激情的牺牲品。在苍白的月光下，用古老而生硬的方式，满怀不可思议的爱慕和绝望去爱。

我希望一夜醒来，成为世界上还活着的最伟大的小提琴家。希望我有许多银器、初版书和绿象牙。

日 食

夏夜，客厅的窗户敞开着，屋子里洒满柔和的月光，缭绕着袭人的花香。我觉得我们的谈话很愉快。这个话题是我最喜欢的话题之一。关于这一点，我有很多发人深思的东西要说。我们被叫到窗口去看木星时，我心有不悦。他们说，木星在夜空闪烁，非常明亮。

我们轮流用望远镜凝望那颗行星。我认为他们有点夸大其词了。不过什么也没说。哪怕给我整个世界，给我这个世界的一切，我都不希望他们猜出我为什么对那颗星星不满意。

英国国教会

我在圣公会教堂做礼拜。星期日下午，坐在那座始建于18世纪的伦敦教堂里，听着没有波澜起伏、抑扬顿挫的声音齐声吟诵。正确的礼拜仪式让人感到温馨，心里踏实，相信我们不会误入歧途，陷入不体面的宗教狂热的危险之中。我们没有在这样的场合聚集在一起，献媚讨好，卑躬屈膝，降低自己的身份，在未曾驯服的宇宙任何邪恶的创造者面前兴高采烈地呼喊：和撒那！这里没有怪异的、创造奇迹的和邪恶骗人的神。我们只对备受世人尊敬的英国国教的神——杰出的、拘谨缄默的、彬彬有礼的神——尽责。我们在不失自尊的情况下，稳重端庄地赞美。

蜘 蛛

该拿什么来比喻我称之为"思想"的这个奇异的东西呢？废纸篓，滤下一层残渣的筛子，还是漂着浮沫的垃圾桶？

不，它真正最像的是颤颤巍巍挂在树叶和细枝上的蜘蛛网，上面沾满露珠和死苍蝇。每当风儿吹过，就会轻轻颤抖。神秘的灵魂像蜘蛛一样，一动不动趴在它的几何中心，永远在思考生存的问题。

我的画像

但我毕竟不是变形虫，不只是酒囊饭袋。我会演讲，会骑自行车，会用列车时刻表查找火车。事实上，我坦然地宣称自己是人——大自然的杰作，时间最高贵的结晶。我是一个理性、礼貌、食肉的人。

宇宙为了创造我，恒星曾经怎样碰撞、燃烧，洪水曾经怎样肆虐，涂炭生灵，天地付出了多么巨大的努力——我难道不是星体时期和宇宙形成过程中应运而生的王者和奇迹吗？

那么，我伟岸的雕像应该安放在哪里的海滨广场或主宰世界的阶地上呢？我的画像的背景——宫殿和凯旋门亮丽的风景在哪里呢？夕阳映照的大理石楼梯不能太窄，不能寒酸，因为我要站在栏杆环绕的楼梯上摆个需要足够空间的姿势。

眩 晕

不过，我还是不喜欢，不能苟同。我一直认为，像我们这样认真努力、道德高尚的思想家，竟然以这样一种不体面的方式在太空匆匆穿行，真令人遗憾。我这把年纪的人，带着参考书、被褥和热水瓶，以每秒十九英里的不可思议的速度被抛向天空，这合适吗？如我所说，我一点儿也不喜欢。这个天文学中旋转的宇宙让我有点头晕目眩。

上帝应该用他永恒的力量推动浩瀚无际的太阳系旋转，嬉戏——这样做岂不是好很多——就像一个大孩子抽陀螺和刻着字母的小陀螺玩一样。这难道不是重大的丑闻吗？不知道我们那些"旋转一神论者"对此作何感想。

伞 下

从伞下，我看见被雨水冲洗过的人行道在脚下滑动，新闻海报沾着污泥躺在十字路口，公共汽车在泥水中留下车辙。我继续走过这个水淋淋的世界。经过多少漫长的岁月，我依然能步履匆匆走过湿漉漉的大街呢——步入中年，也许直到很老的时候？为什么差事奔忙？

读者，我问自己这个问题的时候，从你的视野中消失，走向远方。顶着风，打着伞。

（李尧 译）

15

This Was My Mother

回忆母亲

MARK TWAIN
马克·吐温

(1835–1910)

ABOUT THE AUTHOR

Samuel Langhorne Clemens (1835–1910) was a leading American humorist, journalist, and author whose pseudonym was adopted from the leadsman's call "mark twain" (two fathoms sounded). Born in Hannibal, Missouri, young Samuel worked as a printer and then as an apprentice to a pilot on a steamboat on the Mississippi River. During the Civil War he went to Nevada and California where he wrote for frontier newspapers and first attracted attention by his writing. Soon he became extremely popular and was favorably received by serious critics. After 1894, when he suffered a financial failure, his work began to show a pessimistic quality which was later heightened by the deaths of his wife and two daughters. Of his voluminous writings *Tom Sawyer* (1876) and its sequel *Huckleberry Finn* (1884) are acclaimed as the best for their hilarious humor, youthful vigor, high-spirited exaggeration, and lively colloquialism.

作者简介 塞缪尔·朗赫恩·克莱门斯（1835—1910），美国著名的幽默大师、记者和作家。笔名马克·吐温，源于轮船测深员报告水深两英寻——"mark twain"(two fathoms)的声音。小塞缪尔出生在密苏里州的汉尼拔，当过印刷工人，后来在密西西比河的一艘轮船上给一个领航员当学徒。内战期间，他去了内华达和加利福尼亚，给西部边疆地区报纸撰稿，其作品引起广泛关注，好评如潮。1894年以后，他在经济上受到重创，作品开始显露出悲观的色彩，后来他的妻子和两个女儿相继去世，使得这种色彩更加浓厚。在他大量的作品中，《汤姆·索亚历险记》(1876)及其续集《哈克贝利·费恩历险记》(1884)因其令人捧腹的幽默、昂扬的活力、夸张和生动的口语而被誉为最佳作品。

* **ABOUT THE SELECTION** In simple and lucid prose the author portrays his mother as he remembers her as a typical American matron in the pioneering days in mid-nineteenth century. With a few masterly strokes he succeeds in weaving memorable incidents and characteristic conversations into a delightfully honest sketch of a kind, brave, earthy and robust woman. The racy style is heightened by a touch of humor which spares neither mother nor son. It is this sense of humor and a biographical integrity to tell nothing but the truth that keep such reminiscences from sentimentality.

内容简介 作者用简洁明快的文字将母亲描绘为他记忆中 19 世纪中期"拓荒者时代"典型的美国家庭主妇。他以精巧的笔触,用难以忘怀的往事和颇具特色的对话成功地塑造出一个善良、勇敢、朴实、健壮的女人的形象。而在母子身上均有体现的幽默愈发突显出活泼的风格。正是这种幽默感和作为传记文学的完整性——只讲事实,不言其他,使得这种回忆不致让人感伤。

My mother, Jane Lampton Clemens, died in her 88th year, a mighty age for one who at 40 was so delicate of body as to be accounted a confirmed invalid,¹ destined to pass soon away.² But the invalid who, forgetful of self, takes a strenuous and indestructible³ interest in everything and everybody, as she did, and to whom a dull moment is an unknown thing, is a formidable adversary⁴ for disease.

She had a heart so large that everybody's griefs and joys found welcome in it. One of her neighbors never got over⁵ the way she received the news of a local accident. When he had told how a man had been thrown from his horse and killed because a calf had run in his way, my mother asked with genuine interest, "What became of⁶ the calf?" She was not indifferent to the man's death, she was interested in the calf, too.

She could find something to excuse and as a rule to love in the toughest of human beings or animals—even if she had to invent it. Once we beguiled her into saying a soft word for the devil himself. We started abusing him, one conspirator after another adding his bitter word,⁷ until she walked right into the trap. She admitted that the indictment⁸ was sound, but had he been treated fairly? Who, in 18 centuries, had had the common humanity to pray for the one sinner who needed it most?⁹

She never used large words, yet when her pity or indignation was stirred she was the most eloquent person I have ever heard. We had a little slave boy whom we had hired from someone there in Hannibal.[10] He had been taken from his family in Maryland, brought halfway across the continent,[11] and sold. All day long he was singing, whistling, yelling, laughing. The noise was maddening, and one day I lost my temper, went raging to my mother[12] and said Sandy had been singing for an hour straight, and I couldn't stand it. Wouldn't she please shut him up? The tears came into her eyes and she said:

"Poor thing, when he sings it shows me that he is not remembering, and that comforts me, but when he is still I am afraid he is thinking. He will never see his mother again; if he can sing, I must be thankful for it. If you were older you would understand, and that friendless child's noise would make you glad."

All dumb animals had a friend in her. Hunted and disreputable cats recognized her at a glance as their refuge and champion. We once had 19 cats at one time. They were a vast burden, but they were out of luck, and that was enough. She generally had a cat in her lap when she sat down, but she denied indignantly that she liked cats better than children; though there was one advantage to a cat, she'd say. You could always put it down when you were tired of holding it.

I was as much of a nuisance[13] as any small boy and a neighbor asked her once, "Do you ever believe anything that boy says?"

"He is the wellspring of truth," my mother replied, "but you can't bring up the whole well with one bucket. I know his average,[14] so he never deceives me. I discount him 90 percent for embroidery[15] and what is left is perfect and priceless truth, without a flaw."

She had a horror of[16] snakes and bats, which I hid in pockets and sewing baskets; otherwise she was entirely fearless. One day I saw a vicious devil of a Corsican,[17] a common terror in the town, chasing his grown daughter with a heavy rope in his hand, threatening to wear it out on her.[18] Cautious male citizens let him pass but my mother spread her door wide to the refugee, and then, instead of closing and locking it after her, stood in it, barring the way. The man swore, cursed, threatened her with his rope; but she only stood straight and fine, and lashed him, shamed him, derided and defied him until he asked her pardon, gave her his rope and said with a blasphemous oath that she was the bravest woman he ever saw. He found in her a longfelt[19] want—somebody who was not afraid of him.

One day in St. Louis[20] she walked out into the street and surprised[21] a burly cartman who was beating his horse over the head with the butt of a heavy whip. She took the whip away from him and made such a persuasive appeal that he was tripped into saying he was to blame, and into volunteering a promise that he would never abuse a horse again.

She was never too old to get up early to see the circus procession enter town. She adored parades, lectures, conventions,[22] camp meetings, church revivals[23]—in fact every kind of dissipation[24] that could not be proved to have anything irreligious about it and she never missed a funeral. She excused this preference by saying that, if she did not go to other people's funerals, they would not come to hers.

She was 82 and living in Keokuk[25] when, unaccountably, she insisted upon attending a convention of old settlers of the Mississippi Valley. All the way there, and it was some distance, she was young again with excitement and eagerness. At the hotel she asked immediately for Dr. Barrett, of St. Louis. He had left for home that morning and would not be back, she was told. She turned away; the fire all gone from her, and asked to go home. Once there she sat silent and thinking for many days, then told us that when she was 18 she had loved a young medical student with all her heart. There was a misunderstanding and he left the country; she had immediately married, to show him that she did not care. She had never seen him since and then she had read in a newspaper that he was going to attend the old settlers' convention. "Only three hours before we reached that hotel he had been there," she mourned.

She had kept that pathetic burden[26] in her heart 64 years without any of us suspecting it. Before the year was out, her memory began to fail. She would write letters to school mates who had been dead 40 years, and wonder why they never answered. Four years later she died.

But to the last she was capable with her tongue. I had always been told that I was a sickly child who lived mainly on medicines during the first seven years of my life. The year she died I asked her about this and said:

"I suppose that during all the time you were uneasy about me?"

"Yes, the whole time."

"Afraid I wouldn't live?"

After a recollective pause—ostensibly to think out the facts—"No—afraid you would."

Jane Lampton Clemens's character, striking and lovable, appears in my books as Tom Sawyer's Aunt Polly.[27] I fitted her out[28] with a dialect and tried to think up other improvements for her, but did not find any.

NOTES

1. confirmed invalid: chronic patient given up as incurable.
2. pass away: die.
3. indestructible: that cannot be destroyed.
4. formidable adversary: fearful enemy.
5. got over: recovered from; overcame, (in this case) forgot.
6. became of: happened to.
7. one conspirator after another adding his bitter word: As members of a secret (and usually dishonest) plot, we took turns to scold the devil harshly.
8. indictment: formal accusation. Pronounced (in-dite-ment).
9. the one sinner who needed it most: the devil.
10. Hannibal: a town in NE Missouri, famous as the birthplace of Mark Twain.
11. halfway across the continent: Maryland is a state on the Atlantic coast, and Missouri is an inland state midway between the Atlantic and the Pacific.

12. went raging to my mother: went to my mother angrily.
13. much of a nuisance: a big troublemaker.
14. I know his average: I know the ordinary rate of truth in his words.
15. I discount him 90 percent for embroidery: I dismiss 90 percent of his speech as mere ornaments to the 10 percent truth. A humorously sympathetic way, indeed, to forgive a young liar.
16. had a horror of: had a strong dislike of; feared.
17. Corsican: a native of Corsica, French island in the Mediterranean Sea.
18. to wear it out on her: to beat her fiercely until the rope is worn to shreds.
19. longfelt: felt for a long time.
20. St. Louis: a large city in E Missouri, on the Mississippi River.
21. surprised: came upon suddenly; attacked unexpectedly.
22. conventions: meetings; assemblies.
23. church revivals: special services or efforts made to awaken or increase enthusiasm in religion.
24. dissipation: hilarious amusement or indulgence.
25. Keokuk: a small town in SE Iowa, on the Mississippi River.
26. that pathetic burden: her old, unhappy love affair.
27. Tom Sawyer's Aunt Polly: *Tom Sawyer* is an autobiographical novel whose hero Tom Sawyer frequently maneuvers to outwit his extremely conventional Aunt Polly.
28. fitted her out: equipped her; provided her.

参考译文

我的母亲，简·兰普顿·克莱门斯，八十八岁那年去世。她四十岁的时候就弱不禁风，是公认的病秧子，注定的短命鬼，可结果活到耄耋之年。这个病人全然不把自己放在心上，对周围的任何人、任何事却抱有"锲而不舍"的兴趣。对她而言，闲极无聊是一件闻所未闻的事情。而这一切是战胜疾病最有力的武器。

她心胸那么宽阔，容得下每一个人的悲伤和快乐。有位邻居永远都不会忘记听说当地一起交通事故之后她的反应。那人告诉她，有个人骑着马，被一头小牛挡住去路，从马背上摔了下来,一命呜呼。我母亲兴味盎然地问:"小牛怎么样了?"她并非对那个人的死漠然视之,只是对小牛的结局也同样在意。

即使对那些最粗鲁的人、最凶残的动物,她都能找到原谅他们的理由,而且一如既往地爱他们,哪怕不得不编故事骗自己。有一次我们故意设圈套骗她为鬼说好话。几个同谋便轮番骂鬼,越骂越狠,直到她一脚踏空掉进陷阱。她承认对鬼的指控不无道理,但是这样对待他公平吗?在过去的十八个世纪里,人类有谁曾为那个最需要宽恕的恶棍——鬼——祈祷吗?

她从不咬文嚼字,高谈阔论,然而一旦怜悯或者义愤被激起,就变得口若悬河,成了我见过的最伶牙俐齿的人。我家有个小男仆,是我们在汉尼拔居住时从当地人那儿雇来的。他家乡在马里兰州,横跨二分之一大陆,被卖到汉尼拔。小家伙一天到晚唱歌,吹口哨,大喊大叫,哈哈大笑。聒噪之声简直让我发疯。有一天,我终于发脾气了,怒气冲冲跑到母亲面前,说桑迪已经唱了整整一个小时,我实在受不了了,能不能让他闭上嘴巴?妈妈听了,泪水在眼窝里打转,说道:

"可怜的孩子,在我看来,能唱歌说明他没把伤心事放在心里,我听了舒服。他要是不吱声,我就担心他是在想家。他再也见不到妈妈了,如果还能唱歌,我真要谢天谢地了。等你年纪再大一点就会明白,那个无亲无故的孩子的喧闹声会让你高兴。"

她是所有不会说话的小动物的朋友。那些被人撵得丧魂落魄、四处奔逃的流浪猫一眼就能看出她能给它们"庇护所",会是它们的"守护神"。有一回,我们家同时收留了十九只流浪猫。这个负担可不轻。但是一想到它们的不幸,就没人计较了。通常,她坐着的时候,膝盖上总是卧着一只猫。尽管她忿忿不平地矢口否认自己比喜欢孩子还喜欢猫,但也说,猫有个好处,如果你懒得抱它,随时可以把它放下。

183

回忆母亲
This Was My Mother

小时候，我和别的小男孩一样不招人待见。有一次，一位邻居问母亲："那孩子说的话你都信吗？"

"他可是取之不尽用之不竭的真话的源泉，"母亲回答道，"不过，你不可能用一个桶就把井里的水全打上来。我知道，他说的一般都是真话，从来不会骗我。只不过是用百分之九十的花言巧语修饰剩下的那百分之十罢了。那百分之十可是精而贵、贵而宝的真话，绝无瑕疵。"

她除了怕我藏在口袋和针线篮里的蛇和蝙蝠，别的什么都不怕。有一天，我看见一个魔鬼般的科西嘉人——城里公认的恶棍——手里提着一根很粗的绳子，一边追赶已经是大姑娘的女儿，一边扬言要打她打到绳子磨断。胆小怕事的男人没有一个敢上前阻止。只有我母亲敞开大门，让那姑娘进来躲避。姑娘进来之后，她没有关门上锁，而是站在门口挡住那个家伙的去路。那人恶毒地咒骂着，挥舞着手里的绳子吓唬她。可她直挺挺地站着，一动不动，指责他，羞辱他，嘲弄他，直到那人求她原谅，还把绳子交到她手里，然后对天发誓，声称她是他见过的最勇敢的女人。他终于在她身上实现了自己长久以来的愿望——找到一个不怕他的人。

有一天，在圣路易斯，她正在大街上走，突然看见一个五大三粗的车夫用沉甸甸的鞭柄劈头盖脸地打马的头。她一把夺过马鞭，好言相劝，直到那人不得不承认错误，还表示再也不会虐待马了。

马戏团来城里巡回演出的时候，她都要起大早去看热闹，不管"年事"多高。她喜欢看游行，听讲座，参加集会、野营布道会和教堂举行的各种仪式。总而言之，任何娱乐活动，只要不违反宗教信仰，她都乐意参加。她从不错过任何一个人的葬礼，还给自己的"嗜好"编了一个冠冕堂皇的理由——你不参加别人的葬礼，别人也不会来参加你的葬礼。

八十二岁的时候，母亲居住在克库克。让人百思不得其解的是，她非要去参加密西西比河谷的老定居者聚会。路途遥远，但一上路，她就充满青春活力，兴奋、激动，满怀渴望，溢于言表。一到酒店，她就迫不及待地要见从圣路易斯来的巴雷特医生。但是前台告诉她，那天早晨，巴雷特医生已经退房回家，不再来了。她转身离开，黯然失色，要立马回家。回家之后，默默地坐着，朝思暮想好几天。后来告诉我们，十八岁那年，她爱上一个学医的小伙子，爱得如痴如醉。可是他们之间产生了一些误会，结果小伙子离她而去。为了让人家觉得她满不在乎，一赌气就嫁人了事。从那以后，她再也没有见过那个小伙子，直到从报纸上看到他要去参加"老定居者聚会"的消息。她非常伤心，难过地说："我们到酒店三个小时前，他还在那儿呢。"

这段令人伤感的恋情在她心里埋藏了六十四年，我们谁也不曾起过半点儿疑心。那年，还不到年底，她的记忆力就变得越来越差，经常给已经去世四十年的同学写信，然后就纳闷为什么从来没有收到回信。四年后，母亲就去世了。

不过直到最后，她还能表达心之所想。以前，她常说我小时候病病歪歪，七岁前一直靠吃药活着。她去世那年，我问起这件事情：

"我想，那些年你一定为我操碎了心？"

"没错，无时无刻！"

"怕我活不长？"

她想了一会儿，似乎想弄清楚事实真相，"不是……是怕你会活得长。"

简·兰普顿·克莱门斯性格鲜明，讨人喜欢。这种性格的人物出现在我的书里，比如《汤姆·索亚历险记》中的波莉姨妈就有她的影子。虽然我用方言土语为这个角色增加色彩，还试图让人物更丰满，但没有办法做到。

（李尧 译）

16

On Being Busy

论忙碌

HENRY DAVID THOREAU
亨利·戴维·梭罗

(1817–1862)

ABOUT THE AUTHOR

Henry David Thoreau (1817–1862), American author, was a younger member of the transcendentalist group that flourished in mid-19th century New England; and was probably its best literary artist. Thoreau was born in Concord, Mass., and Concord remained the center of his world, although he spent several years of early childhood in neighboring towns and later lived briefly elsewhere. His college career at Harvard brought him two gifts: the discovery of the world of books and friendship with Emerson, leader of the transcendental movement. Thoreau carried out his well-known experiment in living: the residence at Walden Pond from 1845 to 1847. His life was marked by whimsical acts and unconventional stands on public issues, but his rare nature lore, unusual manual skills, and keen common sense won the admiration of many who had thought him only an oddity. Although Thoreau never earned a living by his pen, his works fill 20 volumes. His first major essay "Civil Disobedience" (1849) developed the idea of passive resistance. The only two books published during his lifetime are *A Week on the Concord and Merrimac Rivers* (1849), and *Walden* (1854) on which his great fame rests. Posthumous works include *Excursions*, *The Maine Woods*, *Cape Cod*, and *A Yankee in Canada*.

作者简介 亨利·戴维·梭罗(1817—1862)，美国作家，是19世纪中期兴起于新英格兰超验主义者团体的年轻成员，优秀的文学艺术家。梭罗出生在马萨诸塞州康科德。康科德一直是他的世界的中心，尽管童年时代有几年他在附近的城镇度过，后来又在其他地方短暂生活。梭罗在哈佛大学读书期间，命运之神给了他两件礼物：一是在书的海洋畅游，二是与超验主义运动领袖爱默生建立了深厚的友谊。1845至1847年，梭罗在瓦尔登湖的住所进行了著名的"生活实验"。他的一生充满了异想天开的行为和对公共事务标新立异的立场。许多人认为他是个古怪反常的人。但广博的自然知识、非常人可比的手工技能和强烈的常识感使他赢得了世人的钦佩。尽管梭罗从未以写作为生，但他的作品却有二十卷之多。他的第一篇重要文章《论公民的不服从》(1849)提出非暴力抵抗的口号。他生前出版过两本书：《在康科德与梅里马克河上一周》(1849)和《瓦尔登湖》(1854)。这两本书使他获得很高的声誉。他的遗作包括《远足》《缅因森林》《科德角》和《美国人在加拿大》。

ABOUT THE SELECTION

On Being Busy, taken from Thoreau's *Life without Principle*, is a statement of part of the author's philosophy of life. During his lifetime, Thoreau put this philosophy into practice and did anything that afforded him a simple livelihood without ever making the work an absolute necessity. To support himself, he made pencils, worked as a hired man, wrote, tutored, lectured, and surveyed. In this essay, Thoreau does not condemn work, but frowns upon those who work for lucre and luxuries and those who labor just to get "a good job." He discriminates between those who toil for money and become the slaves of work and those who toil for the love of work and become the masters of their crafts. He points out that "a man may be very industrious, and yet not spend his time well." A century has passed since Thoreau's death; but the questions that he raised are still pertinent to our society and are worth pondering and discussing. Typical of his other major works, Thoreau's style here tends to be aphoristic. He strives to compress large thoughts into pithy statements. In tone, he is earnest, moral, conversational, and sometimes humorous.

内容简介　《论忙碌》选自梭罗的《没有原则的人生》，是作者人生哲学的一部分。梭罗一生都将这一哲思付诸实践，做任何能让他过上简单生活的工作，而不是把工作变成绝对必要的事情。为了养活自己，他做过铅笔，当过雇工、家庭教师、土地测量员，写作，演讲。在这篇文章中，梭罗并没有对工作本身横加指责，而是对那些为金钱和奢华而工作的人和那些只是为了谋求"一份好工作"而劳动的人嗤之以鼻。他认为，为金钱而成为工作的奴隶的人和因为热爱工作而成为各自行业的大师的人真有天渊之别。他指出："一个人可能非常勤奋，但却没能有效利用时间。"梭罗去世已经一个世纪，但他提出的问题仍然与我们的社会生活息息相关，值得思考和讨论。与梭罗其他重要作品一样，这篇文章的风格倾向于"名言警句"。他努力把宏大的思想压缩成精辟的格言。其语气则是会话式的，既严肃认真、寓意深刻，又不乏幽默。

This world is a place of business. What an infinite bustle! I am awakened almost every night by the panting of the locomotive. It interrupts my dreams. There is no sabbath.[1] It would be glorious to see mankind at leisure for once. It is nothing but work, work, work. I cannot easily buy a blankbook[2] to write thoughts in; they[3] are commonly ruled for dollars and cents.[4] An Irishman, seeing me making a minute[5] in the fields, took it for granted that I was calculating my wages. If a man was tossed out of a window when an infant, or scared out of his wits by the Indians, it is regretted chiefly because he was thus incapacitated for—business! I think that there is nothing, not even crime, more opposed to poetry, to philosophy, ay[6] to life itself, than this incessant business.

There is a coarse and boisterous money-making fellow in the outskirts of our town, who is going to build a bank-wall under the hill along the edge of his meadow. The powers[7] have put this[8] into his head to keep him out of mischief[9] and he wishes me to spend three weeks digging there with him. The result will be that he will perhaps get some more money to hoard, and leave for his heirs to spend foolishly. If I do this, most will commend me as an industrious and hard-working man, but if I choose to devote myself to certain labors which yield more real profit, though but little money, they may be inclined to look on me as an idler. Nevertheless, as I do not need the police[10] of meaningless labor to regulate me, and do not see anything absolutely praiseworthy in this fellow's undertaking any more than in many an enterprise of our own or foreign governments, however amusing it may be to him or them, I prefer to finish my education at a different school.[11]

If a man walk in the woods for love of them half of each day, he is in danger of being regarded as a loafer; but if he spends his whole day as a speculator, shearing off those woods and making earth bald before her time,[12] he is esteemed an industrious and enterprising citizen. As if a town had no interest in its forests but to cut them down!

Most men would feel insulted if it were proposed to employ them in throwing stones over a wall, and then in throwing them back, merely that they might earn their wages. But many are no more worthily employed now. For instance, just after sunrise one summer morning, I noticed one of my neighbors walking beside his team, which was slowly drawing a heavy hewn stone swung under the axle,[13] surrounded by an atmosphere of industry,—his day's work begun,—his brow commenced to sweat, —a reproach to all sluggards and idlers,—pausing abreast the shoulders of his oxen, and half turning round with a flourish of his merciful whip, while they gained their length on him.[14] And I thought, such is the labor which the American Congress exists to protect, —honest, manly toil, —honest as the day is long, —that makes his bread taste sweet, and keeps society sweet, —which all men respect and have consecrated; one of the sacred band,[15] doing the needful but irksome drudgery. Indeed, I felt a slight reproach, because I observed this from a window, and was not abroad and stirring about a similar business. The day went by, and at evening I passed the yard of another neighbor, who keeps many servants and spends much money foolishly, while he adds nothing to the common stock,[16] and there I saw the stone of the morning lying beside a whimsical structure[17] intended to adorn this Lord Timothy Dexter's premises,[18] and the dignity forthwith departed from the teamster's labor, in my eyes. In my opinion, the sun was made to light worthier toil than this. I may add that his employer[19] has since run off, in dept to a good part of the town, and, after passing through Chancery,[20] has settled somewhere else, there to become once more a patron of the arts.[21]

The ways by which you may get money almost without exception lead downward.[22] To have done anything by which you earned money *merely* is to have been truly idle or worse. If the laborer gets no more than the wages which his employer pays him, he is cheated, he cheats himself. If you would get money as a writer or lecturer, you must be popular, which is to go down perpendicularly. Those services which the community will most readily pay for, it is most disagreeable to render. You are paid for being something less than a man. The State does not commonly reward a genius any more wisely. Even the poet-laureate would rather not have to celebrate the accidents of royalty.[23] He must be bribed with a pipe of wine;[24] and perhaps another poet is called away from his muse[25] to gauge that very pipe.[26] As for my own business, even that kind of surveying which I could do with most satisfaction my employers do not want. They would prefer that I should do my work coarsely and not too well, ay, not well enough. When I observe that there are different ways of surveying, my employer commonly asks which will give him the most land, not which is most correct. I once invented a rule for measuring cordwood, and tried to introduce it in Boston; but the measurer there told me that the sellers did not wish to have their wood measured correctly, —that he was already too accurate for them, and therefore they commonly got their wood measured in Charlestown before crossing the bridge.

The aim of the laborer should be, not to get his living, to get "a good job," but to perform well a certain work; and, even in a pecuniary sense, it would be economy for a town to pay its laborers so well that they would not feel that they were working for low ends, as for a livelihood merely, but for scientific, or even moral ends. Do not hire a man who does your work for money, but him who does it for love of it ...

The community has no bribe that will tempt a wise man. You may raise money enough to tunnel a mountain, but you cannot raise money enough to hire a man who is minding his own business. An efficient and valuable man does what he can, whether the community pays him for it or not. The inefficient offer their inefficiency to the highest bidder,[27] and are forever expecting to be put into office.[28] One would suppose that they were rarely disappointed.

Perhaps I am more than usually jealous with respect to my freedom. I feel that my connection with and obligation to society are still very slight and transient. Those slight labors which afford me a livelihood, and by which it is allowed that I am to some extent serviceable to my contemporaries, are as yet commonly a pleasure to me, and I am not often reminded that they[29] are a necessity. So far I am successful. But I foresee that if my wants should be much increased, the labor required to supply them would become a drudgery. If I should sell both my forenoons and afternoons to society, as most appear to do, I am sure that for me there would be nothing left worth living for. I trust that I shall never thus sell my birthright for a mess of pottage.[30] I wish to suggest that a man may be very industrious, and yet not spend his time well. There is no more fatal blunderer than he who consumes the greater part of his life getting his living. All great enterprises are self-supporting. The poet, for instance, must sustain his body by his poetry, as a steam planing mill[31] feeds its boilers with the shavings it makes. You must get your living by loving. But as it is said of the merchants that ninety-seven in a hundred fail, so the life of men generally, tried by this standard, is a failure, and bankruptcy may be surely prophesied.

NOTES
1. sabbath: a time of rest.
2. blankbook: a book of mostly blank pages or of printed forms.

3. they: blankbooks.
4. This implies that, since more people are working, more blankbooks are ruled to enable them to record monetary accounts.
5. minute: note or notes.
6. ay: yes.
7. powers: those who have influence and authority in town.
8. this: the idea of building a bank-wall.
9. Evidently the money-making fellow, being coarse and boisterous, often caused a lot of trouble in town.
10. police: control; regulation.
11. to finish my education at a different school: to live a different way of life.
12. making earth bald before her time: When the woods are cut down, the trees are denied their natural span of life; thus the earth is made bare when she should still be covered with forest.
13. drawing a heavy hewn stone swung under the axle: pulling a heavy stone to be used for building or construction under a cart.
14. they gained their length on him: they (the oxen) moved forward so that their bodies pass him (the neighbor Thoreau saw).
15. sacred band: workers. Work has been traditionally considered noble and sacred (holy); thus workers are also regarded as sacred. Band means group.
16. common stock: commonweal.
17. whimsical structure: queerly, fantastically shaped object to be used as an ornament.
18. this Lord Timothy Dexter's premises: the building and the surrounding grounds of the neighbor whose yard Thoreau passed. Thoreau's tone here is definitely sarcastic.
19. his employer: Lord Timothy Dexter.
20. Chancery: a court of equity in the American judicial system.
21. patron of the arts: benefactor of the arts, one who gives of his means or uses his influence to help or benefit the arts, such as painting, music, literature, etc.
22. lead downward: lower the self-respect of a man.
23. poet-laureate: a poet appointed for life by an English sovereign as a member of the royal household, formerly expected to compose poems on court and national occasions. Accidents of royalty: unexpected royal and national events.
24. The office of poet laureate was first installed in the early 17th

century with the holder being paid on the basis of an annual pension. Later on in the century, in addition to the annual pension the poet laureate was also given a cask of wine. Pipe: cask.
25. called away from his muse: disturbed from his work—composing poems. Muse: poet's inspiration.
26. gauge that very pipe: measure that same cask; consume the wine. A possible reference to Tennyson's succession to poet-laureateship upon the death of Wordsworth in 1850.
27. the highest bidder: the one offering the highest salary or wages.
28. to be put into office: to be placed in a high position.
29. they: referring to the slight labors.
30. sell my birthright for a mess of pottage: give up something invaluable in return for something else, especially foolishly or dishonorably. The proverb "to sell one's birthright for a mess of pottage" has evolved from the story in Genesis in which Esau sold Jacob, his younger brother, his birthright for a bowl of red pottage. See Genesis, XXV:30-33.
31. planing mill: a woodworking establishment in which wood is smoothed, cut, matched, and fitted.

参考译文

这个世界是一个工作之地，永无休止的忙碌！几乎每天夜里火车头的喘息都会把我吵醒，打断我的好梦。从来就没有安息日。倘若看到人们休闲一次，那真是可喜可贺的事。除了工作还是工作、工作。很难买到一个全是白纸的笔记本，记下心之所想。通常那些本子都成了记录几美元几美分的账本。一个爱尔兰人如果看见我拿着笔记本站在田地里写写画画，就理所当然地认为我是在计算工资。如果一个人还是婴儿的时候被扔到窗外，或者被印第安人吓得魂不附体，人们最担心的就是小东西会不会因此丧失工作能力。我认为，没有什么事情（包括犯罪）比无休止的工作更与诗歌、哲学，是的，还有生活本身相悖了。

我们那个镇子郊外有一个俗不可耐、咋咋呼呼、满脑子只想赚钱的家伙。他想在山下沿他家牧场边建一道围墙。这个想法其实是城里那些有权有势的人灌输给他的，目的是让他少祸害别人。他想让我和他一起干三个星期活儿，这样他也许能攒更多的钱，留给后辈儿孙挥霍。如果我这么干了，大多数人会夸赞我勤劳、肯干。可是如果我选择投身于别的赚钱不多，但更有意义的工作，他们或许会把我当成懒汉。不过我不需要那些毫无意义的劳动的条条框框限制自己，也看不出这个家伙的"事业"与我们自己的政府或者外国政府的许多事业相比，有什么值得称道之处。有鉴于此，不管对他或他们而言，那些工作多么有趣，我都情愿过一种全然不同的生活。

如果某人喜欢森林，每天花半天时间在林荫下散步，他就会陷入被斥为懒汉的危险之中。然而倘若他是个投机商，一天到晚砍伐树木，把原本郁郁葱葱的森林夷为平地，反倒被誉为勤奋进取、有胆有识的好公民。好像这个城市对于它的森林全无兴趣，情愿把它们都砍掉。

如果有人雇你把石头从墙里扔到墙外，再从墙外扔到墙里，然后给你几文小钱，大多数人都会觉得受了侮辱。但许多受雇于人的劳工，干的活比这强不了多少。比如，一个夏天的早晨，太阳刚刚升起，我看到一位邻居走在牛车旁边。牛慢慢地拉着车轴上挂着的那块沉重的、晃来晃去的毛石。整个场面笼罩着一种辛勤劳动的氛围：一天的工作已然开始，邻居额头渗出细密的汗珠，吆五喝六，责骂那几头不肯出力的懒鬼。和牛并肩而行的时候，他停下脚步，回转身，挥舞"仁慈的皮鞭"。几头牛连忙加快脚步，走到他前头。我想，这就是美国国会保护的劳动——诚实、辛劳——诚实如朗朗晴空——使面包香甜、社会和谐。所有人都对其恭而敬之，视为神圣。而从事如此神圣工作的人群中的一员正在干这必要但令人厌烦的苦差事。说实话，我有点自责。因为我是趴在窗口看到这一幕的，而不是在国外某地忙于同样的事情。那天过去了，傍晚时分，我从另外一个邻居的院落旁边走过。这家人雇了许多仆人，挥金如土，但绝不会为大众福利花一分钱。我在这儿看到早晨那块毛石扔在一个奇形怪状的物件儿旁边，准备装饰蒂莫西·德克斯特勋爵的庭院。赶车人辛苦劳动的尊严与价值在我眼里顿时荡然无存。在我看来，太阳是为了照耀更有价值的劳动才发光的。我还得补充一句，他的雇主蒂莫西·德克斯特勋爵后来跑了。他欠了城里许多人的债。经过衡平法院审理之后，定居别处，又成了艺术家赞助人。

赚钱的方式几乎无一例外都会降低一个人的自尊。无论做什么事情，如果仅仅是为了赚钱，就没有真正的意义，甚至更糟。如果一个人劳动所获仅仅是雇主付给他的那点工钱，那就不但是被人家骗了，还骗了自己。如果你想靠当作家或演说家赚钱，就必须受欢迎，结果就意味着你得堕落到底。社会上最愿意付费的服务，往往是最令人讨厌的活计。你拿工资是因为你不够强大。国家通常不再想方设法奖励天才。即使桂冠诗人也不愿为皇室突发的大事吟诗作赋、歌功颂德了。必须再额外给他一桶葡萄酒才行。也许另一位诗人会在灵感突发时被召唤来，品尝这桶美酒。至于我的工作，即使尽了最大努力，很满意自己的测量工作，雇主也不以为然。他们宁愿我把活儿干得毛毛糙糙，不要太好，嗯，要做得"不够好"。后来我发现测量有两种办法。雇主们都会问，哪种办法能量出最多的土地，而不是哪种办法最正确。我有一次发明了测量薪材的好办法，想在波士顿试一试。结果那儿的测量员告诉我，卖木材的人压根儿就不愿意测量得那么准。对他们而言，他测量得已经很精准了。所以，他们的木头通常过桥前在查尔斯敦已经测量过了。

劳动者的目的不应该只是谋生，不应该只是想找个"好工作"，而应该是做好一件工作。而且，即使从金钱的意义上说也是如此——一个城镇给工人支付比较高的工资,让他们不觉得自己只是在为养家糊口之类的"低端目的"工作,而是以科学甚至道德为宗旨而工作——也是很合算的。不要雇为钱而工作的人,而是要雇真正热爱这份工作的人……

世上没有什么东西可以诱惑智者。你可以筹集足够的钱开凿隧道穿越大山,但你筹不到足够的钱雇一个专注于自己事业的人。一个有能力、有价值的人会倾尽全力,做好自己热爱的工作,不管能否得到社会的回报。无能的人把他们效率低下的劳动卖给出价最高的人,还总在谋求更高更好的职位。讽刺的是,很多时候他们都能如愿以偿。

也许我比常人更加热爱自由。我觉得我和社会的联系,对社会的责任薄弱而短暂。虽然为了维持生计,我也做过一些微不足道的工作,这些工作在一定程度上也为同时代的人提供了服务,但于我而言,投身其中是一种乐趣,因为很少有人提醒我那些事情非做不可。到目前为止,我是成功的。但我也有先见之明——倘若人的欲望永无止境,为满足这些欲望辛勤劳动就成了一件苦差事。如果我像大多数人那样,把上午和下午的时间都卖给社会,那我应该就没有活下去的理由了。我相信我永远不会为了一碗浓汤而出卖自己与生俱来的权利。我想说的是,一个人可能非常勤奋,但却没有好好利用时间。没有比浪费生命大部分时间用来养家糊口更不幸更愚蠢的了。所有伟大的事业都是自给自足的。就像诗人靠诗歌滋养身体,蒸汽刨木机用它生产的刨花为锅炉提供燃料一样。你必须以爱为生。但是,诚如人们所说,一百个商人中有九十七个是失败者。倘若按照这个标准衡量,一般人的生活都是失败的,破产也是预料之中的事情。

(李尧 译)

17

Man, Play, and Creativity

人、游戏和创造力

Eric Hoffer
埃里克·霍弗

(1902–1983)

ABOUT THE AUTHOR

Eric Hoffer (1902–1983), a self-educated longshoreman, is widely known as a political and social philosopher. He was born in New York City, had little formal education, and was almost blind until he was 15. He became a migratory worker in California from 1920 to 1943 and then a longshoreman. His works include *The True Believer* (1951), *The Ordeal of Change* (1963), *The Temper of Our Time* (1967), and *Working and Thinking on the Waterfront* (1969)—all are brilliant, aphoristic studies of mass movements, ideologies, the workingman and the intellectual. His highly original approach and lucid style have won him hundreds of thousands of readers as well as a part-time position as senior research political scientist at the University of California at Berkeley.

作者简介 埃里克·霍弗（1902—1983），一位自学成才的码头工人，后成为知名的政治和社会哲学家。他出生于纽约市，几乎没有接受过正规教育，在 15 岁之前一直几近失明。1920 至 1943 年他在加利福尼亚当农民工，后来成为一名码头工人。他的作品有《狂热分子》(1951)、《艰难的变革》(1963)、《我们这个时代的气质》(1967)和《水边的工作与思考》(1969)——全部都是有关群众运动、意识形态、工人和知识分子的精彩的格言式研究著作。他令人耳目一新的视角、清晰易懂的文风，为他赢得了成千上万的读者，加州大学伯克利分校也为他提供了一份兼职工作，职位是资深政治研究员。

ABOUT THE SELECTION

This article, which is reprinted from the *Dialogue* magazine, is a socio-historical exemplification of the idea that artists and children have in common a sense of play which is the source of the creative impulse. Creativity is likely to emerge where there is leisure, a fascination with objects, and a delight in tinkering and playing with things.

内容简介　本文发表于《对话》杂志,它从社会历史层面阐述了一个观点:艺术家和孩子都有一种游戏意识,这正是创造力的源泉。在人们有闲暇,对某些物品着迷,喜欢修补和摆弄东西时,创造力才可能会出现。

It is a story worth retelling. In 1879, the Spanish amateur archaeologist the Marquis de Sautuola and his daughter Maria discovered the breathtaking paintings of bison and other animals on the ceiling of the cave at Altamira.[1] The Marquis recognized immediately the significance of the discovery. Moreover, he was 48 years old, and saw here a heaven-sent chance to make his mark[2] as a pre-historian. He was going to write a monograph on the paintings, magnificently illustrated by a good painter.

Everything went swimmingly[3] for a while. The Marquis wrote to his friend Professor Villanova of the University of Madrid. The professor came, saw the paintings, and was swept off his feet.[4] The Madrid newspapers had front page stories and photographs of the momentous discovery. King Alphonso XII[5] visited the cave and stayed at the Marquis' castle in Santillana del Mar. The Marquis also had an artist. He had some time earlier befriended a destitute French painter,[6] afflicted with dumbness,[7] who had been stranded in the neighborhood, and he now put him to work making the sketches required for his treatise.

Then disaster struck out of the blue.[8] At the congress of prehistory held in Lisbon[9] in 1880, the assembled experts and scholars denied the authenticity[10] of the Altamira paintings. Professor Emile Cartailhac of the University of Toulouse thought it was all a hoax[11] perpetrated by the Marquis to obtain cheap renown and make fools of the experts. Anti-Altamira articles began to appear in the press. Professor Villanova eventually went over to the experts. The Marquis tried again at the next congress held in Algiers[12] in 1882. No one would listen to him. The Marquis retired to his estates and died in 1888 at the relatively early age of 57.

The denouement[13] is interesting. Eighteen years after the death of the Marquis, Professor Emile Cartailhac of the University of Toulouse published a beautifully illustrated monograph under the title *La Caverne d'Altamira*.[14]

The story is told here not to demonstrate fallibility of the experts. Actually the experts could not help themselves. Think of it: these paintings which were supposedly done by Paleolithic[15] savages who lived 15,000–30,000 years ago had nothing primitive about them. They were masterpieces unsurpassed in any age, and closer to the feel and understanding of modern man than any ancient art. Moreover, the oil colors, deep reds and the blackest black, were vivid and fresh, and felt damp to the touch. It was natural to suspect that the paintings were the work of a living painter—probably of the French painter in the Marquis' employ.

Equally crucial was the picture the experts had of the Paleolithic savage. He was more primitive than most of the global dropouts[16] who make up the present-day primitive tribes in various parts of the world—at least as primitive as the Australian aborigines. Paleolithic man had only the most rudimentary[17] tools. He could not make a pot, weave cloth or work metals. He had no domesticated animals, not even a dog. What connection could there be between such an utterly primitive creature and works of art which are among the greatest achievements of mankind?

We know that, eventually, around 1900, the experts changed their minds about the cave paintings. Was this due to a drastic revision[18] of their thought on the life of early man? Not that you can notice it. Pick up an armful of books on prehistoric man and you still find the Paleolithic hunter depicted as wholly absorbed in a perpetual, cruel struggle for sheer survival—always one step ahead of starvation; always facing the problem of how to eat without being eaten, never knowing when he fell asleep whether he would be there in the morning. How come, then, the paintings? They were, we are told, an aid in the eternal quest for food; they reflect the deep anxiety of the hunter community about the animals on whose meat they depended for very life; they were part of the magical rites connected with the capture and killing of game.[19] The savage, we are told, had noticed that by imitating, by disguising himself as an animal, he could lure and kill his prey, which led him to believe that likeness was the key to mysterious powers by which to control other creatures. The more lifelike the likeness the greater the magic. Hence the marvelous realism of the paintings.

Now, one can admit the magical connotations[20] of the cave paintings and yet reject the suggestion that Paleolithic art had its origin in magic. Giotto and Michelangelo[21] painted for the church, and many of their paintings had a magical purpose, but no one would maintain that religion was at the root of the impulse, drive, preoccupation and aspiration which animated these artists. We know that the shaman,[22] medicine man, and priest make use of the artist—they subsidize him and enable him to execute momentous works. But magic and religion do not bring forth the artist. The artist is there first. The Paleolithic artists engraved, carved, and modeled in clay long before they executed the animal frescoes[23] in the caves. The artistic impulse is likely to emerge where there is leisure, a fascination with objects, and a delight in tinkering and playing with things.

Plato, Not Play

The first thing I do when I get a book on prehistoric man is go to the index to see whether it has the word *play*. It is not there! You find Plato[24] but not play. The experts take it for granted[25] that man's ability to master his environment has been the product of a grim, relentless struggle[26] for existence. Man prevailed because he was more purposeful, determined and cunning than other creatures. Yet, when we try to trace the origin of a skill or a practice which played a crucial role in the ascent of man, we usually reach the realm of play.

Almost every utilitarian device had its ancestry in a non-utilitarian pursuit or pastime. The first domesticated animal—the dog puppy—was not the most useful but the most playful animal. The hunting dog is a rather late development. The first domesticated animals were children's pets. Planting and irrigating, too, were probably first attempted in the course of play. It is also plausible that the wheel, sail, brickmaking, etc. were invented in the course of play. The Aztecs[27] did not have the wheel, but some of their animal toys had rollers for feet. Ornaments preceded clothing. The bow, we are told, was a musical instrument before it became a weapon.

Seen thus it is evident that play has been man's most useful occupation. It is imperative to keep in mind that man painted, engraved, carved and modeled long before he made a pot, wove cloth, worked metals or domesticated an animal. Man as an artist is infinitely more ancient than man as a worker. Play came before work; art before production for use. Pressing necessity often prompted man to make use of things which amuse. When grubbing for necessities man is still in the animal kingdom. He becomes uniquely human and is at his creative best when he expends his energies, and even risks his life, for that which is not essential for sheer survival. Hence it is reasonable to assume that the humanization of man took place in an environment where nature was bountiful, and man had the leisure and the inclination to tinker and play.

The Paleolithic Painters

Let us return to the Paleolithic hunters who painted the cave masterpieces.

Were their daily lives merely endless cruel struggles for sheer survival?

Actually they lived in a hunter's paradise, a crossroad of the seasonal migrations of huge herds of bison, reindeer, wild horses, musk-ox and deer. The animals filed past in their thousands along well-defined routes. Food was almost no problem. The hunters lived mostly in skin tents and were clad in sable, arctic fox and other fancy furs. Judged by their fine bone needles the Paleolithic hunters were expert tailors. They sported swagger sticks of mammoth ivory[28] beautifully carved and engraved. They wore necklaces of shell and perforated animal teeth, and engraved pendants made of ivory, bone, horn or baked clay. They were sportsmen, their life rich with leisure yet not without tensions and passionate preoccupations. They had leisure to develop and exercise subtle skills not only in carving, engraving and painting but also in elaborating the sophisticated art of fishing with bone fishhooks and sinew[29] lines. They probably had secret societies which met in cave hideouts adorned with engravings and paintings of animals. The shaman injected himself in these sporting activities and gradually endowed them with a pronounced[30] magical connotation.

Almost all the engravings, carvings and paintings of Paleolithic man were of animals. What was his attitude toward animals? He adored and worshipped them. They were his betters.[31] Man among the animals is an amateur among superbly skilled and equipped specialists, each with a built-in[32] tool kit. Man has neither claws, nor fangs, nor horns to fight with, neither scales nor hide to shield him, no special adaptations for burrowing, swimming, climbing or running. He craved the strength, speed and skill of the superior animals around him. When he boasted he likened himself unto an elephant, a bull, a deer. He watched the adored animals with the total absorption of a lover, and could paint them in vivid detail, even on the ceiling of a dark cave.

Man's being an unfinished, defective animal has been the root of his uniqueness and creativeness. He is the only animal not satisfied with being what he is. His ideal was a combination of the perfections he saw in the animals around him. His art, dances, songs, rituals and inventions were born of his groping to compensate himself for what he lacked as an animal. His spirituality had its inception[33] not in a craving to overcome his animality, but in a striving to become a superior animal. In the case of *Les Trois Frères*,[34] the sorcerer, painted high on a ledge above the ground, seems to rule over the world of animals on the walls below, and this sorcerer, whose face is human, is a composite of animals.

The most crucial consequence of man's incurable unfinishedness[35] is, of course, that he cannot truly grow up. Man is the only perpetually young thing in the world, and the playground is the ideal milieu[36] for the unfolding of his capacities and talents. It is the child in man that is the source of his uniqueness and creativeness. Whom the Gods love, said the Greeks, die young—stay young till the day they die.

A Magic Circle

I have always felt that five is a golden age. We are all geniuses at the age of five. The trouble with the juvenile is not that he is not yet a man, but that he is no longer a child. If maturing is to have meaning it must be a recapturing of the capacity for total absorption[37] and the avidity[38] to master skills characteristic of a five-year-old. But it needs leisure to be a child. When we grow up the world steals our hours and the most it gives us in return is a sense of usefulness. Should automation rob us of our sense of usefulness, the world will no longer be able to steal our hours.[39] Banned from the marketplace we shall return to the playground and resume the task of learning and growing. Thus, to me the coming of automation is the coming of a grand consummation: the completion of a magic circle. Man first became human in an Eden playground, and now we have a chance to attain our ultimate destiny, our fullest humanness, by returning to the playground.

When, at the age of 27, I first read how God drove man out of Eden, there flashed before my eyes a tableau: I saw my ancestor Adam get up from the dust after he had been bounced out, shake his fist at the closed gates and the watching angels and mutter, "I shall return!" May it fall to this or the next generation to redeem the promise.[40]

NOTES

1. Altamira: a cave in N. Spain, near Santander, noted for its Stone Age color drawings of animals.
2. to make his mark: to attain success, to achieve his ambition.
3. swimmingly: without difficulty; with great success.
4. swept off his feet: overcome by feeling; filled with enthusiasm.
5. King Alphonso XII: Spanish constitutional monarch who ruled from 1874 to 1885.
6. befriended a destitute French painter: made friends with a very poor French artist.
7. afflicted with dumbness: suffered from disability to speak.
8. Disaster struck out of the blue: Disaster hit unexpectedly.
9. Lisbon: a seaport in and the capital of Portugal, in the SW part of the country.
10. authenticity: genuineness.
11. hoax: a trick.
12. Algiers: one of the former Barbary States in N. Africa, now modern Algeria.
13. denouement: the final disentangling of the intricacies of a plot, as of a drama or novel. Hence the development of the story.
14. *La Caverne d'Altamira*: "The Cave of Altamira" in French.
15. Paleolithic: pertaining to, or characteristic of the cultures of the Pleistocene epoch about 1,000,000–10,000 years ago.
16. the global dropouts: people who disappear from the globe.
17. rudimentary: elementary.
18. a drastic revision: extremely extensive re-examination and reconsideration.
19. game: animals and birds hunted for sport and food.
20. connotations: extended or associative meanings and significance.

21. Giotto and Michelangelo: Giotto di Bondone, Florentine painter, sculptor, and architect who lived 1266?-1337; Michelangelo Buonarroti, Italian sculptor, painter, architect and poet who lived 1475-1564.
22. shaman: a medicine man, acting as both priest and doctor.
23. frescoes: pictures or designs painted on a moist lime plaster surface with colors ground in water or a limewater mixture.
24. Plato: Greek philosopher who lived 427-347 B.C.
25. take it for granted: regard it as true or as certain to happen.
26. a grim, relentless struggle: a stern, pitiless effort.
27. Aztecs: members of a Nahuatl people in Mexico.
28. they sported swagger sticks of mammoth ivory: they amused themselves with short canes for walking, made of pre-historical elephant tusks.
29. sinew: tendon; a strong cord, joining a muscle to a bone.
30. pronounced: strongly marked; decided.
31. They were his betters: Animals were superior than men in hunting skills and equipments.
32. built-in: built so as to be an integral part of a larger construction.
33. inception: start.
34. *Les Trois Frères*: a painting, "The Three Brothers."
35. the most crucial consequence of man's incurable unfinishedness: the most decisive distinction of man's irremediable defect.
36. milieu: environment, social surroundings.
37. capacity for total absorption: ability for maximum and complete assimilation.
38. avidity: enthusiasm.
39. Should automation...steal our hours: If machinery takes man's place of his usefulness, we will have more time of our own.
40. to redeem the promise: to materialize this hope.

参考译文

这是一个大家津津乐道的故事。1879 年，西班牙业余考古学家索图奥拉侯爵和他的女儿玛丽亚在阿尔塔米拉洞穴的顶上发现了令他们震撼的壁画，上面画的是野牛和其他一些动物。侯爵立即意识到这一发现的重要性。他当时已经 48 岁了，觉得这是上天赐予他的良机，让他能以史前学家的身份名垂青史。他准备写一本关于这些壁画的专著，找一位优秀画家配上精彩插图。

开始时，一切都很顺利。侯爵给他在马德里大学工作的朋友比利亚诺瓦教授写信，教授来到洞穴，看到这些壁画后喜不自禁。马德里的报纸在头版刊登了有关这一重大发现的报道和照片。国王阿方索十二世参观了这个洞穴，并住在侯爵位于滨海桑蒂利亚纳的城堡里。侯爵身边也有一位艺术家，那是一位他不久前结交的法国画家，画家身患哑疾，穷困潦倒，滞留在附近，现在侯爵雇他来画专著所需的草图。

然而灾难从天而降。在 1880 年里斯本召开的史前史大会上，与会的专家和学者否认了阿尔塔米拉洞穴壁画的真实性。图卢兹大学的埃米尔·卡泰尔哈克教授认为这都是侯爵为了沽名钓誉愚弄专家而制造的骗局。否认阿尔塔米拉洞穴壁画真实性的文章开始出现在媒体上。比利亚诺瓦教授最终转向了其他专家的阵营。侯爵在 1882 年阿尔及尔举行的另一届大会上再次尝试说服大家，但没有人愿意相信他的话。侯爵退隐到自己的庄园，于 1888 年去世，年仅 57 岁。

故事的结局很有意思。侯爵去世 18 年后，图卢兹大学的埃米尔·卡泰尔哈克教授以《阿尔塔米拉洞穴》为书名出版了一本插图精美的专著。

在这里讲述这个故事并不是为了证明专家会犯错。事实上，专家们也无能为力。试想一下：这些据说是由生活在 15000—30000 年前的旧石器时代的野蛮人所作的画，丝毫没有原始落后的痕迹。它们是任何时代都无法超越的杰作，比任何古代艺术都更接近现代人的感觉和理解。此外，油彩、赭红和最黑的黑色，生动而新鲜，摸起来还有潮湿感。人们怀疑这些画是一位在世画家的作品——可能是侯爵雇佣的法国画家的作品，他们这么想实在情有可原。

同样关键的是专家们对旧石器时代野蛮人的描述。他们比今天世界各地原始部落的大多数人都要原始（这些人已经成为这个世界的弃儿）——至少是和澳大利亚土著一样原始。旧石器时代的人们只拥有最简单的工具。他们不会制作锅具，不会织布，也不会加工金属。他们没有驯养的动物，甚至没有狗。这样一种完全原始的生物与人类最伟大成就之一的艺术品之间能有什么联系呢？

我们知道，最终，在1900年左右，专家们改变了对洞穴壁画的看法。这是因为他们对早期人类生活的看法发生了急剧改变吗？并没有。拿起一摞关于史前人类的书，你仍然会发现，这些书里描绘的旧石器时代猎人无时无刻不在进行残酷的斗争，仅仅是为了能够活下去——他离饥饿总是一步之遥，他总是面临着如何填饱肚子而不是被吃掉的问题，睡着之后永远不知道第二天早晨自己是否还能活着醒过来。那么，怎么会有这些壁画呢？专家告诉我们，这是猎人们不断寻找食物过程中采取的一种手段，反映了猎人群体对这些他们赖以生存的动物的深切忧虑，是与捕杀猎物有关的一种神奇仪式。专家告诉我们，野蛮人已经注意到，通过模仿，通过伪装成动物，他可以诱杀他的猎物，这使他相信，相似性是用来控制其他生物的神秘力量的关键。形象越逼真，魔力越大。因此，这些壁画的逼真程度令人惊叹。

现在，人们可以承认洞穴壁画的神奇内涵，但不接受旧石器时代的艺术起源于魔法的说法。乔托和米开朗基罗为教堂作画，他们的许多画作都有神秘的目的，但没有人会坚持认为宗教是激发这些艺术家的冲动、动力、关注和愿望的根源。我们知道，萨满、巫医和牧师都利用艺术家——他们资助他，使他能够完成重大作品。但魔法和宗教并不能产生艺术家，艺术家是先于它们存在的。旧石器时代的艺术家在创作洞穴中的动物壁画之前，早就用陶土来雕刻和建模了。在人们有闲暇，对某些物品着迷，喜欢修补和摆弄东西时，艺术冲动很可能就会出现。

有柏拉图，但没有游戏

每次我拿到一本有关史前人类的书时，做的第一件事就是去看索引，看看是否有"游戏"这个词。没有！索引里会有"柏拉图"，但没有"游戏"。专家们想当然地认为，人类掌控环境的能力是他们为了生存而进行严酷无情斗争的产物。人类之所以占上风，是因为他比其他生物更有目的性、更坚定、更狡猾。然而，当我们试图追溯那些在人类崛起过程中发挥关键作用的技能或做法源自何处时，我们通常会进入游戏的领域。

几乎每一个实用的器具都能在非实用的消遣或爱好中找到它的祖先。第一种被驯化的动物——小狗——不是最有用的，而是最爱嬉戏的动物，猎狗的出现相当晚。最初被驯化的动物都是孩子们的宠物。种植和灌溉也可能是在游戏过程中首次尝试的。如果说轮子、帆、制砖等是在游戏过程中发明的，这也是说得通的。阿兹特克人没有轮子，但他们的一些动物玩具用滚轮来做脚。装饰品比衣服先出现。我们知道，弓在成为武器之前是一种乐器。

由此可见，游戏一直是人类最有用的职业。我们必须牢记，早在制作锅具、纺衣织布、加工金属或驯化动物之前，人类就开始绘画、雕刻和建模了。作为艺术家的人比作为工人的人要古老得多。游戏出现在工作之前；艺术出现在生产使用之前。迫切的需要常常促使人类去利用原本用来娱乐的东西。在人因为生活所迫而不得不劳作的时候，他仍属于动物界。当他花费精力，甚至冒着生命危险去做那些对于生存本身来说并非必不可少的事情时，他就成了独特的人，并处在他的最佳创造状态。因此，我们有理由认为，人类人性化的环境需要富饶的大自然，同时人要有闲暇，要有修补摆弄东西的意愿。

旧石器时代的画家

让我们回过头再去看那些绘制洞穴杰作的旧石器时代的猎人。他们的日常生活是否只是为了活下去而进行无休止的残酷斗争？

事实上，他们生活在猎人的天堂里，那里是大量野牛、驯鹿、野马、麝牛和鹿季节性迁徙的十字路口。成千上万的各种动物沿着明确界定的路线经过。食物几乎不成问题。猎人们大多住在皮帐篷里，他们身穿黑貂皮、北极狐皮和其他花哨的毛皮。从他们的细骨针来看，旧石器时代的猎人是裁缝专家。他们挥舞着用猛犸象牙制成的雕刻精美的手杖，戴着用贝壳和钻孔的动物牙齿做成的项链，还有用象牙、骨头、牛羊角或烤土加工而成的雕刻吊坠。他们爱好运动，他们的生活充满闲暇，但也不乏紧张的时刻和狂热的痴迷。他们有闲工夫去培养和锻炼精巧的技能，不仅是雕刻和绘画，而且还钻研用骨鱼钩和筋线钓鱼的复杂技艺。他们可能有秘密社团，在装饰着动物雕刻和绘画的隐蔽洞穴里聚会。巫师参与到这些游戏活动中，并逐渐赋予它们明显的魔法内涵。

几乎所有旧石器时代人类的雕刻和绘画都是关于动物的。他对动物是什么态度？他崇拜它们。它们比他高明。置身百兽之中，人就像一个门外汉置身于一群技术精湛、装备精良的专家当中，它们都身揣内置的工具包。人既没有爪子、獠牙或尖角可以用来打架，也没有鳞片或毛皮来保护自己，也没有特殊的适应能力来钻洞、游泳、攀爬或奔跑。他渴望得到周围那些高级动物的力量、速度和技巧。当他吹嘘时，他把自己比作大象、公牛和鹿。他像情人一样全神贯注地观察他所崇拜的动物，生动地描绘它们，甚至是画在黑暗的洞穴顶上。

人是一种未完成的、有缺陷的动物,这是他的独特性和创造性的根源。他是唯一不满足于自己现状的动物。他的理想是要把在身边那些动物身上看到的完美特征集于自己一身。他的艺术、舞蹈、歌曲、仪式和发明都源于他为了弥补自身作为动物的欠缺所进行的摸索。他的灵性不是源于对克服自己身上动物性的渴望,而是源于成为高级动物的努力。在法国的三兄弟洞穴中,巫师被画在离地面很高的悬崖上,仿佛统治着下面岩壁上的动物世界,这个巫师的身体是各种动物的综合体,但他的脸是人的脸。

当然,人这种无法改变的未完成性所产生的最重要的后果是,他不能真正长大。人是世界上唯一永远年轻的东西,而游乐场是他展现能力和天赋的理想环境。正是人身体里的那个孩子成为其独特性和创造性的源泉。希腊人说,诸神所爱的人都会年轻地死去——直到他们死去的那一天他们都会保持年轻。

神奇的循环

我一直觉得,五岁是一个特别美好的年龄,我们在五岁时都是天才。少年的烦恼不在于他尚未成年,而在于他不再是个孩童。如果成熟要有意义,那就必须是重新获得全神贯注的能力和对掌握技能的渴望,这是五岁孩子的特点。但一个人想要成为孩子就得有闲暇。我们长大后,世界偷走了我们的时间,作为交换,它给我们最多的东西是一种有用的感觉。如果自动化剥夺了我们有用的感觉,这个世界将不再能够偷走我们的时间。被禁止进入市场的我们将回到游乐场,继续完成学习和成长的任务。因此,对我来说,自动化的到来是一个完美的结局:一个神奇的循环得以完成。人最初是在伊甸园的游乐场上成为人的,现在我们有机会通过回到游乐场来实现我们的最终命运,实现我们最充分的人性。

在我 27 岁时,第一次读到上帝如何把人赶出伊甸园,我的眼前闪现过一个画面:我看到我的祖先亚当在被赶出伊甸园后从尘土中站起来,对着关闭的大门和监视他的天使挥舞着拳头,喃喃自语道:"我一定会回来的!"但愿我们这一代或下一代人能够兑现这个承诺。

(章艳 译)

18

Away from Home

离 家

PETER KOPER
彼得·科珀

(1947–2022)

ABOUT THE AUTHOR	Peter Koper was a student at Johns Hopkins University, Baltimore, Maryland. This truthful description was written when he went back from vacation as a sophomore.
作者简介	彼得·科珀是美国马里兰州巴尔的摩市约翰斯·霍普金斯大学的一名学生。他就读大二时度假归来，写下了这篇真情实感的文章。

	ABOUT THE SELECTION	Away from Home is a young man's recollective account of the younger generation adapting to the world it faces in getting educated. The selection, a reprint from *Youth U.S.A.: Dreams and Dilemmas*, (English Teaching Division, United States Information Service, 1969), depicts the freshman year on an American university campus.
	内容简介	《离家》是一个年轻人的回忆文章,讲述了年轻一代在面临大学教育时的适应过程。这篇文章发表在《美国年轻人:梦想与困境》(美国新闻处英语教学项目,1969)上,描述了一所美国大学校园里的大一生活。

David, Don, Steve and I met while we were standing in line at the dormitory eating hall on the first day of the first year at college. In the coming months the four of us were to become friends and live together, experiencing the pleasures as well as the ordeals[1] of a freshman in college.

The end of the year was to find Steve married, David an honor student, Don out of school and myself wondering about what had happened to us in that first year.

When I arrived, suitcase in hand, at Johns Hopkins University[2] in Baltimore,[3] Maryland,[4] I looked at my surroundings with a feeling best described as bewilderment. Like an actor going on stage for the first time, I took a deep breath, put on a confident air and walked onto the campus to face a new life.

I was attending an all men's private university. The school was small compared with other universities—only 1,700 undergraduates and about 3,000 graduate students in all the university's many departments. Although Johns Hopkins is located in a large city, its students come from everywhere in the United States. Some of our fellow students came from foreign countries as well. We had 14 countries represented in our freshman class of 470.

A great majority of the freshmen, like myself, could have attended a college or university much closer to their hometown. However, in the United States, high school graduates do not necessarily go to the nearest college. There are many reasons for this. Often a father wants his son, or a mother her daughter, to get the education in his or her alma mater,[5] which may be some distance away; sometimes students like another city better than their own; they frequently look for and find schools where admission requirements are not as high as in others, or where it is easier to get a scholarship. But most of all, any boy or girl, after 17 or 18 years at home, just wants to get away for a try at life.[6]

The entire freshman class at my school is required to live in the campus dormitories for a year so that students have a chance to adjust gradually to the new freedom of living away from home. After the first year the students can live where they please, whether in the campus dormitories or in apartments in the city.

The first time I saw the Georgian-style[7] brick dormitory building, I eyed it with suspicion. It didn't look like a home—but it certainly became one. David, Don, Steve and I lived in the same dormitory hall our first year. The hall divided into eight rooms with each room accommodating[8] two boys. They were comfortable and adequate, but hardly luxurious, furnished with beds, desks, dressers, closets and bookshelves. All of us complained about the color of the walls in our rooms, and Don even hung a few of his paintings, atrocious[9] as they were, on the walls to cover them up. During the first year as we learned to live together, we found that our initial problem was one often encountered by bachelors—how to keep house.

Steve and I were roommates and, after a week's studying, playing and living in the room, there were books, baseballs and clothes scattered throughout. The university had planned on this perhaps; for we had maid service once a week that was provided for in the $900 charge for room and food.

After having been raised on home cooking, the meals we had in the cafeteria tasted bland.[10] The food was nutritious, but it was traditional to complain about dormitory food and we did. (I must admit that our mothers liked to hear how much we missed their cooking.)

David didn't complain about the food as much as we did. As a matter of fact, David was the quietest of the four. His home was in Colorado[11] and this was the first time he had been in the eastern part of the country. His father is a clerk in an accounting firm, and I can tell you that his mother makes good cookies—she sent a box of them to David every month. He was the best organized of us all and had a persevering[12] desire to be a doctor.

If there was ever a complete opposite to David, it could be found in Don. Coming from New York, Don was as much the big city slicker[13] as David was the small town boy. His father is a lawyer and they live in a middle-class neighborhood. He wanted to be a psychiatrist, but his carefree personality and his lack of ambition soon vaporized[14] his dream.

My roommate, Steve, was an even-tempered[15] boy from Virginia[16] where his father is a bus driver. His parents couldn't afford to send him to college because of a large family, and as a result Steve, on the basis of his grades and his need for financial help, had a full scholarship from the university for four years.

This comprised[17] the group of special, inseparable friends that stayed together during that first year of college. Each of us had a scholarship, but less than Steve's. Tuition at our college is $2,000 a year. This is higher than most of other universities because our school is small and privately run. Also, my college is more expensive because it pays a larger salary to professors in order to attract the best possible faculty. The large state-supported schools cost much less and often they charge no tuition at all, although a student must pay room and board (if he lives on campus) and buy his own school supplies. But in both types of school scholarships are plentiful from private and government sources for students who maintain good grades and who could not attend college without financial aid.

The day after the four of us met we put our scholarships to work—it was the first day of classes for us as college students. Lectures for each course are given three times a week and each student usually takes five courses a semester. Therefore, we spent an average of 15 hours a week in lecture halls or smaller classrooms. Steve and David were ambitious and took six classes each. We planned our schedules at the beginning of each term and were free to choose any courses we wished as long as we fulfilled our basic requirements for a degree.

With 10 or 15 books to read for each course, with term papers to write and lectures to attend, we found that most of our time was spent working. Steve studied an average amount, but Don studied very little, preferring to plunk[18] on his guitar. David was by far the best student of us all. Each night he went to the library to study for several hours.

Our library—as at any other university—is the center of academic life. It contains 1,500,000 volumes including a division of rare books and about 5,000 periodicals from all over the world. Don, who always wanted to avoid work anyway, found that he could cover his Shakespeare requirements by merely listening to the recordings of the Bard's plays[19] in the record room. There is a 2,000-record collection in the library along with listening rooms. In another part of the library is a microfilm[20] collection for research. Besides a special map room, there is a large computer in the library that can be used by students working on projects that call for high-speed computation of facts or figures. Don, once again wanting to take advantage of labor-saving devices, found a way to do his mathematics homework on the computer.

Despite our busy schedules, the four of us all suffered a common malady[21]—homesickness. One boy in the dormitory suddenly left school one night for home and never returned to college. None of us, however, had felt loneliness strongly enough to leave school, and after awhile in the busy life we had, we lost our homesickness. All of us, that is, except Steve. He missed his girl friend at home and wrote to her every night. The other three knew he was serious about her, and one night at a "bull session"[22] Steve startled us by saying that he was going to marry her in the summer.

"Bull sessions," I soon found, are a college ritual. They just seem to "happen" when a group of boys sit together late at night, drinking beer and then begin talking about anything. Beer, I will add, is an American college staple,[23] although at parties students usually drink whiskey. The range of subjects one discusses in "bull sessions" is limitless—girls, the New York Yankees baseball team, Bobby Kennedy, *The Catcher in the Rye*,[24] the latest foreign movie in town and anything else that comes to mind.

We talked about girls a lot in our "bull sessions" mostly because we went to an all men's college. We dated students from nearby women's colleges. A few dances are given at my school each year, but the more aggressive Casanovas[25]—which, incidentally, we all considered ourselves—usually made arrangements for other kinds of dates. The university sponsors a concert series that ranges from classical to popular music. The student theatrical group stages excellent plays, and professional productions on tour from New York City are found in the town of Baltimore. Foreign films are very popular among the students. The boys appreciate the movies even more because students can buy tickets at half-price. And you can always puzzle over modern art in the city's galleries. During the spring, of course, we invited girls to the park for a bottle of wine and some bread with cheese.

Watching television in the common rooms[26] of the dormitories was an emotional experience. We booed[27] at villains and cheered the heroes, or vice versa—but we always whistled at pretty girls when they appeared on the screen. In the dormitories there is a snack bar,[28] as well as lounges and a music room. A bachelor's delight—the self-service laundromat[29]—is located in the basement. Whenever David washed his clothes he never failed to put too much soap in the machine and as a result spent most of his time cleaning up the overflow.

Sports are less popular at our school than they are at bigger colleges.

We have a program of sports among Johns Hopkins students, but when our school teams play other schools in such major sports as basketball and baseball, we don't fare too well. Soccer is becoming an extremely popular game in the United States, and our college has adopted the sport with enthusiasm. Our school is famous for lacrosse, a confusing sport invented by the North American Indians. It resembles soccer in some points, tennis in others and football in still other ways. Don played the game well and taught us how.

But everything outside of our studies was forgotten as the end of the first semester arrived and we faced final examinations. Final examinations last three hours for each course and stretch over a week-long examination period. During final examination week we needed all the physical stamina[30] and mental sharpness we could muster up[31] to survive.

That week always separates those who have done their work and those who have not. Steve and Don, not having worked much, had to stay up all night before an examination to study.

With week-old beards and bloodshot eyes we emerged from examination week to find out how we had done. David had made the best grades of all, and Steve and I had done fairly well. We knew Don had done poorly and we waited for him to find out about his marks.

When he arrived, we could tell something had gone wrong. He failed three of his courses and was told that he had to leave the university. We were stunned, knowing that we were losing a friend. We felt empty and depressed as we talked to him for the last time. Now there were only three of us left.

During a week-long winter vacation before the start of the second semester, David and Steve hitchhiked[32] to Florida[33] for some warm weather, while I went home to Arlington,[34] Virginia, to visit my parents.

Before we knew it, second term came around and once again David, Steve and I met at school. This time we felt we knew what to expect from college and how to handle it. Each of the three of us joined a campus activity. David started working in the Student Council, a school government with representatives elected by the students themselves. He was a committee chairman in charge of issuing a report on academic problems bothering the students. The report was later submitted to the university administration and the recommendations were later approved and put into effect. The Student Council also organizes social activities and invites prominent[35] people to lecture on various topics. They often pick controversial speakers and topics—Martin Luther King[36] spoke, as did Alabama's Governor Wallace[37], on segregation.[38] Once President Lyndon Johnson came and later Richard Nixon.

Steve joined Students for a Democratic Society, a political organization, and participated in a demonstration against racial discrimination[39] in a local restaurant. The Students for a Democratic Society also distributed leaflets presenting their point of view and debated rival political groups. Meanwhile I started working on the college newspaper which is put out weekly by the students.

As David, Steve and I became more involved in the college activities, we entirely lost our feelings of loneliness and uncertainty. We met more people and thought seriously about what we wanted to do when we left college. As the year ended we also realized we had learned something intangible.[40] We had learned slowly and in our own way what it was to live in the world without the help of home. We also began to realize our limitations and how to adjust to them.[41]

The three of us parted at the end of the second semester for summer vacation. We said our goodbyes on a sunny day similar to the one almost a year before when we had first met, except that the leaves were green instead of brown. Most of the students, like David, Steve and myself, were going to work during the summer to earn extra money for the start of school the next fall. David went to work as a laboratory assistant in a medical research company. Steve returned home to get married, then went to work for the government until school resumed. I became an ice cream man that summer.

The three of us met again at the beginning of our second year in college. Steve is married now, and all of us live in apartments near the university. Both David and I still often speak of Don, but we also see that each of those four nervous freshmen boys has come out[42] into the world successfully, ready to live on his own.[43]

NOTES

1. ordeals: extremely severe, trying tests, trials, or experiences.
2. Johns Hopkins University: The University, founded in 1876, is a famous private school in the United States. Its undergraduate schools, with the exception of McCoy College, are for men only, but its graduate schools are coeducational. Johns Hopkins is most noted for its Medical Division and the School of Advanced International Studies.
3. Baltimore: a seaport in N. Maryland, U.S.A.
4. Maryland: a state in the E. United States, along the Atlantic.
5. alma mater: a school where one has studied, and usually graduated.
6. It means "to get away from home to try a different life."
7. Georgian-style: the architecture of or in the style of the Georgian era, esp. the period of 1714–1760.
8. accommodating: making or having room for.
9. atrocious: shockingly bad or lacking in taste; execrable.
10. bland: nonirritating; moderate; agreeable.
11. Colorado: a state in the W. United States, whose capital is Denver.
12. persevering: continuing; abiding; persisting.
13. slicker: (slang) a crafty person.
14. vaporized: evaporated; made (his dream) hopeless.
15. even-tempered: calm.
16. Virginia: a state in the E. United States, on the Atlantic coast, part of the historical South.
17. comprised: included; made up.
18. plunk: strike.

19. the Bard's plays: Shakespeare's plays. Shakespeare was a great dramatist as well as bard (poet).
20. microfilm: a film bearing a miniature photographic copy of printed or other graphic matter, usually of a newspaper, document, or book pages made for a library, archive, or the like.
21. malady: any undesirable condition.
22. bull session: (slang) an idle or boastful informal group discussion, especially among male students.
23. staple: a basic or necessary item of food.
24. *The Catcher in the Rye*: It is a novel by J. D. Salinger, an American author. The book became especially popular among American high school and college students. The hero and narrator of the story is Holden Caulfield, a prep school dropout in search of self-understanding and a meaning for life. In the end, Holden learns to face the ugliness in life and the weakness in himself.
25. Casanovas: men with a reputation for having many amorous adventures. Originally, Giovanni Jacopo Casanova (1725-1798) was an Italian adventurer and writer.
26. common rooms: (in schools and colleges) a room or lounge for informal use by all.
27. booed: showed disapproval or contempt by crying "boo" at something.
28. snack bar: a lunchroom or restaurant where light meals are sold.
29. the self-service laundromat: a laundry having coin-operated, automatic machines for the washing and drying of clothes, linens, operated by customers themselves.
30. stamina: strength; power to endure disease or fatigue.
31. muster up: gather up.
32. hitchhiked: traveled by getting free automobile rides and sometimes by walking between rides.
33. Florida: a state in the SE United States between the Atlantic and the Gulf of Mexico.
34. Arlington: a county in NE Virginia, opposite Washington, D.C., site of the U.S. National Cemetery.
35. prominent: celebrated; famous.
36. Martin Luther King (1929-1968): U.S. Baptist minister, civil rights leader and Nobel Peace Prize winner in 1964.
37. George Corley Wallace (1919-1998) served as governor of Alabama from 1963 to 1967, and was elected again in 1970.

38. segregation: racial discrimination; separation.
39. racial discrimination: treatment, or making a distinction in favor of or against a person or thing based on the race to which that person or thing belongs, rather than on individual merits.
40. intangible: unintelligible; immaterial.
41. adjust to them: adapt (ourselves) to (our) limitations.
42. come out: gotten on; emerged.
43. on his own: independently; by himself.

参考译文

大卫、唐、史蒂夫和我是在进大学第一天在宿舍食堂排队时认识的。在接下来的几个月里,我们四个人将成为朋友生活在一起,体验大学新生的快乐和煎熬。

这一年结束时,史蒂夫结了婚,大卫成了优等生,唐退了学,而我正在想着大学第一年我们经历了什么。

当我提着行李箱来到位于马里兰州巴尔的摩市的约翰斯·霍普金斯大学时,看着周围的环境,我当时的感觉只能用迷惘这两个字来形容。我就像一个初次登台的演员,深吸一口气,装出一副自信的样子,走进校园去面对新的生活。

我上的是一所全部是男生的私立大学。与其他大学相比,学校规模很小——全校所有院系加起来一共只有1700名本科生和大约3000名研究生。虽然约翰斯·霍普金斯大学位于大城市,但学生来自美国各地。我们还有一些同学来自外国,在470名新生中,有来自14个国家的学生。

和我一样,绝大多数新生原本可以上离家更近的大学。然而,在美国,高中毕业生不一定会去最近的大学。这有很多原因。通常情况下,父亲会希望他的儿子,或母亲希望她的女儿,在他们的母校接受教育,而这些大学可能会有点远;有时一些学生喜欢另一个城市,而不是他们自己所在的城市；他们经常去寻找入学要求没有其他大学那么高的大学，或者是更容易获得奖学金的大学。但最重要的原因是，任何一个男孩或女孩，在家里待了十七八年后，只想着远走高飞体验新生活。

我们学校的整个新生班级都必须在校园宿舍里住一年，这样学生就有机会逐渐适应离家生活的新自由。第一年结束后，学生们可以住在他们想住的地方，无论是留在校园宿舍还是在城里另找公寓。

第一次看到这幢乔治亚风格的砖砌宿舍楼时，我满眼疑虑。它看起来一点儿也不像个家——但它确实成了我们的家。在我们大学的第一年，大卫、唐、史蒂夫和我住在同一幢宿舍楼里。宿舍楼分为八个房间，每个房间住两个男生。这些房间宽敞舒适，但绝不豪华，配有床、书桌、梳妆台、壁橱和书架。我们所有人都抱怨房间墙壁的颜色太难看，唐甚至把他自己的几幅画挂在墙上来遮盖，虽然这些画本身也是惨不忍睹。在我们学会共同生活的第一年里，我们发现自己面临的第一个问题是单身汉们经常遇到的问题——如何打扫房间。

史蒂夫和我是室友，经过一周的学习、玩耍和生活后，房间里到处散落着书籍、棒球和衣服。大学对此早有准备，因为我们每周有一次女佣打扫服务，这是包含在 900 美元的食宿费里的。

从小到大吃惯了家里的饭菜，食堂里的一日三餐吃起来寡淡无味。那些食物的营养没问题，但抱怨学校食堂的饮食是一种传统，我们也不例外。（我必须承认，我们的母亲一定愿意听到我们说多么怀念她们的厨艺呀。）

大卫不像我们几个那样喜欢抱怨食物。事实上，大卫是我们四个人中最安静的一个。他的家在科罗拉多州，这是他第一次来到美国东部地区。他的父亲是一家会计公司的职员，我告诉你们，他母亲做的饼干太好吃了——她每个月都会给大卫寄一盒。他是我们所有人中做事最有条理的，而且他有一个锲而不舍的愿望，那就是成为一名医生。

如果要找一个与大卫完全相反的人，那就是唐。唐来自纽约，如果说大卫是个安静的小镇男孩，那么唐就是个时髦的都市少年。他的父亲是律师，他们住在一个中产阶级社区。他想成为一名精神病学家，但他无忧无虑随遇而安的性格很快就让他的梦想消失得无影无踪。

我的室友史蒂夫是一个脾气平和的男孩，他来自弗吉尼亚州，父亲是一名巴士司机。由于家里子女多，他的父母没钱送他上大学，凭着自己的成绩，再加上他确实需要经济帮助，他成功申请到了大学四年的全额奖学金。

这就是我们这群关系不同寻常、形影不离的朋友，在大学的第一年里我们一直待在一起。我们每个人都有奖学金，但比史蒂夫的少。我们的学费是每年 2000 美元，这比大多数大学都要高，因为我们学校是个小规模的私立大学。我们的学费更贵的另一个原因是，为了吸引最好的老师，我们大学支付给教授的工资比其他大学更高。国家支持的大型学校费用要低得多，甚至根本不收学费，但学生得支付食宿费（如果他住在校园里的话），并购买自己的学习用品。不过，这两类学校都有大量来自私人和政府的奖学金，提供给那些成绩优异但经济困难的学生。

我们四个人见面后的第二天，就开始发挥奖学金的作用了——这是我们作为大学生上课的第一天。每门课程每周有三次课，每个学生通常一学期要上五门课。因此，我们平均每周要花 15 个小时在报告厅或小一点的教室里。史蒂夫和大卫雄心勃勃，各选了六门课。我们在每个学期开始时就订好时间表，只要我们达到了学位基本要求，就可以自由选择任何课程。

每门课程要读 10 或 15 本书，要写学期论文，要听讲座，我们发现自己的大部分时间都花在学习上。史蒂夫的课业量属于平均水平,但唐很少学习,他更喜欢鼓捣他的吉他。到目前为止,大卫是我们所有人中学习最好的,每天晚上他都会到图书馆学习几个小时。

和其他大学一样,我们的图书馆是学术生活的中心。它拥有150万册图书,包括一个珍藏本区,还有来自世界各地的约5000种期刊。唐总是想尽办法逃避学习,他发现只需要听录音室里的莎士比亚戏剧录音就可以满足对莎士比亚的课业要求。图书馆收藏了2000张唱片,配有听音室。图书馆的另一个区域存放着用于研究的微缩胶卷。除了一个特殊的地图室,图书馆里还有一台大型计算机,可以供那些从事的项目中需要高速运算信息或数字的学生使用。唐又一次想利用省力的设备走捷径,找到了一个在电脑上做数学作业的方法。

尽管我们很忙,我们四个人还是都得了一种共同的病——思乡病。宿舍楼里有个男生某天晚上突然离校回家,再也没有回来上学。但我们四个人中还没有谁的孤独感强烈到要离开学校,过了一段时间的忙碌生活后,我们不再想家了。我们所有人,但不包括史蒂夫。他想念在家乡的女朋友,每天晚上都给她写信。我们三个知道他对她非常用心,在一次"公牛会"[1]上,史蒂夫宣布说暑假他们就结婚,吓了我们一跳。

我很快发现,"公牛会"是大学里的一种仪式。当一群男孩深夜坐在一起,喝着啤酒,然后开始天南海北地聊天时,这种仪式似乎就自然"发生"了。我要补充的是,美国大学生喝的最多的还是啤酒,尽管在派对上学生们通常会喝威士忌。"公牛会"上讨论的话题无边无际——姑娘、纽约洋基棒球队、博比·肯尼迪、《麦田里的守望者》、城里最近放的外国电影以及其他任何想到的东西。

---

1 Bull session,这里为了保留原文的特点,译为"公牛会",实际上就是大学男生寝室里的深夜聊天会。——译者

我们在"公牛会"上经常谈论女生，这主要是因为我们上的是一所全部是男生的大学。我们和附近女子学院的学生约会。我们学校每年都会举办几场舞会，但那些更大胆活跃的浪荡公子——顺便说一句，我们都认为自己是浪荡公子——通常会安排其他类型的约会。学校会赞助一个系列音乐会，从古典音乐到流行音乐什么都有。学生戏剧团体表演优秀的戏剧，纽约市巡回演出的专业剧目在巴尔的摩也能看到。外国电影在学生中很受欢迎。男生们更喜欢看电影，因为学生可以买半价票。市里那些美术馆的现代艺术总会让你觉得不知所云。当然，在春光明媚的日子里，我们会邀请姑娘们到公园里，喝上一瓶葡萄酒，吃些奶酪面包。

在宿舍楼的公共休息室看电视是一种情感体验。我们对着坏蛋发出嘘声，为英雄欢呼，或者是倒过来的反应——不过，只要漂亮姑娘出现在屏幕上，我们总是对着她们吹口哨。宿舍楼里有一个小吃部，还有休息室和音乐室。单身汉的至爱——自助式洗衣机放在地下室里。大卫每次洗衣服都会在洗衣机里放太多的肥皂，结果他要花很多时间清理溢出的肥皂沫。

体育运动在我们学校不如在其他规模更大的大学那么受欢迎。约翰斯·霍普金斯大学的学生有体育项目，但我们的校队在与其他学校进行篮球和棒球这些主要运动的比赛时，表现并不理想。足球在美国正成为一项极为流行的运动，我们大学也满腔热情地开展了这项运动。我们大学以长曲棍球闻名，这是一项由北美印第安人发明的令人费解的运动。它在某些方面像英式足球，另一些方面又像网球，还有些方面像美式足球。唐的长曲棍球打得很棒，还教我们怎么打。

但是，随着第一学期结束，我们面临着期末考试，学习之外的一切都被抛到脑后。每门课程的期末考试时间为三个小时，各种考试加起来前后要持续一周。在期末考试周期间，为了生存，我们得拼上所有体力，让脑子保持敏锐。

离家
Away from Home

谁认真读书，谁没有认真读书，一个考试周就能立见分晓。史蒂夫和唐平时没有用功，考试前就不得不熬夜临时抱佛脚。

一个星期之后，我们胡子拉碴，眼睛里布满血丝，很快就知道自己考得好不好。大卫是我们所有人中成绩最好的，史蒂夫和我也相当不错。我们知道唐考得很差，我们等着他去打听分数。

他一来，我们就知道大事不妙。他有三门课不及格，学校通知他必须退学。我们惊呆了，知道将要失去一个朋友。最后一次与他交谈时，我们心里空落落的，非常沮丧。现在只剩下我们三个人了。

在第二学期开始前那个寒假的最后一周里，大卫和史蒂夫搭便车去佛罗里达州享受温暖的天气，而我则回到弗吉尼亚州阿灵顿的家中看望父母。

不知不觉中，第二学期就到了，大卫、史蒂夫和我又一次在学校见面。这一次，我们觉得已经知道了对大学有什么期望，知道了该如何应对。我们三个人各自参加了一个校园活动。大卫开始在学生会工作，这是一个由学生自己选举代表的学校政府。他是委员会主席，负责发布一份报告，是关于那些让学生们感到困惑的学术问题的。该报告后来被提交给大学管理层，提出的建议后来得到批准并付诸实施。学生会还组织社会活动，邀请知名人士就各种主题进行演讲。他们经常挑选有争议的演讲者和话题——马丁·路德·金和亚拉巴马州州长华莱士都发表过关于种族隔离的演讲。林登·约翰逊总统来过，后来理查德·尼克松也来过。

史蒂夫加入了一个叫"民主社会学生会"的政治组织，并参加了在当地一家餐馆举行的反对种族歧视的游行示威。"民主社会学生会"还分发传单，介绍他们的观点，并与对立的政治团体进行辩论。与此同时，我开始在校报工作，这是由学生负责的报纸，每周发行。

随着大卫、史蒂夫和我越来越多地参与到大学活动中，我们完全没有了孤独感和不确定感。我们认识了更多的人，并认真思考离开大学后想做什么。这一年结束时，我们也意识到自己学到了一些无形的东西。我们慢慢地以自己的方式了解到，没有家人的帮助，生活在这个世界上会是怎样的。我们也开始认识到自己的缺点，认识到应该如何去改正这些缺点。

　　我们三个在第二学期放暑假时分开了。我们在一个阳光明媚的日子里道别，那天的天气与一年前我们第一次见面时的天气差不多，只是树叶是绿色的，而不是棕色的。大多数学生，像大卫、史蒂夫和我一样，暑假期间都要去工作，为秋天开学多挣些钱。大卫去一家医学研究公司做实验室助理。史蒂夫回家结婚，然后去为政府工作，直至学校开学。那年夏天，我成了一个卖冰淇淋的人。

　　我们三个在大学二年级开始时再次聚首。史蒂夫已经是个已婚男人，我们所有人都住在大学附近的公寓里。大卫和我仍然经常提到唐，但我们也意识到，刚进大学时胆怯不安的那四个男孩都成功地迈入了世界，准备好了独立生活。

（章艳 译）

19

College Students and Reading

大学生和阅读

RALPH E. ELLSWORTH
拉尔夫·E. 埃尔斯沃思

(1907–2000)

ABOUT THE AUTHOR

Ralph E. Ellsworth (1907–2000), formerly director of libraries at the University of Iowa, fills that post at the University of Colorado. He is the author of a book and a number of articles dealing with university library policies and problems: The State of the Library Art: Buildings (1960), Planning of College and University Library (1960), The American Right Wing (1960), The School Library: Facilities for Independent Study (1963), The School Library (1964), The Economics of Book Storage (1969), and many others. He is also a professor of Library Science.

作者简介

拉尔夫·E. 埃尔斯沃思（1907—2000），曾任爱荷华大学图书馆馆长、科罗拉多大学图书馆馆长。他有一部专著和多篇文章，都是探讨大学图书馆政策和图书馆相关问题的，包括《图书馆艺术现状：建筑》(1960)、《高校图书馆规划》(1960)、《美国右翼》(1960)、《学校图书馆：独立学习的设施》(1963)、《学校图书馆》(1964)、《图书存储经济学》(1969)等。他也是图书馆学专业的教授。

ABOUT THE SELECTION

It is a general agreement that students read few books while they are in college and even fewer after they graduate. What can we do, then, to help prepare the highly demanded, good, dynamic citizens? Mr. Ellsworth's article is based on a paper prepared for the National Conference on the Undergraduate and the Lifetime Reading Interest, held at Ann Arbor in 1958 under the sponsorship of the University of Michigan and the National Book Committee. It maintains that this can be done only as we develop a more sophisticated and spiritual set of cultural values, as the colleges and universities rid themselves of nonintellectual curricula and activities, as faculties are given permission and time to practice inductive methods, and as the humanities and social sciences demonstrate that they, like sciences, have valid answers to the questions our youth want answered.

内容简介

如今人们似乎有一种相当普遍的共识，大学生在校期间本就读书甚少，毕业后数量更是寥寥。那么，我们能做些什么来帮助培养高素质、优秀且充满活力的公民？本文底稿是埃尔斯沃思先生为1958年"全美大学生和终生阅读兴趣会议"准备的会议论文，该会议受密歇根大学和美国国家图书奖评审委员会赞助在安娜堡举行。文章认为，只有当我们发展出一整套更为成熟和不为物欲所动的文化价值观，当高校摆脱了非智力课程和活动，当教师被允许并有时间实践归纳式教学法，人文学科与社会科学表明它们和自然科学一样能够解答青年的疑惑时，才能真正做到这一点。

There now seems to be a rather general agreement that students read few books while they are in college, and even fewer after they graduate. Gallup polls[1] substantiate this,[2] and Russell Lynes's report on the reading habits of the Yale class of 1932 reveals much the same picture for the graduates of one of the colleges where all the factors that should lead to good reading habits are optimum.[3] In pre-sputnik days[4] this evidence of nonintellectualism[5] seemed sufficiently important to be mentioned only by commencement speakers who were hard pressed[6] for something to say. But now that our general perspective on education is changing, everyone is asking why the taxpayer should support an expensive system of college education if its graduates do not learn, through the reading of important books, how to contribute more to society than the adults who have not attended college. The question is a fair one.

I am quite sure that if a careful, historical comparison were made between the ability of today's college students to extract information from print[7] with that of students of fifty years ago, we would be amazed by the capabilities of our young people. Most graduates of large high schools now come to college well equipped to use library indexes and catalogues, and many are still given substantial instruction on term paper writing during their freshman year. University reference librarians will testify that students of today are so much more sophisticated in their technical ability to read and write reports that they cannot be measured on the same scale with their predecessors.[8] To be sure, their knowledge of literary masterpieces is not so extensive. They do not read as many unassigned books while in college as did their grandfathers. And it may be that they cannot sprinkle their writing with literary quotations, spell, or write clearly and beautifully. But of this there is no question—today's students possess a technical skill in handling the literature of knowledge that is without precedent.

The background for this competence lies in the fact that analysts of the reading process, like Gray of Chicago, have in the last twenty-five years learned how to teach children to read with a much higher degree of success than was possible a generation ago. In addition, well-developed libraries in the generally improved public and private schools have exposed children to a wider range of books and other materials than was available in the secondary schools of fifty years ago.

Why then, in spite of the fact that students come to college better able to read and more experienced in the skills of reading, do they read so little beyond inescapable assignments, and practically stop reading once they leave the campus with a degree?

I am prepared to defend the thesis that their reading behavior as adults is at fault because of four factors: the nature of our culture, particularly our popular culture, the crowding out[9] of an intellectual climate in the college by a vocational or professional climate; the teaching methods college faculties use, or are forced to use, which kill real intellectual development; and, as a result of the instability of our society, the present college generation's rejection of the heritage the older generation tries to pass on to it.

Let us first look at our culture. It is not a reading culture, and it does not bestow its rewards on the reader, with the exception of those few who are satisfied with the spiritual rewards found in teaching or preaching. The quick, big money goes to those who offer something unique and sensational in the entertainment world (for example, Bing Crosby, Elvis Presley, Jack Benny or Miss Monroe),[10] for which the intellectual life is not essential, or to those who gain power or control in finance and business through methods that appear to young people (probably because of the mores[11] of the advertising industry) to be based less on virtue and solid effort than on chance and trickery. The roads to fortune in common use today do not involve the intellectual process or reading of a high, cultural level. Note in the TV dramas, for instance, that the symbols for suggesting success are never the reading of a book or the ability to handle an idea requiring more than six words for expression. Success is indicated by the possession of an expensive car, a large house, a young and slender wife, or by the practiced use of the whisky bottle and the talents of a public relations expert. Hints that the successful man has consulted a psychiatrist are frequently employed, thus implying that TV writers think the American public expects its heroes to be a bit mentally ill, as well as grossly overworked[12] physically—behavior that is not usually associated with the well-educated, mature, disciplined man of the nineteenth century.

The accumulated knowledge displayed on television quiz programs[13] by such persons as Nadler or Van Doren[14] is, of course, greatly admired by the American public, but not nearly so much as little Robert Strom's[15] ability to think with the tools of science. The public knows that when Robert grows up, he and his kind will take us to the moon (if we are not there by the time this article appears), will find a cure for cancer, a cheap way of utilizing sea water, and a safe way of disposing of atomic waste. Nobody cares about Robert Strom's general, cultural reading or, indeed, that of Teller, Von Braun, Fermi, Oppenheimer, Bohr or their Russian counterparts.[16] One can become a great scientist and make powerful bombs and rockets without being a reader of fine novels and plays or history. Knowledge, scientific knowledge, is manna to our society; humanistic learning is not. And to think that youth will forego acting like a scientist in favor of a nineteenth-century English gentleman, even in reading habits, is to walk with one's head in the clouds.[17] It is to the physicist not the philosopher, to Kinsey[18] not St. Paul,[19] that our people turn for guidance. The knowledge they want is frequently more easily obtained from nonbook sources than from books.

And here is the storm center of our worst fears. The best of our scientists and the wisest of our nonscientists know that science as it is today, not what it may be a hundred years from now, cannot be applied to the toughest and most critical problems we face. If only we could be sure of the Russians' intentions, and if they could trust ours, we might view the problem of getting into outer space as important and interesting but not critical. We might be able to persuade the Robert Stroms to devote their lives to fundamental research in the behavioral sciences[20] in an attempt to find out how to teach man to live happily with other men and with himself, which is the big problem for twentieth-century man.

Those who lament the lack of widespread book learning are forgetting, to some extent, that the younger generation today does not turn to traditional, humanistic knowledge for wisdom and guidance, that it has a basic distrust of any statement not proved by science. These young people distrust the whole Western humanistic culture that we older people take for granted,[21] and they show little enthusiasm for reading the books that carry this culture.

Can we blame them? As an eighteen-year-old sees it, the old values have not worked. He measures these values not against the progress that has been made by civilization, but against absolute standards of perfection. Quick annihilation stares him in the face,[22] and he knows it. One too many cocktails for Khrushchev,[23] and everything could be lost. The youth of today resents the obvious failure of Western civilization to produce a stable way of life. He will read the old books when he is required to do so, but not before.

Consider the intellectual climate in most of our colleges today. Fifty years ago it was assumed that the American college and university educated a limited number of students for an intellectual life in the professions that could be learned only from the mastering of many books. There was a commitment to read in all of them. Although this vigorous intellectual training is still there today, to it has been grafted[24] a wide variety of special vocational and professional programs that do not pretend to be intellectual in content and do not carry the serious reading commitment that would develop substantial reading habits carrying over into adult life. Except for the vocational reading[25] done by graduates of such programs, or the prestige reading[26] one's social relationships force, it is unreasonable to expect today's students to be book readers for the simple reason that their college experience creates no strong intellectual appetite in them while they are in college. No one, surely, thinks that reading behavior can rise higher in the individual than his motivations.

One of the problems with these programs is not so much a low requirement for wide reading, although even this is true in the science courses, but that the materials read are sterile and lifeless. They do not have in them the magical quality of generating intellectual curiosity. They offer no challenge, no vistas. They are not the books one takes to bed to read. Another problem is the type of faculty these programs attract. Many of these men have been trained in the same kind of narrow, restrictive professional subjects, and they, like the materials, are dull and lifeless. They motivate no brain-stretching,[27] no yearning for learning for its own sake. Beyond their narrow professional competence, they are as undisciplined as the average high school graduate.

Many people, both within and without the colleges and universities, are dissatisfied with the number of intellectually barren courses that are offered, but I see little evidence that anyone is going to do much about this. There are too many vested[28] interests in the department heads and deans who know that large enrollments in their areas determine salary levels, the number of graduate assistants and other forms of cheap labor that free the senior professors for research. And, of course, one way to keep the enrollment high is to increase the course offerings. (Look, for instance, at the number of courses listed under journalism, personnel psychology, accounting, education, nursing, library science, sociology, public administration, et cetera, in the big state universities.) The top brass[29] in the universities seem to be unable, although they try, to think of any good arguments to use in wringing the water out[30] of the curriculum, just as they seem to be unable to control intercollegiate athletics.[31] The sputnik is the best weapon they have had in years, and they are using it with some good results, but the inertia to be overcome is enormous.

The teaching methods commonly used in colleges and universities too frequently produce nonreaders. Many courses are taught through a combination of formal class lectures and specific reading assignments in fairly rigid textbooks, just as they were before the rotary press made books plentiful. The professor who uses the lecture-textbook method is not concerned with the reading habits his method produces. He is concerned with the problem of teaching knowledge that his students can use in more advanced courses. Such courses are not intended to produce readers, and they certainly do not. A more serious result is that they do not require any real mental exertion on the part of the student. The thinking has been done by the professor and the author of the textbook. Oscar Handlin has commented on this situation with the same conclusion.[32] The student is given no contact with source material, and so he does not learn what it means to evaluate facts and to draw conclusions from them. He merely learns the facts and principles others have developed from source materials. If this method of teaching were used only in introductory courses, the situation would not be so bad. But this is not the case, it permeates[33] the entire college. This method does not teach students to develop judgment or taste in books for the very simple reason that it allows them no practice in handling or reading books. Why bother with reading several books if one textbook can present an adequate summary of current knowledge?

Reliance on the crutches of class lectures or on textbooks and other forms of passive learning is the worst possible kind of preparation for adult life in the America of today. Everyone is bombarded with one-sided, direct pressure statements in the form of magazines, radio and TV programs, house and trade journals, pamphlets and the like, and there is no professor around to say what the correct line is. He who has not formed the habit of evaluating sources is quite likely to be at the mercy of the special pleader.[34]

Deans and other administrators seem to be eager to improve the quality of college teaching, but it is my observation that they usually place the kudos[35] on the professors who do the best lecturing, which usually means the ones who organize and present the material so well that the students have to do almost no reading. The stultifying[36] effect on the student has not seemed to worry professors because they do not really know very much about the reading behavior of students, and they care less. Neither do most of them think very much about the effect of their methods on the preparation of the good citizen. They concentrate on the short-term objectives of their courses. It is only in the honors programs,[37] limited to a few students, that undergraduates are placed in a learning situation where they are forced to develop judgment and taste in the handling of the literature of knowledge.

If we librarians are at fault[38] in this matter of reading, it is in that we should have been shouting loudly that there was something wrong with teaching methods and with the point of view of professors. I know what professors think of this charge. They say that their main concern must be research, that their advancement depends on publication, and that they would have no time for research if they used inductive methods[39] of teaching undergraduates. They would also say that our libraries could not hold up their end[40] of such teaching procedures. They may be right, but that does not lessen the damage done to students.

I am equally concerned that in the big universities the writing of term papers, or any other kind of writing, is almost a thing of the past for undergraduates. Traditionally, it has been the term paper that has driven the student into books on an extensive scale.[41] Many faculties have given up the term paper requirements because they no longer have time to read the papers and because they cannot spend the effort that would be required to detect plagiarism and other forms of student laziness. I know of no substitute for the term paper in motivating reading or in teaching students the virtues of inductive learning in nonlaboratory courses.

We librarians should also have been screaming to the high heavens about the devastating effects that the so-called objective, true-false examinations are having on student reading and writing, If I am accused of flogging a dead horse,[42] I deny that the horse is dead. In the rooms of a university library where reserve books are being read, one can see that students have definite ideas about how to study for these examinations. They think it is better to memorize a small amount of text than it is to read widely and comparatively, and to do their reading just before the examination, on the assumption that it is a test of memory plus luck anyway. Therefore, reading is concentrated into a two-week period just before examinations, and "life adjustment"[43] activities are indulged in the rest of the time.

Everyone agrees that grading essay examination papers is a very subjective business and that the objective examinations are impartial. We also know that the latter can be graded on machines, thus saving faculty time for research and reading. But if it is true that, with all their virtues, these examinations measure the least important part of learning and actually stultify the important parts, of what use is the impartiality or the faculty time thus saved?

Thus, I conclude that one of the worst obstacles to good reading is the faculty itself. As I watch the way in which they make their reading assignments, protect themselves from spending time with students so they can do their own research, use teaching methods that kill whatever natural desire for learning their students bring from high school, refuse to find out what college students are really like, refuse to set a good example by being good readers outside their own specialty, and refuse to believe that students can learn on their own outside the classroom, I reach the inescapable conclusion that we will never produce college graduates who will read as good citizens so long as undergraduates are taught by a faculty primarily interested in research, public service and committee assignments.[44]

Before we are too quick to pass judgment on the lack of general, humanistic book reading among the young, we should realize that in a time of rapid and extensive social change, and in a time when the old values appear to have failed, young people will reject their cultural heritage and turn to themselves to work out their problems. Margaret Mead[45], speaking to this point in 1951, said:

> *We have come to realize that each generation in this country is sufficiently different from each other generation so that they are unknown to each other, and that you can't any longer find out what it is to be a teenager by remembering what it was like to have been one...*
>
> *The young people of today can live comfortably in a world we never knew if only we will let them be free to do so. They must form themselves. That is the whole meaning of an age that is changing so rapidly. Each group must work out its own salvation...*
>
> *There are no books in our libraries that can tell the youth of 1958 how to shape their lives around sex, marriage, military service, a system of business that professes*[46] *traditional honesty but practices trickery and frivolousness,*[47] *a religion they cannot understand, or a civilization that may be blown up*[48] *at any moment. The young must decide these things by*

talking with one another. And this they do. The student union building rather than the library has become the heart of the campus, because here the students gather to talk and learn from one another. In many American universities one will find more students in the union than in the library at any hour of the day. This may be chilling to the hearts of those who think books are the proper carriers of the advice of other generations and who assume that humanistic books are the best carriers, but it was they, not the youngsters, who created the kind of social conditions that are forcing the young to act in this way.

Intellectuals laugh at the "togetherness"[49] slogan of one of the popular magazines, and they worry about the apparent conformity[50] of young adults. They should show more understanding, because these are merely symbols for the manner in which young adults must find the answers to their problems in a society that expects them to find the answers in a heritage the young must reject. They will not read the books of the past because they distrust the past.

It may be that youth is wrong, and that by rejecting the best of their cultural heritage they will wreck themselves and our culture, but this is where the situation rests. The Kinsey reports on sexual behavior will have more influence in creating the new sexual ethics than will all the other books that have been written on the subject from the beginning of recorded history.

It follows, then, that no amount of preaching, wringing of hands,[51] advertising or merchandising tricks[52] will change the reading behavior of college students. This can be done only as we Americans develop a more sophisticated and spiritual set of cultural values, as the colleges and universities rid themselves of nonintellectual curricula and activities, as faculties are given permission and time to practice inductive teaching methods, and as the humanities and social sciences demonstrate that they, as well as the sciences, have valid answers to the questions our youth want answered.

NOTES

1. Gallup polls: a representative sampling of public opinion or public awareness concerning a certain issue.
2. substantiate this: Read "Low Readership Level in U.S. Shown by Gallup Poll," and "One in Five Read Books," *Publishers' Weekly*, 1950.
3. Read "Desire Out From Under the Elms," *Harper's*, 1957.
4. pre-sputnik days: time before the U.S.S.R. launched her man-made satellites into the space.
5. nonintellectualism: a lack of intellectuality and learnedness; or a poor readership.
6. pressed: compelled.
7. print: printed pages.
8. This sentence is comparable to the last sentence of Paragraph 2, "Today's students possess a technical skill in handling the literature of knowledge that is without precedent."
9. crowding out: taking the place.
10. Bing Crosby, Elvis Presley, Jack Benny and Miss Marilyn Monroe: the big entertainers in the 1950's.
11. mores: social codes and customs.
12. grossly overworked: terribly overworked.
13. television quiz programs: television programs in which contestants compete, often for prizes, by answering questions, also called quiz show.
14. Nadler or Van Doren: famous quiz program winners.
15. little Robert Strom: a name representing any American youngster.
16. Edward Teller (1908-2003), American physicist; Wernher von Braun (1912-1977), American rocket expert; Enrico Fermi (1901-1954), Italian physicist; J. Robert Oppenheimer (1904-1967) American physicist; and Niel Henrik David Bohr (1885-1962), Danish physicist; are all leading scientists responsible for the development of atomic energy. "Their Russian counterparts" means "similar leading physicists in Russia".
17. to walk with one's head in the clouds: to do something impractical.
18. Alfred Charles Kinsey (1894-1956): U.S. zoologist and biologist famous for his study of human sexual behavior.
19. St. Paul: known as the "Apostle to the Gentiles," was one of the greatest preachers and organizers of the early Christian Church.
20. behavioral science: a science or branch of learning, as psychology, sociology, etc., deriving its concepts from observations of the

behavior of living organisms.
21. take for granted: accept as proven truth.
22. Quick annihilation stares him in the face: Man faces a sudden destruction.
23. Nikita S. Khrushchev: Russian political leader, premier of the U.S.S.R. in 1958-1964.
24. has been grafted: has been set to.
25. vocational reading: reading in order to obtain information necessary for a vocational training.
26. prestige reading: reading for one's social status.
27. brain-stretching: extension and expansion of the mind.
28. vested: firmly established.
29. brass: officials.
30. wringing the water out: forcing the nonintellectualism out.
31. intercollegiate athletics: athletic competitions among colleges.
32. Read "Textbooks That Don't Teach," *Atlantic Monthly*, 1957.
33. permeates: spreads.
34. at the mercy of the special pleader: easily influenced by a willful enthusiast.
35. kudos: reputation; glory; popularity.
36. stultifying: befooling.
37. honors programs: programs or courses in college or university consisting largely of independent research terminating in a dissertation or a comprehensive examination and earning for the student who passes it a degree with distinction.
38. at fault: guilty.
39. inductive method: a teaching method which enables the students to draw their own conclusions through observation, reasoning, evaluation, etc.
40. end: share.
41. an extensive scale: a large measure.
42. flogging a dead horse: beating and whipping a dead horse; figuratively, criticizing something irreparable, such as the use of true-false examinations.
43. "life adjustment" activities: non-academic engagements.
44. committee assignments: duties as a member of a committee.
45. Margaret Mead: (1901-1978), distinguished U.S. anthropologist.
46. professes: maintains.
47. frivolousness: shallow-wit.
48. be blown up: be destroyed; fail.
49. togetherness: warm fellowship.
50. conformity: agreement; adaptation.

51. wringing of hands: squeezing hands together as a sign of great despair.
52. merchandising tricks: sale tricks.

参考译文

如今人们似乎有一种相当普遍的共识,大学生在校时读书甚少,毕业后更是数量寥寥。盖洛普民意调查就证实了这一点。罗素·林斯关于1932届耶鲁大学学生阅读习惯报告也显示,虽然某个学院的毕业生具备了所有本该促进阅读的积极因素,但结果却并无不同。在人造卫星之前的时代,这种非智主义似乎只有那些搜肠刮肚寻找说辞的毕业典礼演讲者才会认为至关重要、值得一提。但我们的总体教育观正在发生转变,所有人都在质问,如果大学生通过阅读重要的书籍,还不懂得自己对社会应该做出比那些未受过大学教育的人更大的贡献,那么纳税人为何还要支持这一昂贵的大学教育体系呢?这一质疑是合乎情理的。

我非常确信,如果要做严格的历史比较的话,当今大学生与五十年前的大学生,两者从印刷品中获取信息的能力完全不可同日而语,我们一定会惊叹于今天年轻人的能力。现在很多大型高中的毕业生在上大学之前,已经掌握了使用图书馆索引和目录的技能,很多人在大一时还接受了大量的学期论文写作的指导。大学图书馆的咨询馆员都能证明,今日学生的阅读和撰写报告的技能要成熟得多,完全不能用同一标准去衡量他们的前辈。诚然,他们对文学名著知之不多,在大学期间未能像前人那样阅读大量的课外书籍,在自己的文章中也就难以旁征博引,拼写或书写做不到准确而优雅。但有一点是毫无疑问的——今天的学生处理知识文献的技能是前所未有的。

上述能力的变化源于在过去的二十五年间，诸如芝加哥大学的威廉·S.格雷这样的阅读过程研究者，掌握了儿童阅读的教学方法，使得儿童的阅读效率比上一代人大大提升。此外，与五十年前的中学相比，今天的公立和私立学校的条件普遍改善，先进的图书馆让儿童接触到的书籍和其他资料极大丰富。

那么，掌握了更强阅读能力和更多阅读技巧的学生进入大学之后，除了必须完成的作业之外，为何课外阅读量却如此之少，甚至在毕业之后几乎不再读书了呢？

我想为此尝试一辩，大学生成人后的阅读行为之所以会出问题，可以归因于四个方面：我们的文化属性，特别是流行文化；大学里的知识氛围被职业或专业的氛围所取代；大学教师主动或被动使用的教学方法，遏制了学生真正的智力发展；以及由于我们社会的不稳定，当代大学生拒绝接受上一辈人试图传承下去的传统。

首先来看看我们的文化吧。这不是一种阅读文化，除了极少数人从教学或讲道中得到精神慰藉之外，读书无法给人带来什么回报。大笔财富快速流向娱乐圈那些个性独特、追求轰动效应的人物（例如，平·克劳斯贝、猫王、杰克·本尼或梦露小姐），对他们来说，智性生活并不重要；或者流向那些在金融和商业领域有权有势的人，他们获取财富的方式，在年轻人看来（可能受到了广告的影响）不是基于美德和脚踏实地，而是靠投机和欺诈。如今常见的致富之路不再依靠知识的积累或高层次的文化阅读。例如在电视剧中，人们注意到，成功的象征从来不是会读书或者具有表达六个字以上想法的能力。成功的标志是拥有一辆豪车、一栋豪宅、一位身材窈窕的娇妻，或是能熟练地打开威士忌酒瓶再加公关专家的才能。剧中常有成功人士咨询精神科医生的桥段，这表明电视剧编剧认为美国公众希望主角们都有点轻微的精神问题，以及身体严重透支——这与19世纪那些受过良好教育、成熟自律的男性形象相去甚远。

纳德勒或范多伦等人在电视智力竞赛节目上所展示的渊博知识固然令美国公众大为折服，但相比之下，人们更加钦佩小罗伯特·斯特罗姆运用科学工具所展现出的思考能力。人们知道，当罗伯特们长大后，他们将把我们带往月球（尽管本文发表时可能还尚未实现），找到攻克癌症的方法，以低廉的成本利用海水资源，并能安全处理原子能废料。没有人会关心罗伯特·斯特罗姆们读过什么通识文化方面的书籍，事实上，也没人关心泰勒、冯·布劳恩、费米、奥本海默、玻尔或其俄罗斯同行们读过什么书。一个人不必阅读什么优秀的小说戏剧或史书巨著，也可以成为伟大的科学家，能够制造威力巨大的炸弹和火箭。知识，科学的知识，是社会的甘露；而人文知识则不值一提。如果认为年轻人会放弃像科学家一样行事而去模仿19世纪的英国绅士，哪怕只是阅读习惯上的一种效仿，那也是不切实际的妄想。需要指导时，人们求助的是物理学家而非哲学家，求助的是金赛而非圣保罗。他们寻求的知识往往更容易从书本以外的渠道获得。

而这恰恰是我们的心腹之患。最好的科学家和最聪明的非科学家都知道，今天的科学不是百年之后的科学，无法解决我们现在面临的最棘手也最关键的难题。如果我们能确定俄罗斯人的意图，如果他们也能信任我们，那么我们可能会认为探索太空既重要又有趣，而非情势所逼。我们也许能够说服罗伯特·斯特罗姆们将毕生之精力投入到行为科学的基础研究之中，努力去找到人与人、人与自我愉快的相处之道这一20世纪人类的大难题。

那些哀叹今人不够博览群书的人在一定程度上忘记了，今天的年轻一代并不转向传统的人文知识去寻求智慧和指导，他们对任何未经科学证明的说法都抱持怀疑态度。这些年轻人并不信服我们年长的人奉为圭臬的西方人文文化，对阅读承载这种文化的书籍更是兴致索然。

我们该责怪他们吗？在一个18岁的孩子看来，旧的价值观已经不再奏效。他以绝对完美的标准而非文明的进步来衡量这些价值观。从天而降的灾难就在眼前，他心知肚明。假如赫鲁晓夫喝了太多的鸡尾酒，一切都可能灰飞烟灭。当代年轻人对西方文明无法创造稳定的生活方式感到愤怒。除非未来向他们提出要求，否则他们决不会主动去阅读那些传统的书籍。

再来看看如今大多数高校的知识氛围吧。五十年前，人们认为美国的高校培养的是少数精英，他们注定要过一种智性生活，只有阅读大量书籍才能掌握专业知识。那时人人都立志阅读。虽然这种充满活力的智性教育如今仍然存在，但它已被嫁接到各种特殊的职业和专业的课程之中，这些专业在授课内容上并不自诩为智性教育，也没有严格的阅读任务，但恰恰是阅读任务才能让学生养成广泛阅读的习惯，进而影响他们终身。这些专业的毕业生所做的不过是职业阅读，或是社会地位所要求的面子阅读。除此之外，指望今天的学生成为读书人并不合理，原因很简单，他们的大学经历并没有使他们在就读期间产生强烈的求知欲。可以肯定的是，一个人的阅读行为一定不会高于他的阅读动机。

这些专业的一个问题，与其说是对广泛阅读的要求太低（尽管理科课程确实如此），倒不如说是阅读材料的枯燥与乏味。它们不具备激发求知欲的迷人品质，既无挑战性，也无前景展望，也不是人们想要带到床上去看的枕边书。另一个问题则在于这些专业所吸引的教师类型。他们中的许多人所接受的是同样狭隘的、限制性的专业科目的培训，他们与这些材料一样枯燥乏味。他们没有想象力，缺乏对学习本身的渴望。除了狭隘的专业能力外，他们就像普通高中毕业生一样蒙昧无知。

高校内外的许多人都对高校提供的智力课程的乏善可陈感到不满，但我几乎没有看到有人对此采取什么行动。因为太多的系主任和院长都是既得利益者，他们很清楚本专业的高入学率决定着教师的工资水平，能够带来众多的研究生助理和其他形式的廉价劳动力，也才能让资深教授腾出手来去做自己的研究。当然，保持高入学率的方法之一就是增设课程（比如，看看那些规模庞大的州立大学在新闻学、人事心理学、会计学、教育学、护理学、图书馆学、社会学、公共管理等等专业名下所开设的课程，就会一清二楚）。大学的高层管理者似乎绞尽了脑汁，也没有想到好的办法为非智力课程脱水，一如他们无法左右校际体育赛事一样。人造卫星是他们多年来所拥有的最好武器，他们用得心应手、效果不错，但需要克服的惯性也是巨大的。

高校普遍采用的教学方法往往培养出来的都是"非读者"。许多课程的教学方式还是正式的课堂讲座与呆板的教科书中具体阅读任务的结合体，就像轮转印刷机还未问世，书籍尚且稀缺时那样。使用讲座-教科书教学法的教授并不关心这种教学法会导致怎样的阅读习惯，而是偏重于向学生传授他们在更高级课程中所需要的知识。这样的课程不是为了培养读者，当然也培养不出读者来。但它所导致的一个更加严重的后果是——它不需要学生付出任何真正的脑力劳动，因为思考已经由教授和教科书的作者完成了。奥斯卡·汉德林对此发表了同样的看法。学生没有机会接触第一手资料，自然不懂得如何去甄别事实，也推导不出结论。他不过是被动地接受别人从中得出的事实与原理罢了。如果这种教学法只用于入门课程倒也不算太糟，但事实并非如此，它在整个学院蔓延。这种方式无法培养学生对书籍的判断力和品味，原因很简单，它不让学生学着去自主管理或阅读书籍。既然只需一本教科书就能得到对当前知识的详细梳理，为什么还要费心费力去读好几本书呢？

当下美国教育依赖课堂讲座、教科书或其他形式的被动学习法，无疑是对成年生活所做的最拙劣的准备。每个人都被杂志、广播、电视节目、房产金融杂志、广告传单上偏颇和具有煽动性的话语所轰炸，身边也没有教授告诉你如何甄别真伪。没有养成评估信息来源习惯的人很容易受恶意蛊惑者的摆布。

　　院长们和管理层似乎也急于提高教学质量，但在我看来，他们通常只嘉奖那些擅于讲课的教授，这些教授往往是最善于整理和介绍材料的人，学生也就几乎不需要再读书了。教授们似乎并不担心学生会思维钝化，因为他们对学生的阅读行为并不十分了解，也不怎么关心。他们中的大部分人并不过多考虑其教学方法对培养优秀公民的作用，而只是专注于课程的短期目标。只有在少数学生进入的荣誉专业，本科生才会置身于学习的环境之中，被迫在整理知识文献时培养自己的判断力和辨别力。

　　如果说我们图书馆员在这件事上也有过错，那就是我们本应大声疾呼，指出这些教学方法之谬和教授们的观念之误。我很清楚教授们对这项指控会有怎样的看法。他们会说，自己的工作重心必须放在研究上面，因为职务晋升仰赖出版与发表，如果采用归纳法教学就会挤占自己的研究时间。他们还会说，我们图书馆无法提供与这种教学方式相应的服务。此话可能言之有理，但这并不能减轻对学生所造成的伤害。

　　同样让我感到忧心的是，在很多规模庞大的大学中，本科生的学期论文，或其他任何类型的写作，似乎都已成为过去。一直以来，正是学期论文促使学生去大量阅读书籍。现在，许多教师不再要求学生撰写学期论文，因为他们不愿花时间去评阅论文，也不愿花费精力去检查学生是否有抄袭和其他偷懒行为。而我认为，在激励阅读以及在非实验性课程让学生认识到归纳学习的价值方面，学期论文具有无可替代的作用。

　　我们图书馆员也早该大声斥责那些所谓客观的、非对即错的考试了，它们极大地损害了学生的阅读与写作能力。如果有人指责我不过是把死马当活马医，我则坚决否认这是一匹死马。在大学图书馆的馆藏书阅览室，我们可以看到学生深谙备考之道。他们相信，背诵几篇课文比广泛阅读和比较阅读更行之有效，而且直到考前才临时抱佛脚，认为考试无非就是考记忆力，再加上一点运气罢了。因此，阅读全都集中在考前的两周，其余时间则用来"调剂生活"。

每个人都同意，给论文试卷打分相当主观，而客观考试则非常公正。我们还知道，后者还可以借助机器评分，从而节省教师研究和阅读的时间。但即使这些考试确实具备以上优点，它们所衡量的仍然是学习中的旁枝末节，真正重要的部分却变得呆板僵化，如果真是这样，那么公正性或由此节省下来的教师时间又有什么意义？

因此，我的结论是，良好阅读习惯养成的最大障碍之一就是教师本身。一如我所见所闻，他们给学生布置阅读作业，为了保证自己的研究时间而鲜少和学生共处，他们运用的教学方法扼杀了学生高中时拥有的自发学习的欲望，他们拒绝去了解学生的实际情况，拒绝以身作则在自己的专业外做一个好读者，也拒绝相信学生具备课外自主学习的能力。为此，我得出了一个必然的结论，只要本科生是由只在乎学术研究、公职事业和委员会事务的教师授课，那么我们就永远培养不出大学毕业后还会阅读的好公民。

我们先不要着急下结论，认为年轻人普遍缺乏通识性和人文书籍阅读，而首先应该认识到，在这样一个社会变革快速而广泛、旧的价值观念近乎失效的时代，年轻人将会拒绝继承文化传统，而会转向自身去解决他们所面临的各种问题。玛格丽特·米德在1951年谈到这一点时说：

> 我们已经认识到，这个国家的每一代人都与其他任何一代迥然不同，他们彼此之间互不相识，因此你不能通过回忆自己的少年时光来了解现在的年轻人……

只要我们不干预，今天的年轻人就会舒适地生活在一个我们未知的世界里。他们必须自我锻造。这就是一个日新月异的时代的全部意义。每个群体都必须自我救赎……

图书馆里没有一本书能教会1958年的年轻人如何塑造他们的生活，尤其是如何面对性、婚姻、兵役，如何面对表面上宣扬传统诚信但实际上诡诈肤浅的商业体系，如何面对令人费解的宗教，以及随时可能崩塌的文明。年轻人必须通过彼此交流来决定如何理解这些事情。他们也是这么做的。校园的心脏已经不是图书馆，而是学生活动中心，学生们聚集在这里彼此交谈和相互学习。在许多美国的大学中人们都能发现，无论在任何时候，学生活动中心的人流都比图书馆的要多。这可能让一些人感到心寒，因为他们相信书籍承载了世世代代人的智慧，而人文书籍又是其中的最佳载体。但恰恰是他们，而非年轻人，营造了迫使年轻人如此行事的社会环境。

知识分子对某本流行杂志打出的"团结共进"口号嗤之以鼻，他们也对年轻人的从众行为感到担忧。但他们应该表现出更多的理解，因为这正反映了年轻人所处的困境，他们必须要在社会中找到自身所面临问题的答案，而这个社会又期望年轻人从他们决意要摒弃的遗产中找到答案。他们不会去读过去的书，因为他们根本不相信历史。

也许年轻人是错的，也许他们会因为抛弃文化遗产中的精华而毁掉他们自己以及我们的文化，但这就是现实。《金赛性学报告》在建立新的性伦理方面的影响力，胜过有史以来所有书写这一主题的书籍。

因此，要改变大学生的阅读行为，无论怎样说教，怎样绝望的双手紧攥，抑或是采用怎样的推销伎俩都无济于事。只有当我们美国人发展出一整套更为成熟和不为物欲所动的文化价值观，高校摆脱了非智力课程和活动，教师们被允许并有时间实践归纳式教学法，人文学科与社会科学表明它们和自然科学一样能够解答青年的疑惑时，才能真正做到这一点。

（郭英剑 译）

20

The Basis of Education

教育的基础

ROBERT M. HUTCHINS
罗伯特·M. 哈钦斯

(1899–1977)

ABOUT THE AUTHOR

Robert M. Hutchins (1899–1977) is an outstanding American educator and critic of over-specialization, lack of balance in the curriculum, and a failure to maintain the intellectual traditions of the Western world. Born in Brooklyn, he was educated at Oberlin and Yale, and became Dean of the Yale School of Law. He was president of the University of Chicago from 1929 to 1944 and chancellor from 1945 to 1951. His educational reforms have been widely copied but seldom duplicated. He is chairman of the board of Encyclopedia Britannica and editor-in-chief of the Great Books of the Western World program. Politically, he has been president for the Fund for the Republic (set up with Ford Foundation money) and director of the Center for the Study of Democratic Institutions in Santa Barbara, California. In these roles he has been a very controversial public figure.

作者简介　罗伯特·M.哈钦斯（1899—1977）是一位杰出的美国教育家，他批判过度的专业化、课程的失衡以及未能保持西方世界知识传统的教育方式。他出生于布鲁克林，就读于欧伯林学院和耶鲁大学，曾任耶鲁大学法学院院长，并于1929至1951年任芝加哥大学校长。其教育改革被广泛效仿，但难以复制。他曾任《大英百科全书》董事会主席和"西方世界的伟大著作"丛书主编。在政治上，他曾担任（由福特基金会出资设立的）共和基金会主席和加州大学圣塔芭芭拉分校民主制度研究中心主任。在其职业生涯中，他一直是一位极具争议的公众人物。

ABOUT THE SELECTION

This is a good statement on education by a justly famous American liberal. Although Hutchins was only thirty years old when he became the president of the University of Chicago, he soon made it one of the great universities of America, both in terms of its faculty and its graduating students. As this essay demonstrates, he has clear ideas about education. Though he is economically a socialist, he is a traditionalist in terms of learning. This is a somewhat incongruous combination, but it served the University of Chicago well. The selection is taken from *The Conflict in Education* (1953).

内容简介　本文是一位名副其实的美国自由主义者针对教育问题所做的宣言。虽然哈钦斯担任芝加哥大学校长时年仅三十岁,但他很快就使芝加哥大学跃居美国最伟大的大学之列,无论是在师资力量还是在毕业生质量方面,莫不如此。正如本文所示,他对教育有着明确的观点。虽然在经济上他是一位社会主义者,但在教育方面,他却是一位传统主义者。这一看似不协调的组合,却对芝加哥大学的发展颇有助益。本文选自《民主社会中教育的冲突》(1953)。

The obvious failures of the doctrines of adaptation, immediate needs, social reform, and of the doctrine that we need no doctrine at all may suggest to us that we require a better definition of education.[1] Let us concede[2] that every society must have some system that attempts to adapt the young to their social and political environment. If the society is bad, in the sense, for example, in which the Nazi[3] state was bad, the system will aim at the same bad ends. To the extent that it makes men bad in order that they may be tractable[4] subjects of a bad state, the system may help to achieve the social ideals of the society.[5] It may be what the society wants, it may even be what the society needs, if it is to perpetuate[6] its form and accomplish its aims. In pragmatic[7] terms, in terms of success in the society, it may be a "good" system.

But it seems to me clearer to say that, though it may be a system of training, or instruction, or adaptation, or meeting immediate needs, it is not a system of education. It seems clearer to say that the purpose of education is to improve men. Any system that tries to make them bad is not education, but something else. If, for example, democracy is the best form of society, a system that adapts the young to it will be an educational system. If despotism[8] is a bad form of society, a system that adapts the young to it will not be an educational system, and the better it succeeds in adapting them the less educational it will be.

Every man has a function as a man. The function of a citizen or a subject may vary from society to society, and the system of training, or adaptation, or instruction, or meeting immediate needs may vary with it. But the function of a man as man is the same in every age and in every society, since it results from his nature as a man.[9] The aim of an educational system is the same in every age and in every society where such a system can exist: it is to improve man as man.

If we are going to talk about improving men and societies, we have to believe that there is some difference between good and bad. This difference must not be, as the positivists[10] think it is, merely conventional.[11] We cannot tell this difference by an examination of the effectiveness of a given program as the pragmatists propose; the time required to estimate these effects is usually too long and the complexity of society is always too great for us to say that the consequences of a given program are altogether clear. We cannot discover the difference between good and bad by going to the laboratory, for men and societies are not laboratory animals.[12] If we believe that there is no truth, there is no knowledge, and there are no values except those which are validated[13] by laboratory experiment, we cannot talk about the improvement of men and societies, for we can have no standard of judging anything that takes place among men or in societies.

Society is to be improved, not by forcing a program of social reform down its throat, through the schools or otherwise, but by the improvement of the individuals who compose it. As Plato said, "Governments reflect human nature. States are not made out of stone or wood, but out of the characters of their citizens: these turn the scale and draw everything after them." The individual is the heart of society.

To talk about making men better we must have some idea of what men are, because if we have none, we can have no idea of what is good or bad for them. If men are brutes like other animals, then there is no reason why they should not be treated like brutes by anybody who can gain power over them. And there is no reason why they should not be trained as brutes are trained. A sound philosophy in general suggests that men are rational, moral, and spiritual beings and that the improvement of men means the fullest development of their rational, moral, and spiritual powers. All men have these powers, and all men should develop them to the fullest extent.

Man is by nature free,[14] and he is by nature social.[15] To use his freedom rightly he needs discipline. To live in society he needs the moral virtues. Good moral and intellectual habits are required for the fullest development of the nature of man.

To develop fully as a social, political animal man needs participation in his own government. A benevolent despotism[16] will not do. You cannot expect the slave to show the virtues of the free man unless you first set him free. Only democracy, in which all men rule and are ruled in turn for the good life of the whole community, can be an absolutely good form of government.[17]

The community rests on the social nature of men. It requires communication among its members. They do not have to agree with one another; but they must be able to understand one another. And their philosophy in general must supply them with a common purpose and a common concept of man[18] and society adequate to hold the community together. Civilization is the deliberate pursuit of a common ideal. The good society is not just a society we happen to like or to be used to. It is a community of good men.

Education deals with the development of the intellectual powers of men. Their moral and spiritual powers are the sphere[19] of the family and the church. All three agencies must work in harmony; for, though a man has three aspects, he is still one man. But the schools cannot take over the role of the family and the church without promoting the atrophy[20] of those institutions and failing in the task that is proper to the schools.

We cannot talk about the intellectual powers of men, though we can talk about training them, or amusing them, or adapting them, and meeting their immediate needs, unless our philosophy in general tells us that there is knowledge and that there is a difference between true and false. We must believe, too, that there are other means of obtaining knowledge than scientific experimentation. If knowledge can be sought only in the laboratory, many fields in which we thought we had knowledge will offer us nothing but opinion or superstition, and we shall be forced to conclude that we cannot know anything about the most important aspects of man and society. If we are to set about developing the intellectual powers of men through having them acquire knowledge of the most important subjects, we have to begin with the proposition[21] that experimentation and empirical data will be of only limited use to us contrary to the convictions of many American social scientists, and that philosophy, history, literature, and art give us knowledge, and significant knowledge, on the most significant issues.

If the object of education is the improvement of men, then any system of education that is without values is a contradiction in terms.[22] A system that seeks bad values is bad. A system that denies the existence of values denies the possibility of education. Relativism, scientism, skepticism, and anti-intellectualism, the four horsemen of the philosophical apocalypse,[23] have produced that chaos in education which will end in the disintegration of the West.

The prime object of education is to know what is good for man. It is to know the goods in their order. There is a hierarchy[24] of values. The task of education is to help us understand it, establish it, and live by it. This Aristotle had in mind when he said: "It is not the possessions but the desires of men that must be equalized,[25] and this is impossible unless they have a sufficient education according to the nature of things."

Such an education is far removed from the triviality[26] of that produced by the doctrines of adaptation, of immediate needs, of social reform, or of the doctrine of no doctrine at all. Such an education will not adapt the young to a bad environment, but it will encourage them to make it good. It will not overlook immediate needs, but it will place these needs in their proper relationship to more distant, less tangible,[27] and more important goods. It will be the only effective means of reforming society.

This is the education appropriate to free men. It is liberal education. If all men are to be free, all men must have this education. It makes no difference how they, are to earn their living or what their special interests or aptitudes may be. They can learn to make a living, and they can develop their special interests and aptitudes,[28] after they have laid the foundation of free and responsible manhood through liberal education. It will not do to say that they are incapable of such education. This claim is made by those who are too indolent or unconvinced to make the effort to give such education to the masses.

Nor will it do to say that there is not enough time to give everybody a liberal education before he becomes a specialist. In America, at least, the waste and frivolity[29] of the educational system are so great that it would be possible through getting rid of them to give every citizen a liberal education and make him a qualified specialist, too, in less time than is now consumed in turning out uneducated specialists.

A liberal education aims to develop the powers of understanding and judgment. It is impossible that too many people can be educated in this sense, because there cannot be too many people with understanding and judgment. We hear a great deal today about the dangers that will come upon us through the frustration of educated people who have got educated in the expectation that education will get them a better job, and who then fail to get it. But surely this depends on the representations[30] that are made to the young about what education is. If we allow them to believe that education will get them better jobs and encourage them to get educated with this end in view, they are entitled to a sense of frustration if, when they have got the education, they do not get the jobs. But, if we say that they should be educated in order to be men, and that everybody, whether he is a ditch-digger or a bank president, should have this education because he is a man, then the ditch-digger may still feel frustrated, but not because of his education.

Nor is it possible for a person to have too much liberal education, because it is impossible to have too much understanding and judgment. But it is possible to undertake too much[31] in the name of liberal education in youth. The object of liberal education in youth is not to teach the young all they will ever need to know. It is to give them the habits, ideas, and techniques that they need to continue to educate themselves. Thus the object of formal institutional liberal education in youth is to prepare the young to educate themselves throughout their lives.

I would remind you of the impossibility of learning to understand and judge many of the most important things in youth. The judgment and understanding of practical affairs can amount to little in the absence of experience with practical affairs. Subjects that cannot be understood without experience should not be taught to those who are without experience. Or, if these subjects are taught to those who are without experience, it should be clear that these subjects can be taught only by way of introduction and that their value to the student depends on his continuing to study them as he acquires experience. The tragedy in America is that economics, ethics, politics, history, and literature are studied in youth, and seldom studied again. Therefore the graduates of American universities seldom understand them.

This pedagogical[32] principle, that subjects requiring experience can be learned only by the experienced, leads to the conclusion that the most important branch of education is the education of adults. We sometimes seem to think of education as something like the mumps, measles, whooping-cough, or chicken-pox.[33] If a person has had education in childhood, he need not, in fact he cannot, have it again. But the pedagogical principle that the most important things can be learned only in mature life is supported by a sound philosophy in general. Men are rational animals. They achieve their terrestrial felicity[34] by the use of reason. And this means that they have to use it for their entire lives. To say that they should learn only in childhood would mean that they were human only in childhood.

And it would mean that they were unfit to be citizens of a republic. A republic, a true res publica,[35] can maintain justice, peace, freedom, and order only by the exercise of intelligence. When we speak of the consent of the governed, we mean, since men are not angels who seek the truth intuitively[36] and do not have to learn it, that every act of assent on the part of the governed is a product of learning. A republic is really a common educational life in process. So Montesquieu[37] said that, whereas the principle of a monarchy was honor, and the principle of a tyranny was fear, the principle of a republic was education.

Hence the ideal republic is the republic of learning. It is the utopia[38] by which all actual political republics are measured. The goal toward which we started with the Athenians twenty-five centuries ago is an unlimited republic of learning and a worldwide political republic[39] mutually supporting each other.

All men are capable of learning. Learning does not stop as long as a man lives, unless his learning power atrophies because he does not use it. Political freedom cannot endure unless it is accompanied by provision for the unlimited acquisition of knowledge. Truth is not long retained in human affairs without continual learning and relearning. Peace is unlikely unless there are continuous, unlimited opportunities for learning and unless men continuously avail themselves of them. The world of law and justice for which we yearn, the world-wide political republic, cannot be realized without the world-wide republic of learning.[40] The civilization we seek will be achieved when all men are citizens of the world republic of law and justice and of the republic of learning all their lives long.

NOTES

1. Hutchins is criticizing four theories, here called doctrines, of education:
   a. Adaptation: The purpose of education is to help the child / person adapt to his environment.
   b. Immediate needs: The purpose of education is to meet the urgent needs of the student.
   c. Social reform: The purpose of education is to bring about social reform.
   d. We need no doctrine: There should be no purpose in education.
2. concede: admit something at the beginning of an argument.
3. Nazi: German National Socialism led by Adolf Hitler.
4. tractable: easily bent; obedient.
5. Every society has some goals. They might be, for example, the perpetuation of Chinese culture or the strengthening of the German nation.
6. perpetuate: to continue; to pass on through generations.
7. pragmatic: practical.
8. despotism: harsh control by a severe ruler.
9. his nature as a man: The material something is made of determines its use. Something which is composed of man (has the nature of man) has the uses (functions) peculiar to man.
10. positivists: philosophers who say that ethics and ideas are simply subjective opinions and, therefore, have no place in any real world. Only material things are real.
11. conventional: belonging to the customary use of a particular group.
12. laboratory animals: animals which are raised in a laboratory for experimental purposes, such as white mice.
13. validated: proved to be true.
14. This is one of the major assumptions of liberalism. By design man is meant to be free. This is not provable; it is assumed to be true. In the twentieth century many people, including all totalitarians, doubt this.
15. This is another assumption which is not provable, but is generally

assumed to be true.
16. benevolent despotism: a totalitarian control exercised by a kind ruler.
17. Notice Hutchins's support of "democracy" is based on his view of the "nature of man". This includes the belief that man is designed to be free. Powerful totalitarian states, such as Russia, are built on very different assumptions.
18. common concept of man: common idea of what man is and should be like.
19. sphere: area of operation.
20. atrophy: state of death or uselessness because of neglect and lack of use.
21. proposition: in logic a statement that is to be believed, supported, or proved.
22. contradiction in terms: the terms or words which are used to describe something have the opposite meaning to what they are describing.
23. four horsemen of the Apocalypse: The Book of Revelations in the New Testament says that at the doom of the world "four horsemen" will destroy everything. Hutchins says that the four modern destroyers are: (1) relativism—nothing is true or good; everything is approximately the same. (2) scientism—a belief that science can solve all problems including philosophical, religious, and social ones. (3) scepticism—a denial of the belief that things can be solved or improved. (4) anti-intellectualism—the belief that thoughts and thinkers cannot improve any situation; they just make things worse.
24. hierarchy: an order of power or excellence with different ranks from top to bottom.
25. Notice the Buddha said the desires of men must be removed. Aristotle said they must be equalized.
26. triviality: pettiness; attention to unimportant things.
27. tangible: able to be touched or felt.
28. aptitudes: things for which one has special interests and talents.
29. frivolity: triviality; insignificance.
30. representations: the way things are presented or explained.
31. undertake too much: try to do too much.
32. pedagogical: of teachers or teaching.
33. mumps, measles, whooping-cough or chicken-pox: common

childhood diseases.
34. terrestrial felicity: happiness on earth.
35. *res publica*: Latin. *res* (thing, fact or matter). *publica* (female form for publicus: public).
36. intuitively: by knowing something without needing to think about it.
37. Montesquieu (1689-1755): French jurist and philosopher.
38. utopia: an ideal or perfect human society, derived from Thomas More's work of the same title.
39. Notice Hutchins's "liberal" goal is a world government set up on a republican pattern. How practical is this? Many people increasingly feel that this is where the liberals lose contact with the real world.
40. Hutchins is peculiarly modern American when he sees education as the answer to all political and social problems. Most traditional societies see the answer in religion.

参考译文

教育理论如调适论、即需论、社会改革论和理论无用论，其明显的溃败表明，我们需要更好地去界定什么是教育。诚然，任何社会必然存在某种使年轻人顺应其社会和政治环境的制度。若社会是坏的——所谓坏，就是如人所说纳粹国家是坏的含义——那么它的制度也将导向同样坏的目标。制度诱人变坏，让人们成为一个坏的国家所驯服的对象，但它可能有助于实现此社会的社会理想。如果旨在延续社会的形式并实现其目标，这一制度则可能是社会所期望的，甚至是社会所需要的。从实用性来看，就社会的成功而言，它可能是一个"好"制度。

但在我看来，这样说也许更确切，尽管这种制度可以用于训练、指导、调适或满足即需，但它并非是一种教育制度。我们要明确，教育的目的是改善人。任何使人变坏的制度都不是教育，而是其他东西。例如，如果说民主是最好的社会形式,那么使年轻人顺应它的制度即是一种教育制度。如果专制主义是一种糟糕的社会形式,那么使年轻人顺应它的制度就不是教育制度,且其调适功能能越强,教育意义就越小。

每个人都有生而为人的作用。一个公民或臣民的作用可能因社会的不同而发生变化,训练、调适、指导或满足即需的制度同样也可能随之变化。但人之为人的作用在任何时代和任何社会都是相同的,这是由人的本性所决定的。教育制度的目的,无论在任何时代和任何有其存在条件的社会中也都是相同的,即对人的不断改善。

如果要论及对人和社会的改善问题,我们就必须相信人与社会确有好坏之分。这种差别不能像实证主义者所设想的那样,仅仅是一种习惯看法。我们亦无法像实用主义者所建议的那样,通过检验某项计划的效果来辨明这种差别;因为这需要耗费的时间太长,且社会的复杂性太大,所以我们很难得到完全明晰的结论。我们不能通过做实验来辨别好坏,因为人和社会不是小白鼠。如果我们相信世上无真理,社会无知识,除经实验验证的事物外,万物无价值,那么人和社会的改善就无从谈起,因为我们连判断人与人之间或社会中所发生之事的标准都没有。

社会得以改善,不是通过学校或其他方式强制灌输社会改革计划,而是通过改善组成社会的个人。正如柏拉图所说,"政府反映人性。国家不是由木石筑成,而是寓于公民的个性之中:他们左右局势,决定一切。"个体乃社会的核心。

若论及人的改善,我们必须对人是什么有所了解,否则,我们就难以把握何为对其有利,何为对其有害。如果人和其他动物无异,都由兽性主导,那么任何人一旦拥有了凌驾他人的权力,都没有理由不把他们当作畜生去对待。而且,也没有理由不像训练畜生那样去训练他们。健全的哲学一般认为,人是理性的、道德的和精神的存在,人的改善意味着尽可能充分地发展人的理性、道德和精神力量。所有人皆有这些能力，所有人也都应该将这些能力发展到极致。

人的本性自由，而人又是社会动物。人需要规训，才能恰当地运用自由。在社会中生活，人需要德行。德才兼备乃是人的本性得以充分发展的必要条件。

若想充分发展成具有社会性和政治性的动物，人就需要参与到自己政府的治理之中。仁慈的专制主义是行不通的。你不能指望奴隶们展现出自由人的美德，除非你先让他们获得自由。只有民主制度，即所有人为了整个社会的美好生活而轮流统治和被统治的制度，才是最佳的政府形式。

共同体建立在人的社会属性之上，需要其成员之间的沟通与交流。人们不必观点一致，但必须能够相互理解。就总体哲学观而言，他们一定要有能够把共同体凝聚在一起的共同目标和对人与社会的相同理解。文明是对某一共同理想的刻意追求。一个好的社会绝不仅仅是我们碰巧喜欢或恰好适应的社会。它是一个由好人组成的共同体。

教育负责发展人的智力，而道德和精神的发展则由家庭和教会负责。三者必须相互配合，因为尽管一个人拥有三个不同的方面，可他还是一个整体的人。学校不能取代家庭和教会的作用，否则就会让这些机构趋于废弛，学校也无法完成其分内的任务。

尽管我们可以畅谈训练人、娱乐人、调适人，并满足其即需，但我们却无法纵论人的智力，除非我们的哲学告诉我们，这世上有知识，而且知识有真假之分。我们也必须相信，除了科学实验外，人类还有其他获取知识的手段。如果人类只能在实验室里寻求知识，那么在许多我们自认为拥有知识的领域将只能收获想法或迷信，我们也就不得不承认自己对人类和社会最重要的方面一无所知。若要通过让人们获得最重要的学科知识来提高人的智力，我们就必须从这一命题开始——与许多美国社会科学家的信念相悖，实验和经验数据的用处对我们是有限的，而哲学、历史、文学和艺术则能为我们提供知识，而且是关于那些切中要害问题的关键性知识。

如果教育的目标是改善人，那么一切缺乏价值观的教育制度都是自相矛盾的。导向不良价值观的制度是坏制度。否认价值观存在的制度则否定了教育的可能性。相对主义、科学主义、怀疑主义和反智主义，哲学领域的这末日四骑士引发了教育的混乱，最终还将导致西方的土崩瓦解。

教育的首要目的是要了解何为善，也要辨明善的先后次序。价值观有层次结构，而教育的任务就是帮助我们了解它、确立它，并终身笃行。亚里士多德在说这句话的时候，一定想到了这一点，他说：“必须均等的不是财产，而是人的欲望，这就需要通过因材施教让人们接受充分的教育，否则绝无可能实现。”

此种教育与调适论、即需论、社会改革论或理论无用论这类关注细枝末节的理论有着天壤之别。这样的教育不是让年轻人适应恶劣的环境，而是鼓励他们把环境变好。它不会忽视眼前的即时之需，而会恰当地处理它们与更遥远、更抽象，也更重要的善的关系。这将是改革社会的唯一有效手段。

这是适合自由人的教育，也就是人文教育。如果人们想获得自由，就必须要接受这种教育。至于他们如何谋生或是有何特殊兴趣抑或才能，则都是次要的。在接受了人文教育并具备了自由而有担当的品质之后，他们自然可以学习如何谋生，也可以发展其兴趣和才能。那种说人们不能接受这种教育的说法是站不住脚的。它不过是懒惰和猜疑之人的借口，因为他们不愿努力为大众提供这种教育。

那种宣称要先把每个人培养成为专家，因此没有时间让他接受人文教育的说法同样难以成立。至少在美国，教育体制在细枝末节上浪费了太多时间，如果能善加利用，足以让所有公民都接受人文教育并成为合格的专家，所需时间可要比现在培养那些未受过人文教育的专业人才短得多。

人文教育旨在培养理解力和判断力。如此说来，也就不会有太多的人接受人文教育，因为有理解力和判断力的人并不多。如今我们经常能够听到说危机将要降临在我们身上，因为很多人接受了教育之后，本以为会得到一份更好的工作，最后却事与愿违，这让他们备受挫折。但这肯定与我们向年轻人所表述的何为教育有关。如果我们让年轻人相信，教育会给他们带来更好的工作，并鼓励他们以此为目的去接受教育，那么，如果他们接受了教育却没有找到工作，他们自然有权感到沮丧。但是，如果我们说，他们接受教育的目的是"成人"，任何人，无论是挖沟工人还是银行行长，都应该接受这种教育，就因为他是一个人；如此一来，挖沟工人仍有可能会感到懊丧，但决不再是因为接受了教育的缘故。

一个人也不可能接受过度的人文教育，因为人们的理解力和判断力是有限的。但打着人文教育的旗号对年轻人进行过度教育是有可能的。人文教育的目的不是教给年轻人未来所必需的知识，而是教给他们日后自我教育所需要的习惯、思想和技巧。因此，针对青年的正规的制度性人文教育之目标，是要让他们做好终身自我教育的准备。

我想提醒你们注意的是，人在青年时期就想学会理解和判断诸多最重要的事情，那几无可能。如果缺乏处理实际事务的经验，那么对实际事务的判断和理解就无从谈起。有些科目如果没有经验便无法理解，那就不应该教给那些没有经验的人。或者说，这类科目如果要教给那些没有经验的学生，那就必须明确，只能以导论的方式来讲授，至于它们对学生的价值，唯有在学生获取经验后的继续学习中才能得以展现。不幸的是，在美国，人们都是在青年时期学习经济学、伦理学、政治学、历史和文学，此后就抛诸脑后。所以，美国的大学毕业生们很少能真正理解它们。

这一教育学原则，即需要经验的科目只能由富有经验的人来学习，推导出了这样一个结论——教育最重要的分支乃是成人教育。我们有时候似乎认为教育就像流行性腮腺炎、麻疹、百日咳或水痘一样。如果一个人在童年时期接受过教育，他就不需要，事实上也不会再接受教育了。但上述教育学之原则，即人生最重要的知识都是在成人之后才学到的，在健全的哲学中找到了答案。人是理性的动物，通过理性获得现实的幸福生活。而这意味着，他们必须终其一生持续进行理性思考。假如说他们只在童年时学习，那也就意味着他们仅只在童年时才算是个人。

而这就意味着他们不适合成为共和国的公民。在一个共和国，一个真正的共和国中，必须依赖智慧才能维持正义、和平、自由与秩序。当我们谈到被统治者的认同时，我们是在说，既然人不像天使般无需学习仅凭直觉就可以寻求真理，那么，被统治者的每一次认同的行为其实都是学习的产物。共和国实际意味着一种持续的共同教育的生活。所以孟德斯鸠说过，君主政体的原则是荣誉，专制政体的原则是恐惧，而共和政体的原则是教育。

而至于国民共识，人不像天使那般无需学习，只是凭直觉寻求真理。共和国内的每一项共识都是学习所得。

因此，理想的共和国是学习的共和国。它是衡量所有实际政治共和国的乌托邦。我们所要建立的这个目标，始自两千五百年前的雅典人，希冀建立的是一个无限的学习共和国，和一个世界性的政治共和国，两者相互支持，相辅相成。

人人都有学习的能力。生命不息，学习不止，除非他的学习能力因闲弃不用而有所退化。唯有不断地汲取无穷无尽的知识，政治自由才能得以延续和持久。唯有持续的学习和温故知新，真理才会在人类事务中长久地存在。唯有提供持续的、无限的学习机会，并由人们不断地加以利用，人类才能实现和平。唯有出现世界性的学习共和国，我们所渴望的法治与正义的世界，以及世界性的政治共和国才能得以实现。唯有当所有人成为世界法治与正义共和国的公民，亦是学习共和国的终身公民时，我们所追求的文明才终将实现。

（郭英剑 译）

21

Knowledge Viewed in Relation to Learning

从与学习的关系看待知识

JOHN HENRY NEWMAN
约翰·亨利·纽曼

(1801–1890)

ABOUT THE AUTHOR

John Henry Cardinal Newman (1801–1890) was an outstanding Christian preacher and writer in an age of growing disbelief. He attended Trinity College, Oxford and after some university appointments became the preacher at St. Mary's, the collegiate church at Oxford. He reacted to the secular influences of his age, especially after a tour of southern Europe in 1832-1833, by vigorously championing an older Catholicism. He became a national figure both for his preaching and his writing. His bishop resented his outspoken Catholicism, ordered him to cease preaching and writing, and ultimately forced him out of the Church of England. The Roman Catholic Church received him cordially and, after he had stayed in Rome, re-ordained him priest. He established a religious society, The Oratory, and tried unsuccessfully to found the Catholic University in Dublin. He was made a cardinal in 1879.

作者简介　红衣主教约翰·亨利·纽曼（1801—1890）是信仰日益衰微的时代里一名杰出的基督教传教士和作家；他就读于牛津大学三一学院，曾在大学任职，后成为牛津大学主教堂圣玛丽教堂的牧师。他对彼时的世俗影响不满，特别是在1832—1833年南欧之行后大力拥护古老的天主教。纽曼因其布道和写作而成为全国性知名人物。主教憎恶他坦诚的天主教信仰，命令其停止布道和写作，并最终迫使他离开了英国教会。他来到罗马，并留了下来，罗马天主教会热情地欢迎了他，重新任命其为牧师。他建立了一个宗教团体——奥拉托利会，并尝试在都柏林建立天主教大学，但没有成功。1879年，他被任命为红衣主教。

ABOUT THE SELECTION

For the past fifty years *Freshman English Readers* have tried to give students some idea of what it means to be educated. One of the first steps is to learn the crucial distinction between "information" and "knowledge", a distinction which is basic to Western culture and which Newman restates with enthusiasm and clarity. Note, however, in this selection Newman uses "knowledge" to mean "information," and "philosophy" or "enlightenment" to mean "knowledge". Newman spent a good ten years of his life planning and writing about the new university he founded. The university project failed, but his writings about it, *The Idea of a University*, remain the most valuable treatise on education in the nineteenth century. Writing with great care and frequent revisions and commanding a clear, smooth, rich-sounding flow of language as excellent in form as it is in content, Newman is justly regarded as one of the greatest masters of English prose.

内容简介　在过去的五十年里,《大一英语读本》尝试让学生们了解受教育的意义。第一步是了解"信息"和"知识"间的关键差别,这是西方文化的基础,纽曼热诚而明晰地重申了这一点。然而,请注意,在该选段中,纽曼以"知识"代指"信息",以"哲学"或"启蒙"代指"知识"。纽曼花了整整十年规划和撰写他所创办的新大学。大学计划虽然失败了,但他关于这一问题的著作《大学的理念》仍是19世纪最有价值的教育专著。纽曼写作谨慎,时时修订,语言清晰、流畅、丰富,形式和内容都极为出色,他被认为是最伟大的英国散文大家之一。

There is no true culture without requirements, and philosophy presupposes knowledge.[1] It requires a great deal of reading, or a wide range of information, to warrant us[2] in putting forth our opinions on any serious subject; and without such learning the most original mind may be able indeed to dazzle, to amuse, to refute, to perplex, but not to come to any useful result or any trustworthy conclusion. There are indeed persons who profess a different view of the matter, and even act upon it. Every now and then you will find a person of vigorous or fertile mind, who relies upon his own resources, despises all former authors, and gives the world, with the utmost fearlessness, his views upon religion, or history, or any other popular subject. And his works may sell for a while; he may get a name in his day; but this will be all. His readers are sure to find on the long run that his doctrines are mere theories, and not the expression of facts, that they are chaff[3] instead of bread, and then his popularity drops as suddenly as it rose.

Knowledge then is the indispensable condition of expansion of mind, and the instrument of attaining to it;[4] this cannot be denied, it is ever to be insisted on; I begin with it as a first principle; however, the very truth of it carries men too far, and confirms to them[5] the notion that it is the whole of the matter. A narrow mind is thought to be that which contains little knowledge; and an enlarged mind, that which holds a great deal; and what seems to put the matter beyond dispute is, the fact of the great number of studies which are pursued in a university, by its very profession.[6] Lectures are given on every kind of subject; examinations are held; prizes awarded. There are moral, metaphysical, physical Professors;[7] Professors of languages, of history, of mathematics, of experimental science. Lists of questions are published, wonderful for their range and depth, variety and difficulty; treatises are written, which carry upon their very face[8] the evidence of extensive reading or multifarious information;[9] what then is wanting for mental culture to a person of large reading[10] and scientific attainments? what is grasp of mind but acquirement? where shall philosophical repose be found, but in the consciousness and enjoyment of large intellectual possessions?

And yet this notion is, I conceive, a mistake, and my present business is to show that it is one, and that the end of a Liberal Education is not mere knowledge, or knowledge considered in its matter, and I shall best attain my object, by actually setting down some cases, which will be generally granted to be instances of the process of enlightenment or enlargement of mind, and others which are not, and thus, by the comparison, you will be able to judge for yourselves, Gentlemen, whether Knowledge, that is, acquirement, is after all the real principle of the enlargement,[11] or whether that principle is not rather something beyond it.

For instance, let a person, whose experience has hitherto been confined to the more calm and unpretending[12] scenery of these islands,[13] whether here[14] or in England, go for the first time into parts where physical nature puts on her wilder and more awful forms, whether at home or abroad, as into mountainous districts; or let one, who has ever lived in a quiet village, go for the first time to a great metropolis, —then I suppose he will have a sensation which perhaps he never had before. He has a feeling not in addition or increase of former feelings, but of something different in its nature. He will perhaps be borne forward, and find for a time that he has lost his bearings.[15] He has made a certain progress, and he has a consciousness of mental enlargement; he does not stand where he did, he has a new centre, and a range of thoughts to which he was before a stranger.

Again, the view of the heavens which the telescope opens upon us, if allowed to fill and possess the mind, may almost whirl it round and make it dizzy. It brings in a flood of ideas, and is rightly called an intellectual enlargement, whatever is meant by the term.

And so again, the sight of beasts of prey and other foreign animals, their strangeness, the originality (if I may use the term) of their forms and gestures and habits and their variety and independence of each other, throw us out of ourselves into another creation, and as if under another Creator,[16] if I may so express the temptation which may come on the mind. We seem to have new faculties, or a new exercise for our faculties, by this addition to our knowledge, like a prisoner, who, having been accustomed to wear manacles or fetters, suddenly finds his arms and legs free.

Hence Physical Science generally, in all its departments, as bringing before us the exuberant riches and resources, yet the orderly course, of the Universe, elevates and excites the student and at first, I may say, almost takes away his breath, while in time it exercises a tranquilizing influence upon him.

Again, the study of history is said to enlarge and enlighten the mind, and why? because, as I conceive, it gives it a power of judging of passing events,[17] and of all events, and a conscious superiority over them, which before it did not possess.

And in like manner, what is called seeing the world, entering into active life, going into society, traveling, gaining acquaintance with the various classes of the community, coming into contact with the principles and modes of thought of various parties, interests, and races, their views, aims, habits and manners, their religious creeds and forms of worship—gaining experience how various yet how alike men are, how low-minded,[18] how bad, how opposed, yet how confident in their opinions; all this exerts a perceptible influence upon[19] the mind, which it is impossible to mistake, be it good or be it bad, and is popularly called its enlargement.

And then again, the first time the mind comes across the arguments and speculations of unbelievers,[20] and feels what a novel[21] light they cast upon[22] what he has hitherto accounted[23] sacred; and still more, if it gives in to[24] them and embraces them, and throws off as so much prejudice what it has hitherto held, and, as if waking from a dream, begins to realize to its imagination that there is now no such thing as law and the transgression of law,[25] that sin is a phantom and punishment a bugbear,[26] that it is free to sin, free to enjoy the world[27] and the flesh;[28] and still further, when it does enjoy them, and reflects[29] that it may think and hold just what it will, that "the world is all before it where to choose,"[30] and what system to build up as its own private persuasion,[31] when this torrent of willful thoughts[32] rushes over and inundates[33] it, who will deny that the fruit of the tree of knowledge,[34] or what the mind takes for knowledge, has made it[35] one of the gods, with a sense of expansion and elevation,—an intoxication in reality, still, so far as the subjective state of the mind[36] goes, an illumination?[37] Hence the fanaticism of individuals or nations, who suddenly cast off their Maker.[38] Their eyes are opened; and, like the judgment-stricken king in the *Tragedy*,[39] they see two suns, and a magic universe, out of which they look back upon their former state of faith and innocence with a sort of contempt and indignation, as if they were then but fools, and the dupes of imposture.

On the other hand, Religion has its own enlargement,[40] and an enlargement, not of tumult, but of peace. It is often remarked of uneducated persons, who have hitherto thought little of the unseen world, that, on their turning to Good, looking into themselves, regulating their hearts, reforming their conduct, and meditating on death and judgment, heaven and hell, they seem to become, in point of intellect,[41] different beings from what they were. Before, they took things as they came, and thought no more of one thing than another. But now every event has a meaning; they have their own estimate of whatever happens to them; they are mindful of times and seasons, and compare the present with the past; and the world, no longer dull, monotonous, unprofitable, and hopeless, is a various and complicated drama, with parts and an object, and an awful moral.[42]

Now from these instances, to which many more might be added, it is plain, first, that the communication of knowledge certainly is either a condition or the means of that sense of enlargement or enlightenment,[43] of which at this day we hear so much in certain quarters: this cannot be denied; but next, it is equally plain, that such communication is not the whole of the process.[44] The enlargement consists, not merely in the passive reception into the mind of a number of ideas hitherto unknown to it, but in the mind's energetic and simultaneous action upon and towards and among those new ideas, which are rushing in upon it. It is the action of a formative power,[45] reducing to order and meaning the matter of our acquirements,[46] it is a making the objects of our knowledge[47] subjectively our own, or, to use a familiar word, it is a digestion of what we receive, into the substance of our previous state of thought; and without this no enlargement is said to follow. There is no enlargement, unless there be a comparison of ideas one with another, as they come before the mind, and a systematizing of them. We feel our minds to be growing and expanding then, when we not only learn, but refer what we learn to what we know already. It is not the mere addition to our knowledge that is the illumination, but the locomotion, the movement onwards, of that mental centre, to which both what we know, and what we are learning, the accumulating mass of our acquirements, gravitates.[48] And therefore a truly great intellect, and recognized to be such by the common opinion of mankind, such as the intellect of Aristotle, or of St. Thomas, or of Newton, or of Goethe (I purposely take instances within and without the Catholic pale,⁴⁹ when I would speak of the intellect as such) is one which takes a connected view of old and new, past and present, far and near, and which has an insight into the influence of all these one on another; without which there is no whole, and no centre. It possesses the knowledge, not only of things, but also of their mutual and true relations, knowledge, not merely considered as acquirement, but as philosophy.⁵⁰

Accordingly, when this analytical, distributive,⁵¹ harmonizing⁵² process is away, the mind experiences no enlargement, and is not reckoned as enlightened or comprehensive, whatever it may add to its knowledge.⁵³ For instance, a great memory, as I have already said, does not make a philosopher, any more than a dictionary can be called a grammar.⁵⁴ There are men who embrace in their minds a vast multitude of ideas, but with little sensibility about their real relations towards each other. These may be antiquarians, annalists, naturalists, they may be learned in the law; they may be versed in⁵⁵ statistics; they are most useful in their own place; I should shrink from speaking disrespectfully of them; still, there is nothing in such attainments to guarantee the absence of narrowness of mind. If they are nothing more than well-read men, or men of information, they have not what specially deserves the name of culture of mind, or fulfils the type of Liberal Education.

In like manner, we sometimes fall in with⁵⁶ persons who have seen much of the world, and of the men who in their day, have played a conspicuous part in it, but who generalize⁵⁷ nothing, and have no observation, in the true sense of the word. They abound in information in detail, curious and entertaining, about men and things; and, having lived under the influence of no very clear or settled principles, religious or political, they speak of every one and every thing, only as so many phenomena, which are complete in themselves, and lead to nothing, not discussing them, or teaching any truth, or instructing the hearer, but simply talking. No one would say that these persons, well informed as they are, had attained to any great culture of intellect[58] or to philosophy.

The case is the same still more strikingly where the persons in question are beyond dispute men of inferior powers[59] and deficient education. Perhaps they have been much in foreign countries, and they receive, in a passive, otiose,[60] unfruitful way, the various facts which are forced upon them there. Seafaring men, for example, range from one end of the earth to the other; but the multiplicity of external objects, which they have encountered, forms no symmetrical[61] and consistent picture upon their imagination, they see the tapestry of human life, as it were on the wrong side, and it tells no story. They sleep, and they rise up, and they find themselves, now in Europe, now in Asia; they see visions of great cities and wild regions; they are in the marts[62] of commerce, or amid the islands of the South; they gaze on Pompey's Pillar,[63] or on the Andes;[64] and nothing which meets them carries them forward or backward, to any idea beyond itself. Nothing has a drift or relation; nothing has a history or a promise. Every thing stands by itself, and comes and goes in its turn, like the shifting scenes of a show, which leave the spectator where he was. Perhaps you are near such a man on a particular occasion, and expect him to be shocked or perplexed at something which occurs, but one thing is much the same to him as another, or, if he is perplexed, it is as not knowing what to say, whether it is right to admire, or to ridicule, or to disapprove, while conscious that some expression of opinion is expected from him; for in fact he has no standard of judgment at all, and no landmarks to guide him to a conclusion. Such is mere acquisition, and, I repeat, no one would dream of calling it philosophy.

Instances, such as these, confirm, by the contrast, the conclusion I have already drawn from those which preceded them. That only is true enlargement of mind which is the power of viewing many things at once as one whole, of referring them severally to their true place in the universal system, of understanding their respective values,[65] and determining their mutual dependence. Thus is that form of Universal Knowledge,[66] of which I have on a former occasion spoken, set up in the individual intellect, and constitutes its perfection.[67] Possessed of this real illumination, the mind never views any part of the extended subject-matter of Knowledge without recollecting that it is but a part, or without the associations which spring from this recollection. It makes every thing in some sort lead to every thing else, it would communicate the image of the whole to every separate portion, till that whole becomes in imagination like a spirit, every where pervading[68] and penetrating its component parts, and giving them one definite meaning. Just as our bodily organs, when mentioned, recall their function in the body, as the word "creation" suggests the Creator, and "subjects"[69] a sovereign, so, in the mind of the Philosopher, as we are abstractedly conceiving of him, the elements of the physical and moral world, sciences, arts, pursuits, ranks, offices, events, opinions, individualities, are all viewed as one, with correlative functions,[70] and as gradually by successive combinations converging, one and all, to the true centre.

To have even a portion of this illuminative reason and true philosophy is the highest state to which nature can aspire,[71] in the way of intellect, it puts the mind above the influences of chance and necessity, above anxiety, suspense, unsettlement, and superstition, which is the lot of the many. Men whose minds are possessed with some one object, take exaggerated views of its importance, are feverish in the pursuit of it, make it the measure of things which are utterly foreign to it, and are startled and despond[72] if it happens to fail them. They are ever in alarm[73] or in transport.[74] Those on the other hand who have no object or principle whatever to hold by, lose their way, every step they take. They are thrown out, and do not know what to think or say, at every fresh juncture, they have no view of persons, or occurrences, or facts, which come suddenly upon them, and they hang upon the opinion of others,[75] for want of internal resources. But the intellect which has been disciplined to the perfection of its powers, which knows, and thinks while it knows, which has learned to leaven[76] the dense mass of facts and events with the elastic force of reason, such an intellect cannot be partial, cannot be exclusive, cannot be impetuous, cannot be at a loss, cannot but be patient, collected, and majestically calm, because it discerns[77] the end in every beginning, the origin in every end, the law in every interruption, the limit in each delay; because it ever knows where it stands, and how its path lies from one point to another. It is the tetragonous of the Peripatetic,[78] and has the "nil admirari"[79] of the Stoic,[80]—

> *Felix qui potuit rerum cognoscere causas,*
> *Atque metus omnes, et inexorabile fatum*
> *Subjecit pedibus, strepitumque Acherontis avari.*[81]

There are men who, when in difficulties, originate at the moment vast ideas or dazzling projects; who, under the influence of excitement, are able to cast a light, almost as if from inspiration, on a subject or course of action which comes before them; who have a sudden presence of mind equal to any emergency, rising with the occasion, and an undaunted magnanimous bearing,[82] and an energy and keenness which is but made intense by opposition. This is genius, this is heroism; it is the exhibition of a natural gift, which no culture can teach, at which no Institution[83] can aim; here, on the contrary, we are concerned, not with mere nature, but with training and teaching. That perfection of the Intellect which is the result of Education, and its beau ideal,[84] to be imparted to[85] individuals in their respective measures, is the clear, calm, accurate Vision and comprehension of all things, as far as the finite mind[86] can embrace them, each in its place, and with its own characteristics upon it. It is almost prophetic from its knowledge of history; it is almost heart-searching from its knowledge of human nature; it has almost supernatural charity[87] from its freedom from littleness and prejudice, it has almost the repose of faith, because nothing can startle it; it has almost the beauty and harmony of heavenly contemplation,[88] so intimate is it with the eternal order of things and the music of the spheres.[89]

NOTES

1. philosophy presupposes knowledge: there must first be knowledge before philosophy is possible.
2. to warrant us: to give us the right to do something.
3. chaff: The husks of grain are unfit for human food and, therefore, of little value.
4. the instrument of attaining to it: the way to achieve expansion of mind.
5. confirms to them: makes them feel certain that.
6. by its very profession: A university seeks universal knowledge; this is the thing its name requires it to do.
7. moral, metaphysical, physical Professors: nineteenth century terms for professors of ethics, philosophy and science.
8. upon their very face: on their front pages.
9. multifarious information: information which is much and various.
10. what then is wanting for mental culture to a person of large reading: what a great reader lacks in mental development.
11. whether knowledge...is...the real principle of the enlargement: whether knowledge (acquiring information) enlarges the brain.
12. unpretending: unpretentious.
13. these islands: England and Ireland.
14. here: Ireland. Newman was the rector of Catholic University of Ireland when he wrote *The Idea of a University*.
15. lost his bearings: lost his directions.
16. another Creator: The author assumes that God made animals. These animals look so different that they might have been made by another god.
17. a power of judging of passing events: Notice a difference in Newman's grammar. In modern English "events" would be the direct object of the gerund "judging". In Newman events is in a modifying prepositional phrase. Nineteenth-century formal English used more prepositions to show relationships between nouns than

modern spoken English.
18. low-minded: petty; thinking of vulgar things.
19. exerts an influence upon: influences. Formal English often uses verb + object + preposition where spoken English uses a verb.
20. unbelievers: people who do not believe Christian teachings.
21. novel: new.
22. cast light upon: illuminate.
23. accounted: considered.
24. give in to: surrender to.
25. law and the transgression of law: right and wrong.
26. bugbear: an imaginary being (goblin) which people fear.
27. the world: the world of paganism.
28. the flesh: bodily appetites.
29. reflects: considers.
30. "the world is all before it where to choose": a quotation from Milton's *Paradise Lost* meaning a person can do whatever he wants free from any Christian restraints.
31. private persuasion: private belief.
32. willful thoughts: thoughts that are not checked by any consideration of right and wrong.
33. inundates: floods.
34. fruit of the tree of knowledge: In Christian teaching, God told Adam not to eat the fruit of the tree of knowledge. The serpent and Eve seduced Adam to disobey. Man gained knowledge by sinning.
35. it: knowledge.
36. subjective state of the mind: the state of mind when one thinks only of one's self.
37. illumination: a sudden and clear understanding.
38. their Maker: God their Creator.
39. In Bacchae, a play by Euripides, the evil king is punished by suddenly seeing two suns and a magic universe. In other words, by completely losing contact with the real world.
40. Religion has its own enlargement: Religion makes life and the brain larger, fuller, richer.
41. in point of intellect: intellectually.
42. an awful moral: something that illustrates teachings about right and wrong.
43. the communication of knowledge certainly is either a condition

or the means of that sense of enlargement or enlightenment: enlightenment either goes along with knowledge or makes knowledge possible.
44. such communication is not the whole of the process: illumination does not consist only of the passing on of knowledge (information).
45. a formative power: a power which forms or shapes something.
46. the matter of our acquirements: what we have just gotten.
47. the objects of our knowledge: what we have just learned.
48. "What we know" and "what we are learning" are the subjects of the verb "gravitates".
49. Catholic pale: Catholic territory or district.
50. Newman uses the word "knowledge" for "information". After this information has been made part of an organized system he calls it "philosophy". Thus, for Newman, philosophy is organized and systematized knowledge or information.
51. distributive: assigning to their proper places.
52. harmonizing: putting together.
53. Adding information does not enlighten, but taking it apart, assigning it to proper places, and putting things together again in the right order, do enlighten. Philosophy, not information, enlightens.
54. A dictionary merely lists items; a grammar describes an organized system. The former is like information; the latter, like philosophy.
55. be versed in: be familiar with.
56. we sometimes fall in with: we sometimes associate with.
57. generalize: try to discover what general principle this specific thing is related to.
58. culture of intellect: development or cultivation of the mind.
59. men of inferior powers: untalented men.
60. otiose: useless, lazy.
61. symmetrical: balanced; two halves agreeing.
62. marts: markets.
63. Pompey's Pillar: One of the main landmarks of Alexandria, Egypt, it is a commemorative monument dedicated to the Emperor Diocletian and stands at the highest point in Alexandria.
64. the Andes: the high mountain chain that runs from north to south down the west coast of South America.
65. respective values: the value each thing has.

66. Universal Knowledge: the organized system of information which is the collective achievement of a civilization or culture.
67. constitutes its perfection: The mind is made perfect by making its own the universal knowledge of its culture.
68. pervading: passing through; spreading throughout.
69. subject: in a political sense, one who is subject to, or under the control of, a political superior.
70. correlative functions: mutually related functions.
71. the highest state to which nature can aspire: Things are created for a purpose, and this is the highest possible purpose.
72. despond: lose all hope.
73. in alarm: upset; startled.
74. in transport: ecstatic; rapturous.
75. hang upon the opinion of others: uncritically follow what other people think.
76. to leaven: to rise as yeast and spread things apart.
77. discerns: sees.
78. tetragonous of the Peripatetic: The Peripatetic was a follower of one school of philosophy. It accepted the teaching of Aristotle's *Ethics* that the good man must realize all four potentialities and thus become cube-shaped or properly developed.
79. nil admirari: to be amazed at nothing (because one has an organized system of knowledge into which he can fit the new material).
80. The Stoic: a follower of a school of Roman philosophy which taught people to rise above circumstances and be calm in every situation.
81. Happy is he who is able to know the sequences of things, and thus triumphs over all fear, and unchangeable fate, and the roar of greedy Acheron (a river in the land of the dead). Three lines from Virgil's *Georgics*, ii, 490-492.
82. undaunted magnanimous bearing: brave, noble manner.
83. Institution: something founded, here undoubtedly his university.
84. beau ideal: good model or target.
85. imparted to: given to; conveyed to.
86. finite mind: the mind that is limited to this world.
87. supernatural charity: love, understanding, and kindness that are dependent upon religious sources and are above what men commonly possess.

88. contemplation: the calm, peaceful observation of something.
89. music of the spheres: the harmonious operations of the stars, as beautiful in their order as notes of music.

参考译文

没有知识的习得就没有真正的文化修养，哲学以知识为前提。我们需要大量的阅读，或者广泛收集信息，才能确保我们能对任何严肃的议题提出自己的见解；若未经这样的学习，最具独创性的头脑或许能使人赞叹、引人发笑、争长论短、迷乱心神，但却得不出任何有用的结果或可信的结论。当然，有人对此会有不同的看法，甚至还身体力行。你时常会发现一个精力充沛、思想活跃的人，凭借着自己的才智，可以蔑视所有的前人作家，以最无畏的姿态向世人侃侃而谈他对宗教、历史或任何其他流行话题的看法。其作品可能会畅销一时，他本人可能也会名噪一时，但也仅止于此。他的读者终究会发现，他的学说不过是理论空谈而非事实的表述，它们只是糠秕而非面包，因此他的人气来得快去得也快。

因此，知识是开拓心智的必要条件，也是实现它的工具，这一点不容否认，也不可动摇。我以此作为我的首要原则；然而，这也容易引人误入歧途，使他们坚信知识就是一切。人们认为狭隘的心智中知识是匮乏的，而思想开阔者则知识渊博；似乎使这一问题变得无可争辩的是这样的事实：大学就是要从事各种各样的学术研究，这是其职责所在。各学科都在举办讲座，举行考试，颁发奖项。大学有道德教授、形而上学教授、物理教授，还有语言教授、历史教授、数学教授、实验科学教授。他们提出了一系列问题，问题的广度和深度、类别和难度都值得称道；他们撰写了各种论著，著述的封面就足以证明他们不是博览群书就是涉猎广泛。那么，一个博览群书、有科学造诣的人还缺什么精神修养呢？除了获取知识，还能如何充实心灵？除了意识到要获取大量的知识财富并享受这份财富外，何处还能觅得哲学的寄托呢？

然而，我认为，这种观念是错误的，我现在的任务就是要说明它的谬误之处，人文教育的目的不仅仅是获取知识，或者是获得知识的根源；为了能够恰如其分地说明这个问题，我会客观地举出一些例证，其中一些是大家一致公认的思想启蒙或扩宽思维过程的例证，还有一些则不尽然；而通过对比，你们就可自行判断了，先生们，知识的习得究竟是不是拓宽思维的真正原则，还是说这一原则不过是另外的某种东西罢了。

如果一个人，他迄今为止的见识都仅限于此处或者英国那些岛屿上平静而朴素的风景，现在让他第一次走进大自然呈现出更为狂野和可怕形态的地方，无论是国内还是国外，比如走进山区之中；或者让一个一直居住在静谧村庄的人，第一次来到大都市——那么我想，他会获得从未有过的体验。这种全新的体验不是对以往体验的增补，而是有着完全不同的性质。他也许会被裹挟前行，然后发觉一时间迷失了方向。他已有所进步，意识到自己思维的拓展；他不再驻足于从前之地，而是找到了新的中心，打开了他曾全然陌生的视野。

再如，望远镜向我们展现的天体景象占据了我们的大脑，很可能会令我们头晕目眩。它引发的是思想的洪流，也被恰当地称之为心智的拓宽，我们暂且不论这个词的具体涵义究竟是什么。

同样地，观察形形色色的猛兽和其他外来动物，它们的奇异之处，它们原创性的（如果我可以使用这个词语的话）外形、姿态、习性、多样性和相互独立，将我们全身心抛入另一个创造物，宛如身处另一个造物主之下，如果我可以这样来形容它们对心智的诱惑的话。由于知识的增长，我们似乎拥有了新的能力，或者说能力有了新的施展机会，就像一个戴惯了手铐和脚镣的囚犯，猛然间发现自己的胳膊和腿都获得了自由。

因此，一般而言，自然科学及其各个学科，给予了我们丰富的财富和资源，而宇宙的有序进程使学生倍感鼓舞与振奋，而且从一开始，我可以说，就几乎引得他屏息凝神，而随着时间的推移，又让他的心灵得到宁静。

同样，人们说学习历史可以开阔和启蒙思想，原因何在呢？在我看来，这是因为学习历史赋予了人们对过往事件乃至一切事物的判断力，并赋予了心智过去从未有过的一种超脱一切的自觉意识。

与之相仿，人们过去所谓的去见世面，过进取的生活，踏入社会，走遍天下，结识社会的不同阶层，接触并了解各个党派、利益集团和种族群体的行为原则和思维方式，知晓他们的观点、目标、习俗和礼数，洞悉他们的宗教信条和礼拜形式——并从中体会到，人是如此的不同却又如此的相似，都是那样低劣，那样卑下，那样敌对，却又对信念如此的坚定不移；所有这一切都真切影响着人们的心灵，无论好坏，影响都切实存在着，人们通常称之为心智的拓宽。

再者，当心智第一次接触不信教之人的论点和思考时，感到它们给其一直笃信的神圣事物投下了无比新奇的光辉；更重要的是，如果心智屈从并接受它们，抛开以往的偏见，便会如梦初醒般地意识到一切都是想象，即现在不存在法律和违法这回事，罪恶是幻影，惩罚是鬼魅，人们可以肆无忌惮地作恶，尽情地享受这个世界并耽于欲望。更有甚者，当心智已然在享受其中的欢乐，可以想其所想，享其所欲，"世界尽在眼前，哪里都可以选择"，那又该建构何种体系来作为个人的信仰呢？当这恣意的思想激流奔涌而来漫过心智时，谁还会否认智慧之树的禁果，或者说心智所认为的知识，已使心智加冕为神，并得到了拓展和提升——这是对现实的狂喜，同时，就心智的主观状态而言，还是一种顿悟？故此，某些个体或民族突然背弃了其造物主，表现得极为狂热。他们的眼界被打开了；就像《酒神的伴侣》中遭到审判的国王一样，他们看到了两个太阳和一个奇幻的宇宙，因此他们以轻蔑和愤慨的眼光回望自己以前的信仰和纯真之态，仿佛自己当时不过是愚人，是上当受骗的傻子。

另一方面，宗教也有其拓展方式，它不是混乱般拓展，而是以和平的方式实现。人们常言道，未受过教育者很少会思考未知的世界，可当他们转向良善，审视自我，规范内心，匡正行为，冥想死亡和审判、天堂和地狱时，他们似乎变成了在心智上与过去完全迥异的人。之前他们随遇而安，不计较世事。但现如今诸事皆有意义；他们对一切际遇做出了自己的评判；他们关注时间和季节，比较现在与过去；而世界也不再枯燥、单调、无益和无望，变成了一出纷繁复杂的戏剧，有角色有景物，还有一整套严肃的道德准则。

例子还有很多，从这些例子可以看出，首先，显而易见的是，知识的传播无疑是拓宽或启蒙心智的条件或手段，这是我们如今时常耳闻的，它毋庸置疑；但接下来，同样清晰的是，知识传播并不是拓宽心智的唯一途径。拓宽心智不仅仅是被动地输入尚不为人知的新思想，还包括心智为回应涌入的新观念所采取的积极进取的行动。这是一种建构性的行动，将我们所习得的知识归结为秩序和意义，也是我们将所学的知识进行主观内化的过程，或简言之，它把我们所输入的知识消化成为我们先前思想状态的实质；如果没有这一点，就难有拓宽可言。只有在它们出现时去比较心智的各种观念，并将其系统化，才会有拓宽。我们不仅要学习，更要将所学知识与已知内容相参照联系，这样才能感到心智的成长和拓宽。启发我们的不是知识的简单增补，而是精神核心的向前进步，我们的所知和所学，我们所习得的大量的知识，都该被吸引到这个中心中来。因此，那些真正伟大的心智，都是被人类所共同认可的心智，如亚里士多德、圣托马斯、牛顿或歌德的心智（说到心智时，我特意列举了天主教治域之内和之外的例子），他们联结了新与旧、过去与现在、天涯与咫尺，并能洞察以上矛盾双方的相互影响；一旦缺少这样的洞察力，也就没有了整体和中心。这种心智拥有的知识，不仅是对事物本身的认识，也是对它们相互和真实关系的理解；知识不止被认为是习得，更是哲学。

因此，如果缺失了这种分析、分配和协调的过程，无论吸收多少知识，心智也不会得到拓宽，更不会变得开明或透彻。诚如我说过的那样，超群的记忆力并不能造就一名哲学家，就像一本字典不能称之为语法书一样。一些人可能满腹经纶，但对知识间的真正联系却一无所知。他们可能是古文物收藏家、编年史学家、博物学家；他们可能精通法律；他们可能熟知统计学；在自己的专业领域无所不知；我不该对他们妄加评论；但是，在这样的成就中，他们并未摆脱心智狭隘的弊害。如果他们只不过是博览群书的人，或者是知识渊博的人，那么他们就没有特别值得称为心智文化的东西，也未达到人文教育的要求。

同样，我们有时也会遇到这样的人，这些人见多识广，熟知那些在自己的时代扮演了重要角色的风云人物，但他们不知如何归纳，也没有真正意义上的观察力。他们掌握着大量关于人和事的详尽信息，新奇而有趣；此外，由于不受特定或固定的宗教或政治原则的影响，他们只把所谈论的事当作现象，这些现象本身就是完整的，不导向任何结果，既不研讨，也不教谕，也不点拨听众，他们只是闲谈。虽然个个学识渊博，但谁也不会说他们在任何伟大的心智培养或哲学方面有所造诣。

如果我们所讨论的是平庸之辈或缺乏教育者，情形则会更加明显。他们可能长期旅居国外，被动地、无用地、无益地接受了各种强加于他们的事实。例如,航海者从地球的一端来到了另一端;但他们所遇到的外部事物的多样性,并没有在他们的想象中勾勒出一幅对称而一致的图景,他们似乎是从反面看到了人类生活的绚丽织锦,可也说不出个所以然来。他们睡觉,他们醒来,发现自己时而身在欧洲,时而身在亚洲;他们看过大城市和荒野之地的种种景象;他们到过各种商业市场,或南方的岛屿;他们凝望过庞培柱或安第斯山脉,可万事万物都不能带着他们展望未来或者回望过去,无法形成任何超越事物自身的观念。任何事物都是僵化且割裂的,既没有历史也没有未来。万事万物独立存在,朝来暮去,就像戏剧表演中不断变换的场景,徒留观众在原地观望。也许您曾在某个特定的场合接触过这样的人,本以为他会对所发生的事情感到震惊或者困惑;但对他来说,凡事都没有差别,或者说,假如他感到困惑,他也意识到了别人希望他表达意见,可他的表现却是不知道该说些什么,不知道该赞美、嘲笑还是反对;因为事实上,他根本就没有任何判断的标准,也没有任何引导他得出结论的路标。这就是单纯的习得,而且,我重申一遍,绝不会有人想到要把它称之为哲学。

通过对比诸如此类的例子,可以证实我从此前的例证中所得出的结论。心智拓宽的真谛在于它能够同时把许多事物看作一个整体,并把它们分别置于普遍体系中各自正确的位置,理解其各自的价值,并确定它们之间相互的依存性。这就是我在此前某个场合谈到过的普遍知识的形式,它构建于个人的心智之中,并使其达到至善至美。受到这种真正启迪的心灵,在看待知识任何延展的部分时,都不会忘记它只是局部知识,也不会忘记各个部分之间的联系。它使任何事物都在某种程度上与其他事物相连,并将整体的意象传达给每一个独立的部分,直到整体在想象中变成了一种精神,它无处不在并渗透进了所有的组成部分,并赋予了它们一个明确的意义。正如我们提到身体器官时会联想到它们的功能，比如人们默认"创造"一词指向造物主，提到"臣民"难免会联想到君主，当我们抽象地设想哲学家的心智时，物质与道德世界的一切元素，科学、艺术、追求、等级、职务、事件、观点、个性，都被视为一个整体，具有相互关联的功能，并通过连续不断的组合，由整体到所有，逐渐汇集到真正的中心。

　　哪怕只拥有一部分经过启迪的心智和真正的哲学，也已是天性的极致；它让心灵超越了偶然性与必然性的影响，超越了焦虑、疑惑、不安和疑神疑鬼，而这正是大多数人的遭际。有些人一门心思追求某一目标，对其重要性夸大其词，表现得十分狂热，以该目标去衡量与它完全不相干的事物，如果愿望无法达成，就会感到震惊与沮丧。他们时而惊慌失措时而欢天喜地。与之相对，那些没有任何目标或原则可以坚持的人，每走一步都会迷失方向。他们不知所措，在每一个紧要关头都不知该怎么思考或如何表达，对蓦然出现的人、发生的事与显现的事实毫无看法，因为缺乏内在资源，他们只能人云亦云。然而，受过训练的心智，其各方力量已臻完美，它觉知，并在觉知的基础上思考，还一直在学着用理性的弹性力量去拆解事实，这样的心智不偏袒、不排他、不急躁、不迷惘，而是不厌其烦、泰然自若、庄严冷静，因为它能够从开头窥见结局，从结局看到序章，洞悉阻断之规律，参透延迟之极限；因为它永远知道自己所处的位置，知道从一点到另一点的路径。正如逍遥学派理想的四面体，或斯多葛派讲求的"无动于衷"。

　　　　洞悉事物真理的人无比幸运，
　　　　他因此战胜了一切恐惧和不可改变的命运，
　　　　以及贪婪的黄泉的咆哮。

　　有些人遇到困难时，能够迅速构想出宏大的想法或令人眼花缭乱的计划；他们受到刺激，仿佛得到了某种灵感，从而有能力把一束光投射到摆在他们面前的主题或行动方针上；他们在任何紧急情况下都能急中生智，随势而起，且有无所畏惧又宽宏大量的气度，越是遇到反对力量，其精力愈加充沛，敏锐度愈加强烈。这就是天才，这就是英雄主义；这就是自然禀赋的展示，任何文化都无法传授，任何机构都无法培养；恰恰相反，这里我们所关注的，不是纯粹的天性，而是训练和传授。心智的完善乃是教育的结果，其美好的理想，以因材施教的方式传授给个人，即面对所有事物时要具备清晰、冷静、准确的洞察力和理解力，只要有限的心智能够接纳它们，大家都能各得其所，也各有特点。就历史知识而言，它几乎是先知预言；从人性认识来看，它几乎能洞察人心；若摆脱了狭隘与偏见，它算得上具有超自然的仁爱之心，它几乎拥有信仰般的安宁，因为再没有什么能够惊吓到它；它几乎拥有了天堂般的静观之美与和谐意趣，从而与万物的永恒秩序及天体和谐运行的乐曲竟变得如此形影不离。

（郭英剑 译）

22

Gettysburg Address

葛底斯堡演说

ABRAHAM LINCOLN
亚伯拉罕・林肯

(1809—1865)

ABOUT THE AUTHOR

Abraham Lincoln (1809—1865) was the 16th and best loved president of the United States. Born in a log cabin in Kentucky, he grew up on the frontier as the family moved northward. By educating and disciplining himself, Lincoln managed to become successively a lawyer in Springfield, Illinois, U.S. representative (1847-1849), and Republican candidate for U.S. Senate in 1858. He was not an abolitionist, but he regarded slavery as an injustice and an evil and strongly opposed its extension. He was elected President of the United States in 1860 and reelected in 1864. Lincoln's presidency was inseparable from the Civil War. Unprepared by previous experience, he became, within two years, the master of complex and gigantic events, the principal strategist of the northern cause, and the tragic embodiment of the nation's suffering, North as well as South. On the night of April 14, 1865, six weeks after his inauguration, Lincoln was assassinated by John Wilkes Booth in Ford's Theater, Washington. He died the next morning.

作者简介　亚伯拉罕·林肯（1809—1865），美国第 16 任总统，也是最受爱戴的总统。他生于肯塔基州的一个小木屋里，后来跟随家人搬到北方，在边疆长大。林肯勤奋刻苦，靠自学成才，成为伊利诺伊州首府斯普林菲尔德的一名律师，1847—1849 年成为美国众议院议员，1858 年成为美国参议院共和党候选人。他并不是一位废奴主义者，但他认为奴隶制不公平、邪恶，强烈反对它的扩张。1860 年，他当选为美国总统，1864 年连任成功。林肯的总统任期与内战密不可分。虽然缺乏经验，但他在两年内就在复杂宏大的政务上游刃有余，成为北方军队的首席战略家，以及南北方共同认可的国家危难的悲剧象征。1865 年 4 月 14 日晚，他的就职典礼结束后六周，林肯在华盛顿福特剧院被约翰·威尔克斯·布思刺杀，翌日早晨去世。

* **ABOUT THE SELECTION** Gettysburg, founded by James Gettys in 1780, is a town in S. Pennsylvania. During the American Civil War of 1861-1865, it became the site of a decisive battle which hastened the defeat of Confederacy. For three days—July 1-3, 1863—the famous Gettysburg campaign raged on between the Union army under General Meade and the Confederates under General Lee. Though it was the Union that won the battle, both sides suffered heavy losses. The thousands of dead were hastily buried, but part of the battlefield was at once set apart as a national memorial to enshrine the memory of the slain. Dedication ceremonies were announced, and many government dignitaries were invited to attend. Edward Everett, the eminent statesman and orator, was chosen as the speaker. Although Lincoln had been invited to say a few words, it was not supposed that he could spare the time from his presidential duties. After a belated acceptance he composed the first draft of his remarks just before leaving Washington and revised it in Gettysburg the next morning. On November 19, 1863, more than 15,000 people listened while Everett recited from memory a two-hour address in the style of formal oratory of his day. Then Lincoln stood before the throng, and, in two minutes, scarcely glancing at the single page in his hand, spoke the 260 words which posterity was to repeat in its confirmation of freedom and democracy. Gettysburg should be pronounced (get-tis-burg) instead of (gets-burg).

内容简介 葛底斯堡是宾夕法尼亚州的一座小镇，1780 年由詹姆斯·葛底斯创立。1861—1865 年美国内战期间，这里成为一场决定性战役的地点，加快了南部邦联的溃败。1863 年 7 月 1 日至 3 日，著名的葛底斯堡战役爆发，交战双方是米德将军率领的北方联邦军和李将军率领的南方邦联军。尽管最后赢得胜利的是北方联邦军，双方都损失惨重。阵亡的几千名军人被草草埋葬，为了纪念他们，战场上一块区域被划定为国家纪念公墓，并举办了启用仪式，许多政府要人受邀参加。一位杰出的政治家和演讲家爱德华·埃弗里特被选定为主题演讲者。尽管林肯也受邀发表简短讲话，但人们认为他应该无法从繁忙的总统事务中抽身。林肯很晚才接受邀请，离开华盛顿之前他才拟出演讲的初稿，第二天早晨在葛底斯堡又润色了一版。1863 年 11 月 19 日，在参加仪式的 15000 人面前，埃弗里特发表了两个小时的脱稿演讲，是当时流行的慷慨激昂的风格。然后林肯站在众人面前，用了两分钟时间，没怎么看手里那单张纸的稿子，说出了这流传后世的 260 个单词，后人每当需要确证自由和民主都要重复这篇演讲词。葛底斯堡（Gettysburg）的正确发音应当是 get-tis-burg，而不是 gets-burg。

F our score and seven years ago our fathers brought forth on this continent, a new nation, conceived in Liberty, and dedicated to the proposition that all men are created equal.[1]

Now we are engaged in a great civil war, testing whether that nation, or any nation so conceived and so dedicated, can long endure.[2] We are met[3] on a great battlefield of that war. We have come to dedicate a portion of that field, as a final resting place for those who here gave their lives, that that nation might live.[4] It is altogether fitting and proper that we should do this.

But, in a larger sense, we cannot dedicate—we cannot consecrate—we cannot hallow—this ground. The brave men, living and dead, who struggled here, have consecrated it, far above our poor power to add or detract.[5] The world will little note, nor long remember, what we say here, but it can never forget what they did here. It is for us the living, rather, to be dedicated here to the unfinished work which they who fought here have thus far so nobly advanced.[6] It is rather for us to be here dedicated to the great task remaining before us—that from these honored dead we take increased devotion to that cause for which they gave the last full measure of devotion;[7] that we here highly resolve[8] that these dead shall not have died in vain, that this nation, under God,[9] shall have a new birth of freedom; and that government of the people, by the people, for the people,[10] shall not perish from the earth.[11]

NOTES

1. The first paragraph of the address is a reference to the American Declaration of Independence, adopted on July 4, 1776 by delegates from Thirteen Colonies, announcing their separation from Great Britain and making them the United States. Score means a set of twenty. Instead of "eighty-seven years ago" Lincoln said "four score and seven years ago" to begin his address in the impressive Biblical style, (See "four score and six years old", spoken of Abraham in Gen. 16:16.)
2. endure: last.
3. met: gathered.
4. that that nation might live: so that the United States might live.
5. detract: take away (a part).
6. advanced: brought forward; promoted.
7. the last full measure of devotion: their lives.
8. resolve: make up one's mind; decide.
9. under God: These words, not in the earlier manuscript, came to Lincoln's lips as he spoke, and were included in copies of the speech that he later made.
10. government of the people, by the people, for the people: Whether Lincoln knew it or not, Theodore Parker, Boston clergyman and abolition leader, in an antislavery address in 1850 had characterized democracy as "a government of all the people, by all the people, for all the people."
11. shall not perish from the earth: modeled upon the somber phrasing of the Book of Job, where Bildad speaks of the destruction of one who shall vanish without a trace, and says that "his branch shall be cut off; his remembrance shall perish from the earth" (Job 18:16-17).

参考译文

八十七年前我们的先辈在这块大陆上建立了一个新的国家，这个国家在争取自由中诞生，忠于人人生来平等这一信念。

目前我们正进行着一场伟大的国内战争，战争考验着以上述信念立国的我们或其他国家，是否能长期坚持下去。今天我们在这场战争的战场上集会，来把战场的一角奉献给为我们国家的生存而捐躯的人们，作为他们的安息之地。这是我们应该做的事。

但是，从更大的意义上说，我们无权把这块土地奉献给他们，我们不能使这块土地增加光彩，成为圣地。只有那些活着的或已经死去的、曾经在这里战斗过的英雄们才使这块土地成为神圣之土，我们无力使之增减一分。我们在这里说什么，世人不会注意，也不会长久记住，但是英雄们的行动却永远不会被人们遗忘。这更要求我们这些活着的人去继续英雄们为之战斗并使之前进的未竟事业。我们还需要继续为摆在我们面前的伟大的事业献身——更忠诚于先烈们为之献出生命的事业；我们决不能让先烈们的鲜血白流；——我们这个国家在上帝的保佑下，要争得自由的新生；这个民有、民治、民享的政府一定要永远在地球上存在下去。

(《英语世界》译本)

23

A Conquest of
Solitude

战胜孤独

ROBERT V. BRUCE
罗伯特·V. 布鲁斯

(1923–2008)

ABOUT THE AUTHOR   Robert Vance Bruce (1923–2008) is professor of Boston University in Boston, Massachusetts. He has been associated with its faculty since he was awarded a Ph.D. degree in History by the University in 1953. His publications include: *Lincoln and the Tools of War* (1956), *1877: Year of Violence* (1959), *Science, Union, and Democracy, 1846-1876* (1969), *Abraham Lincoln: a New Portrait* (1959), *Lincoln for the Ages* (1960). He is well known as a lecturer and author.

作者简介   罗伯特·万斯·布鲁斯（1923—2008），马萨诸塞州波士顿市波士顿大学教授。1953年获得该大学的历史学博士学位，从此一直与该大学的教师保持联系。布鲁斯的著作包括：《林肯和战争工具》(1956)、《1877：暴力之年》(1959)、《科学、联邦和民主：1846—1876》(1969)、《亚伯拉罕·林肯：新肖像》(1959)、《林肯时代》(1960)等。布鲁斯还是著名的演讲家和作家。

ABOUT THE SELECTION

Before, during, and after the work that made him famous—his invention of the telephone—Alexander Graham Bell was deeply involved in teaching the deaf. It was his first work, and when he was seventy, he wrote that "recognition of my work for and interest in the education of the deaf has always been more pleasing to me than even recognition of my work with the telephone." The impetus for this interest was extremely intimate: both his mother and wife were deaf. In the new biography, *Bell Alexander Graham Bell and the Conquest of Solitude*, published by Little Brown and Company in 1973, the historian Robert V. Bruce describes the life, work and compassionate nature of this extraordinary man. This excerpt starts when Bell, at the age of forty, met a small child—a girl whose face showed "an indefinable, chilling emptiness."

内容简介

发明电话使亚历山大·格拉汉姆·贝尔一举成名,在此项工作之前、期间和之后,贝尔都深入参与聋人教育事业,这可以说是他的第一项工作。七十岁时,贝尔写道:"对我来说,承认我为聋人教育所做的工作和对聋人教育的兴趣,甚至比承认我在电话方面所做的工作更令我开心。"这一兴趣的动力来自贝尔的亲人:贝尔的母亲和妻子都是聋人。历史学家罗伯特·万斯·布鲁斯1973年在利特尔-布朗出版社出版了新传记《亚历山大·格拉汉姆·贝尔:战胜孤独》,书中描述了贝尔这位非凡人物的生活、工作和富有同情心的性情。本篇文字始于贝尔40岁时遇到的一个女孩,女孩脸上透出"难以名状的空虚,令人沮丧"。

Among the deaf were those people who, like Mabel Bell, Alexander Graham Bell's wife, insisted that they would rather live sightless but warmed by voices in the dark than encased[1] in the cold, bright solitude of deafness. Among them also were those for whom even the solitude was dark. They were the deaf-blind.

Bell knew the deaf-blind, too. In February, 1876, he had attended a memorial service to the late Samuel Gridley Howe[2], the educator and reformer who had done pioneer work with the blind. Howe had been head of the Perkins Institution for the Blind in Boston, and his most famous pupil there had been a deaf-blind student named Laura Bridgman. At the age of two Laura had lost her sight, hearing, even most of her sense of smell and of taste. Little remained to make her living body more than the sealed tomb of her mind. But Howe had touched that mind and found it responsive. And so Laura had discovered the existence of the world and had learned something of what it held. At the service[3] for Howe, Bell had "quite a little talk[4]" with Laura—by means of finger spelling—and as Bell wrote at the time, Laura had cried for her dead teacher. "The whole scene was one I shall long remember," Bell wrote.

Years later, in 1887, Captain Arthur H. Keller, a former Confederate officer who had become a newspaper editor in Tuscumbia,[5] Alabama, brought his six-year-old deaf-blind daughter Helen[6] to Bell in Washington. Helen was a healthy child, excited to something like happiness by what she sensed of the novel[7] journey. Bell may have seen irony in the contrast between her eager gropings and her father's sadness. Yet in her well-shaped face, for all its intimations of dormant intelligence,[8] there seemed to be an indefinable, chilling emptiness. Bell listened to the story of the illness that had left Helen completely deaf and sightless at nineteen months. Something in his touch, Helen remembered years later, gave her an impression of tenderness and sympathy. She sat on his knee and felt his watch strike. He understood her rudimentary signs,[9] and she knew it and loved him at once. "But I did not dream," she wrote in later years, "that that interview would be the door through which I should pass from darkness into light."

According to Helen, Bell unlocked that door with the suggestion that Keller write Michael Anagnos, at that time the director of the Perkins Institution. As it happened, Anagnos was already prepared. A friend of Keller's had spoken to Anagnos about Helen's case months earlier, perhaps at the instance of Helen's mother, who had read about Laura Bridgman in Charles Dickens' *American Notes*.[10] Then, on the strength of a tentative inquiry from Keller himself in the summer of 1886, Anagnos had alerted one of his star graduates to the possibility of such a call. She had since been studying Howe's carefully recorded methods in the case of Laura Bridgman and spending much time with Laura. Presumably Bell's encouragement in February, 1887, rekindled Keller's interest or settled his doubts[11] about Helen's educability. At any rate Keller wrote again to Anagnos and thereby initiated the astonishing lifework of Annie M. Sullivan.[12]

Annie was then twenty years old, still haunted by the horrors of her four childhood years in the Tewksbury poorhouse, still suffering from the effects of trachoma,[13] which had once made and would again make her blind, but soon to be called by Mark Twain and others the miracle-worker and by Helen Keller simply Teacher. It was on March 3, 1887, that Annie

Sullivan arrived in Tuscumbia. That day was to be cherished by Helen Keller as her "soul's birthday." It also happened to be the fortieth birthday of Alexander Graham Bell.

"A miracle has happened," wrote Annie on March 20; "the wild little creature of two weeks ago has been transformed into a gentle child." On April 5 came Helen's famous breakthrough to the understanding that things had names, and three months later she was writing letters, Bell followed the Tuscumbia "miracle" with wonder, as did the public after Michael Anagnos sounded the trumpet.[14] Bell himself helped to spread the news, furnishing a New York paper in 1888 with Helen's picture and one of her letters to him. He saw a wider good coming from the dazzling emergence of her mind.[15] "The public have already become interested in Helen Keller," he wrote in 1891, "and through her, may perhaps be led to take an interest in the more general subject of the Education of the Deaf."

In one respect Bell stood alone among Helen Keller's admirers and celebrators. He insisted that what Annie Sullivan and Helen Keller between them had done was not a miracle but a brilliantly successful experiment. "It is... a question of instruction we have to consider," he wrote, "and not a case of supernatural acquirement." He interviewed Helen himself to measure her progress and pressed Annie Sullivan for explanations of it, especially of Helen's command of idiomatic[16] English. From what Annie reported, he found the key in the fact that she constantly spelled natural, idiomatic English into Helen's hand without stopping to explain unfamiliar words and constructions and that she encouraged Helen to read book after book in Braille[17] or raised type with a similar reliance on context to explain new vocabulary. This, as Bell pointed out, was the equivalent of the way a hearing child learned English. And it supported his long-standing emphasis on the use of the English language, rather than sign language, with deaf children. Indeed, he saw the importance of books in the early stages of educating the deaf as "the chief lesson, I think, to be learned from the case of Helen Keller."

At the 1891 summer meeting of the American Association for the Promotion of the Teaching of Speech to the Deaf, an organization started the year before by Bell and some associates, Bell gave each member a copy of a handsomely bound "Helen Keller Souvenir." This book contained accounts of Helen's education by Annie Sullivan and others, among them Sarah Fuller, who had recently given Helen her first lessons in speech. At the association's expense Helen and Miss Sullivan came in person to the 1893 meeting in Chicago, and Helen "saw" the World's Columbian Exposition through the hands of Bell and her teacher; the tour included an exhibit of Bell's telephone. Teachers of the deaf met her and, it was reported, "saw and heard enough to remove all their doubts." A year later, at the AAPTSD[18] Chautauqua meeting,[19] Annie Sullivan delivered—or rather, out of last-minute shyness, asked Bell to deliver for her—an eloquent yet objective account of her work and relations with Helen. And in 1896 the sixteen-year-old Helen herself proudly addressed the AAPTSD. "If you knew all the joy I feel in being able to speak to you today," she said, "I think you would have some idea of the value of speech to the deaf... One can never consent to creep when one feels an impulse to soar."

Helen Keller and Annie Sullivan were, however, much more to Bell than phenomena or specimens. They were his friends, and he was theirs. "It was an immense advantage for one of my temper, impatience, and antagonisms[20] to know Dr. Bell intimately over a long period of time," said Annie in retrospect.[21] "Gifted with a voice that itself suggested genius, he spoke the English language with a purity and charm which have never been surpassed by anyone I have heard speak. I listened to every word fascinated... I never felt at ease[22] with anyone until I met him... Dr. Bell had a happy way of making people feel pleased with themselves. He had a remarkable faculty[23] of bringing out the best that was in them. After a conversation with him I felt released, important, communicative. All the pent-up[24] resentment within me went out... I learned more from him than from anyone else. He imparted knowledge with a beautiful courtesy that made one proud to sit at his feet and learn. He answered every question in the cool, clear light of reason... [with] no trace of animus against individuals, nations, or classes. If he wished to criticize and he often did, he began by pointing out something good I had done in another direction." When asked long after Bell's death what, aside from her feeling for Helen, had enabled her to keep at so exacting a task for so many years, she replied, "I think it must have been Dr. Bell—his faith in me."

Bell's own daughters felt a touch of jealousy at his feeling for Helen Keller. For her part, one of her early letters, written a few months after her teacher first came to her, was to "Dear Mr. Bell," and it said, among other things, "I do love you." And more than thirty years later, when he was seventy-one, she wrote him, "Even before my teacher came, you held out a warm hand to me in the dark... You followed step by step my teacher's efforts... When others doubted, it was you who heartened us... You have always shown a father's joy in my successes and a father's tenderness when things have not gone right."

More than once in those thirty years things did go wrong for Helen Keller, and Bell was there with a helping hand. A short story, "The Frost King," which she wrote in 1891 at the age of eleven for Anagnos' birthday and which Anagnos then published, was found to echo the plot and wording of a children's fairy tale published nearly twenty years earlier, a story unknown to Annie Sullivan and not in the books available to Helen. It turned out to have been read to her at the home of a friend in Annie's absence more than three years earlier. At the Perkins Institution a solemn committee (Mark Twain in his outrage called it "a collection of decayed human turnips") cross-questioned the bewildered and frightened child at great length[25] with Annie Sullivan sent out of the room, before concluding that Helen had unwittingly summoned up the story from her remarkable memory rather than from her imagination as she supposed. The ordeal crushed Helen's spirit and her joy in books for months and shook her confidence in her own originality for years.

The kindly author of the original story, Margaret Canby, wrote that Helen's version was no plagiarism[26] but "a wonderful feat of memory"[27] and an improvement on the source. "Please give her my warm love," added Miss Canby, "and tell her not to feel troubled over it any more." Mark Twain was more emphatic, recalling the time he himself had unconsciously plagiarized a passage from Oliver Wendell Holmes.[28] "To think of those solemn donkeys[29] breaking a little child's heart with their ignorant damned rubbish about plagiarism!" he wrote. "I couldn't sleep for blaspheming[30] about it last night." Bell, who had helped Annie Sullivan trace Helen's exposure to the story, saw further than either Twain or Miss Canby. Like them, he pointed out that "we all do what Helen did," that "our most original compositions are composed exclusively of expressions derived from others." But he also observed that Anagnos had "failed to grasp the importance of the Frost King incident" and that "a full investigation will throw light on[31] the manner in which Helen has acquired her marvelous knowledge of language—and do much good."

After a long talk with Helen in 1894 Bell heartily seconded her "strong desire" to be educated in a school for normal students rather than in a special school for the deaf or the blind. Bell reminded Captain Keller that his daughter would need a special interpreter in any case, so that a school for the handicapped could offer her no practical advantage. He promised to rally Helen's friends to the underwriting of any expenses.[32] Thus Helen went on to achieve what throughout her life would be one of her chief consolations and sources of pride: acceptance as an intellectual and social equal by people who could see and hear.

In 1897 Arthur Gilman, headmaster of the Cambridge School, at which Helen was preparing for Radcliffe College,[33] decided that Miss Sullivan was endangering Helen's health by pressing her too hard in her studies. Having temporarily persuaded Helen's mother of this, he tried to separate Helen from her beloved teacher. Gilman did his best to win Bell's support for the move. But Bell had boundless faith in the wisdom and dedication of Annie Sullivan, and when she appealed to him for help, he dispatched[34] his assistant, the venerable John Hitz, to investigate. Afterward Bell wrote Gilman that nothing could justify parting Helen and Annie except evidence that Annie was in some way unfit for her charge,[35] and as to that, his free conversation with Helen had revealed her to be a "living testimonial to the character of Miss Sullivan." Mrs. Keller hurried to Massachusetts and, finding Helen in excellent health and determined to stay with Annie, agreed with Hitz and Bell that Gilman was wrong. Never again was it to be suggested that Helen and Annie Sullivan should be parted.

Three years later, just as Helen entered Radcliffe College, a well-intentioned friend nearly persuaded her to give up her studies and, together with Annie, to start and direct a school for deaf-blind children. Bell's decided opposition to the scheme, along with that of other friends, kept Helen in Radcliffe and out of what would surely have been a fiasco.[36]

Bell's doubts of his own business acumen[37] led him to decline the suggestion that he administer a trust fund set up for Helen in 1896. Nevertheless, he took a leading part in organizing the arrangement and contributed a thousand dollars to it. Before and after, he helped out on special occasions, sending Helen four hundred dollars when her father died in 1896, a hundred dollars toward a country vacation in the summer of 1899, $194 so that Helen could surprise Annie with a wedding gift when Annie married the writer and critic John A. Macy in 1905. Financial as well as moral support may have led Annie to write early in 1898 that Bell "will never know how deeply grateful I am to him for one of the richest and fullest years we have ever known."

Among Helen's friends and admirers were those who were richer than

Bell and less deeply committed to the support of other causes. In dollar terms their gifts to Helen out-stripped those of Bell.[38] But he gave her things they could not match with money. "More than anyone else, during those [early] years," wrote a friend who knew Helen in later life, "it was Alexander Graham Bell who gave Helen her first conception of the progress of mankind, telling her as much about science as Phillips Brooks[39] told her about religion." Bell thrilled her with stories that paralleled the Greek epics she loved, Promethean[40] tales like that of the laying of the Atlantic cable. One day he placed her hand on a telephone pole and asked her what it meant to her, then explained that the wires it carried sang of life and death, war and finance, fear and joy, failure and success, that they pierced the barriers of space and touched mind to mind throughout the whole of the civilized world.

Bell's mind, and Helen's through his, responded to nature, too. Once, beneath an oak, he placed her hand on the trunk, and she felt the soft crepitation[41] of raindrops on the leaves. For years after that she liked to touch trees in the rain. Then, on another day, he went with her to Niagara Falls and put her hand on the hotel windowpane so that she could sense the thunder of the river plunging over its shuddering escarpment.[42] He drove with her and Annie from Washington into the springtime countryside, where they gathered wild azalea, honeysuckle, and dogwood blossoms.

More than once Helen visited Beinn Bhreagh, the Bells' summer estate in Nova Scotia.[43] She spent one night with Bell's daughters Elsie and Daisy on their houseboat, from which they all climbed down by a rope ladder to swim in the moonlit lake. In the fields overlooking the Bras d'Or Lakes, Bell told her of his kite flying and his hone of giving wings to mankind. "He makes you feel that if you only had a little more time, you, too, might be an inventor," she wrote. One windy day she helped him fly his kites. "On one of them I noticed that the strings were of wire, and having had some experience in bead work, I said I thought they would break. Dr. Bell said

'No!' with great confidence, and the kite was sent up. It began to pull and tug, and lo, the wires broke, and off went the great red dragon, and poor Dr. Bell stood looking forlornly[44] after it. After that he asked me if the strings were all right and changed them at once when I answered in the negative. Altogether we had great fun." Back at Radcliffe that summer of 1901 she wrote Mabel that "the smell of the ocean, and the fragrance of the pines have followed me to Cambridge and linger about me like a benediction.[45]"

Now and then Bell thought about Helen's future course in life. As she made her way through college he began to feel that "with her gifts of mind and imagination there should be a great future open to her in literature." Later he wrote her, "You must not put me among those who think that 'nothing you have to say about the affairs of the universe would be interesting.'" But Helen was more realistic about the limits put upon, her direct apprehension of the world, about her inescapable dependence on the words of others for learning what eyes and ears tell most people. She knew also that to the public her blindness was her foremost characteristic (though personally she agreed with Mabel Bell that deafness was the heavier cross), so her work came to be more and more that of helping the cause of the blind. And because Bell's work lay with the deaf, he and she saw less of each other as the new century wore on.

Each missed the other. When he tried his hand at a letter in Braille while she was in college, she praised him for not making a single mistake. It seemed almost as if you clasped my hand in yours and spoke to me in the old, dear way, she wrote him. In 1907 he wrote her, "I often think of you and feel impelled to write but—as you know—I am a busy man, and...have always lots of back correspondence to make up." Now and then he wrote again in Braille, but not often enough for it to be easy. He spent a few days in Boston once and tried for a long time one day to telephone Helen's house, but Annie heard the ringing too late. "We seem bound[46] every time to miss seeing him," Helen wrote John Hitz on that occasion. As public figures, each knew in a general way what the other was doing. "I suppose," wrote Helen in 1902, "Mr. Bell has nothing but kites and flying-machines[47] on his tongue's end. Poor dear man, how I wish he would stop wearing himself out[48] in this unprofitable way—at least it seems unprofitable to me." But six years later she sent him a note of congratulation on his successes in aviation, to which he replied in proud detail.

In January, 1907, Helen wired Bell "I need you." She was to speak in New York at a meeting for the blind; but Annie, who usually repeated her speech for those who might have difficulty understanding it, was sick. Bell left Washington at once and lent his matchless voice to the occasion.

In the summer of 1918 Helen asked Bell to play himself in a motion picture of her life. He was then seventy-one, in uncertain health, very susceptible to summer heat, and had "the greatest aversion to appearing in a moving-picture." Still, her letter touched him deeply. "It brings back recollections of the little girl I met in Washington so long ago," he wrote her. "You will," he reminded her, "have to find someone with dark hair to impersonate the Alexander Graham Bell of your childhood." But he promised to appear with her in a later scene, when the hot weather was over, if she wanted him to. To his great relief he was not called upon (which was just as well, since the film was a grotesque failure, both as drama and as history).

The drama of Helen Keller's rescue and rise had, after all, been given a far more enduring form in her own autobiography, *The Story of My Life*, fifteen years before. Supplemented by her own and Annie Sullivan's letters, it both recounted and attested[49] to one of history's most moving triumphs. And it began with the words

To
ALEXANDER GRAHAM BELL
Who has taught the deaf to speak

and enabled the listening ear
to hear speech
from the Atlantic to the Rockies,
I Dedicate
this Story of My Life.

NOTES

1. encased: surrounded or covered as with a case; imprisoned.
2. Samuel Gridley Howe (1801-1876): founded the Perkins Institute for the Blind in 1832, and directed the Institute until his death. He was famous for his contributions in many areas of reform.
3. service: the memorial service.
4. quite a little talk: a conversation to some extent.
5. Tuscumbia: a town in NW Alabama.
6. Helen: Helen Adams Keller (1880-1968), is an outstanding example of a person who conquered physical handicaps. She became a world-renowned campaigner for bettering conditions for the blind in underdeveloped and war-ravaged countries. She is the author of many books which have been translated into more than 50 languages.
7. novel: strange; new.
8. intimation of dormant intelligence: indication of intelligence waiting to be developed.
9. rudimentary signs: very simple sign language.
10. *American Notes*: a volume of travel sketches by Charles Dickens (1842). The book was well received in England, but gave great offence in America.
11. settled his doubt: disposed of his uncertainty.
12. Annie M. Sullivan: Helen Adams Keller's teacher (1866-1930).
13. trachoma: infectious eye disease causing inflammation of the inner surface of the eyelids.
14. sounded the trumpet: spread the news, made it known.
15. dazzling emergence of her mind: splendid unfolding of her mind.
16. idiomatic: dialectal.
17. Braille: a system of writing or printing for the blind in which combinations of tangible dots or points are used to represent letters, characters, etc. which are read by touch.

18. AAPTSD: abbreviation for the American Association for the Promotion of the Teaching of Speech to the Deaf.
19. the annual Chautauqua meeting, usually outdoors, provide public lectures, concerts, and dramatic performances during the summer months.
20. antagonisms: disagreements and hostilities.
21. in retrospect: recollectively; reminiscently.
22. at ease: comfortable; at home.
23. faculty: talent, natural gift.
24. pent-up: restrained; shut-in; confined.
25. at great length: in considerable detail.
26. plagiarism: taking and using somebody else's ideas, words, etc. in one's own writing as if they were one's own.
27. a wonderful feat of memory: an extraordinary performance in displaying remarkable memory.
28. Oliver Wendell Holmes (1809-1894): an American writer of essays, poems, and novels, also a physician and a teacher of medicine.
29. those solemn donkeys: the members of the committee at the Perkins Institute, whom Mark Twain in his outrage also called "decayed human turnips".
30. blaspheming: abusing.
31. throw light on: show; explain.
32. Bell promised to bring together all Helen's friends to bear all the expenses.
33. Radcliffe College: It is a private liberal arts college for women in Cambridge, Mass. The school is affiliated with Harvard University, and was founded in 1879 as a result of women's demand to attend courses given by Harvard instructors.
34. dispatched: sent off (to a destination for a special purpose).
35. charge: care; supervision.
36. fiasco: mess; complete failure.
37. acumen: foresight; insight.
38. The gifts from Helen's other friends were more expensive than Bell's.
39. Phillips Brooks (1835-1893): American Episcopal clergyman and bishop, who is best remembered for his Christmas carol *O Little Town of Bethlehem* He was well known for his eloquence, charming personality, and tolerant views.
40. Promethean: (adjective of Prometheus) creative; boldly original; pioneering.
41. crepitation: flicking; crackle.

42. escarpment: bank; a long precipitous cliff-like ridge of land, rock, or the like.
43. Nova Scotia: a peninsula and province in SE Canada, once a part of the French province of Acadia.
44. forlornly: hopelessly.
45. benediction: thanksgiving; praise.
46. bound: certain, sure.
47. flying-machines: airplanes.
48. wearing himself out: making himself tired; wasting his energy.
49. recounted and attested: summed up and testified.

参考译文

有这样一些聋人，比如亚历山大·格拉汉姆·贝尔的妻子梅布尔·贝尔，他们情愿生活在失明的黑暗中，而能感受声音的温暖，也不愿生活在失聪带来的冰冷而明亮的孤独中。对另外一些聋人来说，这种孤独还是黑暗的。这些人就是聋盲人。

贝尔也了解聋盲人。1876年2月，他参加了已故教育家和改革家萨缪尔·格里德利·豪的追悼会。豪为盲人做了一些开创性工作，曾担任波士顿帕金斯盲人学校的负责人，他当时最著名的学生名为劳拉·布里奇曼，也是名聋盲学生。劳拉两岁时就丧失了视觉和听觉，甚至丧失了大部分嗅觉和味觉，活生生的身体简直就像封存她心灵的墓穴。但是豪触摸到了劳拉的心灵，发现这颗心灵是有反应的。就这样，劳拉意识到了世界的存在，开始了解这个世界。在豪的追悼会上，贝尔与劳拉通过手指拼写的方式进行了"相当多的交谈"，正如贝尔当时所记录的那样，劳拉为自己逝去的老师哭泣。贝尔写道："此情此景我将永远铭记。"

几年后，即1887年，亚瑟·H. 凯勒上尉将自己六岁的聋盲女儿海伦带到华盛顿，见到了贝尔。亚瑟·凯勒曾是南部邦联的一名军官，后来在亚拉巴马州的塔斯坎比亚担任报纸编辑。他的女儿海伦身体健康，对这趟新奇的旅程感到激动，几乎可以说是开心。贝尔察觉出，海伦的热切摸索和她父亲的悲伤情绪之间形成了鲜明对比。不过，尽管海伦的面庞线条优美，体现出她内在的智慧，但似乎也透出一种难以名状的空虚，令人沮丧。亚瑟告诉贝尔，海伦19个月时生了一场病，就是这场病让她彻底失聪、失明。多年以后，海伦还记得，贝尔的触摸让她感受到了一种亲切和同情。海伦坐在贝尔的膝盖上，能够感觉到他手表指针在走动。贝尔可以理解海伦最基本的手势，海伦也知道这一点，并且立即喜欢上了他。"但我不是在做梦，"海伦晚年写道，"那次见面堪称一扇门，将我从黑暗引入了光明。"

海伦表示，贝尔打开了那扇门，建议海伦的父亲亚瑟写信给当时帕金斯盲人学校的校长迈克尔·阿纳格诺斯。事实上，阿纳格诺斯已经做好了准备。几个月前，亚瑟的一位朋友就曾向阿纳格诺斯谈起过海伦的情况，也许是应海伦母亲的请求，因为海伦的母亲在查尔斯·狄更斯的《美国纪行》中读到了劳拉·布里奇曼的故事。亚瑟本人于1886年夏天进行了试探性询问，在此之前，阿纳格诺斯已经提醒他的一位优秀毕业生可能会接到这样一个电话，这位毕业生一直在研究豪在劳拉·布里奇曼病例中仔细记录的方法，与劳拉相处了很长一段时间。也许，贝尔1887年2月的鼓励让亚瑟重新燃起希望，或者打消了他对海伦是否可以接受教育的疑虑。总而言之，亚瑟再次给阿纳格诺斯写信，从此开启了安妮·莎莉文令人惊叹的毕生事业。

当时安妮20岁，童年时期曾在蒂克斯伯里救济院生活了四年，这段艰难岁月对她的影响很大，让她多年来一直饱受沙眼的折磨。沙眼曾使她失明，而且将再度使她失明。不过，安妮很快就被马克·吐温等人称为奇迹的缔造者，被海伦·凯勒称为真正的老师。1887年3月3日，安妮·莎莉文抵达塔斯坎比亚。这一天也被海伦·凯勒珍视为自己的"灵魂生日",恰好还是亚历山大·格拉汉姆·贝尔的四十岁生日。

"奇迹出现了,"安妮 3 月 20 日写道,"两周前充满野性的小东西已经变成了一个温柔的孩子。"4 月 5 日,海伦实现了著名的突破,意识到事物有名字,三个月后就开始写信了。贝尔惊奇地关注着塔斯坎比亚的"奇迹",迈克尔·阿纳格诺斯发布这一新闻后,也引起了公众的关注。贝尔本人也帮助传播这一消息,1888 年,他向一家纽约报纸提供了海伦的照片和海伦写给自己的一封信。贝尔看到,海伦的心灵慢慢苏醒,令人惊叹,出现了更多好消息。"公众已经对海伦·凯勒产生了兴趣,"贝尔 1891 年写道,"通过海伦,也许可以引导公众对聋人教育这个更普遍的主题产生兴趣。"

有一点,贝尔与海伦·凯勒的赞赏者和庆祝者观点不同。他坚持认为,安妮·莎莉文和海伦·凯勒所做的一切并非奇迹,而是极为成功的实验。"这是……我们必须考虑的教育问题,"贝尔写道,"并非超自然成就的案例。"贝尔亲自采访了海伦,以衡量她的进步,并敦促安妮·莎莉文对此做出解释,特别是海伦对地道英语的掌握情况。通过安妮的报告,贝尔发现,关键在于,安妮不断在海伦手上拼写自然地道的英语,并没有停下来解释海伦不熟悉的单词和结构,还鼓励海伦阅读一本又一本布莱叶盲文或凸体文字书,同样依靠上下文来解释新词汇。正如贝尔指出,这相当于一个有听力的儿童学习英语的方式,也证实了贝尔长期以来强调对聋儿使用英语而非手语的观点。事实上,贝尔意识到书籍在聋人早期教育阶段的重要性,也是他"认为自己从海伦·凯勒这一案例中得到的主要收获"。

1890 年,贝尔和一些同事创立了美国聋哑人语言教育促进协会(AAPTSD)。1891 年夏季会议期间,贝尔给每位会员发放了一本装帧精美的《海伦·凯勒纪念册》。这本书包含了安妮·莎莉文和莎拉·富勒等人对海伦进行教育的内容。富勒在不久前给海伦上了她生平第一堂言语课。在协会资助下，海伦和莎莉文小姐亲自参加了1893年在芝加哥举行的会议，海伦通过贝尔和她老师的手"看到了"哥伦比亚世界博览会，包括参观贝尔的电话展览。一些从事聋人教育的教师见到了海伦，据说"所见所闻足以消除他们所有的疑虑"。一年后，在美国聋哑人语言教育促进协会肖托夸夏季教育户外集会上，安妮·莎莉文发表了（或者说，因为最后一刻的羞涩，请贝尔替她发表了）一篇洋洋洒洒而又客观的演讲，介绍了自己的工作以及与海伦的关系。1896年，16岁的海伦本人也自豪地在美国聋哑人语言教育促进协会发言，她说："如果你们能感受到我今天对你们讲话所感受到的所有快乐，我想，你们就会了解言语对聋人的价值……一个人内心有了飞翔的冲动，绝不会满足于在地上爬行。"

不过，对贝尔来说，海伦·凯勒和安妮·莎莉文不仅仅是一种现象或样本。她们是贝尔的朋友，而贝尔也是她们的朋友。安妮回忆道："我这个人脾气不好，没有耐心，充满对立情绪，所以，和贝尔博士的关系对我有极大的好处，与生俱来的音色就说明他是一名天才，他的英语非常纯正，迷人的声音超越了我所听到过的任何人。我着迷地听着每个单词……遇到贝尔之前，我与任何人相处都从未感觉到如此轻松……贝尔博士用一种巧妙的方式使人们对自己感到满意。他有一种非凡的天赋，能激发人们内心最美好的东西。与他交谈之后，我觉得释然，感觉自己很重要，可以沟通交流了，内心所有郁结的怨恨都消失了……我从贝尔那里学到的东西比从其他任何人那里学到的都多。他以一种优美的方式传授知识，使人因为跟着他学习而感到自豪。贝尔以冷静、清晰的理性之光回答每个问题……没有丝毫针对个人、国家或阶层的敌意。如果他想批评（也经常这样做）我，首先会指出我在另一方面的出色表现。"贝尔去世很久以后，有人问安妮，除了对海伦的感情，还有什么支持她这么多年坚持完成如此艰巨的任务，她回答道："我想一定是贝尔博士——贝尔博士对我的信任。"

贝尔的女儿因为他对海伦·凯勒的感情而感到一丝嫉妒。海伦开始学着写信的时候，有一封就是写给"亲爱的贝尔先生"的，这封信是海伦的老师第一次来到她身边几个月之后写的，信中写道："我真的爱您。"三十多年后，贝尔71岁时，海伦在给他的信中写道："甚至在我的老师到来之前，您就在黑暗之中向我伸出了一只温暖的手……一步步观察我老师的工作……别人怀疑的时候，是您激励了我们……您总是在我成功时表现出父亲般的喜悦，在事情不顺利时表现出父亲般的温柔。"

在这三十年间，海伦·凯勒确实不止一次遇到问题，而贝尔总是伸出援手。1891年，11岁的海伦为庆祝阿纳格诺斯的生日创作了一篇短篇小说《霜王》，随后阿纳格诺斯将其发表。人们发现，这篇小说的情节和行文模仿了大约二十年前出版的一篇童话。安妮·莎莉文不知道这个故事，海伦读到的书里也没有这个故事。原来，这个故事是三年前安妮不在的时候，别人在一个朋友家读给海伦的。在帕金斯盲人学校，装腔作势的委员会（马克·吐温愤怒地将其称为"一堆腐烂的人形萝卜"）将安妮·莎莉文赶出房间，对海伦这个充满困惑和惊恐的孩子进行了长时间盘问，然后得出结论，海伦不知不觉地从自己非凡的记忆中提取了这个故事，而非她自己认为的那样：是自己想象出来的。这一痛苦的经历压垮了海伦的精神，使其连续好几个月对书本失去了兴趣，并在好几年里都对自己独创能力缺乏信心。

原故事的作者玛格丽特·坎比心地善良，她写道，海伦的版本不是抄袭，而是"记忆力的绝活"，是对原文的改进。坎比还说："请向海伦表达我温暖的爱意，告诉她，不要再为此感到烦恼。"马克·吐温语气更为坚决，他回顾了自己曾无意识抄袭奥利弗·温德尔·霍姆斯一段话的事情。他写道："那些装腔作势的驴子，对什么是抄袭完全一无所知，竟然用该死的废话令一个小孩心碎！昨晚我因为咒骂这件事而无法入睡。"贝尔曾帮助安妮·莎莉文追溯海伦听到的这个故事，比马克·吐温或坎比看得更远。和他们一样，贝尔指出："我们都在做海伦所做的事情，我们最初的作品完全是用源自他人的表达方式写成的。"不过，贝尔也注意到，阿纳格诺斯"没有把握住《霜王》事件的重要性"，而且"全面调查将有助于揭示海伦如何获得了令人惊叹的语言知识——这种做法也大有裨益。"

1894年，贝尔与海伦进行了一次长谈，衷心赞同她的"强烈愿望"，即在接收正常学生的学校而不是接收聋人或盲人的特殊学校接受教育。贝尔提醒凯勒上尉，他的女儿不管怎样都需要一位特殊翻译，因此，残疾人学校无法给她带来任何实际的好处。贝尔答应动员海伦的朋友承担全部费用。因此，海伦进一步获得了一生中最主要的慰藉，也是令她骄傲的源泉，即：视力和听力正常的人将自己视为与他们智力和社会地位平等的人。

1897年，海伦正在剑桥学校为进入拉德克利夫学院做准备，剑桥学校的校长阿瑟·吉尔曼认为莎莉文小姐在学习方面对海伦的要求过高，危及海伦的健康，就暂时说服了海伦的母亲，试图将海伦与她心爱的老师分开。吉尔曼竭力争取贝尔支持这一举措，但贝尔对安妮·莎莉文的智慧和奉献精神充满无限的信心，因此，安妮向贝尔求助时，贝尔派自己的助手（可敬的约翰·希茨）去调查此事。事后，贝尔在写给吉尔曼的信中说道，除了有证据表明安妮在某种程度上有些不称职以外，无法证明将海伦和安妮分开是合理的，至于这一点，他与海伦的自由交谈表明海伦是"莎莉文小姐能力的鲜活证明"。凯勒夫人匆匆赶到马萨诸塞州，发现海伦健康状况很好并决心和安妮在一起，便同意希茨和贝尔的意见，认为吉尔曼是错误的。从此再也没人建议将海伦和安妮·莎莉文分开了。

三年后，海伦进入拉德克利夫学院，就在那时，一位好心的朋友几乎说服了她放弃学业，与安妮一起创办并管理一所盲聋儿童学校。贝尔坚决反对这一计划，加上其他朋友也反对，海伦最终留在了拉德克利夫，避免了一场注定的惨败。

贝尔对自己的商业头脑表示怀疑，这使他1896年拒绝了为海伦管理信托基金的建议。尽管如此，他还是在基金的组织准备工作中发挥了主导作用，并捐款1000美元。在此前后，贝尔总是在特殊时刻提供帮助，1896年，海伦的父亲去世，他送去了400美元，1899年夏天，又送去100美元用于乡村度假，1905年，安妮与作家兼评论家约翰·A.梅西结婚，他送给海伦194美元，使海伦能够为安妮送上结婚礼物，带去一份惊喜。也许正是这种经济和精神上的支持，使安妮于1898年初写道，贝尔"永远不会知道我对他的感激之情有多深，因为他带给我们有史以来最丰富、最充实的岁月"。

海伦的朋友和崇拜者中，有些人比贝尔更富有，但对其他事情的支持力度却没有贝尔那么大，按美元计算，他们给海伦的礼物超过了贝尔，但贝尔给予海伦的一切是他们用金钱无法比拟的。一位晚年认识海伦的朋友写道："（早先）那些年，就是亚历山大·格拉汉姆·贝尔使海伦第一次认识到了人类的进步，她从贝尔那里了解的科学知识和从菲利普斯·布鲁克斯那里了解的宗教知识一样多。"海伦喜欢希腊史诗，贝尔就给她讲述类似的故事，令她陶醉，例如，铺设大西洋电缆的故事，贝尔把它讲得和普罗米修斯的故事一样。有一天，贝尔把海伦的手放在一根电线杆上，询问这对她意味着什么，然后解释说，电线杆上的电线唱出了生命与死亡、战争与金融、恐惧与欢乐、失败与成功之歌，冲破了空间的障碍，促成了整个文明世界的心灵沟通。

贝尔的思想以及贝尔传递给海伦的思想，也对大自然做出了反应。一次，在一棵橡树下，贝尔把海伦的手放在树干上，海伦感觉到了雨滴落在树叶上发出的轻微噼啪声。此后多年,海伦一直喜欢在雨中抚摸树木。还有一天,贝尔和海伦一起去尼亚加拉大瀑布,贝尔把海伦的手放在酒店的窗玻璃上,这样海伦就能感觉到河流冲下颤抖的悬崖发出雷鸣般的响声。贝尔开车带着海伦及安妮一起从华盛顿出发,前往春天的乡村,他们在那里采集野杜鹃花、金银花和山茱萸花。

海伦不止一次到访贝尔在新斯科舍省的美丽山避暑庄园。海伦和贝尔的女儿埃尔希和黛西在居住船上住了一晚,她们沿着绳梯从船上爬下,在月光下的湖中游泳。在远眺布拉多尔湖的田野上,贝尔给海伦讲述了自己放风筝的故事以及他为人类插上翅膀的渴望。海伦曾经写道:"贝尔让你觉得,只需再多给一点时间,你也可能成为一位发明家。"一个有风的日子,海伦帮助贝尔放风筝。"我注意到,其中一个风筝的线用的是电线,我有一些串珠子的经验,因此我说觉得这些线会断掉。贝尔博士非常自信地说'不会!'于是风筝被送上了天。开始收线、放线,看哪,线真的断了,大红龙飞走了,可怜的贝尔博士站在那里惆怅地看着风筝越飞越远。此后,他会问我风筝的线是否合适,如果我的回答是否定的,他马上就会换线。总的来说,我们玩得非常开心。"1901年夏天,回到拉德克利夫之后,海伦在给梅布尔的信中写道:"海洋的气味和松树的香味跟随我来到剑桥学校,犹如幸福的感觉萦绕着我。"

贝尔不时会考虑海伦未来的人生道路。海伦大学毕业时,贝尔开始觉得"凭借注意力和想象力方面的天赋,她在文学领域应该有一个辉煌的未来。"后来,贝尔给海伦写信说:"你一定不要认为我觉得你对世事的评价索然寡味。"但海伦更现实,她认识到自己直接理解世界所受的限制,认识到她不可避免要依靠别人的话语来了解大多数人依靠眼睛和耳朵就能了解的事情。她还知道,对公众来说,失明是自己最重要的特征(尽管她个人同意梅布尔·贝尔的观点，认为失聪是更深重的苦难），因此她的工作越来越多地涉及助盲事业。由于贝尔的工作与聋人有关，进入20世纪后，贝尔和海伦见面的次数越来越少。

他们都很想念对方。海伦上大学时，贝尔曾尝试用盲文给她写信，海伦称赞他没有出现任何错误。"简直就像你紧握住我的手，像以前那样疼爱地对我说话一样。"海伦在信中写道。1907年，贝尔在给海伦的信中写道："我经常想起你，觉得有写信的冲动，但你知道，我很忙……总是要写很多回信。"贝尔有时用布莱叶盲文写信，但次数不多，因为这样写信并不容易。有一次，贝尔在波士顿待了几天，有一天，他试着给海伦家打了很长时间的电话，可是安妮听到铃声的时间太晚了。"我们似乎每次都会错过见到他的机会，"海伦在写给约翰·希茨的信中这样评价此事。作为公众人物，每个人都大致知道对方在忙什么。海伦1902年写道："我猜，贝尔先生的心里只装着风筝和飞行器。可怜的人，我多么希望他不要再以这种无益的方式耗费自己的精力——至少在我看来徒劳无益。"但六年后，海伦给贝尔寄去了祝贺信，祝贺他在航空领域取得的成就，贝尔非常详细地回复了海伦。

1907年1月，海伦给贝尔发来电报："我需要你。"海伦要在纽约的一个盲人会议上发言，但是安妮病了，她一直负责重复海伦的话，帮助人们更好地理解海伦。贝尔立即离开华盛顿前往纽约，献上了他那无与伦比的声音。

1918年夏，海伦请贝尔在一部有关自己生平的电影中扮演贝尔本人。当时贝尔已经71岁，健康状况不稳定，非常容易受夏季高温的影响，而且他"最讨厌出现在电影中"。尽管如此，海伦的信还是深深地打动了他。"这使我回想起很久以前在华盛顿遇到的那个小女孩。"贝尔在信中写道。贝尔提醒道："你应该找一个黑头发的人来扮演你童年时代的亚历山大·格拉汉姆·贝尔。"不过贝尔承诺，如果海伦希望他出现，炎热的天气结束后，他将和海伦一起出现在以后的场景中。令他感到欣慰的是，海伦没有再找他（这也是好事，因为这部电影后来证明无论从戏剧还是历史角度都失败了，有点滑稽）。

但不管怎样，拍摄这部影片的十五年前，海伦·凯勒的自传《我的人生故事》就已经出版，故事讲述了对海伦·凯勒的救赎以及她的励志故事，堪称海伦人生经历更持久的讲述形式。这本书以海伦本人和安妮·莎莉文的信件作为补充，叙述并证实了历史上最感人的胜利。书的开头是这样一段话：

> 谨以《我的人生故事》
> 致敬亚历山大·格拉汉姆·贝尔
> 是他
> 教会聋人说话
> 使倾听的耳朵
> 能够听到从大西洋
> 传到落基山脉的声音。

（彭萍 译）

24

The Natural Superiority of Women

女人天生优越论

Ashley Montagu
阿什利·蒙塔古

(1905–1999)

ABOUT THE AUTHOR

Ashley Montagu (1905–1999) is an anthropologist and social biologist, noted for his works popularizing anthropology and science. He was born and educated in London, but obtained his Ph.D. from Columbia University. He has taught and lectured at a number of schools, including Harvard, Princeton, Rutgers, the University of California, Santa Barbara, and New York University. Besides many other positions, he is also Editor of National Historical Society Series. His recent works include: *Man, His First Two Million Years*, (1969); *Sex, Man, and Society*, (1969); *The Ignorance of Certainty*, (1970); *Immortality, Religion, and Morals*, (1971); *Textbook of Human Genetics*, (1971); *The Elephant Man*, (1971).

作者简介

阿什利·蒙塔古（1905—1999），人类学家和社会生物学家，以其普及人类学和科学的作品而闻名。他在伦敦出生并接受教育，后来获得美国哥伦比亚大学的博士学位。他曾任教于美国多所高校，包括哈佛大学、普林斯顿大学、罗格斯大学、加州大学圣塔芭芭拉分校和纽约大学等。在诸多职位之外，他还是"国家历史学会丛书"的编者。出版有《人类诞生之初的两百万年》(1969)、《性、男人和社会》(1969)、《对确定性的无知》(1970)、《不朽、宗教和道德》(1971)、《人类遗传学教程》(1971) 和《象人》(1971)。

ABOUT THE SELECTION	Women possess many biological advantages and a competence in social understanding. Physically and psychically, they seem to be stronger and more resistant than men. Women have had to be so unselfish, forbearing, self-sacrificing, and maternal that they possess a deeper understanding than men of what it is to be human. Professor Montagu thinks, in this selection, that with this natural superiority, it is the women's function to help men learn (or to teach men) how to be more human. It will always be true that the hand that rocks the cradle is the hand that rules the world; and the love of a mother for her child is the basic patent and model for all human relationships.
内容简介	女人拥有许多生理优势和一种社会理解能力。在生理和心理上，她们似乎更强大，抵抗力比男性更好。正是因为女性不得不无私宽容，不得不自我牺牲，不得不表现出母性，她们对于"何为人"的理解才比男性更深刻。蒙塔古教授在本文中认为，因为女人这种天生的优越性，她的职能是帮助男人学习（或者教导男人）如何做人。摇动摇篮的手就是统治世界的手，这个说法永远是正确的；母亲对孩子的爱是所有人类关系的基本状态和模式。

女人天生优越论
The Natural Superiority of Women

Oh, no! I can hear it said, not superior. Equal, partners, complementary, different, but not superior. I can even foresee that men will mostly smile, while women, alarmed, will rise to the defense of men[1]—women always have, and always will. I hope that what I shall have to say in this article will make them even more willing to do so, for men need their help more than they as yet, mostly, consciously realize.

Women superior to men? This is a new idea. There have been people who have cogently[2] but apparently not convincingly, argued that women were as good as men, but I do not recall anyone who has publicly provided the evidence or even argued that women were better than or superior to men. How, indeed, could one argue such a case in the face of all the evidence to the contrary? Is it not a fact that by far the largest number of geniuses, great painters, poets, philosophers, scientists, etc., etc., have been men, and that women have made, by comparison, a very poor showing? Clearly the superiority is with men? Where are the Leonardos,[3] the Michelangelos,[4] the Shakespeares,[5] the Donnes,[6] the Galileos,[7] the Whiteheads,[8] the Kants,[9] the Bachs,[10] et al.,[11] of the feminine sex? In fields in which women have excelled, in poetry and the novel, how many poets and novelists of the really first rank have there been? Haven't well-bred young women been educated for centuries in music? And how many among them have been great composers or instrumentalists? Composers—none of the first rank. Instrumentalists—well, in the recent period there have been such accomplished artists as Myra Hess and Wanda Landowska.[12] Possibly there is a clue here to the answer to the question asked. May it not be that women are just about to emerge[13] from the period of subjection[14] during which they were the "niggers"[15] of the masculine world?

The Royal Society of London[16] has at last opened its doors and admitted women to the highest honor which it is in the power of the English scientific world to bestow—the Fellowship of the Royal Society. I well remember that when I was a youth—less than a quarter of a century ago—it was considered inconceivable[17] that any woman would ever have brains enough to attain great distinction in science. Mme. Curie[18] was an exception. But the half dozen women Fellows of the Royal Society in England are not. Nor is Lisa Meitner.[19] And Mme. Curie no longer remains the only woman to share in the Nobel Prize[20] award for science. There is Marie Curie's daughter, Irène Joliot-Curie,[21] and there is Gerty Cory (1947) for physiology and medicine. Nobel prizes in literature have gone to Selma Lagerlof,[22] Grazia Deledda,[23] Sigrid Undset,[24] Pearl Buck[25] and Gabriela Mistral.[26] As an artist Mary Cassatt[27] (1845-1926) was every bit as good as her great French friends Degas and Manet[28] considered her to be, but it has taken the rest of the world another fifty years grudgingly[29] to admit it. Among contemporaries Georgia O'Keeffe[30] can hold her own[31] with the best.

It is not, however, going to be any part of this article to show that women are about to emerge as superior scientists, musicians, painters, or the like. I believe that in these fields they may emerge as equally good, and possibly not in as large numbers as men, largely because the motivations and aspirations[32] of most women will continue to be directed elsewhere. But what must be pointed out is that women are, in fact, just beginning to emerge from the period of subjection when they were treated in a manner not unlike that which is still meted out[33] to the Negro in the Western world. The women of the nineteenth century were the "niggers" of the male-dominated world. All the traits that are mythically attributed to[34] the Negro at the present time were for many generations saddled upon[35] women. Women had smaller brains than men and less intelligence, they were more emotional and unstable, in a Crisis you could always rely upon them to swoon or become otherwise helpless, they were weak and sickly creatures, they had little judgment and less sense, could not be relied upon to handle money, and as for the world outside, there they could be employed only at the most menial[36] and routine tasks.

The biggest dent[37] in this series of myths was made by World War I, when women were for the first time called upon[38] to replace men in occupations which were formerly the exclusive preserve of men. They became bus drivers, conductors, factory workers, farm workers, laborers, supervisors, executive officers, and a great many other things at which many had believed they could never work. At first it was said that they didn't do as well as men, then it was grudgingly admitted that they weren't so bad, and by the time the war was over many employers were reluctant to exchange their women employees for men! But the truth was out—women could do as well as men in most of the fields which had been considered forever closed to them because of their alleged[39] natural incapacities, and in many fields, particularly where delicate precision work was involved, they had proved themselves superior to men. From 1918 to 1939 the period for women was one essentially of consolidation[40] of gains, so that by the time that World War II broke out there was no hesitation on the part of anyone in calling upon women to serve in the civilian roles of men and in many cases also in the armed services.

But women have a long way to go before they reach full emancipation[41]— emancipation from the myths from which they themselves suffer. It is, of course, untrue that women have smaller brains than men. The fact is that in proportion to body weight they have larger brains than men, but this fact is in itself of no importance because within the limits of normal variation of brain size and weight there exists no relation between these factors and intelligence. Women have been conditioned[42] to believe that they are inferior to men, and they have assumed that what everyone believes is a fact of nature; and as men occupy the superior positions in almost all societies, this superiority is taken to be a natural one. "Woman's place is in the home" and man's place is in the counting house and on the board of directors. "Women should not meddle in men's affairs." And yet the world does move. Some women have become Members of Parliament and even attained Cabinet rank. In the United States they have even gotten as far as the Senate. They have participated in peace conferences, but it is still inconceivable to most persons that there should ever be a woman Prime Minister or President. And yet that day, too, will come. *Eppure si muove.*[43]

Woman has successfully passed through the abolition[44] period, the abolition of her thraldom[45] to man, she has now to pass successfully through the period of emancipation, the freeing of herself from the myth of inferiority, and the realization of her potentialities to the fullest.

And now for the evidence which proves the superiority of woman to man. But first, one word in explanation of the use of the word "superiority." The word is used in its common sense as being of better quality than, or of higher nature or character. Let us begin at the very beginning. What about the structure of the sexes? Does one show any superiority over the other? The answer is a resounding "Yes!" And I should like this "Yes" to resound all over the world, for no one has made anything of this key fact which lies at the base of all the differences between the sexes and the superiority of the female to the male. I refer to the chromosomal[46] structure of the sexes. The chromosomes, those small cellular bodies which contain the hereditary particles, the genes, which so substantially influence one's development and fate as an organism, provide us with our basic facts.

In the sex cells there are twenty-three chromosomes, but only one of these is a sex chromosome. There are two kinds of sex chromosomes, X and Y. Half the sperm[47] cells carry X and half carry Y chromosomes. All the female ova[48] are made up of X-chromosomes. When an X-bearing sperm fertilizes an ovum the offspring is always female. When a Y-bearing chromosome fertilizes an ovum the offspring is always male. And this is what makes the difference between the sexes. So what? Well, the sad fact is that the Y-chromosome is but an iota,[49] the merest bit, of a remnant[50] of an X-chromosome; it is a crippled X-chromosome. The X-chromosomes are fully developed structures, the Y-chromosome is the merest comma.[51] It is as if in the evolution of sex a particle one day broke away from an X-chromosome, and thereafter in relation to X-chromosomes could produce only an incomplete female—the creature we now call the male! It is to this original chromosomal deficiency that all the various troubles to which the male falls heir can be traced.

In the first place the chromosomal deficiency of the male determines his incapacity to have babies. This has always been a sore point with men, though consciously they would be the last to admit it, although in some primitive societies, as among the Australian aborigines, it is the male who conceives a child by dreaming it, and then telling his wife. In this way a child is eventually born to them, the wife being merely the incubator[52] who batches the egg placed there through the grace of her husband.

The fact that men cannot have babies and suckle them nor remain in association with their children as closely as the wife has an enormous effect upon their subsequent psychological development. Omitting altogether from consideration the psychologic influences exercised by the differences in the hormonal secretions[53] of the sexes, one can safely say that the mother-child relationship confers enormous benefits[54] upon the mother which are not nearly so substantively operative in the necessary absence of such a relationship between father and child. The maternalizing influences of being a mother in addition to the fact of being a woman has from the very beginning of the human species—about a million years ago—made the female the more humane of the sexes. The love of a mother for her child is the basic patent[55] and the model for all human relationships. Indeed, to the extent to which men approximate[56] in their relationships with their fellow men to the love of the mother for her child, to that extent do they move more closely to the attainment of perfect human relations. The mother-child relationship is a dependent-interdependent one. The interstimulation between mother and child is something which the father misses, and to that extent suffers from the want[57] of. In short, the female in the mother-child relationship has the advantage of having to be more considerate, more self sacrificing, more cooperative, and more altruistic[58] than usually falls to the lot[59] of the male.

The female thus acquires, in addition to whatever natural biological advantages she starts with, a competence in social understanding which is usually denied the male. This, I take it, is one of the reasons why women are usually so much more able to perceive the nuances[60] and pick up the subliminal signs in human behavior which almost invariably pass men by.[61] It was, I believe, George Jean Nathan[62] who called woman's intuition merely man's transparency. With all due deference[63] to Mr. Nathan and sympathy for his lot as a mere male, I would suggest that man's opacity would be nearer the mark.[64] It is because women have had to be so unselfish and forbearing and self-sacrificing and maternal that they possess a deeper understanding than men of what it is to be human. What is so frequently termed feminine indecision, the inability of women to make up their minds, is in fact an inverse reflection of the trigger-thinking[65] of men. Every salesgirl prefers the male customer because women take time[66] to think about what they are buying, and the male usually hasn't the sense enough to do so. Women don't think in terms of "Yes" or "No." Life isn't as simple as all that—except to males. Men tend to think in terms of the all-or-none principle, in terms of black and white. Women are more ready to make adjustments, to consider the alternative possibilities, and see the other colors and gradations in the range between black and white.

By comparison with the deep involvement of women in living, men appear to be only superficially so. Compare the love of a male for a female with the love of the female for the male. It is the difference between a rivulet and a great deep ocean. Women love the human race, men are, on the whole, hostile to it. Men act as if they haven't been adequately loved, as if they had been frustrated and rendered hostile, and becoming aggressive they say that aggressiveness is natural and women are inferior in this respect because they tend to be gentle and unaggressive! But it is precisely in this capacity to love and unaggressiveness that the superiority of women to men is demonstrated, for whether it be natural to be loving and cooperative or not, so far as the human species is concerned, its evolutionary destiny, its very survival is more closely tied to this capacity for love and cooperation than with any other. So that unless men learn from women how to be more loving and cooperative they will go on making the kind of mess of the world which they have so effectively achieved thus far.

And this is, of course, where women can realize their power for good in the world, and make their greatest gains. It is the function of women to teach men how to be human. Women must not permit themselves to be deviated from[67] this function by those who tell them that their place is in the home in subservient[68] relation to man. It is, indeed, in the home that the foundations of the kind of world in which we live are laid, and in this sense it will always remain true that the hand that rocks the cradle is the hand that rules the world. And it is in this sense that women must assume the job of making men who will know how to make a world fit for human beings to live in. The greatest single step forward in this direction will be made when women consciously assume this task—the task of teaching their children to be like themselves, loving and cooperative.

As for geniuses, I think that almost everyone will agree that there have been more geniuses for being human among women than there have among men. This, after all, is the true genius of women, and it is because we have not valued the qualities for being human anywhere nearly as highly as we have valued those for accomplishment in the arts and sciences that we have out-of-focusedly[69] almost forgotten them. Surely, the most valuable quality in any human being is his capacity for being loving and cooperative. We have been placing our emphases on the wrong values—it is time we recognized what every man and every woman at the very least subconsciously knows—the value of being loving, and the value of those who can teach this better than anyone else.

Physically and psychically women are by far the superiors of men. The old chestnut[70] about women being more emotional than men has been forever destroyed by the facts of two great wars. Women under blockade, heavy bombardment, concentration camp confinement, and similar rigors withstand them vastly more successfully than men. The psychiatric casualties[71] of civilian populations under such conditions are mostly masculine, and there are more men in our mental hospitals than there are women. The steady hand at the helm[72] is the hand that has had the practice at rocking the cradle. Because of their greater size and weight men are physically more powerful than women—which is not the same thing as saying that they are stronger. A man of the same size and weight as a woman of comparable background and occupational status would probably not be any more powerful than a woman. As far as constitutional strength is concerned women are stronger than men. Many diseases from which men suffer can be shown to be largely influenced by their relation to the male Y-chromosome. From fertilization on more males die than females. Deaths from almost all causes are more frequent in males at all ages. Though women are more frequently ill than men, they recover from illness more easily and more frequently than men.

Women, in short, are fundamentally more resistant than men. With the exception of the organ systems subserving[73] the functions of reproduction women suffer much less frequently than men from the serious disorders[74] which affect mankind. With the exception of India women everywhere live longer than men. For example, the expectation of life of the female child of white parentage in the United States at the present time is over seventy-one years, whereas for the male it is only sixty-five and a half years. Women are both biologically stronger and emotionally better shock absorbers than men. The myth of masculine superiority once played such havoc[75] with the facts that in the nineteenth century it was frequently denied by psychiatrists that the superior male could ever suffer from hysteria. Today it is fairly well known that males suffer from hysteria and hysteriform conditions with a preponderance[76] over the female of seven to one! Epilepsy[77] is much more frequent in males, and stuttering has an incidence of eight males to one female.

At least four disorders are now definitely known to be due to genes carried in the Y-chromosomes, and hence are disorders which can appear only in males. These are barklike skin (ichthyosis hystrix gravior), dense hairy growth on the ears (hypertrichosis), nonpainful hard lesions[78] of the hands and feet (keratoma dissipatum), and a form of webbing of the toes. It is, however, probable that the disadvantages accruing to[79] the male are not so much due to what is in the Y-chromosome as to what is wanting in it. This is well shown in such serious disorders as hemophilia[80] or bleeder's disease. Hemophilia is inherited as a single sex-linked recessive[81] gene. The gene, or hereditary particle, determining hemophilia is linked to the X-chromosome. When, then, an X-chromosome which carries the hemophilia gene is transmitted to a female it is highly improbable that it will encounter another X-chromosome carrying such a gene, hence, while not impossible, hemophilia has never been described in a female. Females are the most usual transmitters of the hemophilia gene; but it is only the males who are affected, and they are affected because they don't have any properties[82] in their Y-chromosome capable of suppressing the action of the hemophilia gene. The mechanism of and the explanation for (red-green) color blindness is the same. About 8 per cent of all white males are color blind, but only half of one per cent of females are so affected.

Need one go on? Here, in fact, we have the explanation of the greater constitutional strength of the female as compared with the male, namely, in the possession of two complete sex chromosomes by the female and only one by the male. This may not be, and probably is not, the complete explanation of the physical inferiorities of the male as compared with the female, but it is certainly physiologically the most demonstrable and least questionable one. To the unbiased student of the facts there can no longer remain any doubt of the constitutional superiority of the female. I hope that I have removed any remaining doubts about her psychological superiority where psychological superiority most counts, namely, in a human being's capacity for loving other human beings.

I think we have overemphasized the value of intellectual qualities and grossly underemphasized the value of the qualities of humanity which women possess to such a high degree. I hope I shall not be taken for an anti-intellectual when I say that intellect without humanity is not good enough, and that what the world is suffering from at the present time is not so much an overabundance of intellect as an insufficiency of humanity. Consider men like Stalin and Hitler.[83] These are the extreme cases. What these men lacked was the capacity to love. What they possessed in so eminent a degree was the capacity to hate. It is not for nothing that the Bolsheviks[84] attempted to abolish the family and masculinize women, while the Nazis made informers of children against their parents and put the state so much before the family that it became a behemoth[85] which has well-nigh destroyed everyone who was victimized by it.

What the world stands so much in need of at the present time, and what it will continue to need if it is to endure and increase in happiness, is more of the maternal spirit and less of the masculine. We need more persons who will love and less who will hate, and we need to understand how we can produce them; for if we don't try to understand how we may do so we shall continue to flounder in the morass of misunderstanding[86] which frustrated love creates. For frustrated love, the frustration of the tendencies to love with which the infant is born, constitutes hostility. Hatred is love frustrated. This is what too many men suffer from and an insufficient number of women recognize, or at least too many women behave as if they didn't recognize it. What most women have learned to recognize is that the much-bruited[87] superiority of the male isn't all that it's cracked up to be.[88] The male doesn't seem to be as wise and as steady as they were taught to believe. But there appears to be a conspiracy of silence on this subject. Perhaps women feel that men ought to be maintained in the illusion of their superiority because it might not be good for them or the world to learn the truth. In this sense this article, perhaps, should have been entitled "What Every Woman Knows." But I'm not sure that every woman knows it. What I am sure of is that many women don't appear to know it, and that there are even many women who are horrified at the thought that anyone can entertain the idea[89] that women are anything but inferior to men. This sort of childishness does no one any good. The world is in a mess. Men, without any assistance from women, have created it, and they have created it, not because they have been failed by women, but because men have never really given women a chance to serve them as they are best equipped to do—by teaching men how to love their fellow men.

Women must cease supporting men for the wrong reasons in the wrong sort of way, and thus cease causing men to marry them for the wrong reasons, too. "That's what a man wants in a wife, mostly," says Mrs. Poyser (in *"Adam Bede"*),[90] "he wants to make sure o'one fool as 'ull tell him he's wise." Well, it's time that men learned the truth, and perhaps they are likely to take it more gracefully from another male[91] than from their unacknowledged betters.[92] It is equally important that women learn the truth, too, for it is to them that the most important part, the more fundamental part of the task of remaking the world will fall, for the world will be remade only by remaking, or rather helping, human beings to realize themselves more fully in terms of what their mothers have to give them. Without adequate mothers life becomes inadequate, nasty, and unsatisfactory, and Mother Earth becomes a battlefield on which fathers slay their young and are themselves slain.

Men have had a long run for their money in running the affairs of the world. It is time that women realized that men will continue to run the world for some time yet, and that they can best assist them to run it more humanely by teaching them, when young, what humanity means. Men will thus not feel that they are being demoted, but rather that their potentialities for good are so much more increased, and what is more important, instead of feeling hostile towards women, they will for the first time learn to appreciate them at their proper worth. There is an old Spanish proverb which has it that a good wife is the workmanship of a good husband. Maybe. But of one thing we can be certain: a good husband is the workmanship of a good mother. The best of all ways in which men can help themselves is to help women realize themselves. This way both sexes will come for the first time fully into their own, and the world of mankind may then look forward to a happier history than it has thus far enjoyed.

NOTES

1. rise to the defense of men: stand up to the protection of men.
2. cogently: well-groundedly; authoritatively.
3. the Leonardos: the great painters. Leonardo da Vinci (1452-1519) was an Italian painter, sculptor, architect, musician, engineer, mathematician, and scientist.
4. the Michelangelos: the great sculptors. Michelangelo Buonarroti (1475-1564) was an Italian sculptor, painter, architect, and poet.

5. William Shakespeare (1564-1616): English poet and dramatist.
6. John Donne (1573-1631): English poet and clergyman.
7. Galileo Galilei (1564-1642): Italian physicist and astronomer.
8. Alfred North Whitehead (1861-1947): English philosopher and mathematician who lived in the United States after 1924. The Whiteheads means the great philosophers.
9. Immanuel Kant (1724-1804): German philosopher.
10. Johann Sebastian Bach (1685-1750): German organist and composer.
11. et al.: and others.
12. Myra Hess and Wanda Landowska: Dame Myra Hess (1890-1965) was an English pianist who won fame for her playing of works by Scarlatti, Bach, and Mozart; Wanda Landowska (1879-1959) was a famous Polish harpsichordist, pianist, and composer.
13. are just about to emerge: are just going to come out.
14. subjection: inferiority.
15. niggers: offended and disparaged people like the American Negroes.
16. Royal Society of London: The Royal Society of London for the Advancement of Science is a society through which the British government has supported scientific investigation since 1662. It awards four annual medals for scientific achievement and merit.
17. inconceivable: unbelievable.
18. Mme. Curie: Madame Marie Curie (1867-1935) was a Polish physicist and chemist in France. She and her husband were the co-discoverers of radium in 1898. She won the Nobel Prize for physics in 1903 and for chemistry in 1911.
19. Lisa Meitner: born 1878, Austrian nuclear physicist.
20. Nobel Prize: one of a group of prizes awarded annually from the bequest of Alfred B. Nobel (Swedish engineer, manufacturer and philanthropist, 1833-1896) for achievement during the preceding year in physics, chemistry, medicine or physiology, literature, and the promotion of peace.
21. Irène Joliot-Curie (1897-1956): daughter of Pierre and Marie Curie, French nuclear physicist who won the Nobel Prize for chemistry in 1935.
22. Selma Lagerlof (1858-1940): Swedish novelist and poet who won the Nobel Prize in 1909.
23. Grazia Deledda (1875-1936): Italian novelist who won the Nobel

Prize in 1926.
24. Sigrid Undset (1882-1949): Norwegian novelist and winner of the Nobel Prize in 1928.
25. Pearl Buck (1892-1973): U.S. novelist and winner of the Nobel Prize in 1938.
26. Gabriela Mistral (1889-1957): Chilean poet and educator who won the Nobel Prize for literature in 1945.
27. Mary Cassatt (1845-1926): U.S. painter.
28. Degas and Manet: Hilaire Germain Edgar Degas (1834-1917), French impressionist painter; Edouard Manet (1832-1883), French painter.
29. grudgingly: reluctantly.
30. Georgia O'Keeffe (1887-1986): U.S. painter.
31. hold her own: maintain her position; be a match, compete successfully.
32. aspiration: ambition.
33. meted out: handed out; given; bestowed.
34. attributed to: assigned to; attached to.
35. saddled upon: burdened on.
36. menial: servile; degrading.
37. dent: impression.
38. called upon: urged.
39. alleged: assumed.
40. consolidation: intensification.
41. emancipation: rescue; liberation.
42. conditioned: stipulated; bound.
43. *Eppurer si muove*: Italian for "And yet it moves."
44. abolition: doing away completely with something.
45. thral(l)dom: slavery; bondage; servitude.
46. chromosomal: adjective of "chromosome" which is any of the several thread-like bodies, consisting of chromatin, found in a cell nucleus, that carry the genes in a linear order.
47. sperm: a male reproductive cell.
48. ova: plural form for "ovum" which is the female reproductive cell.
49. iota: a very small quantity.
50. remnant: a fragment.
51. comma: a small fragment.
52. incubator: egg hatcher; baby keeper.
53. secretion: excretion, bodily discharge.

54. confers enormous benefits: do much good.
55. patent: right.
56. approximate: resemble; similarize.
57. want: deficiency; absence.
58. altruistic: generous; great-hearted; humanistic; philanthropic.
59. lot: destiny or fate.
60. nuances: a subtle shade of expression, meaning, feeling.
61. pass men by: be ignored by men.
62. George Jean Nathan (1882-1958): U.S. drama critic, author, and editor.
63. deference: respect.
64. man's opacity would be nearer the mark: man's obscurity and unclearness would be more relevant.
65. trigger-thinking: heedless, touch-off thinking.
66. take time: be slow or leisurely.
67. deviated from: departed from.
68. subservient: subject; inferior; subordinate.
69. out-of-focusedly: indistinguishably; vaguely; unrecognizably.
70. chestnut: an old or stale joke.
71. psychiatric casualties: people who are harmed by mental and psychiatric sickness.
72. helm: the place or post of control.
73. subserving: being instrumental to.
74. disorders: derangements of physical or mental health or function.
75. havoc: ruinous damage; harm.
76. preponderance: predominance.
77. epilepsy: a disorder of the nervous system, usually characterized by fits of convulsions that end with loss of consciousness.
78. lesions: any localized abnormal structural change in the body.
79. accruing to: falling on.
80. hemophilia: an abnormal condition of the males inherited through the mother, characterized by a tendency to bleed immoderately, as from an insignificant wound, caused by improper coagulation of the blood.
81. recessive: retreating; receding.
82. properties: characteristics; possessions.
83. Lenin, Stalin, and Hitler: Nikolai or Vladimir Ilyich Lenin (1870-1924), Rusian revolutionary and premier; Joseph V. Stalin (1879-

1953), Russian dictator and premier; Adolf Hitler (1889-1945), Nazi dictator of Germany.
84. Bolsheviks: members of the Russian Communist party.
85. behemoth: a monstrous and grotesque thing.
86. flounder in the morass of misunderstanding: stumble and have trouble in the marshy land of misunderstanding.
87. bruited: spread; advertized.
88. it's cracked up to be: it's praised to be; it's supposed to be.
89. entertain the idea: think of; hold the thought.
90. *Adam Bede*: a novel about the tragic love of a young carpenter by George Eliot (1819-1880), an English novelist.
91. another male: the author himself.
92. unacknowledged betters: unthanked, unrewarded superiors, i.e. the women.

参考译文

哦，不可能！我能听到有人在说，女人不可能比男人优越。男女是平等的，男人和女人是伙伴，他们可以互补，女人和男人不同，但不可能比男人优越。我甚至可以预见到，大多数男人的反应是微微一笑，而女人则会惊慌失措地站出来为男人辩护——女人一直是这么做的，而且未来还会一直这么做。我希望我在这篇文章中所说的话会让她们更愿意这样做，因为男人需要她们的帮助，远比她们清醒意识到的多。

女人比男人优越？这是一个新观念。曾经有一些人很中肯地认为女人和男人一样优秀，但他们显然没有足够的说服力。可是，我不记得有谁公开提供过这样的证据，或者甚至认为女人比男人更好或更优越。确实，面对着所有那些完全相反的证据，人们怎么可能提出这样的观点呢？到目前为止，绝大多数的天才、伟大的画家、诗人、哲学家、科学家等等，都是男人，相比之下，女人的表现差强人意，这难道不是事实吗？很明显，优势在男人一边？女性中的列奥纳多、米开朗基罗、多恩、伽利略、莎士比亚、怀特黑德、康德、巴赫以及其他天才在哪里？在女性擅长的领域，如诗歌和小说，有多少真正一流的女性诗人和小说家？几个世纪以来，有教养的年轻女性不是一直在接受音乐教育吗？她们中又有多少人是伟大的作曲家或乐器演奏家呢？作曲家——没有一个是一流的。器乐家——好吧，近几十年有过像迈拉·海丝和旺达·兰多芙斯卡这样有成就的艺术家。关于前面的问题，这里可能有一条线索有助于回答。之所以这样，难道不是因为女人刚刚开始从一个屈从时代中走出来吗？在那个时代，她们是男人世界里的"黑鬼"。

伦敦皇家学会终于敞开大门，允许女性获得英国科学界有权授予的最高荣誉——皇家学会会员资格。我清楚地记得，在我还是个年轻人时——不到四分之一个世纪以前——如果有哪个女人有足够的智慧能在科学领域取得巨大成就，那简直不可想象，那时候居里夫人是个例外。但现在英国皇家学会里的五六个女会员不再是例外，莉泽·迈特纳也不是例外。居里夫人不再是唯一分享诺贝尔科学奖奖项的女性，除了她之外还有她的女儿伊蕾娜·约里奥·居里，以及获得诺贝生理学或医学奖的格蒂·科里（1947年）。诺贝尔文学奖的得主中有塞尔玛·拉格洛夫、格拉齐亚·黛莱达、西格丽德·温塞特、赛珍珠和加夫列拉·米斯特拉尔。作为一名艺术家，玛丽·卡萨特（1845—1926）的优秀程度完全配得上她伟大的法国朋友德加和马奈对她的评价，但这个世界上的其他人又过了五十年才勉强承认这一点。乔治娅·奥·吉弗在同时代的画家中可以和最出色的同行相提并论。

然而，我不打算在这篇文章的任何部分证明女人将成为优于男人的科学家、音乐家、画家或其他的什么家。我相信，在这些领域，她们可以和男人同样优秀，但数量可能没有男人多，主要是因为大多数女人的动机和抱负会继续被引向其他地方。但必须指出的是，事实上，女人刚刚开始摆脱屈从于男人的时期，那时她们得到的待遇与现在西方世界黑人得到的待遇差不多。19世纪的女人是男人主导的世界中的"黑鬼"。我们现在算在黑人头上的所有那些并不存在的特征，在过去的几代都被强加在女人身上。女人的脑容量比男人小，智力比男人低，女人更情绪化，更不稳定，出现危机时，她们总是晕倒或手足无措，她们是软弱而多病的生物，她们缺乏判断力，没有男人理智，不能指望她们管钱，至于在家庭之外的世界里，她们只能从事一些最琐碎常规的工作。

第一次世界大战给这一系列无稽之谈带来了最大的冲击，当时女人第一次被要求取代男人从事过去只属于男人的职业。她们成为公共汽车司机、售票员、工厂工人、农场工人、体力劳动者、管理者、行政官员，以及许多她们原本被认为永远无法从事的工作。起初，人们说她们做得不如男人好，后来勉强承认她们没有那么糟糕，到战争结束时，许多雇主都不愿意把女员工换成男人！但那时人们已经知道了真相——女人在大多数领域都能做得和男人一样好，可是在过去，因为所谓的天生能力不足，人们认为她们永远无法涉足这些领域；在许多领域，特别是涉及精细准确的工作时，她们已经证明自己比男人强。从1918到1939年，对女性来说，这段时期基本上是巩固成果的时期，因此，在第二次世界大战爆发时，人们毫不犹豫地让女人承担男人的文职工作，而且在许多情况下，还让她们加入武装队伍。

但是女人在获得完全解放之前还有很长的路要走——她们要从让自己遭受痛苦的无稽之谈中解放出来。说女人的脑容量比男人小的说法当然不是真的。事实是，按照与体重的比例，她们的脑容量比男人大，但这一事实本身并不重要，因为在脑容量和体重的正常变化范围内，这些因素与智力之间没有关系。女人一直被灌输自己比男人差的观点，她们觉得大家都相信的事情就是理所当然的事实；由于男人在几乎所有的社会中都占据着优越地位，这种优越性被视为理所当然。"女人的位置在家里",而男人的位置在账房和董事会。"女人不应该插手男人的事情"。然而,世界确实在进步。一些女人已经成为国会议员,甚至达到了内阁级别。在美国,她们甚至已经进入了参议院。她们参加了和平会议,但对大多数人来说,他们仍然无法想象会有一位女总理或女总统。然而,这一天也终将到来。Eppure si muove.(然而,它确实在动。)

女人已经成功地度过了废除期,废除了男人对她的奴役,她现在必须成功地度过解放期,把自己从不如男人的无稽之谈中解放出来,并最充分地实现她的潜能。

现在来看证明女人优越于男人的证据。但首先要解释一下"优越"这个词的用法。这个词在普通意义上是指有更好的质量,或具有更高的性质或特征。让我们从头开始说起。两性的结构如何?一种性别是否显示出比另一个性别优越?答案是响亮的"是!"我希望这个"是"能响彻全世界,因为没有人对这个关键事实做出过任何解释,而这个事实是所有性别差异的基础,也解释了女性为什么比男性优越。我指的是两性的染色体结构。染色体是那些含有遗传颗粒的小细胞体,即基因,它对一个人作为有机体的发展和命运有很大影响,它为我们提供了基本信息。

在性细胞中有 23 条染色体,但其中只有一条是性染色体。有两种性染色体,即 X 和 Y。一半的精子细胞携带 X 染色体,一半携带 Y 染色体。所有女性的卵子都是由 X 染色体组成的。当带 X 染色体的精子使卵子受精时,每次的结果都是女孩。当带 Y 染色体的精子使卵子受精时,每次的结果都是男孩。而这正是两性之间的区别所在。那又怎么样呢?好吧,可悲的事实是,Y 染色体是 X 染色体断片的一小部分,只不过是一点点;它是一个有残缺的 X 染色体。X 染色体是充分发展的结构,而 Y 染色体只不过是个断片。这就好像在性的进化过程中,有一天有一个粒子脱离了 X 染色体,这与两个 X 染色体结合的结果相比,只能产生一个不完整的女性——现在被我们称为男性的生物!男性所面临的各种问题都可以追溯到这种原生的染色体缺陷。

首先,男性的染色体缺陷决定了他没有能力生孩子。这一直是男人的痛点,尽管他们绝对不会自觉地承认这一点。不过,在一些原始社会,如在澳大利亚的土著人中,是男性通过做梦怀上孩子,然后告诉他的妻子。通过这种方式,他们最终生下一个孩子,妻子只是一个孵化器,靠她丈夫的恩赐把蛋放在那里让她孵化。

男人不能生孩子,不能给孩子喂奶,也不能像妻子那样与孩子保持密切的联系,这对他们以后的心理发展会产生巨大的影响。如果不考虑两性荷尔蒙分泌的差异所产生的心理影响,我们可以有把握地说,母子关系给母亲带来了巨大的好处,而在父亲和孩子之间注定不存在这种关系,所以他们也无法获得这些好处。从人类诞生之初——大约一百万年前,成为母亲给女人带来的母性就使女性成为更有人性的性别。母亲对孩子的爱是所有人类关系的基本状态和模式。事实上,只要男人在与同伴的关系中接近于母亲对孩子的爱,他们离实现完美的人类关系就会更近一步。母子关系是一种依赖与被依赖的关系。母亲和孩子之间的相互刺激是父亲所没有的,并在一定程度上因为这种缺乏而产生负面影响。简而言之,在母子关系中,女性的优势在于她们不得不比男性更周到,更愿意自我牺牲,更具有合作和利他精神。

这样一来,女性除了天生具有的生理优势外,还获得了男性通常无法获得的社会理解能力。我认为,这就是为什么女性通常更有能力感知人类行为中的细微差别并捕捉到下意识迹象的原因之一,而男性几乎无一例外都不会关注这些。是乔治·让·内森说过吧,女人的直觉不过是男人一眼洞穿的事。出于对内森先生的尊重和对他作为一个普通男性的同情,我想说的是,男人的反应愚钝才更接近事实。正是因为女性不得不无私宽容,不得不自我牺牲,不得不表现出母性,她们对于"何为人"的理解才比男性更深刻。人们常说的女性优柔寡断,女性无法拿定主意,实际上从反面反映了男性一触即发式的草率思维。每个售货员都更喜欢男性顾客,因为女性会花时间反复考虑她们要买什么,而男性通常没有足够的理智这样做。女人不会用"是"或"不是"来思考。生活没那么简单——除了对男性而言。男人倾向于用非此即彼的原则来思考,想问题时非黑即白。女性更愿意做出调整,考虑其他可能性,并看到黑与白之间的其他颜色以及颜色的渐变。

与女性参与生活的深度相比,男性的参与似乎只是表面上的。比较一下男性对女性的爱和女性对男性的爱,这是涓涓细流和浩瀚大海之间的区别。女性热爱人类,男性总体上对人类充满敌意。男人表现得好像他们没有得到充分的爱,好像他们受到了挫折,变得充满敌意具有进攻性,他们说进攻性是天性,女人在这方面不如他们,因为她们往往是温柔的,没有攻击性!但是,正是在这种爱和不具攻击性的能力中,显示了女性比男性优越的事实,因为不管爱和合作的能力是否为天性,就人类物种而言,它演变的未来、它的生存与这种爱和合作的能力密切相关,其密切程度超过与其他任何能力的联系。因此,除非男人向女人学习如何更有爱心和合作精神,否则他们将继续把世界搞得一团糟,在这方面他们已经颇见成果了。

当然,这正是女人能够在这个世界上实现其向善力并取得最大收益的方面。女人的职能是教男人如何做人。女人千万不要因为有人说她们的位置是在家里顺从于男人而偏离这一职能。事实上,是家庭奠定了我们所生活的这种世界的基础,在这个意义上,摇动摇篮的手就是统治世界的手,这个说法永远是正确的。正是在这个意义上,女人必须承担起培养男人的工作,使他们知道如何创造一个适合人类生活的世界。女人要教育她们的孩子像她们自己一样富有爱心和合作精神,当她们有意识地承担起这项任务时，她们在这个方向上就迈出了最大的一步。

至于天赋，我想几乎所有人都会同意，女人在做人方面的天赋要比男人高。说到底这才是女人的真正天赋，但是因为我们对做人品质的重视程度远不及我们对艺术和科学成就的重视程度，所以我们忽视甚至忘记了这些品质。毫无疑问，任何人身上最宝贵的品质就是他有爱和合作的能力。我们一直把重点放在错误的价值上，现在是时候去赞赏每个男人和每个女人至少潜意识里都认可的价值——爱的价值了，以及那些能更好地教人去爱的人的价值。

在生理和心理上，女人远比男人优越。关于女人比男人更情绪化的老生常谈已经被两场大战的事实彻底摧毁。在封锁、猛烈轰炸、集中营禁闭以及类似的严酷环境下，女人比男人更成功地承受了这些考验。在这种条件下，平民中的精神病患者大多是男人，在我们的精神病院里男人比女人多。掌舵的稳健之手是那只摇过摇篮的手。由于男人的体形和体重较大，他们在身体上比女人更有力量——这与说他们更强大是两回事。一个体形体重与女人相同，且背景和职业地位也与女人相当的男人，可能不会比女人更强大。就体质方面的力量而言，女人比男人更强大。男性所患的许多疾病经证明在很大程度上是与男性 Y 染色体的影响相关的。从受精开始，男性的死亡人数就多于女性。不论什么原因造成的死亡，男性的比重在所有年龄段中都更高。尽管女性比男性更经常生病，但她们康复起来比男性更容易，比例也更高。

简而言之，从根本上说，女性的抵抗力比男性更好。除了服务于生殖功能的器官系统外，女性比男性更少受到影响人类的严重疾病的困扰。除印度外，全世界所有地方的女性都比男性长寿。例如，目前在美国，父母是白人的女婴预期寿命超过 71 岁，而男婴的预期寿命只有 65 岁半。女性在生理上比男性更强大，在情感上更能应对冲击。男性优越性的神话曾经混淆视听，以至于在 19

世纪，精神病学家经常会否认高人一等的男性可能会患癌症。今天，众所周知，男性患癌症和类似疾病的比例是女性的 7 倍！这一点是相当清楚的。癫痫在男性中更为常见，男性口吃的发病率是女性的 8 倍。

现在至少有四种疾病被确定为是由于 Y 染色体携带的基因引起的，因此这些疾病只出现在男性身上。这四种疾病是树皮状皮肤（豪猪状鱼鳞病）、耳朵上长有浓密的毛发（多毛症）、手脚上有不痛的硬伤（角化病/角化瘤）以及蹼状趾。然而，很可能的一点是，男性的缺陷与其说是 Y 染色体中的东西造成的，不如说是 Y 染色体中缺少的东西造成的。这一点在血友病等严重疾病中得到了很好的证明。血友病是通过性联隐性基因遗传的。血友病的致病基因或遗传微粒在 X 染色体上。因此，当一条携带血友病基因的 X 染色体遗传给女性时，它不大可能遇到另一条携带同样基因的 X 染色体，因此，女性身上从未出现过血友病，尽管这也不是不可能。女性是血友病基因最常见的传播者，但只有男性会患病，原因是他们的 Y 染色体中没有任何可能够抑制血友病基因作用的特性。（红—绿）色盲的机制和解释是一样的。所有白人男性中约有 8% 是色盲，但女性色盲比例只有 0.5%。

还需要继续说下去吗？事实上，在这里，我们可以解释女性比男性具有更强的体质，即女性拥有两条完整的性染色体，而男性只有一条。这也许不是男性在体质上不如女性的完整解释，也可能没有完整的解释，但它肯定是生理学上最有说服力最不容置疑的解释。对于没有偏见尊重事实的研究者来说，女性在体质上的优越性已不再有任何疑问。如果有人对女性在精神上的优越性尚存疑虑，我希望现在我已经消除了这种疑虑，精神上的优越性在一个人爱其他人的能力方面尤为重要。

我认为我们过分强调了智力素质的价值，而严重低估了女性所拥有的高度人性素质的价值。我认为没有人性的智力是有缺陷的,目前让这个世界遭殃的不是智力过剩而是人性不足,我希望我这么说不会被认为是反智者。想想斯大林和希特勒这些人吧,他们是极端的个案。这些人缺乏的是爱的能力,他们仇恨的能力达到了惊人的程度。布尔什维克试图废除家庭并使女人男性化,而纳粹则让孩子们成为父母的告密者,并将国家置于家庭之上,以至于它成为一个庞然大物,几乎摧毁了所有受害人,他们这么做不是没有缘由的。

如果这个世界要持续下去并变得更加幸福,那么它目前亟需的,而且未来仍然需要的是多一些母性精神,少一些男性精神。我们需要多一些有仁爱之心的人,少一些心存怨恨的人,我们需要了解我们如何能够培养有爱之人;因为如果我们不尝试了解如何才能做到这一点,我们将继续挣扎在因爱受挫所造成的误解的泥潭中。婴儿生而有之的爱的倾向一旦受挫,这种受挫的爱就会成为敌意。仇恨就是受挫的爱。太多的男人都深受其苦,太多的女人没有认识到这一点,或者至少是有太多的女人表现得好像她们根本没有认识到这一点。大多数女人已经学会认识到的是,男人被大肆宣扬的优越性并不全是像被吹嘘的那样。男人似乎并不像她们被灌输认为的那样明智和稳定。但在这个问题上,似乎有一种沉默的共谋。也许女人觉得应该让男人继续停留在他们优越性的幻觉中,因为了解真相对他们和世界都没有好处。在这个意义上,这篇文章的题目也许应该是"每个女人都知道的事实"。但我不确定是否每个女人都知道。我可以肯定的是,许多女人似乎并不了解这一点,甚至有许多女人一想到有人会产生女人绝不比男人差的念头,就会感到惊恐。这种幼稚的表现对谁都没有好处。这个世界正处于混乱之中。男人在没有女人帮助的情况下制造了这种混乱,他们之所以制造了这种混乱,不是因为女人辜负了他们,而是因为男人从来没有真正给女人机会,让她们以最合适的方式为他们服务——教他们如何去爱同伴。

女人必须停止因为错误的理由以错误的方式去支持男人，从而也让男人停止因为错误的理由与她们结婚。"大多数情况下，这就是男人想从妻子那里得到的，"波伊瑟夫人（在《亚当·比德》中）说，"他想确定有一个傻瓜会告诉他，他是聪明的。"好吧，现在该是男人了解真相的时候了，也许从另一个男人那里得知真相会让他们觉得体面些，而不是从那些他们不承认比自己更好的女人那里。同样重要的是，女人也要了解真相，因为重塑世界的任务中最重要的部分、最根本的部分将落在她们身上，因为只有通过重塑，或者说通过帮助人类更充分地实现他们的母亲所能给予的东西，这个世界才能得以改造。没有足够多的母亲，生活就会变得匮乏、令人生厌、让人不满，地球母亲会成为一个战场，在这个战场上，父亲杀死他们的孩子，他们自己也将被杀死。

为了在管理世界事务中获得利益，男人们已历经漫漫长路。现在是时候让女人意识到，男人还要继续管理这个世界一段时间，但她们可以在他们小时候教给他们什么是人性，从而帮助他们更人性化地管理这个世界。这样，男人就不会觉得自己被降级了，而是觉得自己向善的潜力大增，更重要的是，他们不会对女人产生敌意，而是破天荒学会欣赏她们真正的价值。有一句古老的西班牙谚语说，好丈夫塑造好妻子。也许吧。但有一点我们是可以肯定的：一个好丈夫是一个好母亲的作品。在男人能够帮助他们自己的所有方式中，最好的方式是帮助女人实现她们的价值。这样一来，男女双方都将开始完全实现自己的价值，人类世界就可以期待一个比以往任何时候都更幸福的历史。

（章艳 译）

25

Lenses

镜 头

DONALD CULROSS PEATTIE
唐纳德·卡尔罗斯·皮蒂

(1898–1964)

ABOUT THE AUTHOR

Donald Culross Peattie (1898–1964) was an American botanist and author. A native of Chicago and a graduate of Harvard, he had worked for the U. S. Department of Agriculture for four years before he decided to devote himself to writing. The author of more than 30 books of natural science, essays, and fiction, Peattie is best known for his popular nature studies which vividly record the impressions of a sensitive, scholarly mind. In *An Almanac to Moderns* (1935), a journal of his reactions to nature, he perfected that ability to convey an intimate, perceptive, and poetically heightened awareness of nature for which he has been compared to Thoreau. The ancillary *Book of Hours* (1937) was followed by such informative yet stimulating works as *Flowering Earth* (1939), *A Natural History of Trees of Eastern and Central America* (1950) with its sequel on *Western Trees* (1953), and *Sportsman's Country* (1952). *The Road of a Naturalist* (1941) is an autobiography.

作者简介 唐纳德·卡尔罗斯·皮蒂（1898—1964）是美国植物学家、自然文学作家。他在芝加哥出生长大，毕业于哈佛大学。曾在美国农业部工作四年，后成为全职作家。他出版了 30 余部自然科学题材的散文和小说，其中最为人称道的是他的自然观察作品，生动展现了一个敏锐而严谨的学者对自然的印象。在《现代人年鉴》(1935) 这部散文集中，他对自然高度敏锐的感知、亲切而富有诗意的文笔，堪与梭罗相提并论。皮蒂的其他重要作品有《观看自然的 24 小时》(1937)、《鲜花盛开的大地》(1939)、《美国东部和中部树木自然志》(1950)，后者与《西部树木》(1953)、《渔猎者的乡野》(1952) 组成了三部曲。《博物学家的道路》(1941) 是他的自传。

ABOUT THE SELECTION

In *Lenses*, an essay taken from the author's *Green Laurels* (1936), Peattie takes the reader through an account of a rural walk in which he makes several casual observations that finally converge on the microscope and its importance for biology, the investigation of life. The discovery and development of the microscope are then discussed, but the focus of interest is the lens, for it was the lens that first brought living matter to the human eye and revealed the structure of the cell as well as the mystery of fertilization. One of his major themes is "Lenses determine vision." Their revelations of nature have given man a proper perspective of the physical world and started a revolution in biological thinking. As one reads along, one cannot fail to share Peattie's enthusiasm and rapture at taking close looks at nature and its mysteries of life as they emerge under the lens. The author's diction, his vivid images, and his poetic and philosophic insights into the subject matter make *Lenses* a charming and interesting essay.

内容简介 《镜头》一文选自唐纳德·卡尔罗斯·皮蒂的散文集《绿色月桂》(1936)。这篇散文记述了皮蒂的一次乡野漫步,他对途中偶遇几样事物略作观察,最终勾连到显微镜的功用及其在生物学发展史上的意义,联想巧妙而自然。生物学是研究生命的科学,显微镜的发明具有重大意义,而它对于皮蒂最具兴味的便是镜头这个装置,正因有了镜头,人类才第一次看见生命物质,了解细胞构造,发现受精过程的奥秘。本文一个重要的主题是"镜头决定视野",因为镜头所揭示的自然之秘,才让人们对物理世界有了真正的认识,引发了生物学思想的革命。皮蒂透过镜头近距离观察自然及其生命的奥秘,热情和狂喜洋溢于字里行间,富有感染力。他以细腻的文笔描摹出生动的形象,富有诗意和哲思的见解让这篇短小精练的散文拥有了不俗的魅力。

The storm is gone, and here in the country a mild sun has bit by bit argued[1] the cold and snow away. There is the upheaval of a final thaw in the March lawns that are the color of old straw, and in the ponderous black velvet loam,[2] this Illinois sod without a pea-sized pebble in it. Across the roll and dip of the great plain I saw, as I went walking with my blackthorn,[3] the distant woods as blue-black, rainy-looking islands upon the immense watery prairie, and near at hand[4] the young yellow[5] of the willow whips,[6] first brilliance of the year. Now this was a scene a midlander[7] could love, but I went thinking, thinking, wagging that human tail my cane, how all that I saw came to me thus only because of a specified convexity in the cornea of my eye.

My sense of proportion, to say nothing of esthetics,[8] is really superbly egotistic.[9] Matter, to regard it more exactly than humanly,[10] is full of holes. The solidest thing is as a net, the space between the electronic particles is like unto the spaces between the sun and the planets. The trouble with our human concepts is that we are so pitifully small when it comes to the great, and so unbearably gross when it comes to the small. We occupy a position in the scale of things that is somewhat on the trivial side of total mediocrity. Little wonder if our ideas are mediocre too.

A bee, the first of the year, went by with that direct flight of hers—the most practical people in the world, bees, having no eye for scenery and hence no temptation either to wander or to wonder. A hawk cut a great circular glide through the pale blue air above me, balanced, it seemed, upon the tip of one wing, the other wing pointing almost to the zenith. He takes the opposite view of things. He sees all, for miles about, is curious about all, and much of the time appears simply to be enjoying his perspective, save when emotions incomprehensible to me suddenly shake him, and set up a windy metallic clamor.

I cannot ever share the bee's-eye view or the hawk's-eye view. Whatever their God-given lenses showed them of reality, I would never know what it was. I saw the scene in my human way—the roll and dip of the great plain, the black-silver lakes of snow water seeking out unsuspected dimples,[11] the cottonwood stands,[12] very white of bark as they always are at winter's end, looking at a distance lofty and thoughtful, but turning out to be talkative and flimsy.

My swinging cane struck something soft, was delayed in some yielding yet persistent medium.[13] And I knew, even through the blackthorn, that it was living tissue. There is something, about almost any living thing that is plasmic, resilient, and in a way alarming. We say, "I touched something—and it was alive!" There is no such shock in touching that which has never lived. The mineral world is vast, it is mighty, rigid and brittle. But the hand that touches vital matter infallibly recognizes the feel of life and recoils in excitement.

What I had struck was nothing but a big, soggy fungus, a giant puffball[14] persistent[15] from autumn. From the wound I had made in it there was still curling on the airs a smoke of mustard-green powder, I struck it again deliberately, and like a staked snake[16] teased into spewing venom, it coughed forth another belch of spores.[17]

I unscrewed the crystal of my watch, caught a little of the living dust in it, screwed the watch face down upon the upturned glass, and pocketed the whole. At home, at least, I had a pair of eyes that would deprive the infinitely little of half its mystery. Eyes such as neither hawk nor bee possesses, eyes for probing into the nature of Nature, that man has made for himself with monstrous patience, intricate invention piled upon invention.

At my desk, I draw the microscope out of its case, and though it is heavy, it slides out to me, when I grasp it by its middle, with an ease like a greeting. It is a matter of a moment to whisk the fungus spores on a glass slide, a moment more to find them in the lower magnification, and then with a triumphant click to swing the intense myopic[18] gaze of the timer lens upon them.

From a speck as fine as a particle of wandering cigarette smoke, a spore leaps suddenly up at my eyes as a sphere of gold meshed with vitreous green bands that cut up this tiny world, this planetesimal[19] of sealed-up life, into latitude and longitude. Here a living plant has put its substance into minutest compass and launched it upon the air, where only the most wildly improbable chances, really an unbroken series of lucky one-in-a-thousand hazards, would ever see it grow to a puffball. Here was the whole of heredity, here the past and future of a chain of lives.[20] Intricate, formed to a pattern and plan by the stresses[21] within it, organized by the very fact that it had specific form, this frail and tiny speck of life differed, I saw, from the atom of cigarette smoke precisely as the cry of the hawk differed from the squeal of a rusty hinge which it so much resembled.

I would be at a loss to show the difference between the sound made by a living thing and an inorganic noise. But the lens takes soundings[22] for us in the depths of optical dimensions. There is no shock, for the young mind with a bent[23] for science, like the first look through a microscope. I am not likely to forget the moment when I saw the green world of the algae[24] come alive— delicate twisted bands of color in the glassy cell walls, diatoms[25] like bits of carven glass, desmids[26] like a trembling green lace, the hexagonal meshes of the water-net[27] like the work of bobbins, and Oscillatoria,[28] that plant that swims with a slow eel-like motion. Under the lens I witnessed life's crucial event, when I saw the whip-tailed male cells escape from the sack of a sea kelp[29] and assault the great, inert egg cell, like meteors raining upon a ponderous planet. Under that purposeful attack the planet cell began to roll, with a great, a gentle but irresistible momentum, until one dart, predestined, broke through the surface tensions, dropped to the nuclear core like a solid thing descending through a gas, and then the conquered planet ceased its rolling and the rejected meteors dropped away. Life had begun again.

By a coincidence which has no meaning—or perhaps it has every meaning—human fertilization is startlingly like that in the big red seaweed, and who has seen this latter has in effect looked into the very bottom of the well of self.

Because the lens has left scant privacy to Nature, it is difficult for the modern mind to recall what battles were once waged over the subject of fertilization, the sexuality of plants, the structure of the cell. Men without the weapon of the lens tussled then in bootless speculation as the Trojans and Greeks pulled the body of Patroclus this way and that.[30]

One comes at last to feel that the invention of the microscope by Janssen[31] of Holland in the seventeenth century was the beginning of modern natural history, for the lens added a new dimension to our eyes and enabled us literally to see to the heart of many a problem. The sentence I have just written sounds good enough to pass unchallenged. But it sounds better than it is, for it seems to assert that one man invented the microscope, and it leaves us to infer that, once it was invented, men, peering through it, saw truth at last. In fact, however, having seventeenth century minds, they did not in the least make of[32] what they saw what we would. Except for a few larger minds, the early microscopists were largely engaged in watching the antics of fleas.

And the revolution in biological thought consequent on the use of the microscope did not take place in the seventeenth century but in the unfinished century, 1850 to our times. It is the modern technical improvements, coupled with the forward march of allied[33] sciences, that have created the merciful triumphs of bacteriology, carried us into a deep perspective of atomic structure and brought light into the dark mystery of protoplasm itself. The seventeenth century microscopy was necessarily limited by the imperfections of the early instruments, and still more by the state of the allied sciences at the time. But it was, none the less, an era of high adventure in natural history, for the lens, however faulty, gave to all greatly inquisitive minds the first rapturous look at the underworld of structure.

NOTES

1. argued: persuaded.
2. loam: soil.
3. blackthorn: a cane made of the wood of the blackthorn, a European tree or shrub.
4. at hand: near in time or place.
5. young yellow: yellow flowers which have just blossomed.
6. willow whips: whips are tall slender trees unlikely to develop into desirable crop trees and harmful to their neighbors by their swaying. Willow whips refer to willow trees.
7. midlander: one living in the interior or central region of the U. S.
8. esthetics: usually aesthetics, a branch of philosophy dealing with the nature of the beautiful and with the judgment of beauty.
9. egotistic: self-centered.
10. more exactly than humanly: that is, using a microscope. The human eye does not see things exactly.
11. unsuspected dimples: unseen or unknown hollows or depressions in the surface of the land.
12. cottonwood stands: A cotton wood is any of several American trees having a tuft of cottony hairs on the seed. A stand is a group of plants growing in a continuous area.

13. medium: substance.
14. puffball: any of various fungi that discharge ripe spores in a smoke-like cloud when pressed or struck and are often edible.
15. persistent: continuing its existence.
16. staked snake: a snake tied to a piece of wood which is driven into the ground.
17. spores: seeds; 芽孢.
18. myopic: short-sighted.
19. planetesimal: one of numerous small solid heavenly bodies that may have existed at an early stage of the development of the solar system. 微星.
20. The spore is capable of development into a new individual, sometimes unlike the parent, either directly or after fusion with another spore. It is, therefore, the sum of the qualities and potentialities genetically derived from its ancestors (heredity).
21. stresses: forces.
22. takes soundings: takes measurements. A sounding is a measurement of the depth of water ascertained by using a line divided by different markers and weighted at one end with lead.
23. bent: strong inclination or interest.
24. algae: plural for alga; seaweed; water plant.
25. diatom: kinds of minute one-cell water plant usually in easily separable strings when living.
26. desmid: any of numerous one-cell algae.
27. water-net: a freshwater alga.
28. Oscillatoria: a genus of blue-green algae.
29. kelp: any of various large brown seaweeds.
30. In Homer's *Iliad*, Patroclus is the intimate friend of Achilles. When the sulky Achilles withdraws from the fight, and the Greek host is in danger of being routed, he lends Patroclus his armor to fight against the Trojans. Patroclus at first succeeds, but at last is slain by Hector. The Trojans try to carry away his body, but are intercepted by the Greeks.
31. Zacharias Janssen: early seventeenth century Dutch spectacle-maker credited with making first compound microscope.
32. make of: understand; esteem.
33. allied: related.

参考译文

暴雨过后的这片乡野，温和的阳光已将严寒和冰雪一点点劝退。三月的草地是陈年稻草的颜色，地面隆起，土层终于解冻。黑丝绒般的厚重沃土之上，伊利诺伊州的草皮里连一颗豌豆大的石子都没有。我带着黑刺李拐杖出门散步，目光越过连绵起伏的大平原，辽阔润泽的草原上，远方的树林仿佛墨蓝色的群岛，饱含雨意，而近处柳色新黄，是一年中最早呈现的明艳。此番风景正是一个中原居民所爱，而我挥挥手杖这人类的尾巴，心中不断思忖，各色风景以这般模样进入我眼帘，仅仅是因为我眼角膜那个特定的凸面。

且不说审美，我的比例感实在是极度自我中心。若以更精确而非人类的眼光来审视，物质实际上布满了孔隙。最坚固的物质也像一张网，电子粒子之间的空间就像宇宙中太阳与行星之间的空间。我们人类的概念有个问题，倘若论及宏大，我们则渺小得可怜，倘若论及渺小，我们又臃肿不堪。在事物比例的标尺中，我们所处的位置大概是极为平庸、毫不起眼的。难怪我们的想法也平庸。

一只蜜蜂，今年的第一只，她以其特有的轨迹径直飞过。蜜蜂是世上最讲求实际的族群，对风景视若无睹，也就不会受到诱惑而四处漫游惊叹。一只鹰在我头顶的淡蓝色天空绕圈滑翔，似乎是靠着一扇翅膀的尖端平衡自身，另一扇翅膀几乎指向天顶。他的视角恰与蜜蜂相反，能将数英里的土地尽收眼底，对所有事物充满好奇。大部分时间，那只鹰貌似只是在享受它眼中的景观，突然某种难以捉摸的情绪让他身体一颤，发出尖厉如风的啸声。

我永远也无法拥有蜜蜂或是老鹰的视野。上帝所赐的晶状体为其展现的世界，我永远也无法探知。我以人类的方式看见风景——大平原的起起伏伏；银黑色的雪水湖流入不为人知的凹地；成片成片的白杨林，冬日将尽时树皮总是显得格外洁白，远远望去树形高大，气质深沉，其实它们浅薄又饶舌。

我的手杖来回摇摆，戳到了一个软软的东西，陷入某种富有弹性而又坚韧的介质。即使隔着黑刺李手杖，我也知道那是活组织。几乎所有的生物体都有某种原生质，弹性的质地几乎有点吓人。我们会说："我摸到了什么东西——是活的！"若是触摸没有生命的物体，就不会受到这种惊吓。矿物世界浩广无边，能量强大，刚硬易碎。可是当我们触摸到有生命的东西，必然能察觉到那是活物，便会紧张地缩回手去。

我戳到的不过是一大团湿乎乎的真菌，从秋天留存至今的一个大马勃。在我的手杖碰伤的位置，一缕芥末绿色的烟雾静静地在空中缭绕。我故意再戳弄几下，它又咳出一大片孢子，就像一条缠在木桩上的毒蛇被招惹得狂喷毒液。

我拧开怀表的水晶玻璃盖，用它扣住一点活的孢子烟雾，再将表面倒扣，拧紧水晶玻璃盖，然后整个揣进口袋。家里至少还有一双"眼睛"，将能揭开这极尽微小之物的一半神秘。这双眼睛老鹰和蜜蜂都无法拥有，这是探索自然本质的眼睛，是人类以巨大的耐心、层出不穷的复杂发明为自己制造的眼睛。

坐在桌边，我从匣子里取出显微镜，虽然它很重，却滑落下来。我一把抓住镜臂，好像跟它打了个轻盈的招呼。这一刻我需要把真菌孢子轻拂到载玻片上，再花些时间用低倍镜找到孢子，然后咔嗒一声，成功转换到高倍镜，用镜头对准它们。

一颗孢子，这原本细小如缭绕烟雾的微粒，此时突然跃入眼帘，好像一个金色的球体网布着玻璃绿条纹，条纹在这个微小世界——被密封的微星体上——切出经线纬线。这种有生命的植物为组成它的物质安装了最细小的罗盘，然后发射升空。唯有仰赖最微乎其微的可能性，一连串千里挑一的幸运机会，才能看到它发育长成一株马勃。遗传的全部,一条生命链的过去和未来都在此中。这柔弱而微小的点滴生命精妙复杂,内部压力将其塑造成型,其形式本身决定了构造,在我眼里,它有别于香烟烟雾微粒,正如一只鹰的啸鸣有别于与其极为相似的生锈铰链的声音。

我无法展示生命体发出的声音和无机物噪音的区别,但是镜头能够帮助我们测量光学维度的深邃之处。对迷恋科学的年轻人来说,没有什么比透过显微镜看到的第一眼更令人惊叹。我很难忘记看到藻类的绿色世界骤然鲜活的那个瞬间——透明的细胞壁里弯曲精细的色带,硅藻像花雕玻璃的碎片,鼓藻像颤动的绿色蕾丝,水网藻的六边形网状结构像梭编花样,还有颤藻,那以鳗鱼的姿态缓慢游动的藻类。在显微镜的镜头下,我目睹了生命的重大事件,海带那长着鞭毛尾巴的雄性细胞挣脱了囊,对巨大的、惰性的雌性细胞发起攻击,就像流星纷纷撞击一个沉重的行星。在这种意图明确的进攻下,"行星细胞"开始转动,动力强大,它以徐缓却又不可遏止的势头持续,直到一枚"飞镖"命中注定地穿透了表面张力,像一个固体坠入气体那样落入细胞核心,被征服的行星就这样停止了转动,被排斥的流星散落别处。生命再度发生。

人类的受孕和这红色的大海藻惊人地相似,这也许是一桩并无意义的巧合,又或是包含了一切意义。谁目睹过后者的孕育,谁就望穿了自我之井的最深处。

显微镜已经揭开了自然的大部分隐私,因此现代人难以了解受精、植物性别和细胞结构的问题在过去曾引发过怎样的论战。在特洛伊人和希腊人以种种方式挪动帕特洛克罗斯的尸体的时代,还没有镜头装备的人们做出徒劳的猜测,争论不休。

我们渐渐认识到,17世纪荷兰人詹森发明的显微镜是现代博物学研究的开端,因为镜头给肉眼增添了新的维度,让我们能够亲眼看到很多问题的"核心"。我刚写下的这句话听起来足够漂亮，几乎没人会质疑，但是它美化了实际情况，因为这近乎断言显微镜是一个人发明的，而我们便由此推定——有了显微镜，人们透过显微镜观察，便看到了真相。然而事实上，由于 17 世纪人们思维的局限，他们对于看到的东西和我们的反应完全不同。除了少数极为睿智的人士，早期的显微镜学家大部分只是忙于观察跳蚤的可笑动作。

  显微镜的使用引发的生物学思想革命并未在 17 世纪发生，而是在 1850 年至今这个尚未结束的世纪。现代技术发展协同相关科学的进步，创造了细菌生物学的重大胜利，为人类带来福祉，也让我们对原子结构的认识更为深刻，对原生质幽深的秘密世界洞若烛照。早期仪器的缺陷不可避免地限制了 17 世纪显微镜学的发展，相关科学领域的状况更是处处掣肘。但那依然是博物学史上一个重大的开拓时期，因为无论有多少缺陷，借助镜头，所有渴求探索的人们第一次激动万分地看到了生命结构的内部。

（周玮 译）

Religion and Science

宗教与科学

ALBERT EINSTEIN
阿尔伯特·爱因斯坦

(1879–1955)

ABOUT THE AUTHOR   Albert Einstein (1879–1955), leading American theoretical physicist, was born in Germany of Jewish descent. In 1905 he set forth the theory of relativity on electrodynamics of moving bodies and equivalence of mass and mechanical energy. In 1921 he was awarded the Nobel Prize for his contributions to theoretical physics, especially for his work on the photoelectric effect. He fled the Germany of Hitler in 1933 and became a naturalized American citizen. He remained a life member of the Institute for Advanced Study at Princeton University and advocated peaceful use of the atomic energy.

作者简介   阿尔伯特·爱因斯坦(1879—1955)，美籍犹太裔著名理论物理学家，生于德国。1905年，他提出了关于运动物体的电动力学和质能关系的相对论。1921年，他因为对理论物理学的贡献，特别是对光电效应的研究而获得诺贝尔奖。1933年，他逃离了希特勒的德国，成为美国公民。他是普林斯顿高等研究院的终身成员，并倡导和平利用原子能。

ABOUT THE SELECTION

Can a scientist be religious? Can a religious man be a scientist? Religion has always seemed incompatible with science, and medieval history is notorious for religious persecution of scientists whose discoveries were denounced as heresies by the church. Are scientists really atheists totally insensitive to the majestic creation that is nature? Albert Einstein didn't think so. In the article *Religion and Science*, published on November 9, 1930 in the *New York Times Magazine*, the great scientist discussed religious experiences on three levels: those of primitive fear, of social consciousness, and of a cosmic religious sense independent of God, church, and theology. It is only on this last and highest level of religious experience that a true scientist dedicates himself to the cosmic life and order and bows in profound piety to the grand totality of existence. This cosmic religious sense comes very close to the idea of Tao (道) in Chinese philosophy where the law of nature operates on its own without the ministry of God.

内容简介

科学家可以信仰宗教吗？怀有宗教虔诚的人能成为科学家吗？宗教似乎总是与科学格格不入，中世纪的历史因为对科学家的宗教迫害而臭名昭著，这些科学家的发现被教会谴责为异端邪说。科学家果真是对自然这个伟大创造完全不敏感的无神论者吗？阿尔伯特·爱因斯坦并不这样认为。在1930年11月9日发表在《纽约时报》上的《宗教与科学》一文中，这位伟大的科学家从三个层面讨论了宗教体验：关于原始恐惧，关于社会意识，以及关于一种独立于上帝、教会和神学的宇宙宗教意识。只有在这最后的、也是最高层次的宗教体验中，一个真正的科学家才能献身于宇宙的生命和秩序，并以深深的虔诚向伟大的存在整体致敬。这种宇宙宗教意识非常接近于中国哲学的"道"的概念，自然法则无需神的帮助而独立运作。

Everything that men do or think concerns the satisfaction of the needs they feel or the escape from pain. This must be kept in mind when we seek to understand spiritual or intellectual movements and the way in which they develop. For feeling and longing are the motive forces of all human striving and productivity—however nobly these latter may display themselves to us.

What, then, are the feelings and the needs which have brought mankind to religious thought and to faith in the widest sense? A moment's consideration shows that the most varied emotions stand at the cradle[1] of religious thought and experience.

In primitive peoples it is, first of all, fear that awakens religious ideas—fear of hunger, of wild animals, of illness and of death. Since the understanding of causal connections[2] is usually limited on this level of existence, the human soul forges a being, more or less like itself, on whose will and activities depend the experiences which it fears. One hopes to win the favor of this being[3] by deeds and sacrifices, which, according to the tradition of the race, are supposed to appease the being or to make him well disposed to[4] man. I call this the religion of fear.

This religion is considerably stabilized—though not caused—by the formation of a priestly caste[5] which claims to mediate between[6] the people and the being they fear and so attains a position of power. Often a leader or despot, or a privileged class whose power is maintained in other ways, will combine the function of the priesthood with its own temporal rule[7] for the sake of greater security; or an alliance may exist between the interests of the political power and the priestly caste.

A second source of religious development is found in the social feelings. Fathers and mothers, as well as leaders of great human communities,[8] are fallible and mortal. The longing for guidance, for love and succor,[9] provides the stimulus for the growth of a social or moral conception of God. This is the God of Providence,[10] who protects, decides, rewards and punishes. This is the God who, according to man's widening horizons,[11] loves and provides for the life of the race, or of mankind, or who even loves life itself. He is the comforter in unhappiness and in unsatisfied longing, the protector of the souls of the dead. This is the social or moral idea of God.

It is easy to follow in the sacred writings of the Jewish people the development of the religion of fear into the moral religion, which is carried further in the New Testament.[12] The religions of all the civilized peoples, especially those of the Orient,[13] are principally moral religions. An important advance[14] in the life of a people is the transformation[15] of the religion of fear into the moral religion. But one must avoid the prejudice that regards the religions of primitive peoples as pure fear religions and those of the civilized races as pure moral religions. All are mixed forms, though the moral element predominates in the higher levels of social life. Common to all these types is the anthropomorphic character of the idea of God.[16]

Only exceptionally gifted individuals or especially noble communities rise essentially above this level, in these there is found a third level of religious experience, even if it is seldom found in a pure form. I will call it the cosmic[17] religious sense. This is hard to make clear to those who do not experience it, since it does not involve an anthropomorphic idea of God; the individual feels the vanity of human desires and aims, and the nobility and marvelous order which are revealed in nature and in the world of thought. He feels the individual destiny as an imprisonment and seeks to experience the totality of existence as a unity full of significance. Indications of this cosmic religious sense can be found even on earlier levels of development—for example, in the Psalms of David[18] and in the Prophets.[19] The cosmic element is much stronger in Buddhism,[20] as, in particular, Schopenhauer's magnificent essays have shown us.[21]

The religious geniuses of all times have been distinguished by this cosmic religious sense, which recognizes neither dogmas nor God made in man's image.[22] Consequently there cannot be a church whose chief doctrines are based on the cosmic religious experience. It comes about,[23] therefore, that we find precisely among the heretics[24] of all ages men who were inspired by this highest religious experience; often they appeared to their contemporaries as atheists,[25] but sometimes also as saints. Viewed from this angle, men like Democritus,[26] Francis of Assisi[27] and Spinoza[28] are near to one another.

How can this cosmic religious experience be communicated from man to man, if it cannot lead to a definite conception of God or to a theology? It seems to me that the most important function of art and of science is to arouse and keep alive this feeling in those who are receptive.

Thus we reach an interpretation of the relation of science to religion which is very different from the customary view. From the study of history, one is inclined to regard religion and science as irreconcilable antagonists,[29] and this for a reason that is very easily seen. For anyone who is pervaded with the sense of causal law in all that happens, who accepts in real earnest the assumption of causality,[30] the idea of a Being who interferes with the sequence of events in the world is absolutely impossible. Neither the religion of fear nor the social-moral religion can have any hold on him. A God who rewards and punishes is for him unthinkable, because man acts in accordance with an inner and outer necessity, and would, in the eyes of God, be as little responsible as an inanimate[31] object is for the movements which it makes.

Science, in consequence, has been accused of undermining morals[32]—but wrongly. The ethical behavior of man is better based on sympathy, education and social relationships, and requires no support from religion. Man's plight[33] would, indeed, be sad if he had to be kept in order through fear of punishment and hope of rewards after death.

It is, therefore, quite natural that the churches have always fought against science and have persecuted its supporters. But, on the other hand, I assert that the cosmic religious experience is the strongest and the noblest driving force behind scientific reearch. No one who does not appreciate the terrific exertions,[34] and, above all, the devotion without which pioneer creations in scientific thought cannot come into being,[35] can judge the strength of the feeling out of which alone such work, turned away as it is from immediate practical life, can grow. What a deep faith in the rationality of the structure of the world and what a longing to understand even a small glimpse of the reason revealed in the world there must have been in Kepler[36] and Newton[37] to enable them to unravel the mechanism of the heavens[38] in long years of lonely work!

Anyone who only knows scientific research in its practical applications may easily come to a wrong interpretation of the state of mind of the men who, surrounded by skeptical contemporaries, have shown the way to kindred spirits[39] scattered over all countries in all centuries. Only those who have dedicated their lives to similar ends can have a living conception of the inspiration which gave these men the power to remain loyal to their purpose in spite of countless failures. It is the cosmic religious sense which grants this power.

A contemporary has rightly said that the only deeply religious people of our largely materialistic age are the earnest men of research.[40]

NOTES

1. cradle: birth; beginning.
2. causal connection: connection between cause and effect.
3. this being: God; deity.
4. well disposed to: kindly disposed to; well-meaning to.
5. priestly caste: class of priests; priesthood; the clergy.
6. mediate between: be a connection between.
7. temporal rule: earthly rule, rule on the earth and in this life.
8. great human communities: great social institutions or political organizations.
9. succor: help; relief.
10. Providence: God. The word in small letter means the guardianship of a deity.
11. horizons: limits of one's thinking and experience.
12. New Testament: the part of the Bible which contains the life and teachings of Christ recorded by his followers, together with their own experiences and teachings.
13. the Orient: the East; the Asian countries.
14. advance: progress.
15. transformation: change.
16. the anthropomorphic character of the idea of God: the attribution of human form or qualities to God.
17. cosmic: of cosmos, the universe thought of as an orderly harmonious system.
18. the Psalms of David: the Psalms is a book of Old Testament containing 150 poetic pieces, many of which are traditionally ascribed to David, King of Hebrews about 1,000 B.C.
19. the Prophets: religious leaders of Israel such as Isaiah, Jeremiah, Ezekiel, and Daniel.
20. Buddhism: 佛教.
21. Arthur Schopenhauer (1788-1860), famous German philosopher, maintains in his book *The World as Will and Idea* and his essays on a variety of topics that true reality is a blind impelling force, appearing in individual man as will. The constant mutual resistance of various wills causes strife, and the individual cannot satisfy the wants of his will and therefore lives in pain. The only escape is a negation of the will. Schopenhauer believes that Buddhism is profounder than Christianity, because it makes the destruction of the will the entirety of religion, and preaches Nirvana as the goal of all personal development.

22. made in man's image: modeled upon human qualities.
23. comes about: happens; turns out; takes place.
24. heretics: persons who hold beliefs different from the accepted one of his community; dissenters.
25. atheists: people who believe that there is no God. People denounced as atheists by the church, such as Spinoza and Shelley, are often pious persons full of Einstein's cosmic religious sense.
26. Democritus (c. 460-c. 370, B.C.): Greek philosopher who held that the universe is made up of tiny particles.
27. Francis of Assisi: Saint Francis (c.1182-1226 A.D.), a great Christian saint and founder of the Franciscan order.
28. Benedict Spinoza (1632-1677): Dutch philosopher, was excommunicated in 1656 by the Jewish because of his independent thinking.
29. irreconcilable antagonists: enemies who cannot be reconciled.
30. the assumption of causality: the supposition that reality operates by cause and effect.
31. inanimate: lifeless.
32. undermining morals: weakening right conducts gradually.
33. plight: a bad situation or condition.
34. terrific exertions: very great efforts.
35. come into being: come into existence; be realized.
36. Johannes Kepler (1571-1630): German astronomer who evolved the laws of planetary motion.
37. Sir Isaac Newton (1642-1727), English physicist and mathematician who evolved the law of gravitation.
38. to unravel the mechanism of the heavens: to explain the operation of stars.
39. kindred spirits: sympathetic intellects and minds; fellow scientists.
40. the earnest men of research: serious scientists.

参考译文

人类所思所做的一切都关系到满足深切的需要和减轻苦痛。想要理解精神活动及其发展，就要时常记住这一点。情感和渴望是人类一切努力和创造背后的动力，无论呈现在我们眼前的这些努力和创造显得有多么高贵。

那么，将人引到最广义的宗教思想和信仰的情感和需求是什么呢？只要稍作思考，便不难明白，使宗教思想和宗教经验得以产生的乃是各种各样的情感。

在原始人那里，唤起宗教观念的主要是恐惧——对饥饿、野兽、疾病和死亡的恐惧。因为在人类生存的这一阶段，对因果关系的认识通常还不够深入，人们就在头脑中创造出一些与自己多少有些相似的虚幻之物，那些令人恐惧的事情都来自它们的意志和行为。于是人们便努力求得那些虚幻之物的恩宠，按照代代相传的传统，通过一些行动和祭献，以讨好它们，或者使之对人有好感。在这个意义上，我所谈的是恐惧宗教。

这种宗教虽然不是由人创造出来的，但由于形成了一个特殊的祭司阶层，它就具有相当的稳定性；祭司阶层把自己确立为人民和他们所惧怕的鬼神之间的中间人，并且在此基础上建立起一种霸权。在很多情况下，那些靠别的因素而获得地位的首领、统治者或特权阶层，为了巩固其世俗权力，会把这种权力同祭司的职能结合起来；或者，政治上的统治者会与祭司阶层为了各自的利益而进行合作。

社会冲动是形成宗教的另一个源泉。无论是家中的父母还是更大人类共同体的领袖都不免会死和犯错。渴望得到引导、爱和支持，促使人形成了社会或道德意义上的上帝观。这是一个天意的上帝，掌管着保护、处置、奖惩等权力；他按照信仰者目光所及的范围来爱护和抚育部族或人类的生命，甚至是生命本身；他是生者在悲痛和愿望得不到满足时的安慰者，也是死者灵魂的保护者。这便是社会或道德意义上的上帝观。

犹太经典极好地说明了从恐惧宗教到道德宗教的发展，这种发展在《新约》中得到继续。一切文明民族，尤其是东方民族的宗教，主要是道德宗教。从恐惧宗教发展到道德宗教是民族生活的一大进步。但我们必须防止一种偏见，以为原始宗教完全以恐惧为基础，而文明民族的宗教纯粹以道德为基础。事实上，一切宗教都是以上两种宗教的混合，其区别在于：社会生活水平越高，道德宗教就越占主导。所有这些类型的宗教都有一个共同点，那就是它们的上帝观念都有拟人化特征。

一般来说，只有具有非凡天才的个人和品质极高的集体才能大大超越这一层次。但属于所有这些宗教的还有第三个宗教经验阶段，尽管很少能够见到它的纯粹形式：我把它称为"宇宙宗教感情"。要向完全没有这种情感的人阐明它是什么，那是非常困难的，特别是因为没有什么拟人化的上帝观念能与之对应。个人感觉到人的欲望和目标都属徒然，而大自然和思维世界却显示出令人惊异的崇高秩序。他觉得个人的生活犹如监狱，想把宇宙当成一个有意义的整体来体验。宇宙宗教感情的开端早已有之，比如在大卫的《诗篇》和犹太教的某些先知那里。在佛教中，这种情感要素还要强烈得多，我们尤其可以从叔本华的美妙著作中读到。

一切时代的宗教天才皆因这种宗教情感而卓著，它既无教条，也无以人的形象而构想的上帝，因此不可能有哪个教会会把核心教义建立在它的基础上。因此，恰恰在每个时代的离经叛道者当中，我们可以找到充满这种最高宗教感情的人。在很多情况下，他们都被其同时代人视为无神论者，有时也被看作圣人。由是观之，像德谟克利特、阿西西的方济各（Francis of Assisi）和斯宾诺莎这样的人彼此都极为近似。

如果宇宙宗教感情给不出关于上帝的明确观念，也提不出什么神学，它又如何能得到传承呢？在我看来，艺术与科学最重要的功能便是唤醒某些人身上的这种感情，并使之生生不息。

由此可见，我们对科学与宗教关系的看法与通常的看法大不相同。如果从历史角度来看问题，人们总是倾向于认为科学与宗教势不两立、无法调和，其理由显而易见。凡彻底相信因果律发挥着普遍作用的人，对于那种认为神来干预事件进程的想法是一刻也不能容忍的——当然前提是,他对因果性假说是非常认真的。他用不着恐惧的宗教,也用不着社会或道德的宗教。一个有赏罚的上帝是他所无法设想的,理由很简单:一个人的行为是由外在和内在的必然性决定的,因此在上帝眼里,他不必为自己的行为负责,正如一个无生命物体不必对自己的运动负责一样。

有人因此指责科学损害道德,但这种指责是不公正的。一个人的伦理行为可以不需要宗教基础,但应当有效地建立在同情心、教育、社会联系和社会需求上。如果一个人仅仅因为害怕死后受罚和希望死后得到奖赏才去约束自己,那就不好了。

由此不难理解,为什么教会总要与科学作对,并且迫害献身科学的人。另一方面,我认为宇宙宗教感情是科学研究最有力和最高尚的动机。只有认识到理论科学的开创需要付出巨大的努力甚至是献身,才能领会这样一种感情的力量,只有凭借这种力量才能做出那种远离现实生活的工作。为了揭示天体力学的原理,开普勒和牛顿不知默默工作了多少个年头,他们对宇宙合理性的信念该是多么真挚,理解它的愿望又该是多么热切!而宇宙合理性只不过是显示在这世界上的理性的一点微弱反映罢了。

那些主要从实际结果来认识科学研究的人很难正确理解下面一些人的精神状态:他们遭到世人的怀疑,却为志同道合者指明了道路。这种人虽然不多,但世界各地和各个时代都有。只有终生致力于类似目的的人才能深切体会到,究竟是什么在激励这些人并且赋予他们以力量,使其无论经历多少挫折都能矢志不渝。给人以这种力量的正是宇宙宗教感情。

有一个当代人说的不错:在我们这个唯物主义时代,只有严肃的科学工作者才是深信宗教的人。

(张卜天 译)

27

We'll Never Conquer Space

我们永远无法征服太空

ARTHUR C. CLARKE
亚瑟·查尔斯·克拉克

(1917–2008)

ABOUT THE AUTHOR

Arthur C. Clarke (1917–2008) was a member of the Royal Air Force during World War II and a graduate of the University of London; both experiences gave him a background in mathematics and physics. He has earned a living by writing short stories, novels, radio and television scripts, but his background in science has enabled him to do his most distinguished writing on space. The best-known of his twelve nonfiction works is *The Exploration of Space*. But his great popularity rests mainly on the novel *2001: A Space Odyssey*.

作者简介

亚瑟·查尔斯·克拉克（1917—2008），二战期间曾是英国皇家空军成员，毕业于伦敦大学，这两段经历使其拥有数学和物理学背景。克拉克以撰写短篇小说、长篇小说、广播剧和电视剧本为生，理科背景使他能够创作有关太空的优秀作品，12部非虚构作品中最著名的当数《太空探索》，不过《2001：太空漫游》使其名声大噪。

ABOUT THE SELECTION

The exhilaration modern man gets from lunar exploration and the beginning exploration of our solar system should not blind us to the much greater difficulties involved in the conquest of stellar space. The distances involved are of such enormous size that the lifetime of man limits his ability to deal with them. The kind of achievements we expect of our future will not be obtainable because of our human limitations. *We'll Never Conquer Space*, first published in 1966 in *Edge of Awareness*, is a timely and well-stated caution.

内容简介

现代人因探索月球和开始探索太阳系而备受鼓舞，但这不应该使我们对征服恒星太空所面临的更大困难视而不见。探索太空要走过漫长的距离，而人类的寿命限制了探索太空的能力。正是因为人类自身的局限性，我们将无法获得所期望的成就。《我们永远无法征服太空》1966年首次发表于《认识的边缘》，算是一份有理有据的警告，非常及时。

Man will never conquer space. Such a statement may sound ludicrous,[1] now that our rockets are already 100 million miles beyond the moon and the first human travelers are preparing to leave the atmosphere. Yet it expresses a truth which our forefathers knew, one we have forgotten—and our descendants must learn again, in heartbreak and loneliness.

Our age is in many ways unique, full of events and phenomena[2] which never occurred before and can never happen again. They distort[3] our thinking, making us believe that what is true now will be true forever, though perhaps on a larger scale. Because we have annihilated[4] distance on this planet, we imagine that we can do it once again. The facts are far otherwise, and we will see them more clearly if we forget the present and turn our minds toward the past.

To our ancestors, the vastness of the earth was a dominant fact controlling their thoughts and lives. In all earlier ages than ours, the world was wide indeed, and no man could ever see more than a tiny fraction of its immensity.[5] A few hundred mile's—a thousand, at the most—was infinity.[6] Only a lifetime ago, parents waved farewell to their emigrating[7] children in the virtual certainty[8] that they would never meet again.

And now, within one incredible[9] generation, all this has changed. Over the seas where Odysseus[10] wandered for a decade, the Rome-Beirut

Comet[11] whispers[12] its way within the hour. And above that, the closer satellites[13] span the distance between Troy and Ithaca in less than a minute.

Psychologically as well as physically, there are no longer any remote places on earth. When a friend leaves for what was once a far country, even if he has no intention of returning, we cannot feel that same sense of irrevocable[14] separation that saddened our forefathers. We know that he is only hours away by jet liner, and that we have merely to reach for the telephone to hear his voice.

In a very few years, when the satellite communication network is established, we will be able to see friends on the far side of the earth as easily as we talk to them on the other side of the town. Then the world will shrink no more, for it will have become a dimensionless point.[15]

But the new stage that is opening up for the human drama will never shrink as the old one has done. We have abolished space here on the little earth; we can never abolish the space that yawns[16] between the stars. Once again we are face to face with immensity and must accept its grandeur and terror, its inspiring possibilities and its dreadful restraints. From a world that has become too small, we are moving out into one that will forever be too large, whose frontiers will recede[17] from us always more swiftly than we can reach out towards them.

Consider first the fairly modest[18] solar, or planetary, distances which we are now preparing to assault.[19] The very first Lunik[20] made a substantial impression upon them, traveling more than 200 million miles from the earth—six times the distance to Mars.[21] When we have harnessed[22] nuclear energy for spaceflight, the solar system will contract until it is little larger than the earth today. The remotest of the planets will be perhaps no more than a week's travel from the earth, while Mars and Venus[23] will be only a few hours away.

This achievement, which will be witnessed within a century, might appear to make even the solar system a comfortable, homely place, with such giant planets as Saturn[24] and Jupiter[25] playing much the same role in our thoughts as do Africa or Asia today. (Their qualitative differences of climate, atmosphere and gravity, fundamental though they are, do not concern us at the moment.) To some extent this may be true, yet as soon as we pass beyond the orbit[26] of the moon, a mere quarter-million miles away, we will meet the first of the barriers that will separate the earth from her scattered children.

The marvelous telephone and television network that will soon enmesh[27] the whole world, making all men neighbors, cannot be extended into space. It will never be possible to converse with anyone on another planet.

Do not misunderstand this statement. Even with today's radio equipment, the problem of sending speech to the other planets is almost trivial.[28] But the messages will take minutes—sometimes hours—on their journey, because radio and light waves travel at the same limited speed of 186,000 miles a second.

Twenty years from now you will be able to listen to a friend on Mars, but the words you hear will have left his mouth at least three minutes earlier, and your reply will take a corresponding time to reach him. In such circumstances, an exchange of verbal messages is possible—but not a conversation.

Even in the case of the nearby moon, the 2½-second time lag[29] will be annoying. At distances of more than a million miles, it will be intolerable.[30]

To a culture which has come to take instantaneous communication for granted, as part of the very structure of civilized life, this "time barrier" may have a profound psychological impact. It will be a perpetual reminder of universal laws and limitations against which not all our technology can ever prevail.[31] For it seems as certain as anything can be that no signal—still less any material object—can ever travel faster than light.

The velocity[32] of light is the ultimate speed limit, being part of the very structure of space and time. Within the narrow confines[33] of the solar system, it will not handicap us too severely, once we have accepted the delays in communication which it involves. At the worst, these will amount to twenty hours—the time it takes a radio signal to span the orbit of Pluto,[34] the outermost planet.

Between the three inner worlds, the earth, Mars, and Venus, it will never be more than twenty minutes—not enough to interfere seriously with commerce or administration, but more than sufficient to shatter those personal links of sound or vision that can give us a sense of direct contact with friends on earth, wherever they may be.

It is when we move out beyond the confines of the solar system that we come face to face with an altogether new order of cosmic[35] reality. Even today, many otherwise educated men—like those savages who can count to three but lump together all numbers beyond four—cannot grasp the profound distinction between solar and stellar space. The first is the space enclosing our neighboring worlds, the planets; the second is that which embraces those distant suns, the stars, and it is literally millions of times greater.

There is no such abrupt change of scale in terrestrial affairs.[36] To obtain a mental picture of the distance to the nearest star, as compared with the distance to the nearest planet, you must imagine a world in which the closest object to you is only five feet away—and then there is nothing else to see until you have traveled a thousand miles.

Many conservative scientists, appalled by these cosmic gulfs, have denied that they can ever be crossed. Some people never learn; those who sixty years ago scoffed at the possibility of flight, and ten (eyen five!) years ago laughed at the idea of travel to the planets, are now quite sure that the stars will always be beyond our reach. And again they are wrong, for they have failed to grasp the great lesson of our age—that if something is possible in theory, and no fundamental scientific laws oppose its realization,[37] then sooner or later it will be achieved.

One day, it may be in this century, or it may be a thousand years from now, we shall discover a really efficient means of propelling our space vehicles. Every technical device is always developed to its limit (unless it is superseded[38] by something better) and the ultimate speed for spaceships is the velocity of light. They will never reach that goal, but they will get very close to it. And then the nearest star will be less than five years' voyaging from the earth.

Our exploring ships will spread outwards from their home over an ever-expanding sphere of space. It is a sphere which will grow at almost—but never quite—the speed of light. Five years to the triple system of Alpha Centauri,[39] ten to the strangely-matched doublet Sirius A and B,[40] eleven to the tantalizing enigma[41] of 61 Cygni,[42] the first star suspected to possess a planet. These journeys are long, but they are not impossible. Man has always accepted whatever price was necessary for his explorations and discoveries, and the price of Space is Time.

Even voyages which may last for centuries or millennia[43] will one day be attempted. Suspended animation[44] has already been achieved in the laboratory, and may be the key to interstellar travel.[45] Self-contained cosmic arks[46] which will be tiny traveling worlds in their own right may be another solution, for they would make possible journeys of unlimited extent, lasting generation after generation.

The famous Time Dilation[47] effect predicted by the Theory of Relativity, whereby time appears to pass more slowly for a traveler moving at almost the speed of light, may be yet a third. And there are others.

Looking far into the future, therefore, we must picture a slow (little more than half a billion miles an hour!) expansion of human activities outwards from the solar system, among the suns scattered across the region of the galaxy in which we now find ourselves. These suns are on the average five light-years apart; in other words, we can never get from one to the next in less than five years.

To bring home what this means, let us use a down-to-earth analogy.[48] Imagine a vast ocean, sprinkled with islands—some desert,[49] others perhaps inhabited. On one of these islands an energetic race has just discovered the art of building ships. It is preparing to explore the ocean, but must face the fact that the very nearest island is five years' voyaging away, and that no possible improvement in the technique of shipbuilding will ever reduce this time.

In these circumstances (which are those in which we will soon find ourselves) what could the islanders achieve? After a few centuries, they might have established colonies on many of the nearby islands and have briefly explored many others. The daughter colonies might themselves have sent out further pioneers, and so a kind of chain reaction[50] would spread the original culture over a steadily expanding area of the ocean.

But now consider the effects of the inevitable, unavoidable time lag. There could be only the most tenuous[51] contact between the home island and its offspring.[52] Returning messengers could report what had happened on the nearest colony—five years ago. They could never bring information more up to date than that, and dispatches from the more distant parts of the ocean would be from still further in the past—perhaps centuries behind the times. There would never be news from the other islands, but only history.

All the star-borne[53] colonies of the future will be independent, whether they wish it or not. Their liberty will be inviolably[54] protected by Time as well as Space. They must go their own way and achieve their own destiny, with no help or hindrance from Mother Earth.

At this point, we will move the discussion on to a new level and deal with an obvious objection. Can we be sure that the velocity of light is indeed a limiting factor? So many "impassible"[55] barriers have been shattered in the past; perhaps this one may go the way of all the others.

We will not argue the point, or give the reasons why scientists believe that light can never be outraced by any form of radiation or any material object. Instead, let us assume the contrary and see just where it gets us. We will even take the most optimistic possible case and imagine that the speed of transportation may eventually become infinite.

Picture a time when, by the development of techniques as far beyond our present engineering as a transistor is beyond a stone axe, we can reach anywhere we please instantaneously, with no more effort than by dialing a number. This would indeed cut the universe down to size and reduce its physical immensity to nothingness. What would be left?

Everything that really matters. For the universe has two aspects—its scale,[56] and its overwhelming, mind-numbing complexity.[57] Having abolished the first, we are now face-to-face with the second.

What we must now try to visualize is not size, but quantity. Most people today are familiar with the simple notation which scientists use to describe large numbers; it consists merely of counting zeroes, so that a hundred becomes 10^2, a million, 10^6, a billion, 10^9 and so on. This useful trick enables us to work with quantities of any magnitude, and even defense-budget[58] totals look modest when expressed as $\$5.76 \times 10^9$ instead of \$5,760,000,000.

The number of other suns in our own galaxy (that is, the whirlpool of stars and cosmic dust of which our sun is an out-of-town member, lying in one of the remoter spiral arms) is estimated at about 10^{11}—or written in full, 100,000,000,000. Our present telescopes can observe something like 10^9 other galaxies, and they show no sign of thinning out even at the extreme limit of vision.

There are probably at least as many galaxies in the whole of creation as there are stars in our own galaxy, but let us confine ourselves to those we can see. They must contain a total of about 10^{11} times 10^9 stars, or 10^{20} stars altogether. One followed by twenty other digits[59] is, of course, a number beyond all understanding.

Before such numbers, even spirits brave enough to face the challenge of the light-years must quail. The detailed examination of all the grains of sand on all the beaches of the world is a far smaller task than the exploration of the universe.

And so we return to our opening statement. Space can be mapped and crossed and occupied without definable limit; but it can never be conquered. When our race has reached its ultimate achievements, and the stars themselves are scattered no more widely than the seed of Adam,[60] even then we shall still be like ants crawling on the face of the earth. The ants have covered the world, but have they conquered it—for what do their countless colonies know of it, or of each other?

So it will be with us as we spread outwards from Mother Earth, loosening the bonds of kinship and understanding, hearing faint and belated rumors at second—or third—or thousandth-hand[61] of an ever-dwindling fraction at the entire human race.

Though Earth will try to keep in touch with her children, in the end all the efforts of her archivists[62] and historians will be defeated by time and distance, and the sheer bulk of material. For the number of distinct societies or nations, when our race is twice its present age, may be far greater than the total number of all the men who have ever lived up to the present time.

We have left the realm of human comprehension in our vain effort to grasp the scale of the universe, so it must always be, sooner rather than later.

When you are next outdoors[63] on a summer night, turn your head toward the zenith.[64] Almost vertically above you will be shining the brightest star of the northern skies—Vega of the Lyre,[65] twenty-six years away at the speed of light, near enough the point of no return for us short-lived creatures. Past this blue-white beacon, fifty times as brilliant as our sun, we may send our minds and bodies, but never our hearts.

For no man will ever turn homewards from beyond Vega, to greet again those he knew and loved on the earth.

NOTES

1. ludicrous: silly; ridiculous.
2. phenomena: plural form of phenomenon, an observable fact or event.
3. distort: twist (something) out of true shape or meaning.
4. annihilate: kill off; slaughter and leave nothing behind.
5. a tiny fraction of its immensity: a small part of its vastness.
6. infinity: space without end.
7. emigrating: leaving one country to settle in another.
8. in the virtual certainty: perfectly sure.
9. incredible: unbelievable.
10. Odysseus: the hero of *The Odyssey*, an early Greek epic poem, who roamed the Eastern Mediterranean sea between Troy on the Asia Minor and Ithaca off the west coast of Greece.
11. Comet: a variety of modern passenger airplane.
12. whispers: an advertising claim that this type of airplane is noiseless.
13. satellite: a small heavenly body that revolves around a larger one.
14. irrevocable: that cannot be called back again; lost forever.
15. dimensionless point: point without breadth, length or thickness.
16. yawns: opens up wide like the jaws. Here it is used as a metaphor meaning stretching challengingly and ominously.
17. recede: keep moving back.
18. modest: not extreme; not too great.
19. assault: attack a fortified position; (in this case) cover, overcome.
20. Lunik: a Soviet rocket that was developed to reach the moon.
21. Mars: 火星.
22. harnessed: put into a harness; a metaphor for "control".
23. Venus: 金星.
24. Saturn: 土星.
25. Jupiter: 木星.
26. orbit: circular path.
27. enmesh: cover like a net.
28. trivial: tiny; unimportant.
29. time lag: retardation in time.
30. intolerable: unbearable.
31. against which not all our technology can ever prevail: Not all our technology can ever prevail against such limitations. "Prevail against" means "overcome" or "triumph over".
32. velocity: speed.

33. confine: limit.
34. Pluto: 冥王星.
35. cosmic: relating to the cosmos or space beyond our solar system.
36. terrestrial affairs: earthly events; human affairs.
37. its realization: the carrying out of the theory.
38. superseded: replaced.
39. the triple system of Alpha Centauri: the three-star combination of the brightest star in the constellation of Centaur (人马座).
40. the strangely-matched doublet Sirius A and B: the twin-stars that make up Sirius (天狼星).
41. tantalizing enigma: a riddle that tempts us but always remains out of reach.
42. 61 Cygni: star no. 61 in the constellation of Cygnus (天鹅座).
43. millennia: plural of millennium, a thousand year period.
44. suspended animation: keeping physical bodies alive but inert for long periods of time.
45. interstellar travel: travel among the stars.
46. ark: In the Bible, Noah saved pairs of animals from death in a flood by sheltering them in a boat called ark. "self-contained cosmic arks" are spaceships equipped with everything they need.
47. Time Dilation: expansion of time.
48. down-to-earth analogy: practical comparison.
49. desert: uninhabited or uninhabitable.
50. chain reaction: a series of reactions that take place in a certain order, one leading to the other.
51. tenuous: thin; weak.
52. its offspring: the children of the home island.
53. star-borne: carried on stars.
54. inviolably: in a way that shall not be violated.
55. impassible: that which cannot be passed.
56. scale: proportion.
57. mind-numbing complexity: state of being so complex that it makes thinking impossible (renders the mind inactive).
58. defense-budget: budget for national defense.
59. digits: any of the numerals from 0 to 9.
60. the seed of Adam: the offspring of Adam; (in the Western sense) mankind.
61. at thousandth-hand: passed on through a thousand people.
62. archivists: persons who keep government or historical records.

63. next outdoors: out in the open next time.
64. zenith: highest point overhead.
65. Vega of the Lyre: 天琴座织女星. "Lyra" is a formal name for "the Lyre."

参考译文

人类将永远无法征服太空。这样的观点听起来可能荒唐可笑，因为现在我们的火箭已经飞离超月球一亿英里远的距离，第一批人类旅行者正准备离开大气层。然而，这种观点表达了我们祖先都已经明白的一个事实，一个我们却已经忘记的事实，一个我们的后代必须在心碎和孤独中再次学习的事实。

我们的时代在很多方面独一无二，各种活动和现象空前绝后。这些活动和现象扭曲了我们的想法，使我们相信，今天的真理永远都是真理，也许以后持这种想法的人会更多。因为在这个星球上，我们已经消灭了距离，所以认为可以再次消灭距离。事实远非如此，如果我们忘记现在，把目光转回过去，就会更清晰地看到真相。

对我们的祖先来说，地球广袤无垠，这一事实支配着他们的思想和生活。在我们之前的所有时代，世界确实很宽广，人们只能看到巨大世界的一小部分。几百英里，最多一千英里的距离，就令人感觉无限遥远。就在一代人之前，父母挥手告别移民的孩子时，几乎坚信他们再也不会相见。

现在，令人难以置信，仅仅一代人的时间，一切都发生了变化。奥德修斯当年漂泊了十年之久的海洋，罗马至贝鲁特的"彗星"号喷气客机仅需一小时就能悄无声息地飞越。再往高空，近地卫星一分钟之内就能跨越特洛伊和伊萨卡之间的距离。

从身心两方面看，地球上任何两地之间都显得不再遥远。如果一位朋友启程前往曾经看来无比遥远的国家，即使他不打算回来，我们也无法像先辈那样，涌起生离死别的悲感，因为我们知道，这位朋友和我们之间只有喷气式飞机飞行几个小时的距离，我们只需拿起电话就能听到他的声音。

短短几年后，卫星通信网络一旦建成，我们将能够看到地球另一端的朋友，就像与住在城市另一边的朋友交谈一样容易。届时，世界将无法再缩小，因为它将成为一个点，一个没有长宽高的点。

但是，正在为人类活动开辟的新舞台永远不会像旧舞台那样越来越小。在这个小小的地球上我们已经消除了距离，但我们永远无法消除星球之间的距离。再次面对浩瀚无垠的太空，我们不得不承认它的壮丽，心生畏惧，既认识到它激发无限想象的可能性，又承认其令人敬畏的束缚。我们走出了一个已经变得太小的世界，进入一个永远都太大的世界，其边界将飞速远离我们，速度总是超过我们能够接近其边界的速度。

首先考虑一下我们现在正准备征服的日地之间或行星之间相当有限的距离吧。第一个月球探测器使这些距离给人们留下了深刻的印象。探测器飞离地球两亿多英里，相当于到火星距离的六倍。如果利用核能进行太空飞行，太阳系将缩小到比今天的地球稍大一点。从地球出发前往最遥远的行星可能不到一周即可到达，而火星和金星距离将只有几个小时的路程。

这一成就将在一个世纪内得到见证，甚至可能将太阳系变成一个舒适的家园，到时候，在我们的观念里，土星和木星这样巨大的行星就和今天的非洲或亚洲差不多。（这些行星的气候、大气和重力等方面和地球有质的区别，不过这些问题可以暂时不考虑。）在某种程度上，这种设想可能是对的，但是一旦越过距离地球25万英里的月球轨道，我们就会遇到第一个障碍，这个障碍将把地球与它撒向太空的卫星分开。

令人惊叹的电话和电视网络很快就会遍布整个世界，使得地球上的人都能成为邻居，但这个网络无法延伸至太空，地球上的人永远不可能与另一行星上的人对话。

不要误解这种说法。即使用今天的无线电设备向其他星球发送言语也几乎毫无问题，但这些信息途中需要花费几分钟，有时甚至几小时，因为无线电和光波的传播速度均有限，为每秒186000英里。

20年后，你会听到朋友在火星上说话，但是听到的话至少是他三分钟之前说的，而你的答复也将需要同样的时间才能到达朋友那里。这种情况下，话语交流是可能的，但这不能算作是对话。

即使在地球附近的月球，2.5秒的时间滞后也令人生厌。如果距离超过100万英里，时间滞后会令人无法忍受。

我们的文化已将即时通信视为理所当然，并将其视为文明生活的基本组成部分，上述"时间障碍"可能会产生巨大的心理冲击，它将不断提示普遍法则和限制的存在，而我们所有的技术都不可能战胜这些法则和限制，因为似乎可以肯定，没有什么信号会超过光速，更不用说任何物体了。

光速是速度的极限，是空间和时间最基本的组成部分。在太阳系的狭小范围内，一旦我们接受了"时间障碍"带来的通信延迟，这种极限就不会给我们造成太严重的障碍。最糟糕的情况下，这些延迟将达20个小时：这是无线电信号从地球到太阳系最外层行星冥王星轨道所需的时间。

太阳系内层的地球、火星和金星之间，通信延迟永远不会超过20分钟——不足以严重妨碍商业或管理活动，却足以打断个人之间的声音或视觉联系，但正是这种联系使我们和地球上的朋友有一种直接接触的感觉，无论朋友身处地球上的哪一个角落。

一旦离开太阳系的疆界，我们面对的将是全新的宇宙现实秩序。即使在今天，就像弄不清 4 以上数字的未开化原始人一样，很多以其他方式接受教育的人也无法理解太阳系空间与星际空间的巨大差异。太阳系空间是我们附近的空间，由行星组成；星际空间则是由遥远的恒星组成的空间，要比太阳系空间大数百万倍。

地球上的事物不会有如此突然的变化。为了对比我们与最近的恒星和与最近的行星之间的距离，不妨想象一个世界，在这个世界，离你最近的物体只有五英尺远，再远什么都看不见，除非你走到一千英里之外。

巨大的宇宙鸿沟令很多保守的科学家感到惊恐，认为永远不可能跨越这些鸿沟。有些人永远不会吸取教训；60 年前有些人嘲笑飞行的可能性，10 年（甚至 5 年）前有些人嘲笑想前往行星旅行的人，这些人现在都十分确定，我们永远无法到达其他恒星。这一次，他们又错了，因为他们没有吸取我们这个时代的伟大教训——只要理论上可行，没有基本科学法则阻碍其实现，那么上述想法迟早会变成现实。

有一天，可能就在本世纪，也可能是一千年之后，一定会发现一种真正有效的手段来驱动我们的太空飞行器。每种技术手段总是发展到自己的极限（除非被更高的技术手段所取代），而宇宙飞船的极限速度是光速。宇宙飞船永远无法达到这个目标，但会非常接近光速。那时，从地球出发前往最近的恒星，只需飞行不到五年的时间。

我们的探索飞船将从他们的家园向外扩展，穿过一个不断扩大的球形空间。这一球形空间几乎以光速扩展，不过永远不会达到光速，五年后到达半人马座 α 星三星系统，十年后到达奇怪的构成双星系统的天狼星 A 和 B，十一年后到达神秘诱人的天鹅座 61，据猜测这是第一颗伴有行星的恒星。这些旅程虽然漫长，但并非不可能。人类总是愿意为探索和发现付出任何必要的代价，而探索太空的代价就是时间。

有朝一日，人类甚至可能会尝试持续几个世纪或上千年的太空航行。实验室已经成功使生命暂停，而这可能是星际旅行的关键。自给自足的宇宙方舟本身就是一个小小的旅行世界，这可能是另一种解决方案，这些方舟将使无限延续的太空旅行成为可能，可以一代代延续下去。

相对论预言了著名的时间膨胀效应，即对一个几乎以光速移动的旅行者而言，时间似乎过得更慢。时间膨胀效应可能是第三种解决方案，当然还有其他解决方案。

因此，展望未来，我们必须想象人类活动扩张的缓慢过程（略高于每小时5亿英里！），离开太阳系，进入我们现在所处的银河系中散布的恒星之间。这些恒星平均相距5光年的距离；换言之，我们从一颗恒星到达另一颗恒星，至少需要5年时间。

为说清楚这一点，可以打个切实的比方。想象一下，有一片广阔的海洋，到处都是岛屿——有些荒无人烟，有些可能有人居住，在其中一个岛上，一群充满活力的人刚刚掌握了造船技艺，正准备探索海洋，但他们必须面对这样一个事实：前往距离最近的岛屿需要航行五年，造船技术的任何改进都不可能缩短这一时间。

这种情况下（我们很快就会发现，自己也正面临同样的情况），这些岛民能取得什么成就呢？几个世纪后，他们可能已经在附近的很多岛屿上建立了殖民地，并对其他很多岛屿进行了简单探索。这些殖民地也可能会派出更多拓荒者，这种连锁反应将使母岛最初的文化在海洋上得到稳步传播。

但是，现在要考虑一下时间滞后所带来的影响，它是不可避免、必然出现的。母岛与子岛之间实际上仅存在最微弱的联系，信使返回时所报告的最近殖民地所发生的一切也都是五年前的事情，不可能带来更新的信息，而海上更远地方传来的消息则来自更久远的过去，也许来自几百年前。总之，从其他岛传来的消息都不是新闻，只是历史。

未来的所有星际殖民地都将独立，无论它们是否愿意。时间和空间将保护这些星际殖民地，使其自由不受侵犯，它们必须走自己的路，迎接自己的命运，没有来自地球母亲的帮助或阻挠。

说到这里，我们将把讨论转移到一个新的层面，并回应一种很明显的反对意见。我们可以确定光速真的是限制性因素吗？过去有那么多"不可逾越的"障碍都突破了；也许光速也会和其他障碍一样得到突破。

我们不会就这一点展开争论，也不会解释科学家为什么认为光速永远不会被任何形式的辐射或任何物体超越。我们反而要假设与此相反的情况，看看超过光速会带来什么结果。甚至可以设想最乐观的情况，想象传送速度最终会变得没有极限。

想象一下，有这样一个时代，技术的发展远超我们目前的水平，就像晶体管超越石斧的水平，我们可以瞬间到达自己想去的任何地方，如同拨电话号码一样轻松。这确实会缩小宇宙的尺寸，将物理距离缩小至零。那又会怎样呢？

实际上，一切都很重要。因为宇宙有双重特点，一是奇大无比，二是复杂无比，令人惊叹。解决了大小的问题，我们现在面对的是复杂这个问题。

现在在必须尝试想象数量问题而非尺度问题。大多数人都熟悉科学家用来描述大数字的简单记数法；只需计算零的个数，因此一百变成了 10^2，一百万变成了 10^6，十亿变成了 10^9，以此类推。这一窍门十分有用，使我们能够处理任何数量的数值，就连高达 5760000000 美元的美国国防预算用 5.76×10^9 美元表示时也显得不是太多。

银河系（我们所在的银河系由众多恒星和宇宙尘埃组成，呈旋涡状，太阳是旋涡外围的一颗恒星，位于较偏远的旋臂之中）其他恒星的数量约为 10^{11} 颗，完整表达为 100000000000 颗。目前的望远镜可以观察到大约 10^9 个其他星系，即使在我们视野的最大极限内，也看不出星系逐渐稀疏的迹象。

　　整个宇宙中，星系的数量可能至少与我们银河系中恒星的数量一样多，不过，还是让我们局限于自己能够观察到的星系吧。这些星系包含的恒星总数一定为 $10^{11} \times 10^9$ 颗，或者总计 10^{20} 颗恒星。当然，一个数字后面还有 20 个其他数字，真是一个不可胜数的数字。

　　在这样巨大的数字面前，即使是敢于面对光年这一计算单位的人也会感到畏惧。与探索宇宙相比，细数世界所有海滩上的沙粒显得微不足道。

　　因此，让我们回到文章开头的观点。人类可以为太空绘图，可以穿越太空和占领太空，没有任何限制；但人类永远无法征服太空。即使我们的成就登峰造极，人类可以遍布每个星球，我们依然就像地球表面爬行的蚂蚁一样。蚂蚁已遍布全世界，但它们是否征服了世界？它们占领了无数地方，但它们对这个世界了解多少，对彼此又了解多少呢？

　　从地球母亲出发向外扩张也是如此。亲情越来越淡薄，人们之间越来越缺乏相互理解，地球上的人口在宇宙全部人口中所占的比例也在不断减少，我们听到地球人类的消息都是通过二手、三手甚至一千手断断续续传来的，而且早已过时。

　　尽管地球会设法与自己的孩子们保持联系，但最终，地球上的档案管理员和历史学家付出的所有努力都将被时间和距离以及众多材料击败。因为，如果人类迄今的历史再延长一倍，不同社会或国家的数量可能会远远超过迄今为止曾在地球上生活过的总人口数。

　　我们妄图了解宇宙之大，这已经超出了人类所能理解的范围，这种企图永远都是徒劳，我们要认识到这一点，越早越好。

　　夏夜，身处户外，不妨抬头仰望天空。几乎就在你头顶的位置，闪烁着北方天空中最明亮的星星——天琴座织女星，距你 26 光年的距离，对我们这些短命的人类来说，前往这颗星就相当于踏上了一条不归路。经过这颗亮度达太阳 50 倍的蓝白色星球，我们可以把自己的思想和身体送到更远的地方，但永远无法将自己的感情发送过去。

因为一旦越过了织女星，没有人能够再活着回家，再次问候在地球上认识的人和爱着的人。

（彭萍 译）

28

Technology and World Politics

技术与世界政局

EUGENE B. SKOLNIKOFF
尤金·B. 斯柯尼科夫

(1928–)

ABOUT THE AUTHOR Chairman of the political science department at the Massachusetts Institute of Technology (MIT), Eugene Bertram Skolnikoff (born in Philadelphia in 1928) also holds degrees in economics, philosophy and electrical engineering. He has a special interest in the impact of new technology on developing countries, and has served as consultant in this field to the U.S. Agency for International Development.

作者简介 尤金·伯特伦·斯柯尼科夫（1928年生于费城），麻省理工学院政治学系主任，还拥有经济学、哲学和电气工程学位。他对新技术对发展中国家的影响特别感兴趣，并曾担任美国国际开发署该专业领域的顾问。

ABOUT THE SELECTION   The new technologies which can change our physical environment, exploit ocean resources, and send satellites into outer space make it imperative that governments and scientists devise new forms of international control. Professor Skolnikoff offers vivid examples to support his thesis, and explores some of the political implications of global technology. The themes of the essay are developed also in his book, *Science, Technology, and American Foreign Policy* (1967).

内容简介   新技术可以改变我们的物质环境，开发海洋资源，并将卫星送入外太空，因此政府和科学家必须设计新的国际管控形式。斯柯尼科夫教授列举了生动的例子来支持自己的论点，并探讨了全球技术的一些政治含义。这篇文章的主题也在其《科学、技术和美国外交政策》（1967）一书中得到进一步阐述。

With increasing frequency, new technologies are emerging that require the participation or cooperation of many countries, or that have effects that cannot be contained[1] within the boundaries of single states. Many examples of such global technology are at hand[2] or can be confidently predicted for the future. Communications satellites, or other applications of space vehicles, are typical illustrations. So, too, is the likely development of techniques for controlling the weather and for discovery and exploitation[3] of mineral resources under the oceans. All of these will (or already do) require international cooperation and regulation if their benefits are to be realized.[4]

It is not only new technologies that have international implications.[5] Often it is the enlarged scale[6] or intensity of application of well-known technologies that result in world-wide effects. One example is the danger of carbon dioxide accretion[7] in the atmosphere from the burning of fossil fuels[8] that may alter the planet's surface temperature. Another is the potentially poisonous effects on plants and fish and ultimately on man of increased spread of pesticides and herbicides.[9] And a third is the threat to fish resources in the growing efficiency of fishing technology.

A related phenomenon is the improving technical ability to inject ideas and information across borders into other societies, even when attempts are made to prevent such intrusion.[10] The possible development of a satellite able to broadcast radio or television directly to home receivers will give a strong boost to this capability.

The increasing prevalence[11] of technologies whose effects cross national boundaries has important long-term implications for every country's foreign policy, implications that deserve explicit recognition and serious analysis.

Limits to National Action

The steady diminution[12] of a nation's freedom of action to apply science and technology as it sees fit even at times[13] within its own borders, is one such implication. This restriction of action is not basically different from the better-recognized restrictions nations encounter because of the growing interdependence of national economies and societies. But the restrictions on action that flow from technology introduce a physical element that adds a new and compelling dimension[14] to interdependence. The physical aspect makes it more tangible,[15] and to the extent that some of the world-wide effects of technology may be irreversible,[16] can provide a formidable rallying point[17] for public opinion.

This gradual loss of national independence of action is paralleled by a requirement for international means to operate and to regulate global technology, and to provide a forum for airing disputes.[18] Global technology thus tends to force decision making away from the decentralized national government level[19] toward centralized international policy machinery.[20]

In addition, there is the growing mismatch between the requirements of technology and the resources of nation-states. Today, most of the smaller countries of the world are unable to utilize all or even many modern technologies because of their limited national resources. The larger and richer states of Western Europe now find it impossible acting alone to mount meaningful programs in all prominent new technical fields. And even the United States and the Soviet Union find their resources strained in an attempt to compete in large systems fields.

There are already examples of amalgamations[21] or consortia[22] of nations brought together because of the imperatives[23] of new technology: the Common Market[24] efforts in atomic energy, and the broader European cooperation in space are cases in point. Undoubtedly this tendency for joint action, too, will accelerate in the future as it is realized that cooperative undertakings are essential if the benefits as well as the dangers of global technologies are to be met.

Last is the more general observation that technological developments are likely to be even more dramatic in the future than they have been in the recent past. Man's environment almost surely will continue to be altered by conscious design, and too often accidentally, in the years to come as the desire to make "improvements" is matched by available power to do so. And "improvements" undertaken for local objectives may have far broader effects beyond national borders, not always to the approval of other nations.

Let me cite some examples of current or anticipated technological developments that have profound international implications.

Weather and Climate Modification

Man's long quest for climate control is finally moving out of the realm of fantasy. The experimental evidence from cloud-seeding experiments suggests that rainfall can be increased locally by 5 to 20 percent. It takes only a little imagination to anticipate the problems that are sure to arise within countries and between adjacent or nearby countries with regard to[25] water distribution. Eventually, the question will emerge of how to allocate[26] what will be, in effect, a finite resource of atmosphere-borne fresh water supplies.

The capability to modify storms is likely to be operational in the next 10-20 years, raising the prospect that we will be able to divert or suppress Atlantic hurricanes. An ability to modify major storms looks desirable, of course, in the light of[27] the extensive damage they cause. But such an ability raises rather important technical and international issues. For example, tropical storms bred in the Caribbean[28] are a major source of water for parts of the U.S. and the Caribbean region; thus, suppression of storms will be costly. And, if it were even suspected that modification (i.e. strength-reduction) activities had also deflected[29] the course of the hurricane, legal claims for damage or water deprivation could result. In addition, hurricane modification activities must necessarily be carried out[30] in an international environment—even, at times, over several different national territories.

The feasibility of intentionally modifying climate on a large scale is probably too far in the future yet to be a candidate for planning. On the horizon, however, are bold schemes for melting the Arctic ice cap, with the intention of providing increased moisture for the vast Canadian and Siberian regions. The actual effects of removing part of the Arctic ice cover are not agreed upon; some predict catastrophic[31] results from such a step. But it must be realized that, even now, the resources required for such a project may not be beyond the capabilities of a single large state (a Bering Straits[32] dam—one method—is entirely feasible at costs comparable to large continental dams). Moreover, the incentive[33] to proceed could be enormous. And what international machinery does the world have to say that such a project cannot be "allowed" to proceed?

The inadvertent[34] modification of weather and climate resulting from the rapid alteration of the earth's surface and the dispersion[35] of wastes of all kinds into the atmosphere is a clear possibility. The most general kind of global change relevant to climate is the alteration of the planet's radiation balance. What becomes evident upon examination of the present state of knowledge is that the world could be heading for a major catastrophe, but there is neither enough information about what is actually happening, nor enough understanding of the environment, to be sure. The danger period may well be in the remaining years of the century; or at least, quite evident by then.

Pollution

The needs and the wastes of society both grow at exponential[36] rates. An expected world population close to five billion (by 1985) would lead to more than a 40 percent increase in requirements for food, energy, and natural resources just to maintain the present economic levels, unsatisfactory as they are for much of the population. In fact, these requirements will be substantially increased by economic growth in all countries and by the corresponding increase in industrialization. To meet these requirements it will be necessary to use massive quantities of fertilizers and insecticides, transport and burn larger quantities of fuel, dispose of more agricultural and industrial waste, transform more agricultural land into houses and highways, cut down more forests, and find more fresh water supplies.

Disposal of waste is not a single problem, but an enormously complicated interrelationship. The implications of a change in one aspect cannot be seen adequately or approached adequately without consideration of the rest.

Thus we have the need for DDT for health and food, but also its potentially catastrophic effects on animal life; the need for fertilizer to produce adequate amounts of food, but also its effects on the eutrophication[37] of bodies of water; the atmospheric effects of industrial effluents;[38] the dangers of large-scale oil-spills arising from the transport of needed fuel in huge tankers; the radiation, waste-disposal and security problems associated with nuclear power plants.

Much of the task of controlling pollution will be a national responsibility; but there will also be substantial, and growing needs for international action. At the least there is a need for establishing international norms for effluents with global effects, for solid waste disposal, for tanker routing, for actions in the event of ship accidents and so forth. This need for international norms will be most obvious, and will be relatively easily met, when the pollutants clearly cross national borders.

Where the pollution has more subtle effects, and requires for its amelioration[39] unaccustomed domestic limitations in certain fields, the political problems will be more serious—for example, if limitations must be established for the total annual discharge of specific pollutants, or if certain technologies must be banned altogether, or their use rationed.[40]

Similarly, the costs of controlling some industrial wastes will fall unequally. Who should pay—the producer, the consumer, or the nations most offended by the particular pollutant? A nation's competitive position in international trade may be substantially affected by the measures it must take. Regulation must therefore be in some sense international simply to maintain fair competition. But what is "fair"?

The Oceans

The focus of the first attempts at codifying[41] international law, the oceans are today a major area for the application of new technology, and as a result the cause of much rethinking and reshaping of international law. (An international conference on legal regimes for the oceans is planned for 1973.) We need mention briefly only two of the major aspects that must be dealt with: the resources of the seabed, and the living resources of the sea itself.

It is thought that the world's greatest supplies of fossil fuels are likely to be found under the seabed, and particularly under the continental rise (the final section of continental land before reaching the sea floor—generally deeper than 3,000 meters). Other resources of the seabottom are also of potential interest, particularly manganese, nickel, copper, sulphur, gold, tin, platinum and the "detrital" minerals (sand and gravel). At present, except marginally for sand and gravel, the alternative sources of supply on land seem sufficient to preclude rapid economic exploitation of these undersea minerals, by contrast with[42] oil and gas.

The major international questions, of course, have to do with who owns these resources, and thus has rights to their benefits. The Convention on the Continental Shelf of 1958 gives each coastal state sovereign rights for the purpose of exploration and exploitation. The shelf is defined as "the seabed and subsoil...to a depth of 200 meters or, beyond that limit, where the depth of the superjacent waters admits of the exploitation of the natural resources of the said area..." In other words, if you have the technology to go deeper, it is yours.

Whether the existing convention remains in force, or some modification is eventually agreed to (the U.S. has proposed international ownership beyond 200 meters), one can hypothesize the kind of international functions that may have to be performed if private or public interests are to be able to exploit the resources of the seabed with relative security of investment, and if demands for equitable distribution of benefits are to be satisfied.

In essence,[43] the primary question is again that of allocation and benefits. Assuming any resolution of the limitations of sovereignty other than a simple division of the entire oceans among coastal states (which is most unlikely, since it would not conform with[44] present political realities: Russia would get little, Britain, a new empire based on her island possessions), some kind of regime will have to be established for unassigned areas. This regime would not only have to have a means of deciding who has access to[45] what portions of the seabed and under what conditions, but also a procedure for distributing whatever benefits accrue.

The major concern with regard to the sea's living resources is the trends in present fishing practices and technology in relation to the maximizing of yields. It is a controversial issue, but some scientists do not estimate the potential harvest of the sea to be very much greater than the present harvest, about 60 million metric tons per year. Any attempts at really improving the total catch will depend not only on improved technology; they will depend directly on more ecological knowledge,[46] more efficient fishery methods, controlled competition, and conservation. In fact, improved technology and greater fishing effort, uncontrolled, would lead only to depletion[47] of fish resources. It is almost certain that by the 1980's total catch limits will have to be imposed on essentially all species of commercially important fish (as is already the case for several fish species, by agreement in the relevant Fisheries Commissions).

Thus, for fisheries regulation, one sees the same basic functions as for seabed resources. To obtain the protein that the world's population needs, and to prevent the serious depletion of species endangered by overfishing, may well require the limitation of fishing rights on the high seas, and hence create the need for the conscious allocation of a scarce resource.

Outer Space

There will soon be in existence two major international programs probing the atmosphere: the World Weather Watch, and the Global Atmospheric Research Program. Both will employ, among other sensors,[48] weather satellites. These programs, and follow-on[49] operational programs, will have two immediate effects related to resource availability: they will add to the demand for radio frequencies; and they will require "orbital space," which may be scarce if geostationary orbits[50] are needed.

Of greater long-range significance is the fact that as weather forecasting improves there will be an increased degree of dependence on the forecasts, until they become an essential element in many societal activities, especially related to agriculture. The space portion of a world-wide weather-monitoring system[51] will inevitably be a major component of the system. As dependence grows, there will be increasing resistance to relying on systems controlled by any single country. Internationalization will be inevitable.

Orbiting communications relays[52] will grow substantially in channel capacity,[53] and are likely to be increasingly sophisticated, with well-defined geographical coverage, increased power, and specialized capabilities. Once again, the demand for frequencies will add enormously to the problems of spectrum allocation.[54] And, since communications satellites will mostly be in geostationary orbits (to minimize the costs of the ground terminals) the pressure on available parking spaces in that narrow band around the equator 22,300 miles up will sharply increase. Again, the growing importance of communication satellite systems to national economies will stimulate opposition to continued dominance by one nation.

I have had room only to deal with a few broad topics—environment alteration, ocean resources, outer space. One could also add natural resource management, population growth, information-processing,[55] genetic engineering,[56] and, of course, military technology as areas in which the need for some international regulatory machinery is equally clear.

The Political Implications

Thus, science and technology are presenting all nations with a trend toward physical internationalization that, whether consciously appreciated now or not, is likely to force far-reaching changes in the structure of the international political system in the years to come. At the very least, the trend is certain to set up major new political stresses and pressures that are likely to force the pace of political change.

One lesson is obvious: the direction of future developments in science and technology, because of the resources they require, is likely to be increasingly determined in the political arena[57] rather than independently; therefore, it is not amiss[58] for responsible foreign policy officials to work with scientists and engineers now to explore international political initiatives that might provide a means of controlling the development of global technology. This latter point, a somewhat heretical[59] one, deserves further elaboration.

Attempts to suppress basic science are surely unwise and futile. They are unwise because of the penalties paid in the imposition of intellectual control[60] that would be required; unwise because the agreements necessary with other countries to avoid the danger of scientific surprise would be unenforceable except under conditions of extreme and unrealistic intellectual control, and unwise because such a ban would mean forgoing[61] highly desirable technological applications—including some which might ameliorate technology—that arise from scientific discoveries. Attempts to suppress basic science would be futile, for there would be no way of knowing confidently in advance which fields to ban in order to prevent developments in a supposedly undesirable direction. Once launched on such a course of suppression of science, there would be no logical end to the degree and breadth of control that would be required.

But why is this even raised as a question? The answer, of course, is that the accretion of scientific knowledge continues to put ever more power under man's control, power with the potential of actual destruction of the human species or of alteration of the species and the environment in ways incommensurate[62] with present values. The motivation can also be stated in more modest terms: scientific advances often lead to developments that increase the instability of power. Or, more precisely: the unpredictability of scientific advance implies that it is always a potentially destabilizing[63] factor in international relations. The possibility of sudden developments that would make a new weapon system feasible, such as an effective missile defense or a discovery that reduces the cost and complexity of powerful weapons, thereby making them available to smaller countries, are cases in point.

Should Science Be Controlled?

It is a platitude[64] to observe that it is not science itself that is destabilizing and it is not science that is the direct agent for evil. It is, instead, man's technological application of scientific knowledge that should be the focus of attention. But the layman has the right to ask not only whether technology can be controlled but also whether the underlying science that made the technology possible can be controlled.

Scientists have been derelict[65] in refusing to take this question of suppression of science seriously, for the answers are not obvious to nonscientists. Especially are the answers unclear in an era in which many fields of science require massive resources supplied from public funds for their continued progress. A modest prediction may be made that in the future there will be many more challenges to the continued public support of science, especially expensive fields of science, when the beneficial results are not obvious and the potentially harmful effects, though unknown in detail, are feared.

High-energy physics could be one such field, for already there is speculation[66] about new reactions (matter/antimatter) with fantastic releases of energy that are at least theoretically possible. If, in fact, gigantic new particle accelerators[67] may make it possible to obtain the knowledge that would make such a reaction suitable for military use, the layman is asking a legitimate question when he wonders whether he wants his government to spend the money to bring that possibility about. What beneficial gains are likely to be realized that could offset the dangers? Would it not be better to cut off high-energy physics now, especially as the ability to suppress the field appears simple: refuse to build new accelerators?

(And an international agreement not to build any large new accelerators ought to be easy to enforce.)

The major flaw in that argument, leaving entirely aside questions of whether it is wise on other grounds, is that it is impossible to predict not only what beneficial results would be obtained from continued research in high-energy physics but also whether the knowledge that is feared might not be obtained anyway through lower cost research in related fields. Attempting to stifle a science by refusing to provide expensive research equipment is not a certain way to prevent its advance.

Although the conclusion that it is unwise and impractical to interfere with the progress of basic science is easy to arrive at, there may be other measures possible that will make more feasible the control of any subsequent undesirable applications growing from the science.[68]

The Internationalization of Science

One of the major concerns in the development of a powerful new technology is the possibility of its uncontrolled use for narrow national ends.[69] Might it be useful, therefore, to begin to support some sciences—or perhaps all—through international as well as national mechanisms? International sponsorship of science will not remove the danger of use of the resulting knowledge by individual nations, but it may serve to create a presumption[70] that international means are appropriate to its control. Moreover, international sponsorship may help to reduce the fear of scientific or technological surprise because the same scientific information would be known to all. At a minimum, the existence of channels of communication and a habit of cooperation in a given field may make it easier to contemplate some kind of international agreement for the control of a dangerous technology that develops from the work in that field.

Without doubt, the world will face the question of control or suppression of technology increasingly in the future, perhaps with regard to developments even more frightening than nuclear weapons in their power to influence the global environment or human heredity. The issue deserves more concentrated attention and discussion if the history of nuclear proliferation[71] is not to be repeated. And it may well be time to consider more seriously the internationalization of science support as a means of improving the prospects for control of dangerous technology.

An entirely different aspect of the scientific revolution is becoming more evident and more perplexing in its implications for international affairs. For the first time in history it is possible to say that the lack of technical knowledge is no longer a major barrier to solving man's material problems. This does not mean that the physical knowledge is already in hand for all problems of agriculture, energy, exploitation of water and mineral resources, pollution, or overpopulation. It does mean that man now has the tools to seek and find solutions to such problems and has already demonstrated in each category that solutions are possible.

This circumstance would seem to place an added moral responsibility on the scientifically advanced nations to devote more of their scientific resources to the problems of less developed countries. And it raises acutely the pragmatic[72] question of how technology can be more fully and successfully directed toward solving the physical problems that contribute to international tension.

A New Environment for Foreign Affairs

These new trends toward technologies with global implications do more than simply alter the general environment within which policy must operate. They also raise questions about some of the cherished traditions of nationhood, about the assumptions associated with the present organization of the international political system, and about the traditional beliefs surrounding science and technology themselves. In an important sense it can be said that the underlying forces and relationships on which international politics rest have already been altered in basic ways from 19th-century concepts by the scientific revolution.

Yet, foreign and domestic policies proceed about as always, with only sporadic[73] recognition that control of territory has become an uncertain and ambiguous concept, that freedom of national action and inviolability[74] of borders have long since lost so much of their traditional meaning, that the size of the resources of most nation-states are incommensurate with the requirements of modern technology, and that international organizations must fill a more important role than simply amplify[75] big power goals.

And it must not be forgotten that the rapid advances of science and technology until now are but the prelude to even more rapid remaking of man's environment in the future. Technology will spread, will increase the dependence of one country on another, will create wholly new international relationships, will force new degrees of cooperation and dispute, will result in new threats to international stability, and will raise more problems of overpopulation and environmental pollution.

These developments cannot be predicted in detail, but neither are they impenetrable.[76] Moreover, they are likely to force or call for[77] additional, significant, and perhaps fundamental shifts in national attitudes toward both domestic and international affairs. Accordingly, a much greater effort is warranted[78] in attempting to understand the nature of future developments and, most important, to understand their full meaning for international relations.

NOTES

1. contained: controlled.
2. at hand: within reach.
3. exploitation: utilization for profit.
4. realized: made real; gave reality to a hope or a plan.

5. implications: involvement; relationships of a close, intimate nature.
6. scale: extent.
7. accretion: increase; growth.
8. fossil fuels: matter dug out of the earth for maintaining fire, such as coal and oil.
9. pesticides and herbicides: chemical preparations for destroying pests (as flies, mosquitoes etc,) and for killing weeds.
10. intrusion: overstepping; transgression; trespass.
11. prevalence: utilization.
12. diminution: decrease.
13. at times: occasionally; at intervals.
14. dimension: importance; scope.
15. tangible: real or actual rather than imaginary.
16. irreversible: unalterable; constant.
17. formidable rallying point: appalling significance of coming together for common action.
18. airing disputes: having public arguments.
19. decentralized national government level: a level on which the administrative powers are distributed over a less concentrated area.
20. machinery: any system by which action is maintained, as the machinery of government.
21. amalgamation: union; combination.
22. consortia: plural form for "consortium", meaning partnerships or cooperations.
23. imperatives: needs.
24. Common Market: an economic association established in 1958 to abolish barriers to free trade among member nations and to adopt common import duties on goods from other countries. Its official name is European Economic Community. Its original members are Belgium, France, Italy, Luxemburg, the Netherlands, and West Germany.
25. with regard to: in the matter of.
26. allocate: arrange; assign; locate; distribute.
27. in the light of: taking into account; considering.
28. the Caribbean: the Caribbean Sea, a part of the Atlantic Ocean bounded by Central America, the West Indies, and South America.
29. deflected: diverted; changed; turned aside.
30. be carried out: be put into operation; be executed.
31. catastrophic: disastrous.

32. Bering Straits: a strait between Alaska and the Soviet Union in Asia, connecting the Bering Sea and the Arctic Ocean, 36 miles wide.
33. incentive: invitation, stimulus.
34. inadvertent: negligent; inattentive.
35. dispersion: scattering; distribution.
36. exponential: multiple; numerical.
37. eutrophication: an abundant accumulation of nutrients that support a dense growth of plants and animal life the decay of which uses up the oxygen of the shallow waters in the summer.
38. effluents: outflow.
39. amelioration: improvement.
40. rationed: budgeted.
41. codifying: arranging in a systematic collection; putting into the form of a code.
42. by contrast with: unlike.
43. in essence: basically; essentially.
44. conform with: agree with; meet.
45. has access to: has admission to.
46. ecological knowledge: biological knowledge dealing with the relations between organisms and their environment.
47. depletion: exhaustion; consumption.
48. sensors: devices to detect information of something, mechanically, electrically, or photoelectrically.
49. follow-on: subsequent; succeeding.
50. geostationary orbits: travels of man-made satellites around the earth in certain speeds so that they move with the earth and always stay over fixed ground locations.
51. weather-monitoring system: a system that may observe, record and detect weather conditions with instruments that have no effect upon the atmosphere.
52. communications relays: a series of low-altitude, active communications satellites for receiving and transmitting radio and television signals.
53. channel capacity: ability to transmit radio, television, telegram, telephone frequencies for communication.
54. spectrum allocation: the distribution of frequency spectrum.
55. information-processing: treatment and preparation of information.

56. genetic engineering: the science or art of using biological methods in enhancing heredity to design human beings with desired traits.
57. arena: a field of conflict, activity, or endeavor.
58. amiss: wrong; faulty.
59. heretical: unsound.
60. the penalties paid in the imposition of intellectual control: the disadvantages resulting from the exercise of intellectual control and suppression of science.
61. forgoing: giving up.
62. incommensurate: unsatisfying; inadequate; insufficient.
63. destabilizing: having the quality of making things less stable.
64. platitude: a flat, dull trite remark; cliché.
65. derelict: negligent.
66. speculation: meditation; consideration; reflection.
67. particle accelerators: electrostatic or electromagnetic devices that produce high energy particles and focus them on a target. They are also called atom smashers.
68. there may be other possible ways which will make the control of undesirable scientific applications more practical.
69. ends: objectives.
70. presumption: probability; hope.
71. proliferation: growth by multiplication as the division of cells.
72. pragmatic: realistic; practical.
73. sporadic: fitful; irregular.
74. inviolability: sanctity; the prohibiting of violation.
75. amplify: expand; develop.
76. impenetrable: unapproachable; beyond reach, incapable of being comprehended.
77. call for: warrant; require; entail.
78. warranted: justified; rationalized.

参考译文

新技术不断更迭，需要很多国家参与或合作，产生的影响无法控制在一国境内。这种全球性技术随处可见，可以预见未来必然会出现很多。通信卫星或宇宙飞船的其他应用都属于典型例证，天气控制技术以及海底矿产资源勘探和开采技术也会成为典型例证。所有这些均需要国际合作和监管，才能发挥其作用，现在如此，将来亦如此。

具有国际影响的不仅限于新兴技术。常见技术应用规模扩大，应用频率增加，常常也会产生国际影响。例如，化石燃料会造成大气中二氧化碳增加，地球表面温度面临改变的危险。又如，杀虫剂和除草剂使用范围扩大，会对植物和鱼类产生潜在毒性作用，最终会对人类产生潜在毒性作用。再如，捕鱼技术日趋高效，会对鱼类资源造成威胁。

与此相连，思想和信息跨国传播的技术能力不断提高，尽管有人试图阻止这种侵扰。比如，卫星技术可能会不断发展，能够直接向家庭接收器传送广播或电视节目，这将有力提升跨国传播能力。

产生国际影响的技术越来越普及，对每个国家的外交政策都会产生深远而重要的影响，各国需要清楚地认识到这些影响并对其进行认真分析。

对国家行动的限制

影响之一，国家以自认为合适的方式应用科学和技术的行动，其自由度逐步减少，有时甚至在其境内也是如此。这种限制与各国因经济和社会日益相互依存而遇到的公认限制没有本质区别。但是，技术造成的行动限制引入了一个物质因素，为相互依存的关系增加了一个引人注目的新维度。这一物质因素使相互依存变得更加具体，使技术对全球的某些影响变得不可逆转，对凝聚民意具有很强的号召力。

国家行动的独立性逐渐丧失，这就要求使用国际手段进行操作，对全球科技进行监管，针对争议举办论坛进行公开讨论。因此，世界技术往往迫使决策工作从分散的国家政府层面转向集中的国际政策机构。

此外，技术要求与民族国家的资源之间变得越来越不匹配。如今，由于国家资源有限，全世界大多数小国都无法利用全部现代技术，或无法利用很多现代技术。西欧较富裕的大国发现，不可能单独依靠自己在所有重要的新技术领域实施有意义的计划。就连美国和苏联也发现，如果试图在大型系统领域进行竞争，自己的资源就显得紧张。

由于新技术的需要，已经出现了国家联合的实例：欧洲共同市场在核能方面的努力以及欧洲在太空方面更广泛的合作，都是典型例证。毫无疑问，这种联合行动的趋势未来也会进一步加快，因为各国都认识到，如果要获得全球技术带来的利益，应对全球技术带来的威胁，国际合作至关重要。

最后，各国普遍认为，未来技术发展可能会比此前更为迅猛。未来几年，随着人们有能力"改进"技术，人类环境几乎一定会继续被有意识的设计所改变，而且往往非常偶然。为实现地方目标去改进技术可能会产生更广泛的国际影响，但并非总是能够得到其他国家的认可。

以下是一些当前或可能产生深刻国际影响的技术发展例证。

改变天气和气候

长期以来，人类想要控制气候，这终于不再是幻想。实验证据表明，人工降雨可以使局部降雨量增加 5% 到 20%。稍加想象，就可以预见，国家内部及相邻国家之间一定会出现水资源分配方面的问题。最终的问题在于，如何分配实则有限的大气淡水资源。

未来 10 至 20 年，人类可能拥有削弱风暴的能力，提升了我们转移或抑制大西洋飓风的可能性。当然，鉴于大型风暴造成的巨大破坏，削弱这些风暴的能力似乎令人向往，但这种能力也提出了相当重要的技术问题和国际问题。例如，源自加勒比海的热带风暴是美国部分地区和加勒比海地区的主要水源；因此，削弱这些热带风暴将付出高昂的代价。而且，如果怀疑削弱风暴（即降低强度）活动使飓风的路线发生偏移，则可能因飓风造成的损害或水资源丧失而产生法律纠纷。此外，削弱飓风的活动必须在国际环境中进行——有时甚至要在几个不同国家的领土上进行。

有意识地对气候进行大规模改造，可能在遥远的未来才能实现，无法作为候选计划。不过，有一些融化北极冰盖的大胆计划已经提上日程，这些计划旨在使辽阔的加拿大和西伯利亚地区变得更加湿润。各国对消除部分北极冰盖的实际效果并未达成一致意见；一些国家预测这种做法会导致灾难性的后果。但是，必须认识到，即使是现在，这样一个项目所需的资源可能不会超出一个大国的能力（其中一种方法是建造白令海峡大坝，其成本与在大陆修建大坝相当，完全可行）。此外，该项目有巨大的驱动力。那么，世界根据何种国际机制认定不应"允许"实施这样的项目呢？

地球表面迅速变化，各种废物在大气中扩散，都可能导致天气和气候在不知不觉中发生改变。最常见的全球气候变化是地球辐射平衡改变。就目前所了解，世界可能正在陷入一场巨大的灾难，但是，由于对实际情况缺乏足够的信息，对环境也缺乏足够的了解，还不能证明这种观点是否正确。本世纪后期很有可能就会看到上述危险；或者至少在本世纪，危险会变得相当明显。

污　　染

社会需求及废物排放均以指数级速度增长。预计世界人口接近 50 亿时（截至 1985 年），食物、能源和自然资源的需求将增加

40%以上，而这仅仅可以维持目前的经济水平，但大多数人对目前的经济水平并不满意。事实上，各国经济增长和工业化的相应增长会使得这些需求大大增加。为满足这些需求，就要使用大量化肥和杀虫剂，运输和燃烧更多燃料，处理更多工业和农业废弃物，将更多农业用地变成房屋和公路，砍伐更多森林，寻找更多淡水资源。

废物处理并非简单的问题，而是一个极其复杂、相互关联的问题。如果不考虑其他方面，就无法充分认识其中一个方面的变化所产生的影响，也无法充分解决相关问题。

因此，我们因为健康和食物而需要DDT杀虫剂，但也要考虑DDT杀虫剂对动物生命潜在的灾难性影响；我们需要化肥来生产足够多的食物，但也要考虑化肥对水体富营养化的影响；此外，还要考虑工业废水对大气的影响、大型油轮所需燃料运输产生的大规模石油泄漏危险以及核电站辐射、废物处理和安全问题等。

控制污染的任务将成为一项国家责任，对国际行动的需求也将大幅增加。至少有必要为产生全球影响的污水、固体废物处理、油轮航线、船舶事故处置等建立国际规范。如果污染物明显跨越国界，这时就最需要制定国际规范，而且这种需求相对容易满足。

如果污染的影响不易察觉，而且需要国家在特定领域对其进行非常规的限制，就会带来更严重的政治问题——例如，必须限制特定污染物的年度排放总量，完全禁止特定技术，或约束特定技术的应用。

与此相类似，控制某些工业废物的成本分摊也不均衡。谁应该支付成本，生产者还是消费者，抑或是受特定污染物侵害最严重的国家？必须采取的措施可能会对一个国家在国际贸易中的竞争地位产生实质性影响。因此，在某种意义上，为维持公平竞争，这些规则必须是国际规则。但什么是"公平"？

海　洋

最早尝试编纂国际法所关注的焦点就是海洋，现在，海洋是新技术应用的主要领域，因此也有必要对国际法进行再思考和重新修订。（按照计划，1973年将召开一次关于海洋法律制度的国际会议。）在此需要简单提及必须应对的两个主要方面：海床资源和海洋自身的生物资源。

人们认为，世界上规模最大的化石燃料往往储藏在海底，特别是大陆架（延伸至海底的最后一段大陆，深度往往超过3000米）。海底的其他资源也有潜在价值，特别是锰、镍、铜、硫、金、锡、铂和"碎屑"矿物（沙子和砾石）。目前，与石油和天然气相比，除了少量的沙子和砾石，陆地上的替代资源似乎比较丰富，可以阻止这些海底矿物的快速经济开发。

当然，主要国际问题在于哪个国家拥有这些资源并因此拥有获得其收益的权利。1958年的《大陆架公约》赋予每个沿海国家勘探和开发大陆架的主权。大陆架的定义是"海床和底土……深度为200米，或者超过此限度上覆水域深度容许开采其自然资源的上述区域……"换言之，如果拥有开发更深海底的技术，就可以占有这片区域。

无论现存公约继续有效，还是最终达成一致的修改意见（美国已建议深度超过200米的区域所有权归国际公有），如果私人利益集团或公共利益集团能够在投资相对安全的情况下开发海底资源，如果可以满足公平分配利益的需求，那么就要设定必须履行的某种国际职能。

实质上，主要还是分配和利益问题。假定采用主权限制的解决方案而非在沿海国家之间简单划分整个海洋（这几乎不可能，因为不符合目前的政治现实：如果这样，俄罗斯只能得到一点点海洋，而英国因为拥有众多岛屿会成为一个新的帝国），就必须为未分配的地区建立某种制度。该制度不仅要规定方法来决定哪国可以在什么条件下使用海底哪些部分，而且还要规定程序来分配所产生的所有收益。

关于海洋生物资源，关注的重点是目前的捕捞趋势以及使产量最大化的技术趋势。这是一个有争议的问题，但一些科学家估计，海洋的潜在捕捞量不会超出现在每年约6000万吨的捕捞量很多。任何真正提高总捕捞量的尝试不仅取决于技术改进，还将直接取决于更丰富的生态知识、更有效的捕捞方法、受到限制的竞争和海洋保护情况。实际上，改进技术和加大捕捞量不加以控制，只会导致鱼类资源枯竭。几乎可以肯定的是，到20世纪80年代，几乎所有具有商业价值的鱼类都必须实行捕捞总量限制（渔业委员会的相关协议对一些鱼类已经实行了限制）。

因此，对于渔业监管，人们看到了与海底资源相同的基本功能。为了获得世界人口所需的蛋白质，并防止因过度捕捞而濒临灭绝的物种严重枯竭，有充分理由限制公海捕鱼权，从而使人们认识到有必要对稀缺资源进行明确分配。

外 太 空

以下两项探测大气层的重要国际计划很快得到实施：世界天气监测网和全球大气研究计划。除其他传感器外，两项计划都将使用气象卫星。这些计划和后续运行方案将产生与资源可用性有关的两种直接影响，即需要提高无线电频率，还需要"轨道空间"，如果需要地球同步轨道，这些轨道空间可能会变得稀缺。

更具广泛意义的是，随着天气预报不断改进，人们对预报的依赖程度会越来越高，天气预报最终会成为众多社会活动的一个基本要素，特别是与农业有关的活动。世界范围内的天气监测系统的太空部分无疑会成为该系统一个主要组成部分。随着对该系统的依赖性日益增加，人们会愈发反对依赖任何单一国家控制的系统，国际化便不可避免。

在轨通信中继卫星的信道容量将大大增加，而且可能变得越来越复杂，地理覆盖范围划定明确，功率提高，能力进一步专业化。另外，由于通信卫星将主要在地球同步轨道上运行（旨在尽量降低地面终端的成本），赤道周围22300英里狭窄地带的可用部署空间所面临的压力将急剧增加。同样，通信卫星系统对国家经济的作用日益重要，将促使人们反对某一国家继续占主导地位。

由于篇幅有限，这里只能讨论几个宽泛的主题，包括环境改变、海洋资源和外太空问题，实际上还可以加上自然资源管理、人口增长、信息处理、遗传工程等问题，当然还有军事技术问题，这些领域同样需要一些国际监管机制。

政 治 影 响

因此，科学和技术正在向所有国家展示一种实实在在的国际化趋势，无论现在是否有意识地加以重视，都可能迫使国际政治体系的结构未来几年发生深远的变化。至少，这一趋势一定会带来新的巨大政治压力，可能迫使政治加快变革步伐。

一个教训显而易见：因所需资源限制，科学和技术的未来发展方向可能会越来越取决于政治领域，而非由科学和技术独立决定；因此，相关外交政策官员与科学家和工程师合作，探索可能为全球技术发展提供管理手段的国际政治倡议，这一做法十分正确。后一点听起来有些荒谬，需要进一步阐述。

如果企图控制基础科学，那显然既不明智又是徒劳。之所以不明智，是因为实施必要的知识控制需要付出代价；之所以不明智，是因为除非实施极端和不现实的知识控制，否则无法执行必须与其他国家达成的有关避免科学意外危险的协议；之所以不明智，还因为这种禁令意味着放弃来源于科学发现的优良技术应用，包括使技术得到改进的部分应用。企图控制基础科学之所以徒劳，是因为无法事先确定要禁止哪些领域以防止向所谓的不良方向发展。一旦开始了控制科学的进程，就无法合理控制需要控制的程度和广度。

但这为什么会成为问题呢？答案当然是，科学知识的不断积累会不断赋予人类更多的能力，这些能力实际上有可能毁灭人类，或者通过与当前价值观相悖的方式改变物种和环境。这种动机也可以用更温和的语言来表述：科学进步往往会使人类的能力朝着不稳定的方向发展。或者，更确切地说：科学进步的不可预测性意味着科学进步始终是国际关系中一个潜在不稳定因素。突如其来的技术发展可能会使新武器系统变得可行，例如有效的导弹防御或发现可以降低强大武器成本和复杂性，从而使小国也能使用这些武器。这些都是需要考虑的问题。

应该对科学实施控制吗？

破坏稳定局面的不是科学本身，科学也不是邪恶的直接动因，这是老生常谈。相反，人类对科学知识的技术应用才应成为关注的焦点。但是，外行人不仅有权询问是否可以控制技术，更有权询问是否可以控制技术赖以生存的基础科学。

科学家们一直毫不在意，拒绝认真对待有关压制科学的问题，因为答案对非科学家来说并不清晰。尤其是当今时代，答案更不明确，因为很多科学领域需要由公共基金提供大量资源才能继续发展。可以做一个适度的预测，未来，如果科学带来的益处并不明显，而潜在的有害影响虽然未知，却令人担心，那么公众对科学的持续支持将会面临更多挑战，特别是研发成本高昂的科学领域。

高能物理可能就是这样一个领域，因为已经有人推测会发生新的物理反应（物质/反物质），这种反应会释放极高的能量，至少在理论上是可能的。实际上，如果规模巨大的新粒子加速器使人们获得了一定的知识，能够使这种反应适用于军事用途，那么，外行人会自问是否希望政府花钱来实现这种可能性，这是一个合理的问题。比如，可能获得哪些收益来抵消该反应带来的危险？终止高能物理研究不是更好吗，特别是现在压制该领域发展其实很容易。比如，是否可以拒绝建造新的加速器？（应该很容易执行关于不建造任何大型新加速器的国际协议。）

可以完全抛开基于其他各种理由提出是否明智的问题不谈，上述论点的主要缺陷在于，不仅无法预测继续高能物理研究会获得何种有益的结果，更无法预测是否可以通过低成本研究获得令人恐惧的知识。试图通过拒绝提供昂贵的研究设备来扼杀一门科学，并不一定能阻止其发展。

虽然很容易得出以下结论：干预基础科学的发展不明智且不切实际，但可能有其他措施使人们更容易控制因科学产生的不良应用。

科学的国际化

对于开发强大的新技术，人们的主要担忧在于，该技术有可能被不加控制地用于狭隘的国家目的。因此，人们提出疑问：使用国际机制和国家机制支持一些学科（也许是所有学科）是否有益？为科学提供国际赞助，不会消除个别国家使用其产生的知识所带来的危险，但可能会促使人们认为，应该用国际手段来管控科学。此外，国际赞助可能会让人们不再过多害怕科学或技术带来的意外，因为人们都可以获取同样的科学信息。至少，某一领域如存在沟通渠道和合作习惯，就更容易达成某种国际协议，以控制源自该领域工作的危险技术。

毫无疑问，未来世界将越来越多地面临管控或压制技术的问题，也许在影响全球环境或人类遗传能力方面，技术发展甚至比核武器更令人恐惧。如果核扩散的历史不再重演，技术造成的影响问题就应该得到更集中的关注和讨论。而且，现在就应该更认真考虑将科学支持的国际化作为改善管控危险技术前景的一种手段。

在科学对国际事务的影响方面，科学革命一个完全不同方面正变得更加明显，也更加令人困惑。缺乏技术知识不再是解决人类物质问题的主要障碍，这也许是人类有史以来第一次这么认为。当然，这并不意味着人类掌握了有关农业、能源、水和矿产资源开发、污染或人口过剩等所有问题的全部自然科学知识，但确实意味着，人类已经掌握了一定的工具用来寻求和找到这些问题的解决方案，并且各领域均已证明可能存在解决方案。

这种情况似乎赋予了科学发达国家更多的道德责任，使其将更多的科学资源用于解决欠发达国家的问题。这也提出了一个非常实际的问题，即如何更充分、更成功地将技术用于解决导致国际紧张局势的自然科学问题。

外交事务的新环境

具有全球影响的技术呈现出的这些新趋势，不仅仅改变了总体环境，使制定政策来应对环境成为必需，同时还提出了一些问题，涉及人们珍视的国家传统，涉及与目前国际政治体系组织相关的假设，涉及与科学和技术本身相关的传统信念。从某种意义上讲，19世纪出现的科学革命概念基本上改变了国际政治所依赖的根本力量和关系。

然而，外交政策和国内政策一如既往地推行，只是人们偶尔会意识到：对领土的控制已经成为不确定和模糊的概念，国家行动自由和边界不可侵犯早已失去了传统意义，大多数民族国家的资源规模与现代技术要求不相称，国际组织必须发挥更重要的作用，而不仅仅是将大国的目标予以放大。

一定不要忘记，迄今为止，科学技术虽然发展迅猛，也不过是未来更迅猛的人类环境重塑的前奏。技术会传播，会增加一个国家对另一个国家的依赖，会创造全新的国际关系，会使合作进一步发展，争端进一步加剧，会对国际稳定形成新的威胁，引起更多人口过剩问题和环境污染问题。

技术发展的方方面面不可能详细预测，但也并非不可理解。更有甚者，技术发展可能会迫使或要求各国对国内外事务的态度发生更多重大转变，也许是根本性的转变。因此，需要更好地理解技术未来发展的性质，理解其对国际关系的全部意义。

（彭萍 译）

29

Selections from the Analects

《论语》五十节

Confucius
孔 子

(551–479 B.C.)

ABOUT THE AUTHOR

Confucius (551–479 B.C.) is the Latinized form of K'ung Fu-tzu or Master K'ung, the honorific title for the greatest sage of China whose real name was K'ung Ch'iu. He was born in the feudal state of Lu in the middle of the Spring and Autumn Period, when the court of Chou dynasty had lost control of the empire and the feudal lords fought one against another. Trying to bring order and peace to his age, Confucius aspired to be a statesman and toured the various states to offer his service to the right and righteous ruler. In spite of his brief success in his native Lu, his political career on the whole was a failure. Gradually, he gave up politics for education and became a teacher of rare enthusiasm and art. He was said to have had some three thousand students, of whom seventy-two were close personal disciples or known for their virtue and distinction. To his old age has been traditionally ascribed the editing of the so-called Five Confucian Classics: the *Book of Changes*, the *Book of History*, the *Book of Songs*, the *Book of Rites*, and *Spring and Autumn Annals*.

作者简介 孔子（公元前551年—前479年，Confucius是"孔夫子"或"孔子"的拉丁化译名）是对中国最伟大的圣人的尊称。孔子原名孔丘，出生于春秋中期的鲁国，当时周朝王室已经失去了对华夏大地的掌控，诸侯国之间相互征伐。孔子试图给他的时代带来秩序与和平，他渴望成为一名政治家，周游列国时为正直的明君献计献策。尽管他在家乡鲁国取得了短暂的成功，但他的政治生涯在整体上是失败的。孔子逐渐放弃了政治，转而从事教育，成为一名具有罕见热情和人文精神的教师。据说他有大约三千名学生，其中有七十二名是他的亲传弟子，成为以德行和卓越著称的"七十二贤人"。传统上认为，孔子在晚年编辑了所谓的儒家五经:《易经》《尚书》《诗经》《礼记》和《春秋》。

* **ABOUT THE SELECTION** These fifty monologues and dialogues constitute about one tenth of the *Analects*, a record of Confucius's remarks and activities compiled probably by his disciples' disciples. The book is in twenty chapters and 497 verses, some consisting of the briefest aphorisms. It is by these verses that we come to understand Confucius the man, the teacher, and the philosopher. Since Confucianism became widely accepted, the laconic and provocative sentences of this work, difficult though they often are to interpret, have exercised a profound influence upon the thought and language of the peoples of East Asia, while for the last eight hundred years it has been a basic text in Chinese education known to every schoolboy. The English translation is taken from *Sources of Chinese Tradition*, a book of selections from Chinese thinkers with introductions and commentaries compiled by Theodore de Bary, Burton Watson, Yi-pao Mei, and other Sinologues. Figures in parenthesis at the end of each paragraph refer to chapter and verse of the quotation. For example, VII: 4 refers to 论语述而第七之第四节.

内容简介 这五十节独白和对话占《论语》大约十分之一的篇幅，该书是有关孔子言论与活动的记录，可能是由其弟子的弟子编撰的。全书共二十篇，四百九十七章，有些章节由最简短的警句组成。正是通过这些文字我们才理解了哲学家孔子是如何为人为师的。儒家思想被广泛接受以来，这部作品中简洁而富有启发性的句子，尽管常常难以解释，却对东亚民族的思想和语言都产生了深远的影响。在过去的八百年里，它一直都是学校中人尽皆知的基本教材。英译本摘自《中国传统文献》，这是一本由狄百瑞、华兹生、梅贻宝以及其他汉学家编辑的中国思想家作品选集，书中附有导言和评论。每段末尾括号内的数字是引文的篇和章。例如，VII: 4 指的是《论语》第七篇"述而"，第四章。

孔子其人
Confucius the Man

1. 子之燕居，申申如也，夭夭如也。
   In his leisure hours, Confucius was easy in his manner and cheerful in his expression. (VII: 4)

2. 子钓而不纲，弋不射宿。
   Confucius fished but not with a net; he shot but not at a roosting[1] bird. (VII: 27)

3. 厩焚。子退朝，曰："伤人乎？"不问马。
   When the stables were burned down, on returning from court, Confucius asked: "Was anyone hurt?" He did not ask about the horses. (X: 17)

4. 叶公问孔子于子路，子路不对。子曰："女奚不曰，其为人也，发愤忘食，乐以忘忧，不知老之将至云尔。"
   The Duke of She[2] asked Tzu Lu[3] about Confucius, and Tzu Lu gave

him no answer. Confucius said: "Why didn't you tell him that I am a person who forgets to eat when he is enthusiastic about something, forgets all his worries in his enjoyment of it, and is not aware that old age is coming on?" (VII: 19)

5. 子曰:"饭疏食饮水，曲肱而枕之，乐亦在其中矣。不义而富且贵，于我如浮云。"

   Confucius said: "Having only coarse food to eat, plain water to drink, and a bent arm for a pillow, one can still find happiness therein.[4] Riches and honor acquired by unrighteous means[5] are to me as drifting clouds." (VII: 15)

6. 子曰:"苟有用我者，期月而已可也，三年有成。"

   Confucius said: "Were any prince[6] to employ me, even in a single year a good deal could be done, and in three years everything could be accomplished." (XIII: 10)

7. 子曰:"莫我知也夫！"子贡曰:"何为其莫知子也？"子曰:"不怨天，不尤人，下学而上达，知我者其天乎！"

   Confucius said: "Ah! There is no one who knows me!" Tzu Kung asked: "Why do you say, sir, that no one knows you?" Confucius said: "I make no complaint against Heaven, nor do I lay the blame on men. Though my studies are lowly, they penetrate the sublime on high.[7] Perhaps after all I am known—by Heaven." (XIV: 35)

8. 子畏于匡，曰:"文王既没，文不在兹乎？天之将丧斯文也，后死者不得与于斯文也；天之未丧斯文也，匡人其如予何？"

   When Confucius was in jeopardy in K'uang,[8] he said: "Since the death of King Wen,[9] does not the mission of culture rest here with us? If

Heaven were going to destroy this culture, a mortal like me would not have been given such a place in it. And if Heaven is not going to destroy this culture, what can the men of K'uang do to me?" (IX: 5)

9. 颜渊死。子曰："噫！天丧予！天丧予！"

When Yen Hui[10] died, Confucius exclaimed: "Alas, Heaven has destroyed me! Heaven has destroyed me!" (XI: 9)

10. 长沮、桀溺耦而耕，孔子过之，使子路问津焉。

长沮曰："夫执舆者为谁？"

子路曰："为孔丘。"

曰："是鲁孔丘与？"

曰："是也。"

曰："是知津矣。"

问于桀溺。

桀溺曰："子为谁？"

曰："为仲由。"

曰："是鲁孔丘之徒与？"

对曰："然。"

曰："滔滔者天下皆是也，而谁以易之？且而与其从辟人之士也，岂若从辟世之士哉？"耰而不辍。

子路行以告。

夫子怃然曰："鸟兽不可与同群，吾非斯人之徒与而谁与？天下有道，丘不与易也。"

Ch'ang-chu and Chieh-ni[11] were cultivating their fields together. Confucius was passing that way and told Tzu Lu to go and ask them where the river could be forded.[12] Ch'ang-chu said: "Who is that holding the reins in the carriage?" Tzu Lu said: "It is K'ung Ch'iu[13]." He said: "You mean K'ung Ch'iu of the state of Lu?[14]" "Yes," Tzu Lu replied. Ch'ang-chu said: "If it is he, then he already knows where the ford is."[15] Tzu Lu then turned to Chieh-ni. Chieh-ni asked: "Who are you, sir?" Tzu Lu said: "Chung-yu[16] is my name." Chieh-ni said: "You are a follower of K'ung Ch'iu of Lu, are you not?" He said: "That is so." Chieh-ni said: "The whole world is swept as by a torrential flood, and who can change it? As for you, instead of following one who flees from this man and that, you would do better to follow one who flees the whole world." And with that he went on covering the seed without stopping. Tzu Lu went and told Confucius, who said ruefully:[17] "One cannot herd together with birds and beasts. If I am not to be a man among other men, then what am I to be? If the Way prevailed in the world, I should not be trying to alter things."[18] (XVIII: 6)

11. 子曰:"吾十有五而志于学,三十而立,四十而不惑,五十而知天命,六十而耳顺,七十而从心所欲,不踰矩。"

    Confucius said: "At fifteen, I set my heart on learning. At thirty, I was firmly established. At forty, I had no more doubts. At fifty, I knew the will of Heaven. At sixty, I was ready to listen to it. At seventy, I could follow my heart's desire without transgressing what was right." (II: 4)

12. 子在齐闻韶,三月不知肉味,曰:"不图为乐之至于斯也。"

    When Confucius was in Ch'i,[19] he heard the Shao music[20] and for three months he forgot the taste of meat, saying: "I never thought music could be so beautiful." (VII: 14)

13. 子曰:"三人行,必有我师焉;择其善者而从之,其不善者而改之。"

    Confucius said: "When walking in a party of three, I always have teachers. I can select the good qualities of the one for imitation, and the bad ones of the other and correct them in myself." (VII: 22)

14. 子曰:"述而不作,信而好古,窃比于我老彭。"

    Confucius said: "I am a transmitter[21] and not a creator. I believe in and have a passion for the ancients. I venture to compare myself with our old P'eng."[22] (VII: 1)

15. 子绝四:毋意,毋必,毋固,毋我。

    There were four things that Confucius was determined to eradicate:[23] a biased mind,[24] arbitrary judgments,[25] obstinacy,[26] and egotism.[27] (IX: 4)

16. 子曰:"朝闻道,夕死可矣。"

    Confucius said: "Having heard the Way[28] in the morning, one may die content in the evening." (IV: 8)

作为老师的孔子
Confucius the Teacher

17. 子曰:性相近也,习相远也。

    Confucius said: "By nature men are pretty much alike; it is learning and practice that set them apart."[29] (XVII: 2)

18. 子曰:有教无类。

    Confucius said: "In education there are no class distinctions." (XV: 39)

19. 子曰:"后生可畏,焉之来者之不如今也? 四十、五十而无闻焉,斯亦不足畏也已。"

    Confucius said: "The young are to be respected. How do we know that the next generation will not measure up to[30] the present one? But if a man has reached forty or fifty and nothing has been heard of him, then I grant that he is not worthy of respect." (IX: 23)

20. 子曰:"当仁,不让于师。"

Confucius said: "When it comes to acquiring perfect virtue,[31] a man should not defer even to[32] his own teacher." (XV: 36)

21. 子曰:"生而知之者上也,学而知之者次也;困而学之,又其次也;困而不学,民斯为下矣。"

Confucius said: "Those who are born wise are the highest type of people; those who become wise through learning come next, those who learn by overcoming dullness come after that. Those who are dull but still won't learn are the lowest type of people." (XVI: 9)

22. 子曰:"不愤不启,不悱不发。举一隅不以三隅反,则不复也。"

Confucius said: "I won't teach a man who is not anxious to learn, and will not explain to one who is not trying to make things clear to himself. If I hold up one corner of a square and a man cannot come back to me with the other three, I won't bother to go over the point again." (VII: 8)

23. 子曰:"学而不思则罔,思而不学则殆。"

Confucius said: "Learning without thinking is labor lost; thinking without learning is perilous." (II: 15)

孔子的教诲
The Teachings of Confucius

24. 子曰:"赐也！女以予为多学而识之者与？"对曰:"然，非与？"曰:"非也。予一以贯之。"

    Confucius said: "Tz'u,[33] do you suppose that I merely learned a great deal and tried to remember it all?" The disciple replied: "Yes, is it not so?" Confucius said: "No, I have one principle that runs through it all." (XV: 3)

25. 子贡问曰:"有一言而可以终身行之者乎？"子曰:"其恕乎！己所不欲，勿施于人。"

    Tzu Kung[34] asked: "Is there any one word that can serve as a principle for the conduct of life?" Confucius said: "Perhaps the word reciprocity:[35] Do not do to others what you would not want others to do to you." (XV: 24)

26. 樊迟问仁。子曰:"爱人。"

    Fan Ch'ih[36] asked about humanity.[37] Confucius said: "Love men." (XII: 22)

27. 子曰:"不仁者不可以久处约，不可以长处乐。仁者安仁，知者利仁。"

    Confucius said: "Without humanity a man cannot long endure adversity,[38] nor can he long enjoy prosperity.[39] The humane[40] rest in humanity; the wise find it beneficial." (IV: 2)

28. 或曰:"以德报怨，何如？"子曰:"何以报德？以直报怨，以德报德。"

    Someone inquired: "What do you think of 'requiting injury with kindness'?"[41] Confucius said: "How will you then requite kindness? Requite injury with justice, and kindness with kindness." (XIV: 34)

29. 子曰:"仁远乎哉？我欲仁，斯仁至矣。"

Confucius said: "Is humanity something remote? If I want to be humane, behold, humanity has arrived." (VII: 29)

30. 子游问孝。子曰:"今之孝者，是谓能养。至于犬马，皆能有养；不敬，何以别乎？"

Tzu Yu[42] asked about filial piety.[43] Confucius said: "Nowadays a filial son is just a man who keeps his parents in food. But even dogs or horses are given food. If there is no feeling of reverence, wherein lies the difference?" (II: 7)

31. 子夏问孝。子曰:"色难。有事，弟子服其劳；有酒食，先生馔，曾是以为孝乎？"

Tzu Hsia[44] asked about filial piety. Confucius said: "The manner is the really difficult thing. When anything has to be done the young people undertake it, when there is wine and food the elders are served—is this all there is to filial piety?" (II: 8)

32. 子曰:"恭而无礼则劳，慎而无礼则葸，勇而无礼则乱，直而无礼则绞。"

Confucius said: "Courtesy without decorum[45] becomes tiresome. Cautiousness without decorum becomes timidity, daring becomes insubordination,[46] frankness becomes effrontery."[47] (VIII: 2)

33. 林放问礼之本。子曰:"大哉问！礼，与其奢也，宁俭；丧，与其易也，宁戚。"

Lin Fang[48] asked about the fundamental principle of rites.[49]

Confucius replied: "You are asking an important question! In rites at large, it is always better to be too simple rather than too lavish. In funeral rites, it is more important to have the real sentiment of sorrow than minute[50] attention to observances." (III: 4)

34. 季路问事鬼神。子曰："未能事人，焉能事鬼？"
曰："敢问死。"曰："未知生，焉知死？"

Tzu Lu asked about the worship of ghosts and spirits. Confucius said: "We don't know yet how to serve men, now can we know about serving the spirits?" "What about death?" was the next question. Confucius said: "We don't know yet about life, how can we know about death?" (XI: 12)

35. 樊迟问知。子曰："务民之义，敬鬼神而远之，可谓知矣。"

Fan Ch'ih asked about wisdom. Confucius said: "Devote yourself to the proper demands of the people, respect the ghosts and spirits but keep them at a distance—this may be called wisdom." (VI: 22)

36. 子曰："获罪于天，无所祷也。"

Confucius said: "He who sins against Heaven has none to whom he can pray." (III: 13)

37. 子曰："予欲无言。"子贡曰："子如不言，则小子何述焉？"子曰："天何言哉？四时行焉，百物生焉，天何言哉？"

Confucius said: "I wish I did not have to speak at all." Tzu Kung said: "But if you did not speak, Sir, what should we disciples pass on to others?" Confucius said: "Look at Heaven there. Does it speak? The four seasons run their course and all things are produced. Does Heaven speak?" (XVII: 19)

38. 祭如在，祭神如神在。子曰："吾不与祭，如不祭。"

    Confucius sacrificed[51] (to the dead) as if they were present. He sacrificed to the spirits as if they were present. He said: "I consider my not being present at the sacrifice as if I did not sacrifice." (III: 12)

39. 子不语怪，力，乱，神。

    The Master did not talk about weird[52] things, physical exploits,[53] disorders, and spirits. (VII: 21)

40. 子曰："质胜文则野，文胜质则史。文质彬彬，然后君子。"

    Confucius said: "When nature exceeds art,[54] you have the rustic.[55] When art exceeds nature, you have the clerk.[56] It is only when art and nature are harmoniously blended that you have the gentleman." (VI: 18)

41. 司马牛问君子。子曰："君子不忧不惧。"

    曰："不忧不惧，斯谓之君子已乎？"子曰："内省不疚，夫何忧何惧？"

    Ssu-ma Niu[57] asked about the gentleman. Confucius said: "The gentleman has neither anxiety nor fear." Ssu-ma Niu rejoined:[58] "Neither anxiety nor fear—is that what is meant by being a gentleman?" Confucius said: "When he looks into himself and finds no cause for self-reproach, what has he to be anxious about; what has he to fear?" (XII: 4)

42. 子曰："君子道者三，我无能焉：仁者不忧，知者不惑，勇者不惧。"
    子贡曰："君子自道也。"

    Confucius said: "The way of the gentleman is threefold. I myself have not been able to attain any of them. Being humane, he has no anxieties; being wise, he has no perplexities; being brave, he has no fear." Tzu Kung said: "But, Master, that is your own way." (XIV: 28)

43. 子曰："三军可夺帅也，匹夫不可夺志也。"

    Confucius said: "You may be able to carry off from a whole army its commander-in-chief, but you cannot deprive the humblest individual of his will." (IX: 26)

44. 子贡问君子。子曰："先行其言而后从之。"

    Tzu Kung asked about the gentleman. Confucius said: "The gentleman first practices what he preaches and then preaches what he practices." (II: 13)

45. 子曰："君子求诸己，小人求诸人。"

    Confucius said: "The gentleman makes demands on himself; the inferior man[59] makes demands on others." (XV: 21)

46. 子曰："君子周而不比，小人比而不周。"

    Confucius said: "The gentleman is broad-minded and not partisan;[60] the inferior man is partisan and not broad-minded." (II: 14)

47. 子曰："君子有三畏：畏天命，畏大人，畏圣人之言。小人不知天命而不畏也，狎大人，侮圣人之言。"

    Confucius said: "There are three things that a gentleman fears: he fears the will of Heaven, he fears great men, he fears the words of the sages. The inferior man does not know the will of Heaven and does not fear it, he treats great men with contempt, and he scoffs at[61] the words of the sages." (XVI: 8)

48. 季康子问政于孔子。孔子对曰："政者，正也。子帅以正，孰敢不正？"

    Chi K'ang Tzu[62] asked Confucius about government. Confucius said: "To govern is to set things right. If you begin by setting yourself right, who will dare to deviate⁶³ from the right?" (XII: 17)

49. 子曰："道之以政，齐之以刑，民免而无耻；道之以德，齐之以礼，有耻且格。"

Confucius said: "Lead the people by laws and regulate them by penalties, and the people will try to keep out of jail, but will have no sense of shame. Lead the people by virtue and restrain them by the rules of decorum, and the people will have a sense of shame, and moreover will become good." (II: 3)

50. 子贡问政。子曰："足食，足兵，民信之矣。"
    子贡曰："必不得已而去，于斯三者何先？"曰："去兵。"
    子贡曰："必不得已而去，于斯二者何先？"曰："去食。自古皆有死，民无信不立。"

Tzu Kung asked about government. Confucius said: "The essentials⁶⁴ are sufficient food, sufficient troops, and the confidence of the people." Tzu Kung said: "Suppose you were forced to give up one of these three, which would you let go first?" Confucius said: "The troops." Tzu Kung asked again: "If you were forced to give up one of the two remaining, which would you let go?" Confucius said: "Food. For from of old, death has been the lot of all men, but a people without faith cannot survive." (XII: 7)

NOTES

1. roosting: getting settled for the night. The whole sentence means that Confucius did not take unfair advantage of inferior creatures.
2. The Duke of She: 叶公.
3. Tzu Lu: 子路.
4. therein: in it; in that.
5. unrighteous means: sinful way; unjust method.

6. prince: ruler; sovereign.
7. they penetrate the sublime on high: my studies attain to the noble and the majestic in Heaven.
8. in jeopardy in K'uang: in danger in K'uang. Confucius was besieged by the people of K'uang because he looked like Yang Hu, a wicked man who had oppressed them.
9. King Wen: 周文王, founder of Chou culture.
10. Yen Hui: 颜回, also 颜渊, Confucius's favorite disciple.
11. Ch'ang-chu and Chieh-ni: 长沮, 桀溺, two misanthropic hermits.
12. forded: crossed (where the stream is shallow). Ford is a place where a river is not too deep to cross by walking through the water.
13. K'ung Ch'iu: 孔丘.
14. the state of Lu: 鲁国.
15. Ch'ang-chu seemed to imply, sarcastically, that such a wise man as Confucius should know his way and needed no guidance from lowly peasants.
16. Chung-yu: 仲由, name of Tzu Lu.
17. ruefully: sorrowfully.
18. Confucius would rather be a social reformer than a hermit who ran away from the troubled times.
19. Ch'i: 齐.
20. the Shao music: 韶, classical music of the time of the ancient sage-king Shun 舜 (2255-2208 B.C.?)
21. transmitter: one who passes something on to others.
22. old P'eng: 老彭, virtuous minister of Yin dynasty.
23. eradicate: get rid of completely.
24. biased mind: prejudiced mind; mind that is not objective.
25. arbitrary judgments: purely subjective judgments.
26. obstinacy: stubbornness.
27. egotism: preoccupation with oneself; selfishness.
28. the Way: the truth, 道.
29. set them apart: make them different.
30. measure up to: be equal to.
31. perfect virtue: 仁.
32. defer to: yield in judgment or opinion; submit courteously.
33. Tz'u: 赐, given name of Tzu Kung.
34. Tzu Kung: 子贡.
35. reciprocity: 恕.
36. Fan Ch'ih: 樊须, 字子迟.

37. humanity: 仁.
38. adversity: condition of unhappiness, misfortune, or distress.
39. prosperity: good fortune; success.
40. the humane: the kind and merciful people.
41. 'requiting injury with kindness': return injury with kindness, 以德报怨.
42. Tzu Yu: 子游.
43. filial piety: 孝.
44. Tzu Hsia: 子夏.
45. decorum: propriety of action, speech, dress, etc.; 礼.
46. insubordination: disobedience.
47. effrontery: shameless boldness; impudence.
48. Lin Fang: 林放.
49. rites: 礼.
50. minute: detailed, painstaking; careful. Pronounced mai-noot.
51. sacrificed: offered (food to spirits or gods).
52. weird: unearthly; mysterious.
53. physical exploits: bodily daring deeds.
54. When nature exceeds art: When a man shows more sincerity than decorum.
55. rustic: a country person.
56. clerk: petty officials in charge of secretarial matters. This sentence is translated by Ku Hung-ming as: "when the results of education get the better of their natural qualities, they become *literati*."
57. Ssu-ma Niu: 司马牛.
58. rejoined: replied.
59. the inferior man: 小人.
60. partisan: a person emotionally involved in a party or cause.
61. scoffs at: sneers at; laughs at.
62. Chi K'ang Tzu: 季康子.
63. deviate: turn aside (from the right path).
64. essentials: absolutely necessary elements or qualities; fundamental features.

30

Selections from Chuang Tzu

《庄子》五节

Chuang Tzu
庄子

(369?–286? B.C.)

* ABOUT THE AUTHOR Chuang Chou (369?–286? B.C.), honored as Chuang Tzu (Master Chuang) in Chinese culture, is the second great figure in early Taoism, of which Lao Tzu is believed to be the founder. According to Ssu-ma Ch'ien, Chuang Chou was a native of Meng and though he was at one time a minor official, seems to have lived most of his life in seclusion. Apart from that, nothing is known of him except that he was a contemporary of King Hui of Liang and King Hsuan of Ch'i and was a friend of Hui Shih. Where Confucius teaches the cultivation of gentlemanly virtues, Chuang Tzu offers freedom for the assurance of happiness. To him freedom is the cardinal virtue, not so much in a political or social sense as in the spiritual sense that one is free within, free from himself, his own prejudices, fears, desires, and a tendency to judge everything in terms of himself. His book, also called *Chuang Tzu*, contains thirty-three chapters, some of which are believed to have been authored by his disciples and imitators. Rich in metaphor and allegory and irresistible in its wit, eloquence, and imagination, the book has exercised immense influence not only on philosophers but on writers of prose and verse.

作者简介　庄周（公元前369年？—前286年？）在中国文化传统中被尊称为"庄子"，在老子创立的道家体系中，他是第二伟大的人物。根据司马迁的说法，庄周出生于宋国蒙邑，虽然他曾做过漆园小吏，但似乎一生中大部分时间都在隐居。他与梁惠王和齐宣王是同时代的人，也是惠施的朋友。除此之外，有关庄周的其他信息便不得而知了。孔子教导人们要培养君子的美德，而庄子则提出自由是幸福的保障。对他而言，自由是最重要的美德。这种自由与其说是政治或社会意义上的自由，不如说是精神意义上的自由：人的内心是自由的，不自我设限，不受自我偏见、恐惧和欲望的束缚，不以自己为标准来判断一切。他的书名为《庄子》，包括三十三篇，人们认为其中有些内容是由他的弟子和模仿者撰写的。该书比喻丰富，寓意深刻，其中的智慧、雄辩和想象力有着令人难以抗拒的魅力，不仅对哲学家，而且对散文家和诗人都产生了巨大的影响。

*   **ABOUT THE SELECTION** These five selections are parables and allegorical anecdotes taken from *Chuang Tzu*. Imaginary and whimsical as they may seem, these episodes are profound and subtle reflections on life and death presented in such dramatic and memorable ways. The first three are about death: in the first and the third passages, death is viewed as an inevitable phase in the natural process of change which enlightened minds should take with quiet resignation; in the second passage, it is even imagined as a better state than life because of its complete freedom from the cares of life. The fourth passage is so beautiful in its transcendance of distinct forms of life and seems to suggest that persistence upon individual identities in life may be after all but a dream. The last passage is not so much a preference of wretched life to honored death as one of freedom to fettered distinction. The first two passages are from Chapter 18 of *Chuang Tzu* (庄子至乐第十八) and of Arthur Waley's translation. The third is translated from Chapter 6 (大宗师第六) by Burton Watson. The fourth is from Chapter 2, (齐物论第二); the fifth from Chapter 17 (秋水第十七): both are translated by Yi-pao Mei. The reader is advised to refer directly to the Chinese original of *Chuang Tzu* for a better understanding of the selections.

内容简介 这五节文字是选自《庄子》的寓言轶事，虽然看起来天马行空、富于想象，但都以一种令人难忘的戏剧性方式呈现出对生命和死亡深刻而微妙的思考。前三节是关于死亡的内容：在第一和第三节中，死亡被视为自然变化过程中的一个不可避免的阶段，开悟的人应该坦然地接受这个阶段；在第二节中，死亡甚至被想象成比生命更好的状态，因为它完全摆脱了生活的烦恼。第四节文字在超越生命的不同形式方面表现得如此美丽，似乎暗示在生活中坚持个人的独特性可能最终只会是幻梦一场。在最后一节文字中，与其说庄子探讨的是悲惨的生活和荣耀的死亡两者间的取舍，不如说他是在表达对一种不为名利所累的逍遥自在生活的向往。前两节选自《庄子》"至乐"第十八章，由阿瑟·韦利翻译完成。第三节是由华兹生翻译的"大宗师"第六章。第四节选自"齐物论"第二章，第五节选自"秋水"第十七章，这两节都是由梅贻宝翻译的。建议读者直接参考《庄子》原文，以便更好地理解这些选文。

1

庄子妻死，惠子吊之，庄子则方箕踞鼓盆而歌。

惠子曰："与人居，长子、老、身死，不哭，亦足矣，又鼓盆而歌，不亦甚乎！"

庄子曰："不然。是其始死也，我独何能无概然！察其始而本无生；非徒无生也而本无形；非徒无形也而本无气。杂乎芒芴之间，变而有气，气变而有形，形变而有生，今又变而之死，是相与为春秋冬夏四时行也。人且偃然寝于巨室，而我噭噭然随而哭之，自以为不通乎命，故止也。"

——《庄子·至乐》

1

When Chuang Tzu's wife died, Hui Tzu[1] came to the house to join in the rites of mourning. To his surprise he found Chuang Tzu sitting with an inverted[2] bowl on his knees, drumming upon it and singing a song.

"After all," said Hui Tzu, "she lived with you, brought up your children, grew old along with you. That you should not mourn for her is bad enough; but to let your friends find you drumming and singing—that is going too far!"

"You misjudge me," said Chuang Tzu. "When she died, I was in despair, as any man well might be. But soon, pondering on what had happened, I told myself that in death no strange new fate befalls[3] us. In the beginning we lack not life only, but form. Not form only, but spirit. We are blended in the one great featureless indistinguishable mass.[4] Then a time came when the mass evolved[5] spirit, spirit evolved form, form evolved life. And now life in its turn has evolved death. For not nature only but man's being has its seasons, its sequence[6] of spring and autumn, summer and winter. If some one is tired and has gone to lie down, we do not pursue him with shouting and bawling.[7] She whom I have lost has lain down to sleep for a while in the Great Inner Room.[8] To break in upon her rest with the noise of lamentation would but show that I knew nothing of nature's Sovereign Law.[9] That is why I ceased to mourn."

2

庄子之楚,见空髑髅,髐然有形,撽以马捶,因而问之,曰:"夫子贪生失理,而为此乎?将子有亡国之事,斧钺之诛,而为此乎?将子有不善之行,愧遗父母妻子之丑,而为此乎?将子有冻馁之患,而为此乎?将子之春秋故及此乎?"

于是语卒,援髑髅,枕而卧。夜半,髑髅见梦曰:"子之谈者似辩士。视子所言,皆生人之累也,死则无此矣。子欲闻死之说乎?"

庄子曰:"然。"

髑髅曰:"死,无君于上,无臣于下;亦无四时之事,从然以天地为春秋,虽南面王乐,不能过也。"

庄子不信,曰:"吾使司命复生子形,为子骨肉肌肤,反子父母妻子闾里知识,子欲之乎?"

髑髅深矉蹙頞,曰:"吾安能弃南面王乐而复为人间之劳乎?"

——《庄子·至乐》

2

When Chuang Tzu was going to Ch'u[10] he saw by the roadside a skull[11], clean and bare, but with every bone in its place. Touching it gently with his chariot-whip he bent over it and asked, "Sir, was it some insatiable ambition[12] that drove you to transgress the law[13] and brought you to this? Was it the fall of a kingdom, the blow of the executioner's axe[14] that brought you to this? Or had you done some shameful deed and could not face the reproaches of father and mother, of wife and child, and so were brought to this? Was it hunger and cold that brought you to this, or was it that the springs and autumns of your span[15] had in their due course[16] carried you to this?"

Having thus addressed the skull, he put it under his head as a pillow and went to sleep. At midnight the skull appeared to him in a dream and said to him, "All that you said to me—your glib[17], commonplace chatter—is just what I should expect from a live man, showing as it does in every phase a mind hampered by trammels[18] from which we dead are entirely free. Would you like to hear a word or two about the dead?"

"I certainly should," said Chuang Tzu.

"Among the dead," said the skull, "none is king, none is subject.[19] There is no division of the seasons: for us the whole world is spring, the whole world is autumn. No monarch on his throne has joy greater than ours."

Chuang Tzu did not believe this. "Suppose," he said, "I could get the Clerk of Destinies[20] to make your frame anew,[21] to clothe your bones once more with flesh and skin, send you back to father and mother, wife and child, friends and home, I do not think you would refuse."

A deep frown furrowed[22] the skeleton's brow. "How can you imagine," it asked, "that I would cast away joy greater than that of a king upon his throne, only to go back to the toils of the living world?"

3

子祀、子舆、子犁、子来四人相与语曰:"孰能以无为首,以生为脊,以死为尻;孰知死生存亡之一体者,吾与之友矣!"四人相视而笑,莫逆于心,遂相与为友。

俄而子舆有病,子祀往问之。曰:"伟哉夫造物者,将以予为此拘拘也!"曲偻发背,上有五管,颐隐于齐,肩高于顶,句赘指天,阴阳之气有沴,其心闲而无事,胼𨇤而鉴于井。曰:"嗟乎!夫造物者又将以予为此拘拘也!"

子祀曰:"女恶之乎?"

曰:"亡,予何恶!浸假而化予之左臂以为鸡,予因以求时夜;浸假而化予之右臂以为弹,予因以求鸮炙;浸假而化予之尻以为轮,以神为马,予因以乘之,岂更驾哉!且夫得者,时也,

3

Master Ssu, Master Yu, Master Li and Master Lai[23] were all four talking together. "Who can look upon inaction as his head, upon life as his back, upon death as his rump?"[24] they asked. "Who knows that life and death, existence and annihilation,[25] are all parts of a single body? I will be his friend!"

The four men looked at each other and smiled. There was no disagreement in their hearts and so the four of them became friends.

All at once Master Yü fell ill, and Master Ssu went to ask how he was. "Amazing!" exclaimed Master Yü. "Look, the Creator is making me all crooked![26] My back sticks up like a hunchback's so that my vital organs[27] are on top of me. My chin is hidden down around my navel, my shoulders are up above my head, and my pigtail[28] points at the sky, It must be due to some dislocation of the forces of the yin and the yang.[29]"

Yet he seemed quite calm at heart and unconcerned. Dragging himself haltingly[30] to the edge of a well, he looked at his reflection and cried, "My, my![31] Look, the Creator is making me all crooked!"

"Do you resent it?" asked Master Ssu.

"Why no," replied Master Yü. "What is there to resent? If the process continues, perhaps in time he'll transform my left arm into a rooster: in that case I'll herald[32] the dawn with my crowing. Or in time he may transform my right arm into a crossbow pellet[33] and I'll shoot down an owl for roasting. Or perhaps he will even turn my buttocks into cartwheels: then with my spirit for a horse, I'll climb up and go for a ride, and never again have need for a carriage.

"I received life because the time had come, I will lose it because the order of things passes on. If only a man will be content with this time and dwell in this order neither sorrow nor joy can touch him. In ancient times this

失者，顺也；安时而处顺，哀乐不能入也。此古之所谓县解也。而不能自解者，物有结之。且夫物不胜天久矣。吾又何恶焉！"

俄而子来有病，喘喘然将死。其妻子环而泣之。子犁往问之，曰："叱！避！无怛化！"倚其户与之语曰："伟哉造化！又将奚以汝为，将奚以汝适？以汝为鼠肝乎？以汝为虫臂乎？"

子来曰："父母于子，东西南北，唯命之从。阴阳于人，不翅于父母；彼近吾死而我不听，我则悍矣，彼何罪焉！夫大块载我以形，劳我以生，佚我以老，息我以死。故善吾生者，乃所以善吾死也。今之大冶铸金，金踊跃曰'我且必为镆铘'，大冶必以为不祥之金。今一犯人之形，而曰'人耳人耳'，夫造化者必以为不祥之人。今一以天地为大炉，以造化为大冶，恶乎往而不可哉！"成然寐，蘧然觉。

——《庄子·大宗师》

was called 'the freeing of the bound.'[34] Yet there are those who cannot free themselves, because they are bound by mere things. Creatures such as I can never win against Heaven. That is the way it has always been: what is there to resent?"

Then suddenly Master Lai also fell ill. Gasping for breath he lay at the point of death. His wife and children gathered round in a circle and wept. Master Li, who had come to find out how he was, said to them, "Shoo! Get back! Don't disturb the process of change!"

And he leaned against the doorway and chatted with Master Lai, "How marvelous the Creator is!" he exclaimed. "What is he going to make out of you next? Where is he going to send you? Will he make you into a rat's liver? Will he make you into a bug's arm?"

"A child obeys his father and mother and goes wherever he is told, east or west, south or north," said Master Lai. "And the yin and the yang—how much more are they to a man than father or mother! Now that they have brought me to the verge[35] of death, how perverse[36] it would be of me to refuse to obey them. What fault is it of theirs? The Great Clod[37] burdens me with form, labors me with life, eases me in old age and rests me in death. So if I think well of my life, by the same token I must think well of my death. When a skilled smith is casting metal,[38] if the metal should leap up and cry, 'I insist upon being made into a famous sword like the sword Mu-yeh[39] of old!'—he would surely regard it as very inauspicious[40] metal indeed. In the same way, if I who have once had the audacity to take on human form[41] should now cry, 'I don't want to be anything but a man! Nothing but a man!'—the Creator would surely consider me a most inauspicious sort of person. So how I think of heaven and earth as a great furnace and the Creator as a skilled smith. What place could he send me that would not be all right? I will go off peacefully to sleep, and then with a start I will wake up."

4

昔者庄周梦为胡蝶，栩栩然胡蝶也，自喻适志与！不知周也。俄然觉，则蘧蘧然周也。不知周之梦为胡蝶与，胡蝶之梦为周与？周与胡蝶，则必有分矣。此之谓"物化"。

——《庄子·齐物论》

5

庄子钓于濮水，楚王使大夫二人往先焉，曰："愿以境内累矣！"

庄子持竿不顾，曰："吾闻楚有神龟，死已三千岁矣，王以巾笥而藏之庙堂之上。此龟者，宁其死为留骨而贵乎？宁其生而曳尾于涂中乎？"

二大夫曰："宁生而曳尾涂中。"

庄子曰："往矣！吾将曳尾于涂中。"

——《庄子·秋水》

4

Once upon a time, Chuang Chou dreamed that he was a butterfly, a butterfly fluttering about, enjoying itself. It did not know that it was Chuang Chou. Suddenly he awoke with a start and he was Chuang Chou again. But he did not know whether he was Chuang Chou who had dreamed that he was a butterfly, or whether he was a butterfly dreaming that he was Chuang Chou. Between Chuang Chou and the butterfly there must be some distinction. This is what is called the transformation of things.[42]

5

Once Chuang Tzu was fishing in the P'u River[43] when the King of Ch'u[44] sent two of his ministers to announce that he wished to entrust to Chuang Tzu the care of his entire domain.

Chuang Tzu held his fishing pole and, without turning his head, said: "I have heard that Ch'u possesses a sacred tortoise which has been dead for three thousand years and which the king keeps wrapped up in a box and stored in his ancestral temple.[45] Is this tortoise better off[46] dead and with its bones venerated,[47] or would it be better off alive with its tails dragging in the mud?"

"It would be better off alive and dragging its tail in the mud," the two ministers replied.

"Then go away!" said Chuang Tzu, "and I will drag my tail in the mud!"

NOTES

1. Hui Tzu: Master Hui (惠施), a friend of Chuang Tzu and an argumentative logician.
2. inverted: turned upside down.
3. befalls: happens to.
4. one great featureless indistinguishable mass: one great mass which is so blended that it is faceless and we cannot tell one thing from another.
5. evolved: developed gradually.
6. sequence: order of succession.
7. bawling: shouting or crying in a noisy way.
8. the Great Inner Room: 巨室, literally, the Enormous Room; Nature itself.
9. nature's Sovereign Law: the supreme law of nature, 命.
10. Ch'u: 楚.
11. skull: the bone of the head.
12. insatiable ambition: too much ambition that it cannot be satisfied.
13. transgress the law: break the law.
14. executioner's axe: axe with which a law officer puts a criminal to death.
15. the springs and autumns of your span: the full extent of your natural life. "Springs and autumns" indicates age in Chinese usage.
16. in their due course: in their proper, natural process.
17. glib: too smooth and easy to be sincere.
18. hampered by trammels: held back by restrictions or hindrances.
19. subject: person ruled or controlled by others, especially by a monarch.
20. the Clerk of Destinies: official of the underworld who is in charge of man's fate.
21. make your frame anew: make a new body for you.
22. furrowed: wrinkled.
23. Master Ssu, Master Yu, Master Li and Master Lai: 子祀, 子舆, 子犁, 子来.

24. rump: the hind part of the body where the legs join the back.
25. annihilation: complete destruction.
26. crooked: bent; twisted.
27. vital organs: organs necessary to life, such as heart, brain, lungs. Also called the vitals.
28. pigtail: braid of hair hanging from the back of the head.
29. dislocation of the forces of the yin and the yang: disorder of the complementary forces of the yin (阴) and the yang (阳); a state out of sorts.
30. haltingly: in a lame way; hesitatingly.
31. my, my!: exclamation of surprise.
32. herald: announce.
33. pellet: bullet.
34. 'the freeing of the bound': setting the imprisoned free; 县解.
35. verge: edge; brim.
36. perverse: willful; stubborn.
37. the Great Clod: 大块; earth, nature.
38. When a skilled smith is casting metal: When a skillful blacksmith is beating a piece of metal into shape.
39. Mu-yeh: 镆铘, a famous sword.
40. inauspicious: unlucky.
41. the audacity to take on human form: the courage to assume the form of a man; the boldness to accept human life.
42. the transformation of things: 物化, a life taking different forms. Later the term 物化 has come to mean "death" (a changing back to nature, a becoming one with things).
43. P'u River: 濮水.
44. King of Ch'u: 楚王, most probably 楚威王.
45. ancestral temple: temple built in honor of ancestors.
46. better off: in better circumstances.
47. venerated: revered; highly respected.

31

The Biography of General Li Kuang

《史记·李将军列传》

Ssu-ma Ch'ien
司马迁

(145?–90? B.C.)

ABOUT THE AUTHOR

Ssu-ma Ch'ien (145?–90? B.C.), the greatest of Chinese historians, has had tremendous influence not only on historians but on prose writers in general. Like Li Kuang, he was a tragic figure in Han history. During the reign of Emperor Wu, General Li Ling, Li Kuang's grandson, was taken prisoner by the Hsiung-nu and surrendered to his captors. Ssu-ma Ch'ien offended the emperor by his outspoken defence of Li Ling's loyalty and was punished by castration. He took the humiliation with courage and suppressed indignation. Taking shelter from the unhappy present and seeking consolation in immortal fame, he devoted himself to his lifelong work, *Records of the Grand Historian*. The book is divided into five sections: Basic Annals, Chronological Tables, Treatises, Hereditary Houses, and Biographies. It is the last of these that has the widest literary appeal for its profound understanding of human nature and its vivid characterization.

作者简介　司马迁（公元前145年？—前90年？）是中国最伟大的历史学家，他不仅对后世的历史学家而且对大部分散文家都有巨大的影响。与李广一样，司马迁也是汉代历史上的一个悲剧人物。在汉武帝时期，李广的孙子李陵将军被匈奴俘虏后投降。司马迁直言不讳地维护忠诚的李陵，因而触怒了皇帝，被处以阉割的刑罚。他含羞忍辱，直面挫折。为了逃避令人不悦的现状，也为了在不朽的名声中寻求安慰，他将自己的毕生心血投入到《史记》的书写中。该书分为五个部分：本纪、表、书、世家和列传。其中最后一个部分因其对人性的深刻理解和生动的人物描写而具有最广泛的文学魅力。

《史记·李将军列传》
The Biography of General Li Kuang

* ABOUT THE SELECTION   This moving biography is taken from *Records of the Grand Historian* (史记), a monumental work of history begun by Ssu-ma T'an (d. 110 B.C.), Grand Historian under Emperor Wu of Han dynasty, and carried on and brought to completion by his son Ssu-ma Ch'ien, who succeeded him as the official historian. Li Kuang was a famous general of the generation preceding that of Ssu-ma Ch'ien who saw the great soldier in person. The biographer's admiration for his hero was greatly enhanced by sympathy because both had known the bitterness of disgrace in their official careers. Out to the tragic hero who had to save his honor at the expense of his life, went the heart of the biographer in a prose at once simple, forceful, and sublime. Chinese readers are advised to refer to the original Chinese text for a deeper understanding of the work and for an appreciation of the austere beauty of Ssu-ma Ch'ien's style. The English translation, with some slight abridgments, is by Burton Watson, a distinguished Sinologue and professor at Columbia University.

内容简介 这篇动人的传记选自《史记》这部不朽的历史著作。该书由汉武帝时期的太史令司马谈（约公元前110年）开始书写，他的儿子司马迁后来继承了父亲的官职，并最终完成了这部作品。李广是司马迁前一代的著名将领，作者曾见过这位伟大的战士。作者对这位英雄的钦佩因同情而大大增强，因为两人都曾在各自的官场生涯中经历过耻辱的痛苦。李广不得不以生命为代价来挽救自己的荣誉，作者用简单、有力、崇高的文字向这位悲剧英雄表达了自己的心声。建议中国读者阅读时参考原文，以便更深入地理解这部作品，并欣赏司马迁文风中的朴素之美。英译文由杰出的汉学家、哥伦比亚大学的华兹生教授完成，英译文在内容上有所删节。

《史记·李将军列传》
The Biography of General Li Kuang

李将军广者,陇西成纪人也。其先曰李信,秦时为将,逐得燕太子丹者也。故槐里,徙成纪。广家世世受射。孝文帝十四年,匈奴大入萧关,而广以良家子从军击胡,用善骑射,杀首虏多,为汉中郎。广从弟李蔡亦为郎,皆为武骑常侍,秩八百石。尝从行,有所冲陷折关及格猛兽,而文帝曰:"惜乎,子不遇时!如令子当高帝时,万户侯岂足道哉!"

及孝景初立,广为陇西都尉,徙为骑郎将。吴楚军时,广为骁骑都尉,从太尉亚夫击吴楚军,取旗,显功名昌邑下。以梁王授广将军印,还,赏不行。徙为上谷太守,匈奴日以合战。典属国公孙昆邪为上泣曰:"李广才气,天下无双,自负其能,数与虏敌战,恐亡之。"于是乃徙为上郡太守。后广转为边郡太守,徙上郡。尝为陇西、北地、雁门、代郡、云中太守,皆以力战为名。

匈奴大入上郡,天子使中贵人从广勒习兵击匈奴。中贵人将骑数十纵,见匈奴三人,与战。三人还射,伤中贵人,杀其骑且尽。中贵人走广。广曰:"是必射雕者也。"广乃遂从百骑往驰三人。三人亡马步行,行数十里。广令其骑张左右翼,而广身自射彼三人者,杀其二人,生得一人,果匈奴射雕者也。已缚之上马,望匈奴有数千骑,见广,以为诱骑,皆惊,上山陈。广之百骑皆大恐,欲驰还走。广曰:"吾去大军数十里,今如此以百骑走,匈奴追射我立尽。今我留，匈奴必以我为大军之诱，必不敢击我。"广令诸骑曰："前！"前未到匈奴陈二里所，止，令曰："皆下马解鞍！"其骑曰："虏多且近，即有急，奈何？"广曰："彼虏以我为走，今皆解鞍以示不走，用坚其意。"于是胡骑遂不敢击。有白马将出护其兵，李广上马与十余骑奔射杀胡白马将，而复还至其骑中，解鞍，令士皆纵马卧。是时会暮，胡兵终怪之，不敢击。夜半时，胡兵亦以为汉有伏军于旁欲夜取之，胡皆引兵而去。平旦，李广乃归其大军。大军不知广所之，故弗从。

　　居久之，孝景崩，武帝立，左右以为广名将也，于是广以上郡太守为未央卫尉，而程不识亦为长乐卫尉，程不识故与李广俱以边太守将军屯。及出击胡，而广行无部伍行陈，就善水草屯，舍止，人人自便，不击刀斗以自卫，莫府省约文书籍事，然亦远斥候，未尝遇害。程不识正部曲行伍营陈，击刀斗，士吏治军簿至明，军不得休息，然亦未尝遇害。不识曰："李广军极简易，然虏卒犯之，无以禁也；而其士卒亦佚乐，咸乐为之死。我军虽烦扰，然虏亦不得犯我。"是时汉边郡李广、程不识皆为名将，然匈奴畏李广之略，士卒亦多乐从李广而苦程不识。程不识孝景时以数直谏为太中大夫。为人廉，谨于文法。

　　后汉以马邑城诱单于，使大军伏马邑旁谷，而广为骁骑将军，领属护军将军。是时单于觉之，去，汉军皆无功。其后四岁，广以卫尉为将军，出雁门击匈奴。匈奴兵多，破败广军，生得广。单于素闻广贤，令曰："得李广必生致之。"胡骑得广，广时伤病，置广两马间，络而盛卧广。行十余里，广详死，睨其旁有一胡儿骑善马，广暂腾而上胡儿马，因推堕儿，取其弓，鞭马南驰数十里，复得其余军，因引而入塞。匈奴捕者骑数百追之，广行取胡儿弓，射杀追骑，以故得脱。于是至汉，汉下广吏。吏当广所失亡多，为虏所生得，当斩，赎为庶人。

　　顷之，家居数岁。广家与故颍阴侯孙屏野居蓝田南山中射猎。

尝夜从一骑出，从人田间饮。还至霸陵亭，霸陵尉醉，呵止广。广骑曰："故李将军。"尉曰："今将军尚不得夜行，何乃故也！"止广宿亭下。居无何，匈奴入杀辽西太守，败韩将军，后韩将军徙右北平，于是天子乃召拜广为右北平太守，广即请霸陵尉与俱，至军而斩之。

广居右北平，匈奴闻之，号曰"汉之飞将军"，避之数岁，不敢入右北平。

广出猎，见草中石，以为虎而射之，中石没镞，视之石也。因复更射之，终不能复入石矣。广所居郡闻有虎，尝自射之。及居右北平射虎，虎腾伤广，广亦竟射杀之。

广廉，得赏赐辄分其麾下，饮食与士共之。终广之身，为二千石四十余年，家无余财，终不言家产事。广为人长，猿臂，其善射亦天性也，虽其子孙他人学者，莫能及广。广讷口少言，与人居则画地为军陈，射阔狭以饮。专以射为戏，竟死。广之将兵，乏绝之处，见水，士卒不尽饮，广不近水，士卒不尽食，广不尝食。宽缓不苛，士以此爱乐为用。其射，见敌急，非在数十步之内，度不中不发，发即应弦而倒。用此，其将兵数困辱，其射猛兽亦为所伤云。

居顷之，石建卒，于是上召广代建为郎中令。元朔六年，广复为后将军，从大将军军出定襄，击匈奴。诸将多中首虏率，以功为侯者，而广军无功。后二岁，广以郎中令将四千骑出右北平，博望侯张骞将万骑与广俱，异道。行可数百里，匈奴左贤王将四万骑围广，广军士皆恐，广乃使其子敢往驰之。敢独与数十骑驰，直贯胡骑，出其左右而还，告广曰："胡虏易与耳。"军士乃安。广为圜陈外向，胡急击之，矢下如雨。汉兵死者过半，汉矢且尽。广乃令士持满毋发，而广身自以大黄射其裨将，杀数人，胡虏益解。会日暮，吏士皆无人色，而广意气自如，益治军。军中自是服其勇也。明日，复力战，而博望侯军亦至，匈奴军乃解去。汉军罢,弗能追。是时广军几没,罢归。汉法,博望侯留迟后期,当死,赎为庶人。广军功自如,无赏。

初,广之从弟李蔡与广俱事孝文帝。景帝时,蔡积功劳至二千石。孝武帝时,至代相。以元朔五年为轻车将军,从大将军击右贤王,有功中率,封为乐安侯。元狩二年中,代公孙弘为丞相。蔡为人在下中,名声出广下甚远,然广不得爵邑,官不过九卿,而蔡为列侯,位至三公。诸广之军吏及士卒或取封侯。广尝与望气王朔燕语,曰:"自汉击匈奴而广未尝不在其中,而诸部校尉以下,才能不及中人,然以击胡军功取侯者数十人,而广不为后人,然无尺寸之功以得封邑者,何也?岂吾相不当侯邪?且固命也?"朔曰:"将军自念,岂尝有所恨乎?"广曰:"吾尝为陇西守,羌尝反,吾诱而降,降者八百余人,吾诈而同日杀之。至今大恨独此耳。"朔曰:"祸莫大于杀已降,此乃将军所以不得侯者也。"

后二岁,大将军、骠骑将军大出击匈奴,广数自请行。天子以为老,弗许;良久乃许之,以为前将军。是岁,元狩四年也。

广既从大将军青击匈奴,既出塞,青捕虏知单于所居,乃自以精兵走之,而令广并于右将军军,出东道。东道少回远,而大军行水草少,其势不屯行。广自请曰:"臣部为前将军,今大将军乃徙令臣出东道,且臣结发而与匈奴战,今乃一得当单于,臣愿居前,先死单于。"大将军青亦阴受上诫,以为李广老,数奇,毋令当单于,恐不得所欲。而是时公孙敖新失侯,为中将军从大将军,大将军亦欲使敖与俱当单于,故徙前将军广。广时知之,固自辞于大将军。大将军不听,令长史封书与广之莫府,曰:"急诣部,如书。"广不谢大将军而起行,意甚愠怒而就部,引兵与右将军食其合军出东道。军亡导,或失道,后大将军。大将军与单于接战,单于遁走,弗能得而还。南绝幕,遇前将军、右将军。广已见大将军,还入军。大将军使长史持糒醪遗广,因问广、食其失道状,青欲上书报天子军曲折。广未对,大将军使长史急责广之幕府对簿。广曰:"诸校尉无罪,乃我自失道。吾今自上簿。"

至莫府,广谓其麾下曰:"广结发与匈奴大小七十余战,今幸从大将军出接单于兵,而大将军又徙广部行回远,而又迷失道,岂非天哉!且广年六十余矣,终不能复对刀笔之吏。"遂引刀自刭。广军士大夫一军皆哭。百姓闻之,知与不知,无老壮皆为垂涕。而右将军独下吏,当死,赎为庶人。

广子三人,曰当户、椒、敢,为郎。天子与韩嫣戏,嫣少不逊,当户击嫣,嫣走。于是天子以为勇。当户早死,拜椒为代郡太守,皆先广死。当户有遗腹子名陵。广死军时,敢从骠骑将军。广死明年,李蔡以丞相坐侵孝景园墙地,当下吏治,蔡亦自杀,不对狱,国除。李敢以校尉从骠骑将军击胡左贤王,力战,夺左贤王鼓旗,斩首多,赐爵关内侯,食邑二百户,代广为郎中令。顷之,怨大将军青之恨其父,乃击伤大将军,大将军匿讳之。居无何,敢从上雍,至甘泉宫猎。骠骑将军去病与青有亲,射杀敢。去病时方贵幸,上讳云鹿触杀之。居岁余,去病死。而敢有女为太子中人,爱幸,敢男禹有宠于太子,然好利,李氏陵迟衰微矣。

李陵既壮,选为建章监,监诸骑。善射,爱士卒。天子以为李氏世将,而使将八百骑。尝深入匈奴二千余里,过居延视地形,无所见虏而还。拜为骑都尉,将丹阳楚人五千人,教射酒泉、张掖以屯卫胡。

数岁,天汉二年秋,贰师将军李广利将三万骑击匈奴右贤王于祁连天山,而使陵将其射士步兵五千人出居延北可千余里,欲以分匈奴兵,毋令专走贰师也。陵既至期还,而单于以兵八万围击陵军。陵军五千人,兵矢既尽,士死者过半,而所杀伤匈奴亦万余人。且引且战,连斗八日,还未到居延百余里,匈奴遮狭绝道,陵食乏而救兵不到,虏急击招降陵。陵曰:"无面目报陛下。"遂降匈奴。其兵尽没,余亡散得归汉者四百余人。

单于既得陵,素闻其家声,及战又壮,乃以其女妻陵而贵之。

汉闻，族陵母妻子。自是之后，李氏名败，而陇西之士居门下者皆用为耻焉。

太史公曰：传曰"其身正，不令而行；其身不正，虽令不从"。其李将军之谓也？余睹李将军悛悛如鄙人，口不能道辞。及死之日，天下知与不知，皆为尽哀。彼其忠实心诚信于士大夫也！谚曰"桃李不言，下自成蹊"。此言虽小，可以谕大也。

参考译文

General Li Kuang was a native of Ch'eng-chi in Lung-hsi Province. Among his ancestors was Li Hsin, a general of the state of Ch'in, who pursued and captured Tan, the crown prince of Yen. The family originally lived in Huai-li but later moved to Ch'eng-chi. The art of archery had been handed down in the family for generations.

In the fourteenth year of Emperor Wen's reign (166 B.C.) the Hsiung-nu entered the Hsiao Pass in great numbers. Li Kuang, as the son of a distinguished family, was allowed to join the army in the attack on the barbarians. He proved himself a skillful horseman and archer, killing and capturing a number of the enemy, and was rewarded with the position of palace attendant at the Han court. His cousin Li Ts'ai was also made a palace attendant. Both men served as mounted guards[1] to the emperor and received a stipend[2] of eight hundred piculs[3] of grain. Li Kuang always accompanied Emperor Wen on his hunting expeditions. The emperor, observing how he charged up to the animal pits, broke through the palisades, and struck down the most ferocious beasts, remarked, "What a pity you were not born at a better time! Had you lived in the age of Emperor Kao-tsu, you would have had no trouble in winning a marquisate[4] of at least ten thousand households!"

When Emperor Ching came to the throne, Li Kuang was made chief commandant of Lung-hsi; later he was transferred to the post of general of palace horsemen. At the time of the revolt of Wu and Ch'u, he served as a cavalry commander under the grand commandant Chou Ya-fu, joining in the attack on the armies of Wu and Ch'u, capturing the enemy pennants, and distinguishing himself at the battle of Ch'ang-yi. But because he had accepted the seals of a general from the king of Liang without authorization from the Han government, he was not rewarded for his achievements when he returned to the capital.

Following this he was transferred to the post of governor of Shang-ku Province, where he engaged in almost daily skirmishes[5] with the Hsiung-nu. The director of dependent states Kung-sun K'un-yeh went to the emperor and, with tears in his eyes, said, "There is no one in the empire to match Li Kuang for skill and spirit and yet, trusting to his own ability, he repeatedly engages the enemy in battle. I am afraid one day we will lose him!" The emperor therefore transferred him to the post of governor of Shang Province.

At this time the Hsiung-nu invaded Shang Province in great force. Emperor Ching sent one of his trusted eunuchs[6] to join Li Kuang, ordering him to train the troops and lead them in an attack on the Hsiung-nu. The eunuch, leading a group of twenty or thirty horsemen, was casually riding about the countryside one day when he caught sight of three Hsiung-nu riders and engaged them in a fight. The three Hsiung-nu, however, began circling the party[7] and shooting as they went until they had wounded the eunuch and were near to killing all of his horsemen. The eunuch barely managed to flee back to the place where Li Kuang was, "They must be out hunting eagles!" said Li Kuang, and galloped off with a hundred horsemen in pursuit of the three Hsiung-nu. The Hsiung-nu, having lost their horses, fled on foot. After they had journeyed twenty or thirty li, Li Kuang caught up with them and, ordering his horsemen to fan out[8] to the left and right of them, began to shoot at them. He killed two with his arrows and took the third one alive. As he had guessed, they were eagle hunters.

Li Kuang had bound his prisoner and remounted his horse, when he spied several thousand Hsiung-nu horsemen in the distance. The Hsiung-nu, catching sight of Li Kuang and his men, supposed that they were a decoy[9] sent out from the main body of the Han forces[10] to lure them into combat. They made for[11] a nearby hill in alarm and drew up their ranks on its crest.

Li Kuang's horsemen were thoroughly terrified and begged him to flee back to camp as quickly as possible, but he replied, "We are twenty or thirty li away from the main army. With only a hundred of us, if we were to try to make a dash for it,[12] the Hsiung-nu would be after us in no time[13] and would shoot down every one of us. But if we stay where we are, they are bound to think we are a decoy from the main army and will not dare to attack!"

Instead of retreating, therefore, Li Kuang gave the order to his men to advance. When they had reached a point some two li from the Hsiung-nu ranks, he told his men, "Dismount and undo[14] your saddles!"

"But there are too many of them and they are almost on top of us!" his men protested. "What will we do if they attack?"

"They expect us to run away," said Li Kuang. "But now if we all undo our saddles and show them we have no intention of fleeing, they will be more convinced than ever that there is something afoot."[15]

The Hsiung-nu in fact did not venture to attack, but sent out one of their leaders on a white horse to reconnoiter.[16] Li Kuang mounted again and, with ten or so of his horsemen, galloped after the barbarian leader and shot him down. Then he returned to his group and, undoing his saddle, ordered his men to turn loose their horses and lie down on the ground. By this time night was falling and the Hsiung-nu, thoroughly suspicious of what they had seen, still had not ventured to attack. They concluded that the Han leaders, having concealed soldiers in the area, must be planning to fall upon[17] them in the dark, and so during the night the Hsiung-nu chiefs and their men all withdrew. When dawn came Li Kuang finally managed to return with his group to the main army, which, having no idea where he had gone, had been unable to follow him.

After this Li Kuang was assigned to the governorship of several other border provinces in succession, returning finally to Shang Province. In the course of these moves he served as governor of Lung-hsi, Pei-ti, Tai, and Yün-chung Provinces and in each won fame for his fighting.

After some time, Emperor Ching passed away and the present emperor[18] came to the throne. The emperor's advisers informed him of Li Kuang's fame as a general, and he made Li Kuang the colonel of the guard of the Eternal Palace, while allowing him to retain the governorship of Shang Province.

At this time Ch'eng Pu-chih was the colonel of the guard of the Palace of Lasting Joy. Ch'eng Pu-chih had been a governor in the border provinces and a garrison general at the same time as Li Kuang. When Li Kuang went out on expeditions to attack the Hsiung-nu, he never bothered to form his men into battalions and companies. He would make camp wherever he found water and grass, leaving his men to set up their quarters[19] in any way they thought convenient. He never had sentries circling the camp at night and beating on cooking pots, as was the custom, and in his headquarters he kept records and other clerical work down to a minimum. He always sent out scouts some distance around the camp, however, and he had never met with any particular mishap.

Ch'eng Pu-chih, on the other hand, always kept his men in strict battalion and company formation. The sentries banged on the cooking pots, his officers worked over their records and reports until dawn, and no one in his army got any rest. He likewise had never had any mishaps. Ch'eng Pu-chih once expressed the opinion, "Although Li Kuang runs his army in a very simple fashion, if the enemy should ever swoop down on him[20] suddenly he would have no way to hold them off. His men enjoy plenty of idleness and pleasure, and for that reason they are all eager to fight to the death for him. Life in my army may be a good deal more irksome, but at least I know that the enemy will never catch me napping!"

Li Kuang and Ch'eng Pu-chih were both famous generals at this time, but the Hsiung-nu were more afraid of Li Kuang's strategies, and the Han soldiers for the most part preferred to serve under him and disliked being under Ch'eng Pu-chih's command. Ch'eng Pu-chih advanced to the position of palace counselor under Emperor Ching because of the outspoken advice he gave the emperor on several occasions. He was a man of great integrity and very conscientious in matters of form and law.

Some time later, the Han leaders attempted to entice the Shan-yü (leader of the Hsiung-nu) into entering the city of Ma-yi, concealing a large force of men in the valley around the city to ambush the Hsiung-nu. At this time Li Kuang was appointed cavalry general under the command of Han An-kuo, the leader of the supporting army. As it happened, however, the Shan-yü discovered the plot and escaped in time, so that neither Li Kuang nor any of the other generals connected with the plot achieved any merit.

Four years later (129 B.C.) Li Kuang, because of his services as colonel of the guard, was made a general and sent north from Yen-men to attack the Hsiung-nu. But the Hsiung-nu force he was pitted against[21] turned out to be too numerous and succeeded in defeating Li Kuang's army and capturing him alive.

The Shan-yü had for a long time heard of Li Kuang's excellence as a fighter and had given orders, "If you get hold of Li Kuang, take him alive and bring him to me!" As it turned out, the barbarian horsemen did manage to capture Li Kuang and, since he was badly wounded, they strung a litter between two horses and, laying him on it, proceeded on their way about ten li. Li Kuang pretended to be dead but managed to peer around him and noticed that close by his side was a young Hsiung-nu boy mounted on a fine horse. Suddenly he leaped out of the litter and onto the boy's horse, seizing his bow and pushing him off the horse. Then, whipping the horse to full gallop, he dashed off to the south. After traveling twenty or thirty li he succeeded in catching up with what was left of his army and led the men back across the border into Han territory. While he was making his escape, several hundred horsemen from the party that had captured him came in pursuit, but he turned and shot at them with the bow he had snatched from the boy, killing several of his pursuers, and was thus able to escape.

When he got back to the capital, he was turned over to the law officials, who recommended that he be executed[22] for losing so many of his men and being captured alive. He was allowed to ransom his life and was reduced to the status of commoner.[23]

Following this, Li Kuang lived in retirement for several years, spending his time hunting. His home was in Lan-t'ien, among the Southern Mountains, adjoining the estate of Kuan Ch'iang, the grandson of Kuan Ying, the former marquis of Ying-yin.

One evening Li Kuang, having spent the afternoon drinking with some people out in the fields, was on his way back home, accompanied by a rider attendant, when he passed the watch station at Pa-ling. The watchman, who was drunk at the time, yelled at Li Kuang to halt.

"This is the former General Li," said Li Kuang's man.

"Even present generals are not allowed to go wandering around at night, much less former ones!" the watchman retorted, and he made Li Kuang halt and spend the night in the watch station.

Shortly after this, the Hsiung-nu invaded Liao-hsi, murdered its governor, and defeated General Han An-kuo. Han An-kuo was transferred to Yu-pei-p'ing, where he died, and the emperor forthwith summoned Li

Kuang to be the new governor of Yu-pei-p'ing. When he accepted the post, Li Kuang asked that the watchman of Pa-ling be ordered to accompany him, and as soon as the man reported for duty Li Kuang had him executed.

After Li Kuang took over in Yu-pei-p'ing, the Hsiung-nu, who were familiar with his reputation and called him "The Flying General," stayed away from the region for several years and did not dare to invade Yu-pei-p'ing.

Li Kuang was out hunting one time when he spied a rock in the grass which he mistook for a tiger. He shot an arrow at the rock and hit it with such force that the tip of the arrow embedded[24] itself in the rock. Later, when he discovered that it was a rock, he tried shooting at it again, but he was unable to pierce it a second time.

Whatever province Li Kuang had been in in the past, whenever he heard that there was a tiger in the vicinity he always went out to shoot it in person.[25] When he got to Yu-pei-p'ing he likewise went out one time to hunt a tiger. The beast sprang at him and wounded him, but he finally managed to shoot it dead.

Li Kuang was completely free of avarice. Whenever he received a reward of some kind he at once divided it among those in his command,[26] and he was content to eat and drink the same things as his men. For over forty years he received a salary of two thousand piculs of grain, but when he died he left no fortune behind. He never discussed matters of family wealth. He was a tall man with long, ape-like arms. His skill at archery seems to have been an inborn talent, for none of his descendants or others who studied under him was ever able to equal his prowess.[27] He was a very clumsy speaker and never had much to say. When he was with others he would draw diagrams on the ground to explain his military tactics or set up targets of various widths and shoot at them with his friends, the loser being forced to drink. In fact, archery remained to the end of his life his chief source of amusement.

When he was leading his troops through a barren region and they came to water, he would not go near it until all his men had finished drinking. Similarly he would not eat until every one of his men had been fed. He was very lenient with his men and did nothing to vex them so that they all loved him and were happy to serve under him. Even when the enemy was attacking, it was his custom never to discharge his arrows unless his opponent was within twenty or thirty paces and he believed he could score a hit.[28] When he did discharge an arrow, however, the bowstring had no sooner sounded than his victim would fall to the ground. Because of this peculiar habit he often found himself in considerable difficulty when he was leading his troops against an enemy, and this is also the reason, it is said, that he was occasionally wounded when he went out hunting wild beasts.

Sometime after Li Kuang was made governor of Yu-pei-p'ing, Shih Chien died, and Li Kuang was summoned to take his place as chief of palace attendants.

In the sixth year of *yüan-so* (123 B.C.) Li Kuang was again made a general and sent with the general in chief Wei Ch'ing to proceed north from Ting-hsiang and attack the Hsiung-nu. Most of the other generals who took part in the expedition killed or captured a sufficient number of the enemy to be rewarded for their achievements by being made marquises, but Li Kuang's army won no distinction.

Three years later Li Kuang, as chief of palace attendants, was sent to lead a force of four thousand cavalry north from Yu-pei-p'ing. Chang Ch'ien, marquis of Po-wang, leading ten thousand cavalry, rode out with Li Kuang but took a somewhat different route. When Li Kuang had advanced several hundred li into enemy territory, the Hsiung-nu leader known as the "Wise King of the Left," appeared with forty thousand cavalry and surrounded Li Kuang's army. His men were all terrified, but Li Kuang ordered his son Li Kan to gallop out to meet the enemy. Li Kan, accompanied by only twenty or thirty riders, dashed straight through the Hsiung-nu horsemen, scattering them left and right, and then returned to his father's side, saying, "These barbarians are easy enough to deal with!" After this Li Kuang's men were somewhat reassured.

Li Kuang ordered his men to draw up in a circle with their ranks facing outward. The enemy charged furiously down on them and the arrows fell like rain. Over half the Han soldiers were killed, and their arrows were almost gone. Li Kuang then ordered the men to load their bows and hold them in readiness, but not to discharge them, while he himself, with his huge yellow crossbow,[29] shot at the subcommander[30] of the enemy force and killed several of the barbarians. After this the enemy began to fall back a little.

By this time night had begun to fall. Every one of Li Kuang's officers and men had turned white with fear, but Li Kuang, as calm and confident as though nothing had happened, worked to get his ranks into better formation. After this the men knew that they could never match his bravery.

The following day Li Kuang once more fought off the enemy, and in the meantime Chang Ch'ien at last arrived with his army. The Hsiung-nu forces withdrew and the Han armies likewise retreated, being in no condition to pursue them.[31] By this time Li Kuang's army had been practically wiped out. When the two leaders returned to the capital, they were called to account before the law.[32] Chang Ch'ien was condemned to death for failing to keep his rendezvous[33] with Li Kuang at the appointed time, but on payment of a fine he was allowed to become a commoner. In the case of Li Kuang it was decided that his achievements and his failures canceled each other out and he was given no reward.

Li Kuang's cousin Li Ts'ai had begun his career along with Li Kuang as an attendant at the court of Emperor Wen. During the reign of Emperor Ching, Li Ts'ai managed to accumulate sufficient merit to advance to the position of a two thousand picul official, and under the present emperor he became prime minister of Tai. In the fifth year of *yüan-so* (124 B.C.) he was appointed general of light carriage and accompanied the general in chief, Wei Ch'ing, in an attack on the Hsiung-nu "Wise King of the Right." His achievements in this campaign placed him in the middle group of those who were to receive rewards and he was accordingly enfeoffed[34] as marquis of Lo-an. In the second year of *yüan-shou* (121 B.C.) he replaced Kung-sun Flung as chancellor of the central court. In ability one would be obliged to rank Li Ts'ai very close to the bottom, and his reputation came nowhere near to equaling that of Li Kuang.[35] And yet, although Li Kuang never managed to obtain a fief[36] and never rose higher than one of the nine lower offices[37] of the government, that of colonel of the guard, his cousin Li Ts'ai was enfeoffed as a marquis and eventually reached the position of chancellor, one of the three highest posts. Even some of Li Kuang's own officers and men succeeded in becoming marquises.

Li Kuang was once chatting with Wang So, a diviner[38] who used configurations[39] of the sky to foretell the future, and remarked on this fact. "Ever since the Han started attacking the Hsiung-nu, I have never failed to be in the fight. I've had men in my command who were company commanders or even lower[40] and who didn't even have average ability, and yet twenty or thirty of them have won marquisates on the strength of their achievements in attacking the barbarian armies, I have never been behind anyone else in doing my duty. Why is it I have never won an ounce of[41] distinction so that I could be enfeoffed like the others? Is it that I just don't have the right kind of face for a marquis? Or is it all a matter of fate?"

"Think carefully, general," replied Wang So. "Isn't there something in the past that you regret having done?"

"Once, when I was governor of Lung-hsi, the Chiang tribes in the west started a revolt, I tried to talk them into surrendering and, in fact, persuaded over eight hundred of them to give themselves up. But then I went back on my word[42] and killed all of them the very same day. I have never ceased to regret what I did. But that's the only thing I can think of."

"Nothing brings greater misfortune than killing those who have already surrendered to you," said Wang So. "This is the reason, general, that you have never gotten to be a marquis!"

Two years later general in chief Wei Ch'ing and general of swift cavalry Ho Ch'ü-ping set off with a large force to attack the Hsiung-nu. Li Kuang several times asked to be allowed to join them, but the emperor considered that he was too old and would not permit him to go. After some time, however, the emperor changed his mind and gave his consent, appointing him general of the vanguard.[43] The time was the fourth year of *yüan-shou* (119 B.C.).

Li Kuang accordingly joined the general in chief, Wei Ch'ing, and set off to attack the Hsiung-nu. After the group had crossed the border, Wei Ch'ing captured one of the enemy and learned the whereabouts of the Shan-yü. He therefore decided to take his own best troops and make a dash for the spot,[44] ordering Li Kuang to join forces with[45] the general of the right, Chao Yi-chi, and ride around by the eastern road. The eastern road was rather long and roundabout and, since there was little water or grass in the region, it presented a difficult route for a large army to pass over. Li Kuang therefore asked Wei Ch'ing to change the order. "I have been appointed general of the vanguard," he said, "and yet now you have shifted my position and ordered me to go around by the east. I have been fighting the Hsiung-nu ever since I was old enough to wear my hair bound up, and now I would like to have just one chance to get at[46] the Shan-yü. I beg you to let me stay in the vanguard and advance and fight to the death with him!"

Wei Ch'ing had been warned in private by the emperor that Li Kuang was an old man and had already had a lot of bad luck in the past. "Don't let him try to get at the Shan-yü, or he will probably make a mess of things!" the emperor had said. Also, at this time Kung-sun Ao, who had recently been deprived of his marquisate, was serving as a general under Wei Ch'ing, and Wei Ch'ing wanted to take him along with him in his attack on the Shan-yü so that Kung-sun Ao would have a chance to win some distinction. For these reasons he removed Li Kuang from his post of general of the vanguard.

Li Kuang was aware of all this and tried his best to get out of obeying the order, but Wei Ch'ing refused to listen to his arguments. Instead he sent one of his clerks to Li Kuang's tent with sealed orders to "proceed to your division[47] at once in accordance with[48] the instructions herein." Li Kuang did not even bother to take leave of Wei Ch'ing but got up and went straight to his division, burning with rage and indignation; then, leading his troops to join those of general of the right Chao Yi-chi, he set out by the eastern road. Lacking proper guides, however, they lost their way and failed to meet up with Wei Ch'ing at the appointed time. Wei Ch'ing in the meantime engaged the Shan-yü in battle, but the latter fled and Wei Ch'ing, unable to capture him, was forced to turn back south again. After crossing the desert, he joined up with the forces of Li Kuang and Chao Yi-chi.

When Li Kuang had finished making his report to Wei Ch'ing and returned to his own camp, Wei Ch'ing sent over his clerk with the customary gifts of dried rice and thick wine for Li Kuang. While the clerk was there, he began to inquire how it happened that Li Kuang and Chao Yi-chi had lost their way, since Wei Ch'ing had to make a detailed report to the emperor on what had happened to the armies. Li Kuang, however, refused to answer his questions.

Wei Ch'ing sent his clerk again to reprimand Li Kuang in the strongest terms[49] and order him to report to general headquarters[50] at once and answer a list of charges[51] that had been drawn up against him. Li Kuang replied, "None of my commanders was at fault.[52] I was the one who caused us to lose our way. I will send in a report myself."

Then he went in person to headquarters and, when he got there, said to his officers, "Since I was old enough to wear my hair bound up, I have fought over seventy engagements, large and small, with the Hsiung-nu. This time I was fortunate enough to join the general in chief in a campaign against the troops of the Shan-yü himself, but he shifted me to another division and sent me riding around by the long way. On top of that,[53] I lost my way. Heaven must have planned this! Now I am over sixty— much too old to stand up to[54] a bunch of petty clerks and their list of charges!" Then he drew his sword and cut his throat.

All the officers and men in his army wept at the news of his death, and when word reached the common people,[55] those who had known him and those who had not, old men and young boys alike, were all moved to tears by his fate. Chao Yi-chi was handed over to the law officials and sentenced to death, but on payment of a fine he was allowed to become a commoner.

The Grand Historian remarks: One of the old books says, "If he is an upright person, he will act whether he is ordered to or not, if he is not upright, he will not obey even when ordered."[56] It refers, no doubt, to men like General Li.

I myself have seen General Li—a man so plain and unassuming[57] that you would have taken him for a peasant,[58] and almost incapable of speaking a word. And yet the day he died all the people of the empire, whether they had known him or not, were moved to the profoundest grief, so deeply did men trust his sincerity of purpose. There is a proverb which says, "Though the peach tree does not speak, the world wears a path beneath it."[59] It is a small saying, but one which is capable of conveying a great meaning.

NOTES
1. mounted guards: guards on horseback.
2. stipend: salary.

3. picul: a Chinese unit of weight equal to 133,33 pounds.
4. marquisate: the rank and territory of a marquis.
5. skirmish: slight fight between small groups of soldiers.
6. eunuch: a castrated man in charge of a harem or the household of an emperor, especially in Oriental countries.
7. the party: the group of soldiers.
8. fan out: spread out like a fan.
9. decoy: person or thing used to lead or tempt (the enemy) into danger.
10. the Han forces: the army of Han.
11. made for: went in the direction of; set out for.
12. make a dash for it: (in this case) run for life.
13. in no time: immediately.
14. undo: unfasten; untie.
15. something afoot: something going on.
16. reconnoiter: make a survey (of the enemy) in order to gain information or military purposes.
17. fall upon: attack.
18. the present emperor: Emperor Wu.
19. quarters: place to live.
20. swoop down on him: come on a sudden, swift attack on him.
21. pitted against: set to fight against; set as a match against.
22. executed: put to death according to law.
23. commoner: person who is not a nobleman.
24. embed: fix or enclose in a surrounding mass.
25. in person: (in this case) himself.
26. in his command: under his command.
27. prowess: courage; superior skill or strength in battle.
28. he could score a hit: he could surely hit.
29. crossbow: a weapon with a bow and a grooved stock in the middle to direct the arrows.
30. subcommander: subordinate commander.
31. being in no condition to pursue them: being unable to pursue them; being in too bad a shape to pursue them.
32. called to account before the law: demanded to give an explanation to the court-martial.
33. to keep his rendezvous: to keep his appointment.
34. enfeoffed: conferred a title (as a nobleman).
35. his reputation came nowhere near to equaling that of Li Kuang:

his reputation was no match at all to that (the reputation) of Li Kuang.
36. fief: feudal state.
37. office: position in the public service; position of a government official.
38. diviner: person who is able to foretell future events or reveal occult knowledge through supernatural agency.
39. configurations: the arrangement of the parts, outlines, contours.
40. or even lower: or even lower officials.
41. an ounce of: little.
42. went back on my word: broke my word; broke my promise.
43. vanguard: foremost division of an advancing army.
44. make a dash for the spot: rush to the spot.
45. to join forces with: to meet and unite with (friendly forces).
46. to get at: to reach; to seize; to deal with.
47. division: part of an army commanded by a major general.
48. in accordance with: according to.
49. in the strongest terms: in the severest words; most severely.
50. general headquarters: the office of the commander in chief.
51. answer a list of charges: receive a list of formal accusations (in court-martial).
52. at fault: to blame.
53. on top of that: in addition to that; furthermore.
54. stand up to: meet with courage.
55. when word reached the common people: when news reached the common people.
56. This is a quotation from the *Analects of Confucius*. It is translated by Ku Hung-ming as "If a man is in order in his personal conduct, he will get served even without taking the trouble to give orders. But if a man is not in order in his personal conduct, he may give orders, but his orders will not be obeyed."
57. unassuming: modest. "Assuming" means presumptuous.
58. would have taken him for a peasant: would have supposed him to be a peasant.
59. "Though the peach tree does not speak, the world wears a path beneath it": The peach tree cannot speak, but its blossoms and fruits attract people to it so that their frequent visits wear a path beneath it. This is symbolic of the fact that it was General Li's sincerity, and not his speech, that made him a hero.

The following is a list, arranged in alphabetical order, of the names of persons, places, reigns, titles, etc. and their originals in Chinese.

Chang Ch'ien, marquis of Po-wang 博望侯张骞
Ch'ang-yi 昌邑
Chao Yi-chi 赵食其
Ch'eng-chi 成纪
Ch'eng Pu-chih 程不识
Ch'iang 羌
Ch'in 秦
Chou Ya-fu 周亚夫
Ch'u 楚
Emperor Ching 汉孝景帝
Emperor Kao-tsu 汉高祖
Emperor Wen 汉孝文帝
Eternal Palace, the 未央宫
Han 汉
Han An-kuo 韩安国
Ho Ch'ü-ping 霍去病
Hsiao Pass 萧关
Hsiung-nu, the 匈奴
Huai-li 槐里
Kuan Ch'iang 灌强
Kuan Ying 灌婴
Kung-sun Ao 公孙敖
Kung-sun Hung 公孙弘
Kung-sun K'un-yeh 公孙昆邪
Lan T'ien 蓝田
Li Hsin 李信

Li Kan 李敢
Li Ts'ai 李蔡
Liang 梁
Liao-hsi 辽西
Lung-hsi 陇西
Ma-yi 马邑
marquis of Lo-an 乐安侯
marquis of Ying-yin 颍阴侯
Palace of Lasting Joy, the 长乐宫
Pei-ti 北地
Shan-yü 单于
Shang-ku 上谷
Shang Province 上郡
Shih Chien 石建
Southern Mountains, the 南山
Tai 代
Tan, the crown prince of Yen 燕太子丹
Ting-hsiang 定襄
Wang So 王朔
Wei Ch'ing 卫青
Wu 吴
Yen-men 雁门
yüan-shou 元狩
yüan-so 元朔
Yu-pei-p'ing 右北平
Yün-chung 云中

32

Chinese and
Western
Civilization
Contrasted

中西文明的比较

BERTRAND RUSSELL
伯特兰·罗素

(1872–1970)

ABOUT THE AUTHOR

Bertrand Arthur William, 3rd Earl Russell (1872–1970), came from a distinguished family. His grandfather Lord John Russell was the Liberal Prime Minister and a historian. Educated privately and at Trinity College, Cambridge, he became successively fellow (1895) and lecturer (1910) of that school. Pacifist activities resulted in his six months' imprisonment in 1918, during which he wrote *An Introduction to Mathematical Philosophy*. Among other honors, he was awarded the Order of Merit (1944) and the Nobel Prize for Literature (1950). Bertrand Russell was a philosopher, mathematician, social thinker, and notably one of the intellectual leaders of the twentieth century. His major works include *Principia Mathematica* (1910-1913 in collaboration with A. N. Whitehead), *A History of Western Philosophy* (1945), *Authority and the Individual* (1949), and *Satan in the Suburbs* (1953).

作者简介 伯特兰·亚瑟·威廉,第三代罗素伯爵(1872—1970),出身于贵族家庭。他的祖父约翰·罗素勋爵是自由党人,曾担任英国首相,也是一位历史学家。他在私立学校接受教育,后进入剑桥大学三一学院,他先后成为这所学院的研究员(1895)和讲师(1910)。1918年他因为和平主义活动被判处监禁六个月,其间写出了《数理哲学导论》。他获得了许多荣誉,包括嘉行勋章(1944)和诺贝尔文学奖(1950)。伯特兰·罗素是一位哲学家、数学家、社会思想家,更是20世纪一位知识分子领袖。他的主要著作有《数学原理》(与怀特海合著,1910—1913)、《西方哲学史》(1945)、《权威与个人》(1949)和《郊区的撒旦》(1953)。

ABOUT THE SELECTION

In 1920, when he was forty-eight, Bertrand Russell came to China as a visiting professor of philosophy at Peking University. This comparison was made retrospectively in the light of his personal observations in China. Russell analyzes Western civilization in its three elements of Greek culture, Christianity, and industrialism, and points out that Chinese culture is, by contrast, destitute of religion and science. The insatiable pursuit of progress, encouraged by the rapid development of industrialism at the expense of peace of mind, is attributed by Russell to a restlessness and pugnacity in the Western temperament. On the other hand, he also deplores the Chinese preoccupation with the contemplative virtues to the neglect of "the indispensable minimum of practical efficiency." He wishes that contact between the two civilizations would lead to a judicious adoption of each other's merits instead of defects. Great thinkers are often objective but outspoken critics of their own societies. It would be interesting to compare Russell's criticism of Western civilization with Toynbee's in *Why I Dislike Western Civilization*.

内容简介 1920年，伯特兰·罗素48岁时，作为北京大学的哲学访问教授到访中国。这篇中西文明比较的文章，是根据他对中国的亲身观察写成的回顾性文章。罗素用希腊文化、基督教和工业主义三个元素分析了西方文明，指出中国文化与之相反，它是缺乏宗教和科学的。工业主义的迅速发展激励了人类对进步永不止步的追求，却是以牺牲心灵的宁静为代价，罗素将这归因于西方人性情当中的躁动与好战。另一方面，他也哀叹中国人太过沉溺于沉思的智慧，忽视了"起码的、不可少的效率"。他希望这两个文明的接触会让它们明智地汲取彼此的长处而非缺点。伟大的思想家通常是其所处社会客观而坦率的批判者。将罗素对西方文明的批评与汤因比在《我为什么不喜欢西方文明》中的批评对照来看，是颇有趣味的。

There is at present in China a close contact between our civilization and that which is native to the Celestial Empire.[1] It is still a doubtful question whether this contact will breed a new civilization better than either of its parents,[2] or whether it will merely destroy the native culture and replace it by that of America. Contacts between different civilizations have often in the past proved to be landmarks in human progress. Greece learned from Egypt, Rome from Greece, the Arabs from the Roman Empire,[3] medieval Europe[4] from the Arabs, and Renaissance Europe[5] from the Byzantines.[6] In many of these cases, the pupils proved better than their masters. In the case of China, if we regard the Chinese as the pupils, this may be the case again. In fact, we have quite as much to learn from them as they from us, but there is far less chance of our learning it. If I treat the Chinese as our pupils, rather than vice versa,[7] it is only because I fear we are unteachable.

I propose in this chapter to deal with the purely cultural aspects of the questions raised by the contact of China with the West.

With the exception of Spain and America in the sixteenth century,[8] I cannot think of any instance of two civilizations coming into contact after such a long period of separate development as has marked those of China and Europe. Considering this extraordinary separateness, it is surprising that mutual understanding between Europeans and Chinese is not more difficult. In order to make this point clear, it will be worth while to dwell for a moment on the historical origins of the two civilizations.

Western Europe and America have a practically homogeneous[9] mental life, which I should trace to three sources: (1) Greek culture; (2) Jewish religion and ethics; (3) modern industrialism, which itself is an outcome of modern science. We may take Plato,[10] the Old Testament,[11] and Galileo[12] as representing these three elements, which have remained singularly separable down to the present day. From the Greeks we derive literature and the arts, philosophy and pure mathematics; also the more urbane[13] portions of our social outlook. From the Jews we derive fanatical[14] belief, which its friends call "faith"; moral fervor, with the conception of sin; religious intolerance, and some part of our nationalism. From science, as applied in industrialism, we derive power and the sense of power, the belief that we are as gods, and may justly be the arbiters[15] of life and death for unscientific races.[16] We derive also the empirical method,[17] by which almost all real knowledge has been acquired. These three elements, I think, account for most of our mentality.

No one of these three elements has had any appreciable[18] part in the development of China, except that Greece indirectly influenced Chinese painting, sculpture and music. China belongs, in the dawn of its history, to the great river empires, of which Egypt and Babylonia[19] contributed to our origins, by the influence which they had upon the Greeks and Jews. Just as these civilizations were rendered possible by the rich alluvial[20] soil of the Nile,[21] the Euphrates, and the Tigris,[22] so the original civilization of China was rendered possible by the Yellow River. Even in the time of Confucius,[23] the Chinese Empire did not stretch far either to south or north of the Yellow River. But in spite of this similarity in physical and economic circumstances, there was very little in common between the mental outlook of the Chinese and that of the Egyptians and Babylonians.

Lao-Tze[24] and Confucius, who both belong to the sixth century B.C., have already the characteristics which we should regard as distinctive of the modern Chinese. People who attribute everything to economic causes would be hard put to it[25] to account for[26] the differences between the ancient Chinese and the ancient Egyptians and Babylonians. For my part, I have no alternative theory to offer, I do not think science can, at present, account wholly for national character. Climate and economic circumstances account for parts, but not the whole. Probably a great deal depends upon the character of dominant individuals who happen to emerge at a formative period, such as Moses,[27] Mohammed,[28] and Confucius.

The oldest known Chinese sage is Lao-Tze, the founder of Taoism.[29] "Lao-Tze" is not really a proper name, but means merely "the old philosopher." He was (according to tradition) an older contemporary of Confucius, and his philosophy is to my mind far more interesting. He held that every person, every animal, and every thing has a certain way or manner of behaving which is natural to him, or her, or it, and that we ought to conform to this way ourselves and encourage others to conform to it. "Tao" means "way," but used in a more or less mystical sense, as in the text:[30] "I am the Way and the Truth and the Life."[31] I think he fancied that death was due to departing from the "way," and that if we all lived strictly according to nature we should be immortal, like the heavenly bodies. In later times Taoism degenerated[32] into mere magic, and was largely concerned with the search for the elixir of life.[33] But I think the hope of escaping from death was an element in Taoist philosophy from the first.

Lao-Tze's book, or rather the book attributed to him,[34] is very short but his ideas were developed by his disciple Chuang Tze,[35] who is more interesting than his master. The philosophy which both advocated was one of freedom. They thought ill of government, and of all interferences with nature. They complained of the hurry of modern life, which they contrasted with the calm existence of those whom they called "the pure men of old.[36]" There is a flavor of mysticism in the doctrine of the Tao, because in spite of the multiplicity of living things the Tao is in some sense one, so that if all live according to it there will be no strife in the world. But both sages have already the Chinese characteristics of humor, restraint, and understatement.[37] Their humor is illustrated by Chuang-Tze's account of Po-Lo[38] who "understood the management of horses," and trained them till five out of every ten died. Their restraint and understatement are evident when they are compared with Western mystics.[39] Both characteristics belong to all Chinese literature and art, and to the conversation of cultivated[40] Chinese in the present day. All classes in China are fond of laughter, and never miss a chance of a joke. In the educated classes, the humor is sly and delicate, so that Europeans often fail to see it, which adds to the enjoyment of the Chinese. Their habit of understatement is remarkable, I met one day in Peking a middle-aged man who told me he was academically interested[41] in the theory of politics; being new to the country, I took his statement at its face value, but I afterward discovered that he had been governor of a province, and had been for many years a very prominent politician. In Chinese poetry there is an apparent absence of passion, which is due to the same practice of understatement. They consider that a wise man should always remain calm, and, though they have their passionate moments (being in fact a very excitable race), they do not wish to perpetuate[42] them in art, because they think ill of them. Our romantic movement,[43] which led people to like vehemence, has, so far as I know, no analogue[44] in their literature. Their old music, some of which is very beautiful, makes so little noise that one can only just hear it. In art they aim at being exquisite, and in life being reasonable. There is no admiration for the ruthless strong man, or for the unrestrained expression of passion. After the more blatant[45] life of the West, one misses at first all the effects at which they are aiming; but gradually the beauty and dignity of their existence become visible, so that the foreigners who have lived longest in China are those who love the Chinese best.

The Taoists, though they survive as magicians, were entirely ousted from the favor of the educated classes by Confucianism. I must confess that I am unable to appreciate the merits of Confucius. His writings are largely occupied with trivial points of etiquette, and his main concern is to teach people how to behave correctly on various occasions. When one compares him, however, with the traditional religious teachers of some other ages and races, one must admit that he has great merits, even if they are mainly negative. His system, as developed by his followers, is one of pure ethics,[46] without religious dogma; it has not given rise to a powerful priesthood, and it has not led to persecution.[47] It certainly has succeeded in producing a whole nation possessed of exquisite manners, and perfect courtesy. Nor is Chinese courtesy merely conventional, it is quite as reliable in situations for which no precedent[48] has been provided. And it is not confined to one class, it exists even in the humblest coolie.[49] It is humiliating to watch the brutal insolence of white men received by the Chinese with a quiet dignity which cannot demean itself to answer rudeness with rudeness. Europeans often regard this as weakness, but it is really strength, the strength by which the Chinese have hitherto conquered all their conquerors.

There is one, and only one, important foreign element in the traditional civilization of China, and that is Buddhism. Buddhism came to China from India in the early centuries of the Christian era,[50] and acquired a definite place in the religion of the country. We, with the intolerant outlook which we have taken over from the Jews, imagine that if a man adopts one religion he cannot adopt another. The dogmas of Christianity and Mohammedanism, in their orthodox forms, are so framed that no man can accept both. But in China this incompatibility[51] does not exist, a man may be both a Buddhist and a Confucian, because nothing in either is incompatible with the other. In Japan, similarly, most people are both Buddhists and Shintoists.[52] Nevertheless, there is a temperamental difference between Buddhism and Confucianism, which will cause any individual to lay stress on one or the other even if he accepts both. Buddhism is a religion in the sense in which we understand the world. It has mystic doctrines and a way of salvation and a future life. It has a message to the world intended to cure the despair which it regards as natural to those who have no religious faith. It assumes an instinctive pessimism only to be cured by some gospel. Confucianism has nothing of all this. It assumes people fundamentally at peace with the world, wanting only instruction as to how to live, not encouragement to live at all. And its ethical instruction is not based upon any metaphysical[53] or religious dogma; it is purely mundane.[54] The result of the coexistence[55] of these two religions in China has been that the more religious and contemplative natures turned to Buddhism, while the active administrative type was content with Confucianism, which was always the official teaching, in which candidates for the civil service were examined. The result is that for many ages the government of China has been in the hands of literary skeptics,[56] whose administration has been lacking in those qualities of energy and destructiveness which Western nations demand of their rulers. In fact, they have conformed very closely to the maxims of Chuang-Tze. The result has been that the population has been happy except where civil war brought misery; that subject nations have been allowed autonomy;[57] and that foreign nations have had no need to fear China, in spite of its immense population and resources.

Comparing the civilization of China with that of Europe, one finds in China most of what was to be found in Greece, but nothing of the other two elements of our civilization, namely, Judaism[58] and science. China is practically destitute of[59] religion, not only in the upper classes, but throughout the population. There is a very definite ethical code, but it is not fierce or persecuting, and does not contain the notion "sin." Except quite recently, through European influence, there has been no science and no industrialism.

What will be the outcome of the contact of this ancient civilization with the West? I am not thinking of the political or economic, but of the effect on the Chinese mental outlook. It is difficult to dissociate the two questions altogether, because of course the cultural contact with the West must be affected by the nature of the political and economic contact. Nevertheless, I wish to consider the cultural question as far as I can in isolation.[60]

There is, in China, a great eagerness to acquire Western learning, not simply in order to acquire national strength and be able to resist Western aggression, but because a very large number of people consider learning a good thing in itself. It is traditional in China to place a high value on knowledge, but in old days the knowledge sought was only of the classical literature. Nowadays it is generally realized that Western knowledge is more useful. Many students go every year to universities in Europe, and still more to America, to learn science or economics or law or political theory. These men, when they return to China, mostly become teachers or civil servants or journalists or politicians. They are rapidly modernizing the Chinese outlook, especially in the educated classes.

The traditional civilization of China had become unprogressive, and has ceased to produce much of value in the way of art and literature. This was not due, I think, to any decadence[61] in the race, but merely to lack of new material. The influx[62] of Western knowledge provides just the stimulus that was needed. Chinese students are able and extraordinarily keen. Higher education suffers from lack of funds and absence of libraries, but does not suffer from any lack of the finest human material. Although Chinese civilization has hitherto been deficient[63] in science, it never contained anything hostile to science, and therefore the spread of scientific knowledge encounters no such obstacles as the Church put in its way in Europe. I have no doubt that if the Chinese could get a stable government and sufficient funds, they would within the next thirty years, begin to produce remarkable work in science. It is quite likely that they might outstrip[64] us, because they come with fresh zest and with all the ardor of a renaissance. In fact, the enthusiasm for learning in Young China reminds one constantly of the renaissance spirit in fifteenth-century Italy.

It is remarkable, as distinguishing the Chinese from the Japanese, that the things they wish to learn from us are not those that bring wealth or military strength, but rather those that have either an ethical and social value, or a purely intellectual interest. They are not by any means uncritical of our civilization. Some of them told me that they were less critical before 1914, but that the war[65] made them think there must be imperfection in the Western manner of life. The habit of looking to the West for wisdom was, however, very strong, and some of the younger ones thought that Bolshevism[66] could give what they were looking for. That hope also must be suffering disappointment, and before long they will realize that they must work out their own salvation by means of a new synthesis.[67] The Japanese adopted our faults and kept their own, but it is impossible to hope that the Chinese will make the opposite selection, keeping their own merits and adopting ours.

The distinctive merit of our civilization, I should say, is the scientific method; the distinctive merit of the Chinese a just conception of the ends of life. It is these two that one must hope to see gradually uniting.

Lao-Tze describes the operation of Tao as "production without possession, action without self-assertion, development without domination."[68] I think one could derive from these words a conception of the ends of life as reflective[69] Chinese see them and it must be admitted that they are very different from the ends which most white men set before themselves. Possession, self-assertion, domination, are eagerly sought, both nationally and individually. They have been erected into a philosophy by Nietzsche,[70] and Nietzsche's disciples are not confined to Germany.

But, it will be said, you have been comparing Western practice with Chinese theory; if you had compared Western theory with Chinese practice, the balance would have come out quite differently. There is, of course, a great deal of truth in this. Possession, which is one of the three things that Lao-Tze wishes us to forgo, is certainly dear to the heart of the average Chinaman. As a race, they are tenacious of[71] money—not perhaps more so than the French, but certainly more than the English or the Americans. Their politics are corrupt, and their powerful men make money in disgraceful ways. All this it is impossible to deny.

Nevertheless, as regards the other two evils, self-assertion and domination, I notice a definite superiority to ourselves in Chinese practice. There is much less desire than among the white races to tyrannize over other people. The weakness of China internationally is quite as much due to this virtue as to the vices of corruption and so on which are usually assigned as the sole reason. If any nation in the world could ever be "too proud to fight," that nation would be China. The natural Chinese attitude is one of tolerance and friendliness, showing courtesy and expecting it in return. If the Chinese chose, they could be the most powerful nation in the world. But they only desire freedom, not domination. It is not improbable that other nations may compel them to fight for their freedom, and if so, they may lose their virtue and acquire a taste for empire. But at present, though they have been an imperial[72] race for two thousand years, their love of empire is extraordinarily slight.

Although there have been many wars in China, the natural outlook of the Chinese is very pacifistic.[73] I do not know of any other country where a poet would have chosen, as Po-Chui[74] did in one of the poems translated by Mr. Waley,[75] called by him "The Old Man with the Broken Arm,"[76] to make a hero of a recruit who maimed himself to escape military service. Their pacifism is rooted in their contemplative outlook, and in the fact that they do not desire to change whatever they see. They take a pleasure—as their pictures show—in observing characteristic manifestations of different kinds of life, and they have no wish to reduce everything to a preconceived pattern. They have not the ideal of progress which dominates the Western nations, and affords a rationalization of our active impulses. Progress is, of course, a very modern ideal even with us; it is part of what we owe to science and industrialism. The cultivated conservative Chinese of the present day talk exactly as their earliest sages write. If one points out to them that this shows how little progress there has been, they will say: "Why seek progress when you already enjoy what is excellent?" At first, this point of view seems to a European unduly indolent;[77] but gradually doubts as to one's own wisdom grow up, and one begins to think that much of what we call progress is only restless change, bringing us no nearer to any desirable goal.

It is interesting to contrast what the Chinese have sought in the West with what the West has sought in China. The Chinese in the West seek knowledge, in the hope—which I fear is usually vain—that knowledge may prove a gateway to wisdom. White men have gone to China with three motives: to fight, to make money, and to convert the Chinese to our religion. The last of these motives has the merit of being idealistic, and has inspired many heroic lives. But the soldier, the merchant, and the missionary are alike concerned to stamp our civilization upon the world; they are all three, in a certain sense, pugnacious.[78] The Chinese have no wish to convert us to Confucianism; they say "religions are many, but reason is one," and with that they are content to let us go our way. They are good merchants, but their methods are quite different from those of European merchants in China, who are perpetually seeking concessions,[79] monopolies,[80] railways, and mines, and endeavoring to get their claims supported by gunboats. The Chinese are not, as a rule, good soldiers, because the causes for which they are asked to fight are not worth fighting for, and they know it. But that is only proof of their reasonableness.

I think the tolerance of the Chinese is in excess of[81] anything that Europeans can imagine from their experience at home: We imagine ourselves tolerant, because we are more so than our ancestors. But we still practice political and social persecution, and what is more, we are firmly persuaded[82] that our civilization and our way of life are immeasurably better than any other, so that when we come across a nation like the Chinese, we are convinced that the kindest thing we can do to them is to make them like ourselves. I believe this to be a profound mistake. It seemed to me that the average Chinaman, even if he is miserably poor, is happier than the average Englishman, and is happier because the nation is built upon a more humane and civilized outlook than our own. Restlessness and pugnacity not only cause obvious evils, but fill our lives with discontent, incapacitate[83] us for the enjoyment of beauty, and make us almost incapable of the contemplative virtues. In this respect we have grown rapidly worse during the last hundred years. I do not deny that the Chinese go too far in the other direction; but for that very reason I think contact between East and West is likely to be fruitful to both parties. They may learn from us the indispensable minimum[84] of practical efficiency, and we may learn from them something of that contemplative wisdom which has enabled them to persist while all the other nations of antiquity have perished.

When I went to China, I went to teach, but every day that I stayed I thought less of what I had to teach them and more of what I had to learn from them. Among Europeans who had lived a long time in China, I found this attitude not uncommon, but among those whose stay is short, or who go only to make money, it is sadly rare. It is rare because the Chinese do not excel in the things we really value—military prowess and industrial enterprise. But those who value wisdom or beauty, or even the simple enjoyment of life, will find more of these things in China than in the distracted and turbulent West, and will be happy to live where such things are valued. I wish I could hope that China, in return for our scientific knowledge, may give us something of her large tolerance and contemplative peace of mind.

NOTES

1. the Celestial Empire: China.
2. either of its parents: either Western or Chinese civilization.
3. Roman Empire: the empire of ancient Rome, dating from 27 B.C. and divided into the Eastern Empire and the Western Empire in A.D. 395.
4. medieval Europe: Europe during the Middle Ages, approximately 500-1450.
5. Renaissance Europe: Europe during the 14th, 15th, and 16th centuries when classic arts, letters, and learning were revived.
6. Byzantines: people of the Eastern Roman Empire. The name is derived from Byzantium, capital of the empire.
7. vice versa: making an interchange of positions (Latin).
8. Spain and America in the sixteenth century: Columbus discovered America in 1492 under the patronage of Queen Isabella of Spain. Spanish civilization was naturally the first European civilization to come into contact with American civilization.
9. homogeneous: of the same kind or nature.
10. Plato: a great Greek philosopher (427?-347 B.C.).
11. the Old Testament: the major part of Christian Bible containing records of Mosaic covenant.
12. Galileo (1564-1642): Italian physicist and astronomer.
13. urbane: courteous; refined.
14. fanatical: unreasonably enthusiastic; extremely active for a cause.
15. arbiters: judges.
16. unscientific races: peoples who have not developed science.
17. the empirical method: method characterized by undue reliance on experience, experiment, and observation, with little regard for science or theory.
18. appreciable: perceptible.
19. Babylonia: ancient empire in Western Asia.
20. alluvial: pertaining to alluvium, a deposit of sand, mud, etc., formed by flowing water.
21. the Nile: the great river of Egypt.
22. the Euphrates, and the Tigris: two main rivers in Babylonia.
23. Confucius (551-479 B.C.): Chinese philosopher and educator. See "about the author" of *Selections from the Analects*.
24. Lao-Tze: also Lao-tse or Lao-tzu (老子), honorific title for Li Erh (李耳), Chinese philosopher and founder of Taoism.
25. be hard put to it: be in difficulties.

26. account for: explain.
27. Moses: the great leader and lawgiver of the Israelites.
28. Mohammed (570-632): Arabian founder and prophet of Islam or Mohammedanism.
29. Taoism: 道教.
30. text: short passage of Scripture, especially one chosen in proof of a doctrine, as the subject of a sermon, etc.
31. "I am the Way and the Truth and the Life": John XIV, 6, New Testament.
32. degenerated: declined; grew worse.
33. elixir of life: alchemic preparation for prolonging life.
34. or rather the book attributed to him: With regard to Lao-Tze, the book which bears his name is of doubtful authenticity and was probably compiled two or three centuries after his death. See Giles, *Civilization in China*. (Bertrand Russell's own note).
35. Chuang-Tze (369?-286? B.C.): also Chuang Tzu (庄子), honorific title for Chuang Chou (庄周), Chinese philosopher of the Taoist school.
36. "the pure men of old": " 古之真人 ". See 庄子大宗师篇 .
37. understatement: saying less than the full truth; saying less than one means.
38. Po-Lo: 伯乐 . See the first passage of 庄子马蹄篇 .
39. mystic: person who believes that truth or God can be known through spiritual insight.
40. cultivated: well-educated; enlightened.
41. academically interested: interested scholarly or only in theory.
42. perpetuate: make permanent.
43. our romantic movement: literary and artistic movement in Europe in early nineteenth century, characterized by a return to nature, exaltation of emotion and the senses over intellect, and a revolt against eighteenth-century rationalism.
44. analogue: something comparable.
45. blatant: loudly obtrusive.
46. ethics: study of moral conduct, duty, and judgment.
47. persecution: oppression; punishment.
48. precedent: former case that may serve as an example.
49. coolie: a laborer who does hard work (from the Chinese term 苦力).
50. Buddhism came to China from India in the early centuries of the

Christian era: during the reign of Emperor Ming (汉明帝) of Eastern Han dynasty.
51. incompatibility: lack of harmony.
52. Shintoists: followers of the Shinto religion (神道教), the native religion of Japan which practices nature worship and ancestral worship.
53. metaphysical: of metaphysics, a branch of philosophy that tries to explain reality and knowledge.
54. mundane: worldly.
55. coexistence: existing side by side.
56. skeptic: person who questions the truth of theories or apparent facts.
57. autonomy: right of self-government.
58. Judaism: religious system of the Jews.
59. destitute of: having no; without.
60. in isolation: by itself; not in relation to other things.
61. decadence: deterioration.
62. influx: flowing in.
63. deficient: incomplete; defective.
64. outstrip: pass in progress.
65. the war: the First World War of 1914-1918.
66. Bolshevism: communism.
67. synthesis: combining of elements, parts or ingredients into a system or whole.
68. "production without possession, action without self-assertion, development without domination.": "生而不有，为而不恃，长而不宰." See 道德经第十章.
69. reflective: thoughtful.
70. Friedrich Wilhelm Nietzsche (1844-1900): German philosopher and writer whose ill health and nervous afflictions developed into lunacy in 1889. The main features of his doctrine include a contempt for Christianity with its compassion for the weak, a hostility to the asceticism of Schopenhauer, and an exaltation of the "will to dominate" and of the "superman", a pitiless demigod who tramples on the feeble.
71. tenacious of: clinging tightly to.
72. imperial: of an empire.
73. pacifistic: peace-loving.
74. Po-Chui (772-846): also Po Chü-i (白居易), Chinese poet of T'ang

dynasty.
75. Mr. Waley: Arthur Waley, noted English Sinologue and translator.
76. "The Old Man with the Broken Arm": 新丰折臂翁, a poem by Po Chü-i descriptive of cruelties of war.
77. unduly indolent: excessively lazy.
78. pugnacious: fond of fighting; quarrelsome.
79. concessions: something granted by a government.
80. monopolies: exclusive control of a commodity or service.
81. in excees of: greater than.
82. we are firmly persuaded: we firmly believe.
83. incapacitate: make incapable.
84. indispensable minimum: absolute necessity which cannot be further reduced.

参考译文

在今日之中国，我们西方的文明同中国本土文明之间产生了密切的联系。这种联系是否会产生一种比纯中国或纯西方更好的新文明，或是只会破坏本土文化而代之以美国文化，这仍然是一个值得怀疑的问题。历史上，不同文明之间的联系曾被证明是人类进步的里程碑。希腊曾经向埃及学习，罗马曾经向希腊学习，阿拉伯人曾经向罗马帝国学习，中世纪的欧洲曾经向阿拉伯人学习，文艺复兴时期的欧洲曾经向拜占庭学习。在多数情况下，做学生的往往是青出于蓝而胜于蓝。就中国而论，如果我们把中国视为学生，那他很可能会超过先生；事实上，我们能向他们学习的东西很可能和他们能向我们学习的东西一样多，但是我们向他们学习的可能性却小得多。如果我们只愿意把中国人当作我们的学生，而不愿把我们当作他们的学生，那只是由于我们担心自己"不可教也"。

在本章中，我要涉及的是中西关系中的纯文化问题。

除了16世纪的西班牙和美国之外，我想不出任何先例像中国和欧洲这样在经历了长时期隔绝状态之后才开始发生联系的两种文明。考虑到这是一种异乎寻常的隔绝,我们就会惊奇地发现:中国人同欧洲人之间的相互了解却并不因此而更感困难。为了更清楚地解释这一点,我们应该停下一会儿,略微论及这两种文明的历史渊源。

西欧和美国有着同样的精神生活,其渊源有三:(1)希腊文化;(2)犹太宗教和伦理;(3)现代工业主义,而工业主义本身又是现代科学的产物。我们可用柏拉图、《旧约全书》和伽利略代表这三种文化渊源,这三者直到今天都停留在各自分离的状态中。从希腊人那里我们获得了文学、艺术、哲学、纯数学以及我们的社会观中比较文雅的那一部分内容。从犹太人那里我们得到了狂热的信仰(也可以友善地称其为"信心")、道德热诚和罪恶观、宗教的不容忍性,以及我们的民族主义中的一部分内容。从科学那里(我指的是应用于工业主义的科学),我们获得了权力,并且对权力的含义产生了认识;同时还获得了一种自视为神的信心;面对那些不懂科学的种族,我们仿佛是手握生死予夺大权的法官。我们也从科学那里得到了验证的方法,而一切真实的知识都是从验证法中获得的。我认为,我们思想中的大部分内容是可以用这三种要素来解释的。

在上述三要素中,没有任何一种曾对中国的发展起过重要作用,只是希腊曾间接地影响过中国的绘画、雕刻和音乐。在中国历史的初始时期,中国属于大河帝国。在那些大河帝国中,埃及和巴比伦曾经通过对希腊和犹太人的影响,而对我们的文明渊源做出了贡献。正如同尼罗河、幼发拉底河和底格里斯河那肥沃的冲积平原所产生的埃及、巴比伦文明一样,黄河孕育了早期的中国文明。即使到了孔子时代,中华帝国也没有远离过黄河南北地域。然而,虽然在地域和经济方面中国人同埃及、巴比伦人之间有着相同之处,但他们的思想却是迥异的。公元前6世纪的老子和孔子就已经具有了我们所认为的现代中国人的特性。那些把一切都归因于经济的人们,很难用经济原因去解释古代中国人与古埃及人、古巴比伦人之间的不同点。就是我也无法提供另外一种学说。我认为,目前,科学还无法对一国的特性做出全部的解释。气候和经济条件能够解释一部分原因,但不能解释清楚全部原因。也许,一国的特性主要取决于这一特性形成期间偶然出现的重要人物的性格特征,例如摩西、穆罕默德和孔子。

我们所知道的最早的中国哲人是老子——道家创始人。老子并不是姓名,而是老哲学家的意思。据说他是孔子的同时代人,但比孔子年长。我认为他的哲学远比孔子的哲学有趣。他认为,每一个人、每一只动物、每一样东西,各自都有一种适合自己的处世之道或行为方式。我们自己必须遵循这种行为方式,而且也应鼓励别人按此行事。"道"的意思是道路,但是多多少少被用于神秘的意义中,一如《圣经》里所写的:"我就是道路,真理,生命。"老子认为,偏离了"道"就会导致死亡。假如我们严格地遵守自然法则生活,我们就会永生,一如天体。后来道教退化了,沦为巫术,只注重炼丹求仙。但是我认为,道教自始便希望逃避死亡,这种希望是道教的要义。

老子的著作,或者说一般人都认为是他的著作,是很简短的,但他的思想得到了他的学生庄子的发挥,而庄子是一个比他的老师更有趣的人。他们师徒二人所主张的哲学是一种自由的学说。他们认为,政府以及一切对自然的干涉都是不好的。他们把匆匆忙忙的当世人的生活同古代真人的宁静生活加以比较,并对忙乱的生活投之以批评。道教的学说中有种神秘主义的气息,因为在道教看来,世间虽有万物,但在一定意义上,万物皆备于道,所以如果万物皆能循道而生,世界上就不会再有争斗。这两位哲人已经具有中国人幽默、婉约、含蓄的特性。他们的幽默在庄子的"伯乐治马"中表现出来。伯乐自命长于治马,但经过他训练的马,十匹中只剩下五匹活马。当我们把老庄同西方的神秘主义者加以比较时，就会发现他们的婉约和含蓄是显而易见的。既幽默又婉约、含蓄，这些特性表现在中国的文学、艺术中，也体现在今日中国知识分子的谈吐上。中国每个阶层的人都喜欢放声大笑，而且从不放过开玩笑的机会。在受过教育的中国人中间，幽默是狡黠微妙的，因此欧洲人常常体察不到这样的幽默，而中国人反倒更觉有趣。中国人的含蓄是明显的。有一天，我在北平遇见一位中年人，他告诉我，他对于政治学抱有学术兴趣。因为我刚到中国，就按照这话的表面意思去理解了。我后来才知道他曾经做过省主席，而且是一位成名多年的政治家。中国诗虽然在表面上缺乏热情，但那也是由于含蓄。他们认为，一个聪明人应该永远镇静，虽然他们也有热情的时刻（事实上，中国人也是很容易激动的民族），但他们不愿在艺术作品中使瞬间的冲动变为永恒，因为他们觉得那是不好的。那种导致西方人喜爱强烈感情的浪漫主义运动，据我所知，在中国文学中是没有类似现象的。中国的古典音乐有些非常优美，其声音是那么宁静，宁静得几乎只是隐约可闻。在艺术上，他们讲求美妙；在生活上，他们追求合理。他们不宗凶残的强人，也不喜爱一览无余的直白的热情。在习惯了西方喧闹的生活之后，最初我们对于中国人寻求的效果会全无所察，但是渐渐地他们生活方式中的美感和尊严就变得越来越清晰，因此，在中国居住得最久的外国人也就成了最喜爱中国的人。

以巫师身份残存的道教人士是儒教知识阶层所不齿的。我必须承认，我无法欣赏孔子的优点。他的著作只着重礼仪的细微末节，他最关切的事情是教人如何在不同的场合下正确行事。然而，当人们把孔子和其他时代、其他种族的宗教大师们加以比较时，就必须承认孔子的长处，即使这些长处有很多是消极的。他的制度，如同他的弟子们所发挥的，是纯粹的伦理制度，而没有宗教学说。他的制度不曾产生强有力的教士职位，也没有导致宗教性的迫害。这一制度成功地使整个中华民族具有优美的仪态和完美的礼貌。中国人的礼貌不仅只是依照惯例行事的习俗,而且在没有惯例可循的情况下,他们也有可靠的礼貌。中国人的礼貌不只是限于某一阶层之内,即使在最卑贱的苦力中间也是讲礼貌的。当中国人以一种沉默的尊严冷对白种人的傲慢时,我们西方人应感到羞愧,因为中国人不愿用以牙还牙的态度贬低自己的身份。欧洲人以为那是中国人的懦弱,其实那正是他们的力量,中国人曾经以此征服了所有的征服者。

在传统的中国文化中只有一种外来的重要影响力,那就是佛教。佛教在公元初期从印度传入中国,并且在中国的宗教领域中获得了确定的地位。我们西方人认为,如一个人接受了一种宗教的话,他就不能再接受另外一种宗教,这是因为我们从犹太人那里继承了一种不宽容的态度。基督教和伊斯兰教的正统教义都规定任何人不能同时接受两种宗教。但是在中国,却不存在这种不可兼容的状况。一个中国人可以同时相信佛教和儒教,因为二者之间没有矛盾。在日本,大多数人同样可以既相信佛教又相信神道教。但是,佛教和儒教有着气质上的不同,即使一个人同时相信二者,他也必然会着重其中之一。佛教具有宗教的意味,它有着神秘教义,可以救赎人们脱离苦海,相信来生。它为这个世界带来福音,以医治绝望的心理。佛教认为,没有宗教信仰的人必定会产生绝望的心态。它认为,只有依靠某种福音才能医治本能的悲观主义。而这一切都是儒教所没有的。在本质上,儒教认为人类应当与世界和平相处,人类只需要学习如何生活,而不需要促进生活。它的伦理教义不是基于形而上学或宗教教条之上,而是全然世俗的。由于这两种宗教在中国并存的结果,更倾向于宗教或沉思默想的人们就转向了佛教;活跃的行政类型人才则转向儒教。而儒教是官方的指导课程,那些想成为文官的士子们必须接受儒教的考试。其结果是,在相当长的岁月中,政治一直落在无神论知识分子手中,他们的行政缺乏效力和破坏性,而这两种品质却是西方国家要求统治者必备的素质。事实上，这些无神论的文化人严格地遵守庄子的格言，结果是中国大众都很快乐，却难免遭受内战带来的痛苦，中国的臣属国得到了自治；而且，尽管中国人口众多，资源丰富，外国也不必害怕中国。

比较中国与欧洲两种文明，人们会发现，中国文明中的许多内容在希腊文明里也存在，但中国文明中却不存在另外两种构成西方文明的成分，即犹太教和科学。实际上，中国缺乏宗教，不仅是在上等社会里，即或在整个民众中也是如此。中国有确定的伦理法则，但它既不凶残可怕，也不会置人于死地。在这种伦理中不存在"原罪"一说。中国也不曾有过科学和工业主义，只是最近一个时期在欧洲的影响下，情况才有所改变。

中国古老的文明同西方文明之间的联系将会产生何种结果，现在，我并不想讨论这种联系会在政治或经济上产生什么样的结果，而是想讨论它在中国人的思想观念上将产生的影响。当然，把政治、经济问题完全剥离开是困难的事情，因为中西文化的联系必然会受到中西政治、经济关系的影响。然而，我希望尽量把文化问题同政治、经济分开来加以讨论。

中国人如今急迫地要获得西方的学问，并不仅仅是为了增强国家实力和为了抵抗外国的侵略，而主要是因为大多数中国人认为学问本身是个好东西。重视学问是中国人的传统，但在过去，人们所追求的学问只限于古典文学。如今，人们已经普遍地认识到，西方的学问更具实用性。每年有许多学生去欧洲留学，更多的人是去美国学习科学、经济学、法律或政治学。这些人归国后大都做教授、文官、新闻记者或政治家。他们正在迅速地使中国人的观念更新，特别是使知识阶层快速转向现代观念。

中国的传统文明早已停滞不前了，已经不再对文学和艺术有新的贡献了。我认为，导致这种状况的原因不是由于种族的衰退，而只是因为缺少新的信息。西方知识的输入正为中国人提供了他们所需要的刺激因素。中国学生的能力很强,而且非常聪敏。中国的高等教育缺的是基金和图书馆,但并不缺少优秀的人才。虽然中国文明迄今为止还缺少科学,但是它对科学并不仇视,因此科学在中国的传播将不会受到阻碍,而在欧洲,教会曾经为科学的传播制造了很多障碍。我深信,中国如能有稳定的政府和充足的资金,就会在三十年之内对科学做出卓越的贡献。很可能中国会超过我们西方,因为中国人有崭新的热诚和复兴的渴望。事实上,中国青年的学习热情之高,常使我们想起15世纪意大利的文艺复兴精神。

值得注意的是,中国人不同于日本人,他们要向我们学习的不是富国强兵之道,而是有着伦理意义和社会价值的东西,或是纯粹的学术情趣。中国人对我们的文明绝非一概照搬。有些中国人对我说,1914年以前,他们还很少对我们的文明持批评意见,但是,战争使他们觉得西方人的生活方式并非那么完美。中国人已经养成了很深的习惯要向西方学习智慧,一些年轻人认为,布尔什维克主义也许能够向中国提供他们所寻求的东西。但是这个希望肯定是会落空的,也许不用很长时间,中国人就会认识到他们必须按照新的综合疗法,为解救自己配制良方。日本人曾经既接受了我们的缺陷,又保留了自己的短处,只怕中国人也很难做出相反的选择:既保留自己的优点,又吸收他人之所长。

我认为,我们西方文明最显著的长处是讲求科学的方法;而中国文明最突出的优点是对人生目的具有洞见。我们希望看到的,正是二者的结合。

老子把道的运行描述为"生而不有,为而不恃,长而不宰"。我想,人们可以从这几句话中概括出善于思考的中国人眼中的人生观;而且我们必须承认,这一人生观是同绝大多数白种人所树立的人生目的大相径庭的。在西方,不论是国家还是个人,所热衷追求的正是占有、自恃,以及统治。这些观念已经树立在尼采的哲学之中，而尼采的门徒并不仅限于德国。

也许有人会说，你一直在拿西方的实践同中国的理论作比照，如果比较一下西方的理论和中国的实践，天平的高低就会不同了。确实，这话很有几分道理。老子希望我们放弃的三种东西之一"占有"，恰恰是普通中国人所珍爱之物。作为一个种族，中国人是贪财的，虽说也许不比法国人更爱钱，但确实比英美人有过之。他们的政治腐败，有权势的大人物常采取卑劣手法搞钱。这些都是不能否认的。

然而，在"自恃、统治"这两种邪恶上，我发现中国人确实在实践中比我们做得好。中国人不像白种人那样想统治其他民族。中国在国际上之所以软弱无力，一半是因为它不想统治别国，一半是因为它的政治腐败和其他原因，但通常人们只把腐败说成是中国之所以软弱的唯一原因。如果世界上哪个国家可以说是如此之骄傲，以至于"不屑于打仗"的话，这个国家就是中国。中国人生来就有着友善和宽容的态度，他们对别人有礼貌，也希望对方还之以礼。如中国人愿意，他们就可以成为世界上最强大的民族。但他们只想自由自在，而不愿统治别人。外国很可能强迫中国人为自身的解放而战斗，如果这样的话，中国人就会失去他们的美德而爱好统治。但是就目前而言，虽然中华帝国已有两千年的历史，但中国人对于统治的爱好却极为淡漠。

尽管中国发生过多次战争，但中国人非常爱好和平。我不知道哪个国家会有一个诗人把逃兵作为英雄来歌颂，一如白居易在《新丰折臂翁》中所描写的那个自伤其臂而逃避兵役的人，韦利曾把此诗译成英文，取名"The Old Men with the Broken Arm"。中国人的和平主义植根于他们善于沉思的态度，也植根于他们不愿改变的事实。就像中国画所表现的那样，中国人喜欢从观察各种生活的不同情趣中获得陶然乐趣，而不愿把一切都注入事先定好的模式之中。那种支配着西方人并使其勃勃野心具有合理色彩的进步观，在中国人之中是不存在的。当然，即使对于我们西方人来说，追求进步也是一个非常现代化的理念，它的出现应该部分地归因于科学和工业主义。在今天，保守的中国知识分子说起话来就像古代贤哲写文章一样。如果有人告诉他们，这么做只是表明了中国业已取得的进步真是太少了，这时，保守的读书人会回答："汝既享有美好之物，何复追求进步耶？"刚开始，欧洲人会觉得这种观念太懈怠了，可是当他们渐渐变得聪明后，又逐渐怀疑起自己来，开始自问：我们所谓的进步，在很大程度上是否只是无休止的变动，而并不能使我们接近理想中的目标。

把中国人在西方所追求的事情同西方人在中国所寻求的东西作一比较，是桩很有趣的事。中国人在西方寻求知识，并且希望知识能够成为通向智慧的大门——但是我却担心这一希望十之八九会落空。白种人奔赴中国的动机有三：打仗、赚钱，以及使中国人皈依我们的宗教。传教作为三者中的最后一个动机，具有理想主义的精神，曾经激发过许多英雄主义者。但是，军人、商人和传教士都一样致力于在世界上留下我们的文明印记。从某种意义上说，这三种人都是好战分子。但是中国人却没有也要我们改变成孔教徒的意愿，他们认为宗教是多种多样的，而理性却是唯一的，因此他们乐于让我们走自己的路。中国人是好心的商人，他们用的方法完全不同于在中国经商的欧洲人。欧洲商人一味地寻求租界、垄断、铁路、矿权，而且致力于用炮舰维护他们的索取。一般说来，中国人不是好战士，因为他们知道让他们参军打仗实在毫无道理。但这只能证明他们是有理性的人。

我认为中国人的宽容程度超过了欧洲人基于国内经验所能想象的任何事情。我们自认为自己已经很宽容了，因为我们的容忍力已经超过了我们的前辈。但是，我们仍在施行政治和社会迫害，而且更为严重的是，我们深信自己的文明和生活方式远胜于其他民族。所以，当我们遇见一个像中国人那样的民族时，就会认为我们所能够做的善事是把他们改变成为像我们一样的人。我认为，这是一个极大的错误。在我看来，一个普通的中国人即使很贫穷也要比一个普通的英国人更快乐。他之所以更快乐，乃是因为他的民族是建立在一个比我们更合乎人性、更文明的人生观基础之上的。躁动与好战不仅会产生明显的邪恶，而且使我们的生活充斥着不满足感，令我们不能享受审美的情趣，还几乎使我们不再具有沉思的美德。在这些方面，近百年来我们越做越差。我并不否认，中国人在相反的方向上走得太远了一些，但正由于这个原因，我才认为中西文化的结合对于双方都是有益的。他们应当向我们学习起码的、不可少的效率，而我们应当向他们学习某种沉思的智慧。这种睿智使他们得以延续至今，而其他的古国却都消亡了。

  我到中国来，原是为了教学。但是，我在这里待的时间越长，在向中国人教学方面就想的越少，而在向他们学习方面就想的越多。那些久居中国的欧洲人中间，我发现这样的态度并不罕见。但是到中国小住和赚钱的欧洲人之中，不幸的是，这种态度却很少。我们之所以认为中国人没有什么值得可学的地方，乃是由于中国人不擅长我们所重视的东西——军事上的勇武和工业上的进取。但是，那些重视智慧和审美的人，或者那些只是想享受人生的人，却能够在中国找到智慧、美感和人生乐趣，并且乐于居住在重视这些东西的国度中，因为中国在这些方面要胜过烦躁、纷乱的西方。我希望中国为了酬谢我们的科学知识，能回赠给我们一些她那宽大的容忍和沉思的恬静心境。

（商务印书馆译本）

33

Why I Dislike
Western
Civilization

我为什么不喜欢
西方文明

ARNOLD TOYNBEE
阿诺德·汤因比

(1889-1975)

ABOUT THE AUTHOR

Arnold Joseph Toynbee (1889-1975) is an English historian whose *Study of History* attempts a comprehensive analysis of twenty-one world civilizations. Born in London and educated at Winchester and Oxford, he taught history at Oxford and the University of London, and from 1925 to 1955 was research professor of international history at the Royal Institute of International Affairs. In 1971 he came to Taiwan for a brief visit and exchanged views on the world situation with the local historians.

作者简介

阿诺德·约瑟夫·汤因比（1889—1975）是一位英国历史学家，他的著作《历史研究》试图对世界上的 21 个文明社会进行全面分析。汤因比出生于英国伦敦，先后就读于温切斯特学院和牛津大学，并先后在牛津和伦敦大学教授历史学。1925 至 1955 年任英国皇家国际事务研究所国际史研究教授。1971 年到中国台湾进行短暂访问，并同当地的历史学者交流了对世界形势的看法。

	ABOUT THE SELECTION	In the nineteenth and twentieth centuries liberalism replaced Christianity as the dominant ideology of Western civilization. As Toynbee explains, one illustration of the bankruptcy of liberalism is its repudiation by totalitarian states in Europe, and then most of the newly independent nations of Africa and Asia. Another important illustration is the fact that, whereas one generation ago liberals were confidently promising a Utopian future, now they complain about the present they have succeeded in creating. Promises have turned to regrets; this looks like a modern repetition of Pandora's Box. Notice Toynbee does not blame these failures on "liberalism" but on "Western civilization", which is quite typical.
	内容简介	19世纪末20世纪初,自由主义取代了基督教教义成为西方社会意识形态领域的主流思想。正如汤因比所阐释的那样,欧洲的集权主义国家以及亚非两洲绝大多数新独立的国家都拒绝接受自由主义思想,这是表明自由主义破产的一个例子。此外,还有一个重要的例子也能表明这一趋势。上一代的自由主义者信誓旦旦地(向西方人民)承诺了一个乌托邦式的未来,如今他们却喋喋不休地抱怨自己成功开创的社会。当承诺变成遗憾时,这就像是潘多拉魔盒的悲剧在现代社会重演。值得注意的是,汤因比并没有将这些失败归责于"自由主义"而是归责于"西方文明",这种观点很有代表性。

When I say baldly¹ that I dislike contemporary Western civilization, I am, of course, saying this partly to tease my fellow Westerners. The stand that I take is partly a joke, but it is also partly serious.

My dislike of the West, though genuine as far as it goes, cannot really be unmitigated.² If it were, I should not feel lost—as I know that I should—if I did not have a *pied-à-terre*³ in London. I am a Londoner born and bred, but I have not reacted against my native city; and, though I dislike the congestion⁴ of the mechanized traffic there, I know that this pest⁵ is just as bad in all the other great cities of the postwar world.

If I were to be hounded out⁶ of London by some (non-existent) British counterpart⁷ of the House Committee on Un-American Activities,⁸ I expect I could make myself at home in Edinburgh or Melbourne or Rome or Hamburg or Boston, Mass. (my great-grandfather's farm was in sight of Boston Stump, the tapering⁹ tower of St. Botolph's Church in Boston, England). I should not feel at home as a permanent resident in New York or Chicago or Pittsburgh or Glasgow or Manchester or Milan. And I do not suppose that I could strike root in Kyoto or in Damascus or in Istanbul or even in Athens, though I love and admire each of these beautiful non-Western cities.

In ancient Greece, the navel¹⁰ of the earth was marked by a monolith¹¹ at Delphi.[12] The navel of my earth is not in Greece (though my heart and mind reside there). My world-navel is the Albert Memorial in Kensington Gardens.[13] This British monument may be comically ugly but, to me, it is reassuringly familiar. I used to play around its steps when I was a tiny child. Its frieze[14] taught me the names of the great poets, artists and thinkers of the past; the group of figures at the four corners put the four continents on the map for me.

Yes, one is a prisoner of one's time and place. I belong to the presyncopation age.[15] Classical Western music is music for my ears. When I hear jazz, I become uneasy and turn hostile. I feel my traditional world being victoriously invaded by tropical Africa. Politically, I am on the side of Africa against the Western colonial powers, but when it comes to music, Africa's cultural colonialism makes me cherish the West's pre-African musical past.

To be the prisoner of one's time and place is one of our human limitations. A human being has roots, like a tree, and these roots tether[16] him—though, unlike a tree's roots, they are emotional and intellectual roots, However, it is characteristic of our human nature that we rebel against our human limitations and try to transcend them. I myself, besides being human, happen to be a historian, and a historian's special form of human rebellion is to try to shake himself free of his own parochial[17] blood and soil (to use Hitler's hateful but expressive words). A historian's métier[18] is to move freely through time and space.

What a bore one's own native civilization is. It is dull just because it is familiar. I had the good fortune to be educated in Greek and Latin. This education served me as a magic carpet[19] on which I wafted[20] myself from the twentieth century of the Christian era to the third century B.C., and from the North Atlantic to the Eastern Mediterranean. I hated having to learn the names and dates of the Kings of England. The kings of Israel and Judah were almost as bad, since the Old Testament in the King James version has become virtually part of English literature. But I enjoyed finding my way among the Ptolemies[21] and the Seleucuses.[22] English constitutional history? One glance at the syllabus[23] of the Oxford school of medieval and modern history was enough to put me off reading for that. But the history of Islam, the history of Buddhism—these opened up fascinating new worlds.

Contemporary Western civilization annoys me, not because it is Western, but because it is mine and because I am a historian. The contemporary West holds me fast entangled in its coils. It prevents me from getting back behind the machine age and from getting out into Russia, Dar-es-Salaam, the Hindu world, Eastern Asia. My inescapable Westernness makes it impossible for me to become culturally acclimatized[24] in any of these other contemporary civilizations. This is a limitation on my human freedom that I resent.

However, I have a more formidable[25] reason for disliking the West than any that I have mentioned so far. Since I have been grown-up (I am now turned 75), the West has produced two world wars, it has produced Communism, Fascism and National Socialism, it has produced Mussolini and Hitler and McCarthy. These Western enormities[26] make me, as a Westerner, feel insecure. Now that my German fellow-Westerners have murdered six million Jews, how can I be certain that my English fellow-country-men might not do something equally criminal? We did murder some thousands of defenseless civilians at Port Said in 1956.[27] What might we not go on to do after that? What might I not be capable of doing myself, if this contemporary Western criminal lunacy were to waylay[28] me?

I shiver and shake. Old-fashioned Christian humility, please come to my rescue. Please save me from contemporary post-Christian Western self-complacent sinfulness. I should feel my spirits rise if, instead of being Hitler's fellow-Westerner—as I am—I could be Gandhi's fellow-Hindu. Yes, I believe I could even stomach[29] Benares[30] as the price of being liberated from Hitler's company. But I cannot escape Hitler. This fellow-

Westerner of mine (of the same age to within a week) is going to haunt me for the rest of my West-bound life.

Apart from contemporary Western crimes, there are other blemishes on contemporary Western life that I find repulsive.[31] Though I dislike the former enslavement of the individual to the community in Japan, I also dislike, and this perhaps even more, the lengths to which contemporary Western individualism has gone. The contemporary West is callous[32] toward the aged. This is, I believe, the first civilization, so far, in which the aged have not had a place, as a matter of course, in their adult children's homes. Looking at this Western callousness with de-Westernized eyes, I find it shocking.

I also dislike the contemporary Western advertising business. It has made a fine art out of taking advantage of human silliness. It rams[33] unwanted material goods down surfeited[34] throats when two-thirds of all human beings now alive are in desperate need of the bare necessities of life. This is an ugly aspect of the affluent[35] society; and, if I am told that advertising is the price of affluence, I reply without hesitation, that affluence has been bought too dear. Another item in the price of affluence is the standardization of mass-produced goods and services. This is, in itself, a deplorable impoverishment[36] of the material side of human culture, and it brings spiritual standardization with it, which is still worse.

Looking back into the past history of the West—a past which was still present when I was a child—1 admire the nineteenth-century West's success in postponing the age of sexual awakening, of sexual experience and sexual infatuation[37] far beyond the age of physical puberty.[38] You may tell me that this was against nature; but to be human consists precisely in transcending nature—in overcoming the biological limitations that we have inherited from our prehuman ancestors.

All human societies overcome death by creating and maintaining institutions that are handed on from one generation to another. Sex is a still more awkward feature of our biological inheritance than death, and our nineteenth-century Western society handled sex with relative success. By postponing the age of sexual awakening, it prolonged the length of the period of education. It is this, together with the seventeenth-century Western achievement of learning to think for oneself instead of taking tradition on trust, that accounts for the West's preeminence in the world during the last few centuries.

Nineteenth-century Westerners condemned with justice the Hindu institution of child-marriage, and they deplored, also with justice, the spectacle of an intellectually promising Moslem boy being allowed to commit intellectual suicide by sexual indulgence at the age of puberty. The twentieth-century West is now imitating the non-Western habits that the nineteenth-century West rightly—though perhaps self-righteously—condemned.

Our irrational contemporary Western impatience and our blind adulation[39] of speed for speed's sake are making havoc,[40] today, of the education of our children. We force their growth as if they were chicks in a pullet[41] factory. We drive them into a premature[42] awareness of sex even before physical puberty has overtaken them. In fact, we deprive our children of the human right of having a childhood. This forcing of sex-consciousness started in the United States, it has spread to Britain, and who knows how many other Western countries this perverse[43] system of miseducation is going to invade and demoralize?[44]

Our whole present policy in the upbringing of the young is paradoxical.[45] While we are lowering the age of sexual awareness—and frequently the age of sexual experience, too—to a veritably Hindu degree, we are at the same time prolonging the length of education. We force our boys and girls to become sex-conscious at twelve or thirteen, and then we ask them to prolong their postgraduate studies till they are nearly thirty. How are they to be expected to give their minds to education during those last sixteen or seventeen sex-haunted years?

We are proud of ourselves for providing secondary education, college education, postgraduate education for everybody. But we shall be plowing the sands[46] if we do not simultaneously revert to our grandparents' practice of prolonging the age of sexual innocence. If we persist, in this vital matter, on our present Hindu course, our brand-new would-be[47] institutions for higher education will become, in practice, little more than social clubs for sexual mating.

This relapse[48] into precocious sexuality is one of the moral blemishes of the contemporary Western civilization. One of its intellectual blemishes is its insistence on splitting up the universe into smaller and smaller splinters.[49] It has split up the human race into a host of sovereign[50] independent national states. It has split up knowledge and understanding into a host of separate watertight[51] disciplines.[52] I dislike nationalism and I dislike specialization, and both are characteristically Western aberrations.[53]

When I was about sixteen years old, I stayed with an uncle who was a specialist on Dante,[54] while his wife was a specialist on Horace Walpole.[55] Their library was less specialized than they themselves were, and I browsed in it with excitement and delight. When I was due to leave, my uncle said to me: "Arnold, your aunt and I think you are allowing your interest to be too general. You ought to specialize." I said nothing, but I was instantaneously certain that I was not going to follow this advice; and, in fact, I have consistently[56] done the opposite throughout the sixty years that have passed since then.

What a world to find oneself born into. Since as early as I first became conscious of my native Western environment, Western technology has been inventing new and ever more complicated machines. I did learn to ride a bicycle. How can one be expected, in just one lifetime, to go on to learn to ride a motorcycle or to drive a car? I started shaving in the age of the cutthroat razor, and Mr. Gillette's invention[57] came as a great relief to me. But how can I be expected to go on to use an electric razor? How could I know about volts and ohms and transformers? An American friend did give me an electric razor. This lies safely tucked away in a drawer, and whenever I unearth it, it alarms me.

I do now travel about the world in cars and airplanes. The better these get at covering the distance, the worse they get at allowing an inquisitive passenger to see the view. I did my first traveling in Greece in 1911-1912. I did it on foot with a rucksack[58] on my back. I was as free as a bird. I could go where even mules could not go. I could see the world as I pleased. I have never traveled so satisfactorily as that since then.

The other day, I had a three-hour mule ride from an airstrip to the rock-cut churches at Lalibela in Ethiopia.[59] Once again I was seeing the real world, the unmechanized pre-Western world in which I feel truly at home. Machinery perplexes and dismays me, and I have been born into the Western machine age. Why was I not born in the third-century-B.C. Syria or seventh-century-A.D. China? I should not then have been harassed[60] by machinery as I am in the contemporary West. I heartily dislike this side of contemporary Western life, and, in the eyes of the rest of the world, mechanization is what the contemporary West stands for.

Well, these are some of the reasons why I dislike the contemporary Western civilization. But, as I have said at the beginning of this article, my dislike is not undiluted.[61] My grandchildren, after all, are Westerners, and I certainly like them. Moreover, I want them, in their turn, to have grandchildren who will have grandchildren. I should be desolated[62] if I believed that Western man was going to commit mass suicide by engaging in a third world war that, this time, would be fought with atomic weapons.

To discover the existence of the atom and to go on to discover how to split it has been the chef d'oeuvre[63] of Western science and technology. I do not love Western science for having made these deadly inventions, but I have just enough faith in Western man's political commonsense to expect that he will not liquidate⁶⁴ himself. So perhaps, after all, I do not rate my native Western civilization so low as I fancy that I do in my moments of acute exasperation⁶⁵ at the West's more uncongenial vagaries.⁶⁶

NOTES

1. baldly: openly.
2. unmitigated: not made milder.
3. *pied-à-terre*: a bit of earth to put one's foot on; a base.
4. congestion: a being too crowded; blocked passage.
5. pest: an undesirable nuisance.
6. hounded out: driven out, as by a fierce dog.
7. counterpart: equivalent.
8. House Committee on Un-American Activities: a committee of the House of Representatives appointed to investigate the activities of dissident radicals in America; a prime target of all liberals.
9. tapering: getting thinner as it gets longer, like a finger.
10. navel: the place where the umbilical cord attaches an unborn child's body to the mother's body, hence, by extension, the place one comes from.
11. monolith: a column made of a single stone.
12. Delphi: an important religious center in ancient Greece, site of Apollo's temple.
13. Albert Memorial in Kensington Gardens: an important London monument, site of an important British museum.
14. frieze: an ornamental band of carved figures on a monument or building.
15. the presyncopation age: the characteristic beat of jazz (syncopation) is a delayed third note in a four-note measure. The presyncopation age refers to the age before that of jazz, namely, classic age.
16. tether: to tie, especially an animal, to a post.
17. parochial: of a parish; limited; narrow.
18. métier: profession or calling.
19. magic carpet: In the *Arabian Tales of a Thousand and One Nights*, a flying carpet transported people quickly to distant places.
20. wafted: to be carried aloft by the wind.
21. Ptolemies: a ruling dynasty in Egypt.

22. Seleucuses: a ruling dynasty in the Near East.
23. syllabus: a list of required readings.
24. acclimatized: used to the climate.
25. formidable: strong and difficult to overcome.
26. enormities: great wickednesses; monstrosities.
27. Toynbee, like other liberals, politically disapproved of the English-French occupation of the Suez canal in 1956.
28. waylay: to lay in wait by the side of the road and attack unsuspecting travelers.
29. stomach: (verb) to stand; to eat without vomiting.
30. Benares: the holy city of the Hindus on the Ganges River.
31. repulsive: repelling; causing a feeling of disgust.
32. callous: thick-skinned; unfeeling, inhuman.
33. ram: to push matter through a passage, often with a stick.
34. surfeited: over-fed; hence, not hungry.
35. affluent: rich. Its noun is "affluence".
36. deplorable impoverishment: lamentable poverty.
37. infatuation: preoccupation, exclusive attention to.
38. puberty: the beginning of development of adulthood.
39. adulation: worship; excessive praise.
40. havoc: widespread damage; destruction.
41. pullet: a hen less than one year old.
42. premature: not yet mature.
43. perverse: wilfully choosing a wrong course.
44. demoralize: cause a person to lose confidence in himself and the world.
45. paradoxical: self-contradictory.
46. plowing the sands: a useless activity because crops will not grow in the desert.
47. would-be: intended but not yet actually existing.
48. relapse: fall back.
49. splinters: small, thin pieces of wood.
50. sovereign: the highest authority; hence nations without any higher authority. Also used as an adjective.
51. watertight: a ship whose compartments can keep out water (watertight) is unsinkable. Watertight is thus a symbol of blocked communication.
52. disciplines: separate studies.
53. aberrations: abnormalities; disorders.

54. Dante (1265-1321): greatest Italian poet.
55. Horace Walpole (1717-1797): English author and wit.
56. consistently: without change or stopping.
57. Gillette's invention: the safety razor.
58. rucksack: canvas bag carried on the back.
59. Ethiopia: modern name for Abyssinia, a kingdom in east Africa.
60. harassed: troubled; worried; persecuted.
61. undiluted: unmixed with water; hence, not weakened.
62. desolated: left feeling alone and hopeless.
63. chef d'oeuvre: the main piece of work.
64. liquidate: to turn into liquid, a polite and indirect word for "kill".
65. exasperation: severe vexation.
66. uncongenial vagaries: unpleasant extravagant actions or ideas.

参考译文

当我说自己很不喜欢当代的西方文明时，当然有一种跟我的西方同胞开玩笑的戏谑之意，但同时它也确实是我内心的真实想法。

虽然我确实不喜欢当代西方文明，但也不至于对其全盘否定。若真如此，我就不会像现在这样感到迷茫了。当然，如果不是居住在伦敦的话，那我确实会感到迷失。我是个土生土长的伦敦人，从来没有"反对"过这座城市。虽然我打心眼儿里不喜欢这里拥挤的交通，但我也知道，二战后这种糟糕的现象在几乎所有大城市中都十分普遍。

要是哪天英国也设立了类似"众议院非美活动委员会"这样的机构，并且把我无情地驱逐出伦敦，我觉得我应该会在爱丁堡、墨尔本、罗马、德国汉堡或者美国马萨诸塞州的波士顿这些城市中找一处安身之所（话说在我曾祖父的农场可以看到位于英国波士顿圣博托尔夫教堂的锥形塔——波士顿树桩！），而不会居住在美国纽约、芝加哥、匹兹堡，英国格拉斯哥、曼彻斯特或者意大利的米兰，成为这些城市的永久居民,因为在这些地方我无法感到轻松自在。同时,尽管我很欣赏和喜爱京都、大马士革、伊斯坦布尔、雅典这些美丽的东方城市,但我却也不会想到在这些地方安家。

在古希腊,人们将德尔菲的巨石视为"地球的肚脐"。但在我心中,"地球的肚脐"并不在希腊(尽管她是令我心驰神往的地方),而是在肯辛顿花园的阿尔伯特纪念碑。尽管这个纪念碑看起来可能有些滑稽,甚至是不好看,但对我来说那却是个让我感到熟悉和安心的地方。当我还是个幼童时,就时常在那里的台阶上玩耍。通过圆柱饰带上刻着的名字,我认识了历史上许多伟大的诗人、艺术家和思想家。纪念碑外围的四个角上各矗立着一座塑像,分别刻画了不同地区身着不同服饰的人与动物,正是这些塑像让我对地球上的另外四个大洲有了初步印象。

诚然,人总是因其所处的时代与地域而被束缚。像我就觉得自己属于"切分法"规则之前的时代。西方的古典音乐更符合我的品味。当我听爵士乐时,整个人就会变得烦躁不安,怀有敌意。我感觉热带非洲的音乐已经成功地入侵了我原来的音乐世界。在政治上,我支持非洲国家反抗西方的殖民统治,但就音乐领域而言,非洲的文化殖民主义让我很怀念过去纯粹的未受非洲音乐影响的西方音乐风格。

受制于所生活的时代与地域,这是我们人类的一种局限性。就像树木有自己的根一样,人也有自己的"根",即与某个地方保持着紧密的联系。但与树木不同,人与某个地方的联系往往是情感和思想上的。同时,人总是反抗并寻求突破自身的局限性,这也是人的天性。我除了是一个普通的人之外,还是一个历史学家。历史学家总是试图摆脱狭隘的血缘和区域观念(用希特勒令人厌恶但却富有表现力的话来说),通过这种特殊的方式对抗人必须受制于一定时空的局限性。历史学家擅长让自己的目光在不同的时空间自由穿梭。

对个人而言，本土文明是多么无趣。之所以说无趣，是因为我们对于本土文明太过熟悉。我有幸接受过希腊语和拉丁语的教育。这种教育对我来说像是一张魔毯一样，我可以坐着它随风而行，从 20 世纪的基督教时代穿越到公元前 3 世纪，从北大西洋飞越到东地中海。我讨厌必须要记住历代英格兰国王的名字和任期。自从英王詹姆斯译本《圣经》("钦定版"《圣经》)成为英国文学的一分子，曾经为我喜爱的以色列国王和犹大的形象就变了味，犹如英国国王一样令人讨厌。我喜欢研究古埃及的托勒密王朝和位于亚洲的塞琉古王朝的历史。要是问我是否喜欢研究英国的宪政历史，我会坦率地说，一打开牛津中世纪和现代历史学院列出的必读书单，我就会感到兴趣索然，提不起半点研究热情。但是，阅读伊斯兰和佛教的历史则能令我着迷，它为我开启了一扇奇妙的新世界之门。

我对当代的西方文明感到恼怒，这倒不是因为它是"西方"的文明，而是因为它是我的本土文明，而我又恰好是个历史学家。当代西方文明将我牢牢地束缚在它的各种陷阱之中，让我无法回到机械化之前的时代，无法让我进入俄罗斯、达累斯萨拉姆、印度教国家和地区以及东亚地区。我身上固有的西方化特征使我无法适应任何其他文明的文化。这无疑限制了我作为人类的自由天性，我因此而恼怒。

但是，上述原因之外，还有一个更加恐怖的理由让我厌恶西方文明。自我成年后（我今年 75 岁了），西方世界爆发了两次世界大战，产生了共产主义、法西斯主义和国家社会主义等思潮，出现了墨索里尼、希特勒、麦卡锡等领导人物。在西方世界发生的种种恶行让作为一个西方国家公民的我深感不安，我的同为西方人的德国同胞居然屠杀了 600 万犹太人，我要如何确信我的英国同胞不会犯下同样的罪行？毕竟 1956 年我们确实在塞德港屠杀过数千名手无寸铁的平民。在这一事件后，还有什么恶行是我们做不出来的？如果当代西方文明中疯狂的犯罪思想劫持了我，那我是否有能力奋起反抗，或保持清醒，拒绝作恶？

想到这里我不寒而栗，传统基督徒的虔诚与谦逊，请来拯救我吧！请把我从当代西方后基督教时代的自满罪恶中拯救出来吧！求求了！如果我可以选择不成为希特勒的西方世界同胞而成为印度甘地的同胞，那我应该会感觉好受一些。是的，只要可以洗刷希特勒的同胞这个身份，哪怕让我忍受贝拿勒斯（印度东北部城市）的音乐我也心甘情愿。但事实是，我无法洗刷这个身份。希特勒就是我在西方世界的同胞，甚至与我年龄相差仅在一周之内，这个事实将会一直困扰着我身为西方人的余生。

除了上述种种罪行之外，当代西方世界的生活中还有其他令我感到厌恶的污点。尽管我不喜欢此前日本社会中盛行的极端集体主义思想，但我也不喜欢甚至极度厌恶当代西方文明中越发离经叛道的个人主义思潮。当前西方世界对老人的生活漠不关心，老人们在他们成年子女的家中无法拥有一席之地，我想迄今为止没有哪个文明社会是这样的不可理喻。从非西方的视角看，这种对待老人的冷漠态度是不可接受的。

我也不喜欢当代西方文明中的广告业。通过充分利用人类的无知，广告已成为了一种无孔不入的、精美的艺术形式。当前全球有三分之二的人都迫切需要得到最基本的生活保障，而广告商却机关算尽地把商品推销给一些根本不需要的人，就像是往一个饱汉的喉咙里填塞食物一样，这无疑是一个富裕社会丑陋的一面。如果有人告诉我，广告就是生活富裕的代价，我会毫不犹豫地回答，那现在真是富裕过头了。生活的富裕也导致了商品的批量化和服务的标准化。这种标准化反映出人类物质文明的极度贫瘠，这一事实令人痛心疾首。同时，这种标准化还导致了精神文明的标准化，这无疑是雪上加霜的后果。

回顾西方世界以往的历史——一段我在孩童时期经历过的历

史，19世纪西方社会文明曾成功地使人在一段漫长的生理青春期后才萌发性意识，发生性行为，形成对性的冲动，这令我十分钦佩。你也许会说，这样有违人的天性。但是，作为"人"就必须突破由天性带来的制约，克服从人类的动物祖先那里遗传过来的生物学缺陷。

所有人类社会都会形成和维持各种风俗习惯，并代代相传，以此来对抗死亡。相较于死亡，人的性（冲动）作为一种遗传的生物本能显得尤为尴尬。19世纪的西方文明较好地克服了这种尴尬。通过推迟个人萌发性意识的年龄，延长了个人接受学业教育的时间。正是这种对性意识的克制以及17世纪形成的打破传统、独立思考的观念，使得西方社会在过去几个世纪都领先于其他文明。

19世纪的西方人以正义之名谴责印度教的童婚制度。由于伊斯兰教纵容青春期男孩的性行为，一个处于青春期的聪明过人的穆斯林男孩可能因为纵欲过度而扼杀了自己的才智。西方人也曾同样以正义之名，公开谴责这种令人匪夷所思的现象。但是，20世纪的西方社会似乎在堕落，正在效仿这种自己曾经义正词严、理直气壮批判过的其他文明的风俗习惯。

当前西方社会表现出来的非理性的浮躁以及对追求速度的盲目吹捧，正在祸害我们的儿童教育。我们人为地加快儿童的成长速度，就好像是把雏鸡催化为小母鸡一样。我们让这些远未到青春期的孩子过早地萌发性意识，这事实上是在剥夺他们享受童年时光的权利。这种对儿童进行催化式性启蒙教育的做法起始于美国，如今已经蔓延到了英国。谁知道这种固执而错误的教育思想还会影响和摧毁多少西方国家原本的教育理念。

从整体来看，我们当前培养年青一代的教育政策是自相矛盾的。一方面，我们不仅降低对儿童进行性启蒙教育的年龄要求，还同时把允许青少年性行为的年龄降低到和印度教的风俗习惯一样；另一方面，我们希望延长青少年接受学业教育的时间。我们的教育让孩子们十二三岁的时候就早熟，萌发性意识，而后又要求延长研究生学习年限，使得他们直至近30岁方可毕业。就在这十六或十七年间，性欲的渴望一直萦绕在他们脑海里，如此一来我们又如何能指望他们专心于学业？

我们可以为每个人提供中小学教育、大学教育和研究生教育，这使我们感到自豪。但与此同时，如果不恢复我们祖父母那辈人的做法，提高对青少年进行性启蒙教育的年龄要求，那么我们的教育很可能是徒劳无功的。在这个至关重要的问题上，如果我们仍然坚持像印度教传统那样的做法，那么很可能之后新兴的高等教育机构，实际上比那些以促进男女配对为目的的社交俱乐部好不到哪里去。

性早熟观念的复辟是当代西方文明的一个道德缺陷。其理性上的缺陷在于它坚持将宇宙分割成越来越小的碎片，把人类分裂成许多主权独立的民族国家，把知识分类形成许多独立而严密的学科。我不喜欢民族主义和专业化，我认为两者都是西方社会典型的反常现象。

大约在十六岁的时候，我在叔叔家住了一段时间。叔叔是个研究但丁的专家，而婶婶则是研究霍勒斯·沃波尔的专家。他们家阁楼里的藏书非常丰富，不仅仅局限于他们所研究的领域。我常常沉浸在各种书籍中流连忘返。当我准备离开叔叔家时，叔叔告诫我说："阿诺德呀，我和你婶婶都觉得你的兴趣太宽泛了，你应该选择一个领域进行专门研究呀。"当时我并没有分辩什么，但那一瞬间我内心坚定地认为，不能听从他们的建议。事实上，在此后的六十年里，我一直都在做着完全相反的事情。

我出生在一个多么美好的世界。自我第一次意识到自己生活在西方世界时起，科技不断革新，许多新发明的精密机器不断涌现。我学会了骑自行车，但那时候谁又能想到，这辈子还要学会开摩托车和小汽车呢？我开始刮胡子时，那时还只有长刀片式刮胡刀，之后吉列先生发明的安全剃须刀让我倍感轻松。此后谁又能想到，我现在还可以使用电动剃须刀呢？我又怎么会知道"电压""电阻"和"变压器"这些概念呢？我的一个美国朋友曾送给我一个电动剃须刀，如今它还完好无损地躺在抽屉里。每次打开抽屉，它都会让我感到震惊。

我现在可以乘坐飞机和小汽车环游世界。交通工具越是能让人轻易地跨越遥远的距离，就越不能满足乘客观赏沿途风景的好奇心。1911到1912年的希腊之旅是我（人生中）的第一次旅行。那时的我背着帆布包徒步走在路上，感觉自己像鸟儿一样自由。我甚至可以去到那些连骡子都到不了的地方，随心所欲地欣赏这个世界。后来，我再也没有过那样心旷神怡的旅行体验。

前几天，我骑了三个小时的骡子从埃塞俄比亚的简易机场到拉利贝拉岩石教堂，我又一次看到了真实的世界，一个未被机械化改造的，让我真正感到宾至如归的世界。我出生在一个西方机械化的时代，机器时常让我感到困惑和沮丧。为什么我就不能出生在公元前三世纪的叙利亚或者公元后七世纪的中国呢？那样的话我就不会像现在这样对西方世界的各种机械化感到疲惫不堪了。我发自内心地厌恶当代西方世界机械化的一面，然而，在世界其他文明的人看来，机械化恰恰是当代西方文明的代名词。

好吧，以上就是一些我不喜欢当代西方文明的原因。但就像我在文章开头所说的那样，我对当代西方文明并不只有厌恶。毕竟，我的孙子孙女们也是西方人，我肯定是喜爱他们的。而且，我希望他们也能够传宗接代，子孙满堂。一想到西方人可能会因为参加第三次世界大战（这次将是利用原子武器发动战争），最终自取灭亡，我就会感到悲伤和绝望。

发现原子的存在并继续探索如何使之分裂一直是西方科技发展的主要方向。虽然我不喜欢西方的科技，因为它创造了这些致命的发明，但我对西方人的政治常识有着足够的信心，我相信他们不会自取灭亡。因此，也许我对本土文明的评价终究没有想象中的那么低，只是在被西方世界一些不合宜的变化激怒时才会如此。

(罗选民 译)